OH,
HOW THEY PLAYED
THE GAME

ROB1

OH, HOW THEY PLAYED THE GAME

The early days of football and the heroes who made it great

by **ALLISON DANZIG**

THE MACMILLAN COMPANY, NEW YORK, NEW YORK

COLLIER-MACMILLAN LIMITED, LONDON

The Macmillan Company
866 Third Avenue, New York, N.Y. 10022
Collier-Macmillan Canada Ltd., Toronto, Ontario

Library of Congress Catalog Card Number: 73-163227

First Printing

Printed in the United States of America

The author wishes to thank the following individuals and organizations for their kind permission to reprint material in *Oh, How They Played the Game*:

The Liberty Library Corporation, for "Football Now and Then" by George Ade, © 1929, Liberty Weekly, Inc.

Assembly Magazine, alumni quarterly of the U. S. Military Academy, for "How Football Came to West Point" by John McA. Palmer.

The New York Times, for an article by Jack Doyle from John Kieran's "Sports of the Times" column, © 1937 by The New York Times Company; for two articles by Allison Danzig, © 1931 and © 1962 by The New York Times Company; for an article on the death of William Roper, © 1933 by the New York Times Company.

Esquire Magazine, for an article on Red Grange, © 1936 (renewed 1964) by Esquire, Inc.

The Saturday Evening Post, for "Touchdown" by Amos Alonzo Stagg, © 1926 (renewed 1954), The Curtis Publishing Company; for "That's My Story" by Mike Thompson, © 1931 (renewed 1959), The Curtis Publishing Company; for "Is The Notre Dame System Slipping?" by Glenn S. Warner, © 1934 (renewed 1962), The Curtis Publishing Company; for two George Halas articles, © 1947 and © 1957, The Curtis Publishing Company.

A. S. Barnes and Company, for an article by John W. Heisman from *Frank Menke's Encyclopedia of Sports.*

The St. Louis Post-Dispatch, for two articles by Ed Wray and an article by Eddie Cochems.

The Associated Press, for an article by John W. Herbert and an article by Charles (Gus) Dorais.

The Baltimore Sun, for articles by Arthur Poe and E. Edward Sparrow, as well as an article on the Princeton-Yale game of 1899.

Mamie Doud Eisenhower, for an interview with General Dwight D. Eisenhower in 1968.

The Oregonian, for an article by Lee Cranmer from L. H. Gregory's column in 1928.

The Michigan Daily, for an account of the January 1, 1902 Rose Bowl Game from *The Michigan Daily News.*

The Detroit Free Press, for an article by W. W. Edgar, © 1936 by *The Detroit Free Press.*

The Boston Herald-Traveler Corporation, for an article by Bill Cunningham from *The Boston Herald.*

Mrs. James Thurber, for an article originally published in the newspaper *P.M.* © 1940 James Thurber. © 1968 Helen W. Thurber and Rosemary Thurber Sauers.

College Athletics Publishing Service, for an article by Alvin (Bo) McMillin from the 1941 *Football Guide;* for three articles by Parke Davis, from the 1925, 1927, and 1934 *Football Guides;* for the resolution setting forth Walter Camp's contribution to American rugby football from the 1924 *Football Guide.*

The Yale University Athletic Department, for an article by William H. (Pa) Corbin from the 1939 Yale-Army program; for an article by Allison Danzig from the 1958 Cornell-Yale program; for an article by Leverett Saltonstall from the Harvard-Yale program of 1939.

The Harvard University Varsity Club, for an article by Martin Cate from the first " 'H' Book of Harvard Athletics."

The Princeton Department of Public Relations and Dan Coyle for Dan Coyle's interview with Henry Green Duffield.

The W. C. C. Publishing Company, Inc., for an article by Stanley Woodward, © 1940 by New York Herald Tribune, Inc.; for an article by Red Smith, © 1945 by New York Herald Tribune, Inc.

The author also wishes to thank those individuals who granted him permission to reprint the texts of personal letters.

ACKNOWLEDGMENTS

THE EVOLUTION of American football and the legendary teams, players, coaches, and games of roughly the first half-century of intercollegiate competition are the subject of this work.

Some of the story is related firsthand by those who had a part in the action or were eyewitnesses to it. Most of the pioneers, including Camp, Stagg, Heffelfinger, Yost, Zuppke, Haughton, Heisman, Warner, Heston, Rockne, Dorais, Harper, Woodruff, and Dr. Williams, have passed on. To get the authentic record the only recourse in many instances was to turn to letters to the author, or to interviews, as well as to personal accounts in magazine and newspaper articles and books dating back to the 1920's.

Some of these interviews and letters have been previously published in part, or, in a few instances, in full, in the author's *History of American Football*, now out of print. They were an indispensable source. Acknowledgment is gratefully made of the author's indebtedness for permission to reprint both this material and additional material from *The Saturday Evening Post, Collier's Weekly, The New York Times,* and other publications.

The author is grateful, too, for the generous assistance he has had in collecting the pictures to illuminate football's early years. Particular acknowledgment is made to Yale University, the United States Military Academy, Princeton University, the University of Illinois, the University of Michigan, the University of Notre Dame, the National Football Foundation and Hall of Fame, Hamilton Fish, and Jerome Brondfield, editor of Scholastic Magazines and Book Services in New York.

ALLISON DANZIG

Roslyn, New York, May 28, 1971

CONTENTS

Part Two

INTRODUCTION

THE FIRST GAME OF intercollegiate football in the United States was played between Princeton and Rutgers on November 6, 1869, at New Brunswick, New Jersey. It may come as a shock to some followers of the game played today before vast crowds on the campus and by professional teams that that first contest of more than a century ago was football of an altogether different variety. It was soccer, or association football, with twenty-five men to a side. Running with the ball and passing it by hand were strictly forbidden.

Soccer was the game played everywhere on the American campus in 1869, except at one college. It might have remained the only football, or at least *the* game of football, played to this day had it not been for the fact that at Harvard they had come up with a variety of football that had elements of rugby. In rugby football, running with the ball is allowed, as is passing the ball by hand laterally or backward (but never forward).

It was by sheer chance that the rugby style of football came about in 1823. That year a student at the famous English school Rugby took it in his head during a game of soccer to run with the ball. As the lad, William Webb Ellis, caught a ball kicked by the opposing team, the first stroke of five o'clock sounded on a nearby bell. All activity on the playing fields had to cease at five, and so, instead of heeling the ball and taking a free kick, William Webb Ellis decided, on the spur of the moment, to run with it as the only means of scoring a goal that would avert defeat before five strokes sounded on the bell.

The brash fellow was branded a blackguard, a cad, for his shocking violation of the rules. But in time, as they thought about it, it was decided that William Webb Ellis had something and that running with the ball was worth looking into. A tablet on a wall at Rugby commemorates his historic exploit, perpetuating his fame for what was first judged an act of infamy.

Such was the genesis of another great game of football—rugby. And it was from rugby—not soccer, except indirectly—that, by chance again, evolved the American style of football.

Harvard, because it played a style of football different from that of the game (soccer) at Yale, Princeton, Columbia, and

Rutgers, declined to join these schools when they met in New York on October 19, 1873, and formulated the first intercollegiate rules in the United States—rules modeled after the code of the London Football Association, which played soccer. It looked elsewhere for competition and found an opponent in McGill University of Montreal, which played rugby under the rules of the English Rugby Union. Two games were played at Harvard in Cambridge, Massachusetts, on May 14 and 15, 1874—the first under Harvard's rules (more soccer than rugby) and the second under McGill's. Harvard won the first, 3 goals to 0, and the second ended in a scoreless tie. They also played a third game in October in Montreal, won by Harvard, 3 touchdowns to 0.

The Cantabs weren't easily to be persuaded as a general rule that anybody knew or did anything better than they did. But they went for McGill's game—real rugby—hook, line, and sinker.

For some years Harvard and Yale had been trying in vain to get together on the football field, but were thwarted by the differences in their rules. Now finally, on October 16, 1875, their representatives met at Springfield, Massachusetts, and adopted what they called "Concessionary Rules," and on November 13, 1875, their teams met on the field in Hamilton Park in New Haven, Connecticut, and played a hybrid game that was part soccer and part rugby. Harvard won by 4 goals to 0. That was the start of the most famous rivalry in college football, the Harvard-Yale game, which became the holy of holies, known as The Game. (Prior to this Harvard and Tufts College had met in June, Tufts winning by a goal and a touchdown to nothing for Harvard.)

Now it was Yale's turn to get religion. It went whole hog for rugby, except that it did not like playing with 15 men on a side, as rugby rules called for. From the time it had met an eleven-man team of "Eton Players" from England in 1873 in New Haven, Yale was sold on eleven-man teams, and it fought for them, finally having its way in 1880.

So in 1876 Harvard and Yale played rugby as Oxford and Cambridge, Eton and Harrow and Rugby and all other English "public" schools played it. At the 1875 game Princeton representatives had been observers, and they were so taken with rugby that they went back to Nassau and called a meeting. There was a near-riot when they proposed that Princeton switch from soccer to rugby, so entrenched was the older game, but their powers of persuasion prevailed and Princeton went along. The Big Three stood together. After that, on Princeton's initiative, the Intercollegiate Football Association was formed on November 23, 1876, at Massasoit House in Springfield, with Columbia also represented, and the rules of the English Rugby Union were adopted with modifications.

So English rugby was now the American game in 1876, a hundred years after the Declaration of Independence had renounced allegiance to an English king.

It was not until four years later that the American style of football game began to evolve.

One man, above all others, was responsible for the evolution. That man was Walter Camp, the "Father of American Football."

Camp was from Yale, one of the succession of immortal figures the Elis contributed to the game's legends. Others were to be Amos Alonzo Stagg, William Walter (Pudge) Heffelfinger, and Frank Hinkey, "the Disembodied Spirit."

It was in the conventions and rules committee meetings that Camp, year after year, recommended the changes that, as they were adopted, brought about a complete metamorphosis in the game of football played in the United States.

The first and most fundamental changes came in 1880 in the substitution of "scrimmage" for rugby's scrummage, or "scrum," as it was commonly known, marking the introduction of what was to be the game's most glamorous figure, the quarterback, and, in 1882, the institution of the system of downs.

With scrimmage and the system of downs, the principle of possession of the ball was established, to change the whole basic concept and structure of the game, leading to planning an attack and strategy. In the English "scrum" the ball was thrown in by the referee between two opposing packs of forwards who, with arms locked around necks, endeavored to heel the ball backward to their backs. The back getting it then would run with it and/or lateral it to another back. As soon as he was tackled, the man with the ball had to get rid of it, kicking it or dropping it to the ground, whereupon another scrum followed. The ball might change hands in a matter of seconds over and over. With scrimmage and the system of downs, the ball was given into the possession of a team, which retained possession as long as it advanced 5 yards in three downs (in 1906, 10 yards in three downs, and then, in 1912, 10 yards in four downs) until it had scored, or fumbled the ball away, or kicked it far down the field to the opposition.

The other innovations that brought about the evolution of the American game of football are dealt with in Chapter 2 on Camp.

Cheerful sport between the aesthetic young gentlemen of Princeton and Yale.

They include the reduction in the number of players on a team from fifteen to eleven; the introduction of signals and a numerical scoring system; awarding points for touchdowns, field goals, goals after touchdowns, and safeties; the establishment of the neutral zone; and permitting tackling below the waist (which led to the close-order formation and the original T). Later, in 1906, after President Theodore Roosevelt had called in representatives of Harvard, Yale, and Princeton and asked that they do something to end the brutality of the game, which was causing a clamor for the banning of football from the campus, Camp was a leading figure with Captain Palmer E. Pierce of West Point in the rules committee meetings that adopted the far-reaching changes to curb roughness and reduce the hazards and open up the game. The most significant of these changes was the legalization of the forward pass.

Far more than anything else, the forward pass changed the

character of the game to transform it from an elementary, prosaic, close-order test of brawn and muscle into a contest of skill and intelligence, as well as physical prowess—a swiftly gaited game of speed, deception, faking, manual dexterity, flanking movements, and spectacular passing operations, with every member carrying out an assigned role in an attack of daring, imagination, and split-second timing that challenged the defense as never before. The forward pass was the last big turning point—the turning away from the heavy-handed, unimaginative mass assault of brute force and labored progress, toward the open, quick-striking attack that was so much more appealing to both the player and the spectator.

There have been many changes in the game since 1906, including the introduction of a fourth down in which to make 10 yards, raising the value of the touchdown from 5 to 6 points and changing the length of the field from 110 yards to 100 yards, with end zones —all in 1912; setting the goal posts back from the goal line to the rear line of the end zone, in 1927; permitting free substitution, in 1941 (ended in 1953, followed by the gradual restoration of two-platoon football by 1965); introducing the 2-point conversion after touchdown by running or passing (by kicking, 1 point), in 1958; and widening the distance between the goal posts, in 1959. But all of these changes have been minor compared to the legalization of the forward pass and the innovations introduced by Camp to bring about the evolution from rugby.

Camp died at the rules committee meeting early in 1925. The scope of this volume, roughly football's first half-century, comes within virtually his lifetime of connection with the game as player, coach, and rules maker. It was at the time of his death that football was entering upon the period of the greatest growth it had known, in the Golden Twenties, when the country went sports-mad after the First World War, and the professional side of the game was organizing and doing the spadework that was to bring undreamed-of riches to the National Football League players, coaches, and club owners in the 1950's and 1960's, when college attendance rose from 16,681,731 in 1953 to 29,465,604 in 1970.

Contributing to the skyrocketing of interest in college football in sports' Golden Age, the 1920's, were Knute Rockne, the Four Horsemen, and George Gipp and Jack Cannon of Notre Dame; Red Grange and Bob Zuppke of Illinois; Hurry-Up Yost and Benny Friedman, Harry Kipke and Bennie Oosterbaan of Michigan; Pop Warner and Ernie Nevers at Stanford; Bronko Nagurski and Fat Spears, Minnesota Gophers; Brick Muller and Andy Smith's Wonder

Teams at California; Tad Jones and his great 1923 Yale team with Century Milstead, Win Lovejoy, Mal Stevens, and Bill Mallory; Gil Dobie's Cornell steamrollers of 1921, 1922 and 1923 with George Pfann, Eddie Kaw, and Sunny Sundstrom; Bill Roper's 1922 Princeton Team of Destiny with Mel Dickenson, Charley Caldwell, Herb Treat, Pink Baker and Johnny Gorman; Charlie Moran's 1921 Centre College Praying Colonels with Bo McMillin, Red Weaver and Red Roberts, and Bill Alexander's great Georgia Tech team of 1928 with Pa Lumpkin.

Also, Chick Meehan's New York University powerhouses with Ken Strong, Al Lassman, Len Grant and a military huddle; Howard Jones' Iowa invincibles of 1921 and 1922 with Aubrey Devine, Gordon Locke, Duke Slater and Leland Parkin; Hugo Bezdek's unbeaten 1921 Penn State eleven with Glenn Killinger, Light Horse Harry Wilson and Charley Way; Bob Neyland's Tennessee juggernauts with Herman Hickman, Gene McEver, Buddy Hackman and Bobby Dodd; Wallace Wade's all-conquering Alabama teams of 1925 and 1926 with Johnny Mack Brown and Pooley Hubert; Howard Jones' Southern California Trojans with Morley Drury; Jesse Hawley's great Dartmouth champions of 1925 with Swede Oberlander, Nate Parker and Dutch Diehl; Jock Sutherland's Pittsburgh Panthers with Gibby Welch and Joe Donchess; Chris Cagle, Biff Jones' Army ace; Tom Hamilton, pride of Bill Ingram's unbeaten 1926 Navy team; Major Frank Cavanaugh's Boston College teams of 1920 and 1926, including Joe McKenney; Herb McCracken's amazing 1926 Lafayette invincibles with Charley Berry; Tuss McLaughry's Brown Iron Men; Albie Booth, Mal Stevens' Little Boy Blue at Yale; Eddie Tryon and Tiny Welch, Dick Harlow's Colgate aces; Bernie Bierman's Tulane teams with Jerry Dalrymple; Slip Madigan's toughies at St. Mary's; Greasy Neale's West Virginia Mountaineers; Dana Bible's Texas A. & M. masterpiece with Joel Hunt; Harry Mehre and Catfish Smith at Georgia; Ray Morrison's "passing fools" at Southern Methodist with Gerald Mann; Homer Hazel of Rutgers, Rags Matthews of Texas Christian, George Wilson of Washington, Herb Joesting of Minnesota, Lloyd Brazil of Detroit.

Other great teams, players and coaches have risen since— among the coaches, Frank Leahy, Bud Wilkinson, Earl Blaik, Lou Little, Homer Norton, Andy Kerr, Dan McGugin, Matty Bell, Dutch Meyer, Jess Neely, Fritz Crisler, Carl Snavely, Frank Howard, Clark Shaughnessy, Frank Thomas, Eddie Anderson, George Munger, Charley Caldwell, Lefty James, Johnny Vaught, Jim Tatum, Jim Crowley, Francis Schmidt, Dick Harlow, Red Sanders, Rip Engle,

Buck Shaw, Jack Mollenkopf, Jordan Olivar, Don Faurot, Bobby Dodd, Bowden Wyatt, Wally Steffen, Chuck Taylor, Pappy Waldorf, Harry Kipke, John Wilce, Bernie Moore, Tiny Thornhill, Henry Frnka, Dick Hanley, Glenn Dobbs, Jimmy Phelan, Bill Murray, Babe Hollingbery, Bob Higgins, Edward Robinson, Morley Jennings, George Sauer, Bill Spaulding, Ossie Solem, Clarence (Fat) Spears, Glenn Thistlethwaite, Charlie Bachman, Gus Henderson, Ike Armstrong, Frank Murray, John McEwan, Wally Butts, Pete Cawthon, Biggie Munn, Harvey Harman, Jack Meagher and Lone Star Dietz.

Others are Dud De Groot, Curley Byrd, Dick Romney, Art Guepe, Frank Dobson, Andy Gustafson, Clipper Smith, Wayne Hardin, Eddie Erdelatz, Douglas (Peahead) Walker, Bo McMillin, Dick Colman, Elmer Layden, Harry Stuhldreher, Adam Walsh, Hunk Anderson, Arnold Horween, Herb Kopf, Larry Bankart, George Hauser, Eddie Casey, Dutch Bergman, Lloyd Jordan, Eddie Cameron, Frank Kimbrough, Clyde Littlefield, Frank Bridges, Bert Bell, Rae Crowther, Gus Dorais, Terry Brennan, Joe Kuharich, Howard Harpster, Fred Dawson, Hugh Devore, Herman Hickman, George Little, Bert LaBrucherie, Wes Fesler, Otto Graham, Stu Holcombe, Red Strader, Speedy Rush, Lou Young, Lew Elverson, Pete Elliott, Chalmers Elliott, Forest Evashevski, Carroll Widdoes, Ray Eliot, Tom Hamilton, Ralph Sasse, Gar Davidson, Phil Dickens, Hooks Mylin, Bennie Oosterbaan, Benny Friedman, Abe Martin, Harold Lahar, Ed McKeever, Jack Hagerty, Stub Allison, Buff Donelli, Jack Curtice, Dan Jessee, Len Casanova, Tom Nugent, Swede Larson, Tad Wieman, Ducky Pond, Noble Kizer, Arthur Sampson, and on down to the present.

Currently there are Darrell Royal, John McKay, Woody Hayes, Paul (Bear) Bryant, Ara Parseghian, Frank Broyles, Duffy Daugherty, Bob Devaney, Bob Blackman, Joe Paterno, Ben Schwartzwalder, Harry Prothro, Paul Dietzel, Ralph Jordan, Bo Schembechler, Charles McClendon, John Ralston, Murray Warmath, Dan Devine, Bill Battle, Jim Owens, Chuck Fairbanks, Ben Martin, Vince Dooley, Bill Dooley, John Pont, Hayden Fry, Bob DeMoss, Doug Dickey, Pepper Rodgers, Dee Andros, Bill Peterson, Bill Murphy, Alex Agase, Bud Carson, Bill Yeoman, Tom Cahill, Jack Musick, John Yovicsin, Carmen Cozza, Jake McCandless, Tom Harp, Eddie Crowder, John Bateman, Bill Meek, Bob Odell, Frank Navarro, Rick Forzano, Earle Edwards, Charley Shira, Ray Nagel, Fred Dunlap, Joe Yukica, Ray Willsey, Vince Gibson, Frank Kuse, Len Jardine, John Ray, Floyd Gass, Jerry Frei, Harold Hagan, Bill Hess, Charlie Tate, Joe McMullen, Fred Taylor, Rod Rust, Carl

Ohio State vs. North-western in 1916.

DePasqua, Don Coryell, Roy Lester, Frank Jones, Neil Wheelwright, Dave Puddington, Bill Mallory, John Majors, Homer Smith, Jim Valek, Bill Whitton, John McVay, Jim Parker, Bill Beall, Bob Weber, Alva Kelley, Howdy Myers, Joe Scannella, Vic Fusia, John Toner, Clary Anderson, Jim Ostendarp, Don Russell, John Bell, Don Miller, Fred Prender, Jim Butterfield, Harold Raymond, Jim Lentz, Lawrence Catuzzi, and Harry Gamble.

The great college players since the 1920's have included Sammy Baugh of Texas Christian; Tom Harmon of Michigan; Don Hutson of Alabama; Doc Blanchard, Glenn Davis, and Pete Dawkins of Army; Doak Walker of Southern Methodist; Byron (Whizzer) White of Colorado; Angelo Bertelli, Johnny Lujack, Paul Hornung, George Connor, and Leon Hart of Notre Dame; Roger Staubach and Joe Bellino of Navy; Frank Sinkwich of Georgia; Gayle Sayers of Kansas; Larry Kelley and Clint Frank of Yale; Dick Butkus of Illinois; Jim Parker and Howard Cassady of Ohio State; Alex Karras of Iowa; Tommy Nobis of Texas; Ernie Davis and Jim Brown of Syracuse; Dick Kazmaier of Princeton; Jim Weatherall and Billy Vessels of Oklahoma; Gary Beban of UCLA; George Webster of Michigan State; and, more recently, O. J. Simpson of Southern California, Leroy Keyes of Purdue, Steve Owens of Oklahoma, Terry Hanratty of Notre Dame, and Jim Plunkett of Stanford.

Listing the great teams, there were, in the 1930's, Wallace Wade's all-conquering Alabama teams of 1930 and 1934; Bernie Bierman's national champion Minnesota teams of 1934 and 1936 and also his 1935 varsity, which had a perfect record; Fritz Crisler's Princeton Tigers of 1933, 1934, and 1935, which lost one game, in 1934; Harry Kipke's Michigan Wolverines, national champions in 1932 and 1933; Howard Jones' Southern California Trojan champions of 1931, who ended Notre Dame's three-year winning streak after trailing by 0–14 in the final period; Carl Snavely's Cornell invincibles of 1939, who shocked Ohio State, and his 1940 team, which maintained its winning streak until it forfeited victory to Dartmouth in the next to last game with an unprecedented renunciation when it was found that the winning score on the last play had come on an illegal fifth down.

Also, Matty Bell's 1935 Southern Methodist Mustangs, first team of the Southwest to be recognized as national champions; Dutch Meyer's 1938 Texas Christian eleven, which also was ranked at the top; and then Homer Norton's Texas A. & M. Aggies, who kept the Lone Star at the top in 1939. Wallace Wade's Duke Blue Devils of 1938 won every game and were unscored on. Also unscored on were Andy Kerr's 1932 Colgate Red Raiders, "unbeaten, untied, unscored on—and uninvited" (to any bowl). Jock Sutherland's Pittsburgh Panthers of 1937, with Marshall Goldberg, were national champions, and their toughest foe was Jimmy Crowley's unbeaten Fordham Rams of the "Seven Blocks of Granite," with whom they played a scoreless tie for the third successive year. Notre Dame started off the decade as national champion, as it had been also in 1929 under Rockne, who was to lose his life in the crash of an airplane early in 1931. Tulane, coached by Bierman before he went to Minnesota, had a perfect record in 1931, as it had in 1929, and Oklahoma, too, won every game in 1938.

Bob Neyland led Tennessee to perfect records in 1938 and 1939 and he made it three in a row to start off the 1940's. But the national championship in 1940 went to Bierman's Minnesota Gophers, who were to go to the top again in 1941. The year 1940 was notable for the performance of Stanford in winning every game with the new T formation introduced by Clark Shaughnessy, who had worked it out with George Halas and his Chicago Bears, perpetrators of an astonishing 73–0 massacre of the Washington Redskins that same year with the T.

The 1940's were featured, too, by the great rivalry between Army and Notre Dame and by the rise of Oklahoma under Bud Wilkinson. Frank Leahy went to Notre Dame in 1941 and Earl (Red) Blaik was called to Army the same year. In 1943 Leahy turned out what was regarded as Notre Dame's greatest team up to that time. With Angelo Bertelli at quarterback until he was called into the Marines, and Johnny Lujack then taking over, the Fighting Irish beat every foe until, in the final game, on the last play, the Great Lakes Naval Training Station completed a last-ditch pass of some 50 yards for a touchdown and victory, 19–14. Starting in 1944, Blaik led Army to the greatest record in West Point history. With Doc Blanchard and Glenn Davis, "Mr. Inside and Mr. Outside," in the backfield, the cadets won every game in 1944 and 1945. In 1946 they maintained their invincibility until they came up against Notre Dame, to which Leahy had returned after having been in the service. The teams played to a scoreless tie.

Leahy continued to compile a record of success almost the equal of Rockne's as Notre Dame won every game in 1947 to repeat as national champion, lost out by a shade to Michigan for top honors in 1948, was back on the pinnacle in 1949, and had stood unbeaten for thirty-nine games when it crashed in 1950 and lost

1896 cigar-box heroes.

The 1896 West Point team.

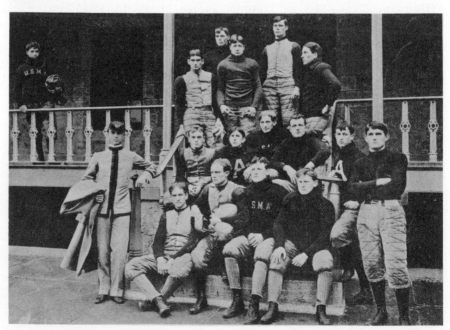

to Purdue. That same year, Army, whose thirty-two-game invincible streak had been ended by Columbia in a shocker in 1947 and which then lost also to Notre Dame in their last meeting for a decade, came to the end of a twenty-eight-game unbeaten streak in 1950 in a stunning setback by a Navy team that had lost six games. The cadets won every game in 1948 except for a tie with Navy, had a perfect season in 1949, and won every game in 1950 until the finale with the midshipmen.

Under Wilkinson, Oklahoma lost its opening game in 1948 and then won thirty-one games in a row for perfect seasons in 1949 and 1950, when it was recognized as national champion for the first time. Ohio State, under Paul Brown, was champion in 1942 and the Buckeyes had a perfect season in 1944. Michigan put great records back to back, in 1947 under Fritz Crisler and in 1948 under Bennie Oosterbaan, both getting the Coach of the Year award. The 1947 team lost out to Notre Dame for the championship award but the 1948 Wolverines were the pick over the Fighting Irish. Duke, under Wallace Wade, had a perfect record in 1941 and lost to Oregon State in the Rose Bowl game, moved as a wartime measure to the Duke campus in Durham, North Carolina. Alabama, Boston College (under Leahy), California, Clemson, Georgia, Lafayette, Penn State, Purdue, Tulsa, and the University of California at Los Angeles had perfect seasons in the 1940's, California repeating, and in 1941 Texas had its best team up to that time, though it was beaten.

The 1950's were dominated by Wilkinson's Oklahoma Sooners, with Princeton, Maryland, Ohio State, Tennessee, Michigan State, UCLA, Syracuse, and Louisiana State sharing in the honors. For three years in a row, 1954 through 1956, Oklahoma won every game, and it continued to win in 1957 until it had set an all-time record with forty-seven successive victories dating from 1953. The streak ended in a 7–0 loss to Notre Dame, the foe to which it had last lost, in 1953. The Sooners had started the decade with a perfect season.

Charley Caldwell's Princeton Tigers, with Dick Kazmaier, one of its greatest backs of all time, at tailback, won every game in 1950 and 1951 en route to a twenty-four-game unbeaten sequence. Under Biggie Munn, Michigan State won every game in 1951 and then repeated in 1952 for its first national championship. Jim Tatum brought Maryland its first national title in 1953, after his Terrapins had won every game in 1951, and they had another perfect season in 1955. Under Neyland, Tennessee was crowned champion in 1951, and under his successor, Bowden Wyatt, the Volunteers won every game in 1956. Woody Hayes' Ohio State Buckeyes had a perfect record in 1954 and were picked as national champion in The Associated Press poll, while Red Sanders' all-winning UCLA Bruins were the choice of United Press International. In 1957 the Buckeyes again shared the title, with Auburn, which, under Ralph (Shug) Jordan, had its first perfect season and was the choice of the A.P. Neither Auburn nor UCLA had ever been national champions before.

In 1958 Louisiana State, with Paul Dietzel at the helm, and Billy Cannon in the backfield, won every game for the first time in half a century and found itself national champion for the first time. The deep South was winning recognition as never before. The next year it was Syracuse's turn to be awarded its first national diadem, as Ben Schwartzwalder's varsity enjoyed the first perfect season the Orange had known in seventy-one years. Wyoming had a perfect record in 1950 and in 1956, Georgia Tech in 1952, San Francisco in 1951, and Arizona State in 1957.

Darrell Royal's Texas Longhorns, John McKay's Southern California Trojans, Alabama under Bear Bryant, Ohio State under Woody Hayes, Notre Dame under Ara Parseghian, and Michigan State under Duffy Daugherty were the big winners in the 1960's. Penn State under Joe Paterno, Arkansas under Frank Broyles, Murray Warmath's Minnesota Gophers, and Bob Devaney's Nebraska Cornhuskers also stood forth.

Texas won the national championship for the first time in 1963, marking the first Southwest Conference team to be so honored since Texas A. & M. in 1939. The Longhorns, unbeaten (but tied) in 1962 for the first time since 1923, had their first perfect record since 1920 in 1963, and they had another in 1969 to repeat as national champions after a thrilling last-minute victory over Arkansas, followed by another over Notre Dame in the Cotton Bowl—the first appearance of the Fighting Irish in a bowl game since the Four Horsemen of 1924 beat Stanford in the Rose Bowl on January 1, 1925. In 1970 Royal's Texans again won every game and were ranked as national champions in both the AP and UPI polls. After they had lost in the Cotton Bowl to Notre Dame, which put on an astonishing defense, the AP took another poll and Nebraska was awarded the top spot.

Devaney's Cornhuskers, who had ranked third at the end of the regular season, beat LSU in the Orange Bowl, while in the Rose

Bowl, Ohio State, which had won every game during the season and ranked second to Texas, suffered a stunning setback against Stanford. The UPI stood on its ranking (Texas, Ohio State, Nebraska). The National Football Foundation and Hall of Fame awarded the MacArthur Bowl jointly to Texas and Ohio State. The Football Writers Association of America in a post-bowl ballot voted the Grantland Rice Award to Nebraska. In the post-bowl AP poll Notre Dame was promoted to second place, behind Nebraska. Texas was third and Tennessee was in fourth place, ahead of Ohio State.

Notre Dame, which came within an eyelash of beating Texas in the Cotton Bowl on January 1, 1970, was ranked first in both the AP and UPI polls in 1966. The MacArthur Bowl was awarded jointly to the Fighting Irish and Michigan State, which played a 10–10 tie before some 33 million television viewers in one of football's most celebrated games. In 1964 Notre Dame had a perfect record up to the last ninety seconds of the season, when it was beaten by Southern California, 21–17, after having led by 17–0. Because of their record in Parseghian's first season as head coach, the Fighting Irish were awarded the MacArthur Bowl, but the A.P. and U.P.I. ranked Alabama first.

Alabama was national champion in 1961 with its first perfect record since 1945. In 1964, with Joe Namath at quarterback, it was national champion again but lost to Texas in the Orange Bowl. In 1065, it was moved up to No. 1 in the A.P. post-bowl ranking after Michigan State, Arkansas, and Nebraska, all of which had perfect records, were beaten in bowl games. In 1966 Bryant led the Crimson Tide to another perfect season and the national championship.

John McKay in 1962 piloted Southern California to its first national championship since 1931, the year it ended Notre Dame's three-year winning streak. This was the first time the Trojans had had a perfect season since 1932. They were champions again with O. J. Simpson in 1967, though they lost to Oregon, 3–0. The 1966, 1967, 1968, and 1969 teams all played in the Rose Bowl, setting a record. The 1969 eleven won every game except for a tie with Notre Dame.

Ohio State in 1968 had a perfect record. In 1969 Woody Hayes' Buckeyes were picked to finish on top again, but in their final game they suffered a stunning defeat by Michigan. In 1970, picked with Texas as the two top teams, they fulfilled their destiny, taking vengeance on Michigan and finishing with a perfect record, only to fall before Stanford in the Rose Bowl. The 1961 Ohio State team was unbeaten but tied, and ranked second.

Michigan State won every game in 1965 and was ranked as champion, but after it lost in a bowl game the AP ranked Alabama No. 1. In 1966 Duffy Daugherty led his team to another perfect record except for the 10–10 tie with Notre Dame and shared the MacArthur Bowl with the Fighting Irish, who were first in the AP and UPI lists.

Joe Paterno directed Penn State to its first perfect record since 1947 in 1968. In 1969 the Nittany Lions were again invincible and offered a challenge to Texas' claim to the national championship. Frank Broyles' Arkansas Razorbacks put together two perfect seasons in 1964 and 1965 and their rivalry with Texas became one of the most dramatic in football. Minnesota, under Murray Warmath, won the national championship in 1960 for the first time since 1941. Nebraska had its first perfect season since 1915 in 1965, after winning its conference title for the first time in 1963. Mississippi won every game for the first time in 1962. Navy gave Wayne Hardin his fifth victory in a row over Army in 1963 and ranked second to Texas. Georgia in 1968 had its first undefeated team since 1946.

Other teams with perfect records in the 1960's were Yale in 1960, Rutgers in 1961, Dartmouth in 1962 and 1965, Princeton in 1964, Wyoming in 1967, Ohio University in 1968, and San Diego State and Toledo in 1969. Another team that distinguished itself was Indiana, which, under its new coach, John Pont, qualified in 1967 to go to the Rose Bowl for the first time. Still another standout was UCLA. The Bruins, under their new coach, Tommy Prothro, could give Southern California fits, as in 1967, when, with Gary Beban, they lost to the Trojans, 21–20 and again in 1969, in a 14–12 defeat.

These two games were among the most exciting of the 1960's. For sheer drama it would be difficult to surpass the 1969 Texas-Arkansas game, which Texas won with its last-ditch rally, 15–14, to be acclaimed in the dressing room by President Richard M. Nixon as a true champion. The Texas-Notre Dame game that followed in the Cotton Bowl was almost a carbon copy. Perhaps no other game in history during the regular season has commanded the national attention as did the 1966 meeting between Notre Dame and Michigan State, both all-victorious at the time. In 1968 Harvard and Yale met for the umpty-umpth time since 1875 in

The Game, and there could not possibly have been any other in the series that had such an impossible, utterly fantastic ending. Yale led 22–0 in the second period and was ahead 29–13, with 42 seconds left—and was tied, believe it or not. Harvard, with an unknown substitute at quarterback, Frank Champi, scored two touchdowns and passed twice for 2 points on each conversion, and came off with a tie as 40,000 went stark mad from joy or grief. Both teams had come into the game untied and unbeaten for the first time since 1909, and Yale had won sixteen games in a row. It had more penalties and lost more fumbles in the second half than usually happens to a team in a whole season.

Other memorable games of the 1960's were Michigan's 24–12 defeat of Ohio State in 1969—one of the upsets of all time; Arkansas's 27–24 defeat of Texas in their 1965 seesaw, the Razorbacks going 80 yards for the winning touchdown in the closing minutes; Southern California's 20–17 defeat of Notre Dame in 1964, the Trojans, after trailing 17–0 at half time, scoring two touchdowns in two minutes and ten seconds; UCLA's 14–12 shocker over Michigan State in the 1966 Rose Bowl game; Texas' 21–17 victory in the 1965 Orange Bowl game over Alabama, whose Joe Namath gave a great performance at quarterback on a badly weakened knee; and Navy's 21–15 triumph over Army in 1963, winning the Heisman Trophy for Roger Staubach and accolades for Wayne Hardin's fifth successive victory over Army.

In a poll taken for the National Collegiate Athletic Association by a panel of football writers and broadcasters from around the country in 1969 on the 100th anniversary of college football, the Notre Dame-Ohio State game of 1935 was voted to be the outstanding game of the century. In that game Andy Pilney led the Fighting Irish to an 18–13 victory in an unforgettable comeback that ended in the winning touchdown on a long pass on the final play of the game from Notre Dame's Bill Shakespeare to Wayne Millner as Pilney was being carried off on a stretcher. All of Notre Dame's points were scored in the fourth period.

The 10–10 Notre Dame-Michigan State tie of 1966 and the 29–29 Harvard-Yale tie of 1968 were among the other games selected. Also nominated were the Southern California-Notre Dame game of 1931, in which the Trojans, trailing 0–14 in the final quarter, pulled out victory at 16–14; Columbia's sensational 7–0 victory over Stanford in the 1934 Rose Bowl game; Tennessee's 6–0 defeat of Georgia Tech in 1956; Illinois' 39–14 trouncing of Michigan in 1924, when Red Grange scored four touchdowns the

"A Game of Football," painted by Henri Rousseau in 1908.

first four times he carried the ball in the first twelve minutes; SMU's 20–14 defeat of Texas Christian in 1935, earning Matty Bell's Mustangs the national championship—the first team from the Southwest Conference to be so honored. Also, the Army-Navy game of 1946 in which the great Blanchard-Davis era almost ended in defeat as the cadets held off the midshipmen inside their 5-yard line as the game ended for a 21–18 victory; the Boston College-Georgetown game of 1940, in which Frank Leahy's B.C. Eagles saved victory by giving up a safety to run out the clock and win, 19–18; Alabama's Rose Bowl victory in 1926 over Washington, 20–19 as Johnny Mack Brown and Dixie Howell did their thing; the Army-Notre Dame scoreless tie in 1946, the only checkmate to Blanchard and Davis in three years, and LSU's 7–3 victory over Mississippi in 1959.

HOW IT ALL STARTED
(PRINCETON-RUTGERS, 1869)

The following article was written for The Associated Press in 1933 by the late JOHN W. HERBERT *of the Rutgers Class of 1872, a prominent corporation lawyer in New York, who was a member of the Rutgers side of twenty-five players who defeated Princeton University in the first game of intercollegiate football in the United States, in 1869. It was sent out by the A.P. for publication in the newspapers of November 23, 1933. It was reprinted in the Cornell-Rutgers football program of 1968 by Ben Mintz, the Cornell program director.*

NEW BRUNSWICK, N.J. (AP)—The first intercollegiate game of football, not only in the United States but in the world, was played November 6, 1869, at New Brunswick between Rutgers College and Princeton University. I had the proud distinction of having participated in that game on the Rutgers team.

The challenge for the game was issued by Rutgers to Princeton. In the preliminary arrangements it was agreed that there should be twenty-five players on each side and that three games should be played, the side winning the first six goals in the game to be declared the winner of that game. The two captains worked out the rules that were to govern the game.

The captain of the Princeton team was the late William S. Gummere, who served as Chief Justice of the Supreme Court of New Jersey from 1901 until his death in 1932. The captain of the Rutgers team was William J. Leggett, who became a distinguished clergyman of the Dutch Reformed Church. These two men were each over six feet in height, fine athletes and well matched physically.

The game was called at 3 o'clock and started with a free kick-off from the tee, the same as now. It was played on the commons (where the Rutgers gymnasium now stands). On the arrival of the players, a few minutes before the game was called, they laid aside their hats, coats and vests. Neither team was in uniform, although some Rutgers players wore scarlet stocking-caps.

The players lined up on each side, the organization of the twenty-five being the same on both sides. Two men were selected by each team to play immediately in front of the opponent's goal and were known as captains of the enemy's goal.

The remainder of each team was divided into two sections. The players in one section were assigned to certain tracts of the field which they were to cover and not to leave. They were known as "fielders." The other section was detailed to follow the ball up and down the field. These latter players were called "bulldogs." They were easily recognizable in the evolution of the game as the forerunners of the modern rush line. I played in this division as I was a good wrestler and fleet of foot.

The toss of the coin for advantage gave Princeton the ball and Rutgers the wind. Amid a hush of expectancy among the spectators Princeton "bucked" or kicked the ball, but the kick was bad and the ball glanced to one side. Parke H. Davis in his "Football, the American Intercollegiate Game," then describes the game as follows:

"The light, agile Rutgers men pounced upon it like hounds and by driving it by short kicks and dribbles, the other players surrounding the ball and not permitting a Princeton man to get near it, quickly and craftily forced it down to Old Nassau's goal, where the captains of the enemy's goal were waiting and these two latter sent the ball between the posts amid great applause.

"The first goal had been scored in five minutes of play. During the intermission, Captain Gummere instructed Michael (the late Jacob E. Michael, Princeton '71), who was to become Dean of the Faculty at the University of Maryland), a young giant of the Princeton 25, to break up Rutgers' massing around the ball. Sides were changed and Rutgers 'bucked.' In this period the game was fiercly contested. Time and time again Michael, or 'Big Mike,' charged into Rutgers' primitive mass play and scattered the players like a burst bundle of sticks. On one of these plays Princeton obtained the ball and by a long accurate kick scored the second goal."

The third goal or "game," as it was then called, went to Rutgers, and the fourth was kicked by Princeton, "Big Mike" again bursting up a mass out of which Gummere gained possession of the ball and, with Princeton massed about him, easily dribbled the ball down and through the Rutgers goal posts, making the score once more a tie.

The fifth and sixth goals went to Rutgers, but the feature of this latter period of play in the memory of the players after the lapse of many years is awarded to "Big Mike" and Large (the late State Senator George H. Large of Flemington, a Rutgers player). Someone, by a random kick, had driven the ball to one side, where it rolled against the fence and stopped. Large led the pursuit for the ball, closely followed by Michael. They reached the fence, on which the students were perched, and, unable to check their momentum, in a tremendous impact struck the fence, which gave way with a crash, and over went its load of yelling students to the ground.

Every college probably has the humorous tradition of some player who has scored against his own team. The tradition of Rutgers dated from this first game, for one of her players, whose identity is unknown, in the sixth period started to kick the ball between his own goal posts. The kick was blocked, but Princeton took advantage of the opportunity and soon made the goal. This turn of the game apparently disorganized Rutgers, for Princeton also scored the next goal after a few minutes of play, thus bringing the total up to four-all.

At this stage Rutgers resorted to that use of craft which has never failed to turn the tide of every close battle. Captain Leggett had noticed that Princeton obtained a great advantage from the taller stature of their men, which enabled them to reach above the others and bat the ball in the air in some advantageous direction. Rutgers was ordered to keep the ball close to the ground. Following this stratagem the Rutgers men determinedly kicked the ninth and tenth goals, thus winning the match six goals to four and with it the distinction of a victory in the first game of intercollegiate football played in the world.

Eighty years after this historic game, the following appeared in the Report From Rutgers, *a monthly publication, in the issue of September, 1949:*

If Wellington was right that the Battle of Waterloo was won on the playing fields of Eton, then it's a good bet that the battles of the Marne, Chateau Thierry, Guadalcanal and Anzio were won on playing fields that trace their histories back to some goings on in New Brunswick on an afternoon long ago.

A cold wind skittered across College Field that frosty November 6 in 1869. It failed to chill the enthusiasm of the fifty assorted

Rutgers and Princeton students, however, who had come together for a special occasion. No less eager were a hundred curious on-lookers watching from their buckboards or precarious perches on a frail, wood fence surrounding the field.

A crotchety old Rutgers professor pedalled up to the scene on his bicycle. After a moment of viewing the proceedings he brandished his umbrella and stalked away shouting, "You men will come to no Christian end."

What the free-wheeling professor missed was the birth of America's autumn madness.

Eighty years ago, on the campus of the State University, Rutgers and Princeton met in the first intercollegiate football game. Rutgers won the famous encounter, 6 goals to 4.

(No one "died for dear old Rutgers" then—or later. That story grew out of an 1892 game when an injured player said he'd die for a drink of water. Imagination took it from there.)

Teams from the two New Jersey colleges met for another game a week later, this time with Princeton winning. The following year Rutgers introduced Columbia University to the new pastime. Other Eastern colleges soon put teams on the gridiron.

From its crude and rustic beginning on College Field . . . college football has spread into every corner of the nation and become an intrinsic part of the American scene.

Just as the academic training of the classroom develops the mental attitude in youth's approach to life, the fundamental training of the athletic field flexes and tones the physical and mental character. The qualities it develops in a boy—sportsmanship, honor, skill and stamina, poise, loyalty and teamwork, courage, cooperation, persistence—are football's contribution to the individual.

Football's contribution to a college is just as important, though perhaps less tangible. It is a unifying factor within the University family. It serves as a focal point of thought and activity—a common bond linking a widely diversified student body, faculty, administration and alumni.

It is doubtful that those Rutgers and Princeton lads had anything like that in mind when they started to mix it up on College Field eighty years ago. Their actions were motivated by the boundless high spirit of American youth seeking an outlet.

When teams from the two great universities meet this fall on the 80th anniversary of their notable invention, many things will be changed—the game, the rules, the spectators, the surroundings

—even the ball itself. But one thing remains unchanged—the same blazing competitive spirit that prompted twenty-five Princetonians to invade New Brunswick eighty years ago in answer to a challenge issued by twenty-five Rutgers students.

That love for rugged action and fierce will-to-win is the gridiron's trademark and football's priceless gift to America.

In 1949, DAN COYLE, *then in the Princeton Department of Public Relations and later assistant to the president of the university, interviewed Henry Green Duffield, a Princeton graduate and former officer, who, as a boy, had witnessed the second meeting between the Tiger and Rutgers in 1869. Coyle's release to the press for October 28, 1949, follows.*

New Jersey's game of the year, the 42nd renewal of the Princeton-Rutgers rivalry in Palmer Stadium Saturday afternoon, will be a great deal more than the 80th anniversary of the first game in the nation's oldest series to a 90-year-old Princeton alumnus who will see the encounter from his car, parked near the stadium scoreboard just off the playing field.

To Henry Green Duffield, a member of the Princeton Class of 1881 and treasurer emeritus of Princeton, Saturday's meeting for the mythical gridiron championship of the state will be another milestone in one of the most remarkable attendance records in the history of American sport, and certainly the most remarkable in the annals of intercollegiate football.

Just eight decades ago as a youngster of ten, Henry Green Duffield, the son of a Princeton professor, wandered away from his Princeton home without parental permission, climbed a rickety fence several blocks from his house and watched Princeton avenge the 6–4 loss it had sustained a week earlier at New Brunswick in helping bring American football into being. His recollections of that far-off afternoon of November 13, 1869, the day that produced Nassau's first football victory, 8 goals to 0, are as clear as if he were describing an event that took place yesterday.

"The game was played on Conover's Field at the foot of Chambers Street, about a block north of Nassau Street," Mr. Duffield recalls. "It wasn't much more than a cow pasture but the hay had been mowed, goal lines drawn and posts erected. It was about a quarter mile from where Palmer Staduim now stands," Mr. Duffield, one of Princeton's all-time baseball greats, went on to say.

"Under the rules of 1869," Mr. Duffield points out, "you could catch the ball but you couldn't run with it. If you did, it was a foul and the ball had to be thrown free up in the air. It could be advanced by batting it with your fist, by kicking it as in soccer or even by dribbling it as in basketball today.

"The ball was not an oval but was supposed to be completely round. It never was, though—it was too hard to blow up right. The game was stopped several times that day while the teams called for a little key from the sidelines. They used it to unlock the small nozzle which was tucked into the ball, and then took turns blowing it up. The last man generally got tired and they put it back in play somewhat lopsided. . . ."

The friend of every Princeton coach who has ever sent a team onto a playing field, Mr. Duffield, since witnessing the second classic of 1869, has seen some 565 of the 628 games the Tigers have played down through the decades. Just twice since 1884, or twice in 64 years, and both times on doctors' orders, has he missed a an eminent mathematician, and the brother of the late Edward D. Princeton home game. . . . The son of Professor John T. Duffield, Duffield, acting president of Princeton in 1932–1933, Duffield joined Princeton's administrative staff in 1885 and stepped into emeritus ranks in 1930. . . .

WALTER CAMP, FATHER OF AMERICAN FOOTBALL

Walter Camp was one of the giants of football in the United States. He stands with Stagg, Rockne, Thorpe, Warner, Heffelfinger in the imprint they made upon the game and their everlasting fame.

He stands first among them, for it was he who sired the game as it is played in the United States—the game that evolved from the soccer (association) and rugby football of England. He played as a Yale freshman in the first Yale-Harvard game of rugby in 1876, when the Intercollegiate Football Association was formed among Harvard, Princeton, Yale and Columbia and adopted the code of the Rugby Union of Britain with modifications. From then on, his was the fertile, inventive mind and guiding leadership that brought about the evolution of the American style of football from rugby, which had displaced soccer (the game played by Princeton and Rutgers in 1869) through the circumstance that Harvard alone chanced to depart from soccer and stood firm for its semi-rugby style of play.

Step by step Camp, who credits his 1876 Yale captain, Eugene V. Baker, with sowing "the first germs of real football at Yale . . . and taught me the best part of football as I know it," led the rules conventions through the evolution. Paramount among the changes he sponsored were the substitution of scrimmage for the rugby scrummage (scrum) and the adoption of the system of downs and yards to gain (first 5, then 10). These two innovations completely changed the basic structure, format and concept of the game, establishing the principle of possession of the ball (as contrasted with the constant flux of exchanges in rugby) and leading to the development of planning and strategy.

Scrimmage was adopted at the convention in 1880 and with it appeared the quarterback, who received the snapback in the scrimmage but could not run with the ball. That same year too Camp won his fight for eleven men on a side instead of the fifteen of rugby. Yale had advocated eleven since it played the Eton "Players" from England, who employed only eleven, in 1873. It was Camp who came up with the arrangement of the eleven men that was settled upon: seven men in the line, a quarterback, two halfbacks and a fullback. This became the standard alignment.

In 1882 the system of downs was adopted, the team in possession of the ball being required to gain five yards in three downs (later in 1906, to 10 yards, and in 1912 a fourth down was added in which to gain 10 yards). With this change, the field was marked with horizontal lines 5 yards apart, giving it the appearance of a gridiron.

Also in 1882 the rules makers adopted Camp's system of signals —at first sentences, then letters, then numbers. In 1883 he brought about the introduction of a numerical scoring system, points being awarded for each method of scoring—safety 1 point, touchdown 2, goal after touchdown 4, and goal from field 5. In 1885 Camp offered a resolution for the establishment of a neutral zone between the lines of the opposing teams, to lessen the violence of the game, but it was not adopted until 1906.

In 1888 Camp introduced another important change, permitting tackling below the waist to as low as the knees. This change and the prohibition against linemen blocking with extended arms, requiring them to keep their arms at their sides, necessitated a change in the deployment of the team in possession of the ball and brought about the close-order formation of American football. The line, which had extended pretty much across the field, was now constricted and the backs, who had been spread wide to carry out the lateral passing movements characteristic of rugby, had to come in close also, for protection against the deadly low tackle.

So was born the T formation, which now became the standard or regular alignment, replacing the spread.

The year 1906 was one of the most momentous in the history of football and Camp played a leading role in its deliberations and far-reaching legislation. The game was under heavy fire the country over for the brutality of its close-order, mass-momentum play, *in which physical force was all-important, and skill and science had little part. As the leader of the American Football Rules Committee, Camp cooperated with Captain Palmer E. Pierce of West Point, the head of a new organization known as the Intercollegiate Athletic Association of the United States (which changed its name on December 29, 1910, to the National Collegiate Athletic Association). The two organizations met jointly in New York January 12, 1906, merged under the name of the American Intercollegiate Football Rules Committee and adopted the far-reaching changes that opened up the game, introduced the forward pass that brought about a revolutionary change in the pattern of play that was to add immensely to its popularity, and so saved the game.*

Thus, Walter Camp was not only the sire of American football but also a savior. For almost half a century, from 1876 until his death on March 14, 1925, this noble character was a prominent figure on the football scene and for most of the years he led in giving the game shape and character, and in setting and enforcing standards of fair play and sportsmanship.

At Yale, he played halfback for six years and was captain of the team two years and he excelled also in baseball, track, tennis, gymnastics, and water sports. He was Yale's first football coach (unpaid) and from 1876 until 1910 he played an important role in the direction of the technique and strategy of Yale football. He was a member of every rules convention or committee from 1879 until his death. He was chairman of the rules committee until 1911, when he was succeeded by Edward K. Hall of Dartmouth. His all-America teams (originated by Caspar Whitney in 1889), published in Collier's *for the years 1898 through 1924, were recognized as official. But most of all, his fame rests upon the fact that he, above all others, was responsible for conceiving and bringing into being the game of football which typifies the American competitive spirit in its premium upon imagination, speed, strategy and daring, as well as upon sheer physical ability and durability.*

PARKE H. DAVIS, one of the game's foremost historians, who also was a successful coach and player, wrote the following tribute to Camp for the 1925 Football Guide.

Walter Camp, father of American football.

WALTER CAMP . . . originated this book. In the intercollegiate convention of December 5, 1883, a motion casually was adopted authorizing "Mr. Camp to copyright and to print the football rules." With the extraordinary talent for invention which characterized all of his activities, Mr. Camp seized the opportunity to give to the sport this official handbook. For forty-two years competently and graciously he has presided as editor of its pages, and in its features for many, many long years will he live. We, who at one time and another in the past full five decades have sat with him in football's legislature, originally the old intercollegiate "conventions" and later the "rules committees," and we, who have collaborated with him in the production of these pages, deeply feel that this book should present at this time a record of the principal achievements of the man who for fifty years has been the central figure of intercollegiate football.

Walter Camp pre-eminently was a philanthropist in American sport. His was the genius to play his country's games surpassingly well; to improve and increase their technique; to surround them with customs and features that added intensely to their attraction; to accompany them with a code of chivalry and nobleness that coincidentally trained players and spectators in American manhood at its best; and his was the talent so to popularize these games that from casual pastimes of schoolboys and collegians they became national institutions of entertainment, recreation and culture.

In his youth he was famed as a player, par excellence, in baseball, in track and water sports, in tennis and in gymnastics, but it was in football that he achieved the masterpieces for which he will be given a place among the most useful citizens of his country. To Yale, his alma mater, he gave—and gave without reservation —time, talent, labor, loyalty and devotion, yet in the depth and breadth of his transcendental genius he wrought for all America.

The present type of intercollegiate football began its career in the fall of 1876. Walter Camp played halfback upon the Yale team in that initial year and continued so to play for six years, in two of which he served as captain. He represented Yale in 1878 in the intercollegiate convention and thereafter sat in every session of football's legislatures, intercollegiate conventions and rules committees, until the session of March 14, 1925, in attending which he died. So continuous and so commanding were his activities in this long period of time that his biography constitutes a history of these teeming five football decades.

Walter Camp was born in the city of New Haven April 17, 1859. He was the son of Leverett L. and Ellen Cornwell Camp. He prepared at Hopkins Grammar School in New Haven and entered and graduated at Yale in the class of 1880. Subsequently he spent two years in the Yale Medical School, but gave up that profession to enter business. In 1888 he married Alice Graham Sumner. Their children were two, Walter Camp, Jr., Yale 1913, a football player of distinction, and Janet Camp Hobson. Mr. Camp was singularly successful as a business man, working his way from a position in the sales force of the New Haven Clock Company through the posts of assistant treasurer, treasurer, general manager, president and chairman of the board of directors. He gave generously of his time to the civic and charitable movements of·the city of New Haven. His extraordinary creative and administrative talent made a success of every enterprise in which he engaged.

Among his schoolboy companions, Walter Camp was a leader in sports afield and on the water. His were the fleetest feet in the schools of all New Haven. His arm was among the first and the best to master the new art of pitching a curve with a baseball. He was as adept in the water sports upon the Sound, powerful and versatile as a swimmer and diver and able to bend and to feather an oar with the best of the watermen of the harbor. Thus, when he entered Yale in 1876 he instantly became one of the best all-around athletes in the university. In his undergraduate days he made every varsity team that existed in that period. He was pitcher and captain of the nine. He was halfback and captain of the eleven. He ran the hurdles and is credited at Yale with having invented the present hurdle step. In swimming he repeatedly won races from short distances up to five miles. In the rising game of tennis he was a leader. He rowed upon his class crew. This memorial, however, must be limited to his career in football.

There was a zest in football at Yale in the fall of 1876. For three years Yale had been playing a modification of the "association" game and in the previous year had waged a battle with Harvard in a modification of Rugby. In the fall of 1876, however, Princeton stirred the football men at Yale by issuing an invitation to Columbia, to Harvard and to Yale to meet them in a convention at Springfield for the purpose of forming an intercollegiate football association, of adopting the Rugby Union rules and for the purpose of scheduling a set of games, all of which was done. And so, when Eugene V. Baker, captain of the Yale football squad in 1876, called for candidates for a Rugby team he was promptly confronted by the lithe, rugged youngster, Walter Camp. The latter easily won the position of halfback.

As a player Walter Camp was exceptionally fast and extraordinarily strong. He was a long distance punter and a drop and place kicker who will stand comparison with the stars of later years. His most conspicuous characteristic, however, was his flashing mind, resourceful, courageous, thinking continually in terms of football, swiftly solving new situations, and indomitable.

No player in the history of the game contended against greater misfortune in his scoring plays than Walter Camp. Four times in his career he actually accomplished scoring plays only to have them nullified. The first of these catastrophes occurred in the Princeton-Yale game of 1877. When Columbia, Harvard, Princeton and Yale adopted the Rugby Union code in 1876 they introduced only one change. That was in the method of scoring. Our English comrades computed the score by goals alone. The American pioneers of 1876 changed this rule so as to make four touchdowns equal to a goal. This change Yale in the convention of that year stoutly resisted. Consequently, in the preliminaries to the game with Princeton in 1877, Captain Eugene V. Baker of Yale exacted the special rule that touchdowns should not count at all in determining the score, but that the latter should be based upon goals alone. As the playing eventuated, Walter Camp, in the first half, catching a long, sailing punt, dashed 80 yards up the field through the entire Princeton team and made a touchdown. In the second half, getting the ball out of "scrum," Camp again dashed up the field, fifty yards. As he was crossing Princeton's line, he was sharply tackled by McNair, Minor and Clarke and thrown, but, rising to his feet, he shook off his tacklers and by the great strength that was his forced his way over the line for a second touchdown. In both instances the try was missed. No score by either side occurred and the game technically thus ended in a draw, 0 to 0.

His third misfortune came in the Harvard-Yale game of 1878. It is near the end of the first half. Wetherbee of Harvard has carried the ball almost to the Yale goal line, where it is lost. Watson and Camp of Yale, alternately carrying the ball, sweep down the field. Finally Camp bursts away and carries the ball to a point thirty-five yards from Harvard's goal line. Here, as he is about to be tackled, he suddenly stops in his flight, drops the ball and, with a drop kick, lifts it high in the air. The ball spins down its groove directly towards Harvard's goal. While it is in the air the whistle sounds the end of the half. The ball continues accurately on its way and cleaves the posts high above the cross-bar. The rule in that period, however, terminated the half the instant the whistle sounded, and thus this brilliant goal was nullified.

The fourth of these curious coincidences came in the Harvard-Yale contest of 1879. Again it was in the closing moments of the first half. The ball is directly in front of Harvard's goal, but forty-five long and difficult yards away. Camp gets the ball out of "scrum" and essays to conquer the long distance by a goal from the field. He drops the ball, lifts it with a powerful kick, and the ball, spinning and tumbling, covers the long flight and crosses squarely between the posts. The referee, Bland Ballard of Princeton, however, has detected holding, and so the beautiful goal which would have won an otherwise scoreless game went for naught.

It was now 1880. Walter Camp had graduated, but was continuing his studies in the Yale Medical School. At that time the idea of undergraduates only manning representative teams had not been conceived. Indeed, Fate was tardily waiting for the arrival of the fall of 1889 to launch that reform and grimly had selected Walter Camp himself as her leader to undertake the racking revolution to accomplish that reform. Therefore, in 1880 Walter Camp continued at his old position of halfback and reappeared at the same position in 1881. In the former year in the Yale-Harvard game he achieved another scoring play and this time it counted. In the closing five minutes of play he made the first score of the game by sending a place kick thirty-five yards through Harvard's goal posts.

Great as he was as a player, he was still greater as an architect of the American intercollegiate game. Sitting as Yale's representative specifically, but of intercollegiate and interscholastic America generally, in every session of football's legislatures from 1878 to 1925, it was his resourceful mind that conceived and constructed the majority of the basic changes which made a distinctively American game out of the classic, old English Rugby.

He was still a junior at Yale when he began his long and brilliant career. He appeared in the game's second "convention," as the legislative assemblages of Columbia, Harvard, Princeton and Yale were called, held in the old Massasoit House in Springfield, October 9, 1878. He promptly and aggressively took a position of leadership by moving to abolish the Rugby institution of fifteen players upon a side and to substitute therefor the number of eleven. This proposition the convention rejected. With the persistency that ever is one of the marks of genius, in 1879 he renewed the motion, but again it was rejected. In the latter convention he set in motion

1879 Yale team. Walter Camp, captain.

his second reform, which was to count safeties as scoring plays, but adversely to the side that made them. This suggestion also at that time was rejected.

During these years, the closing years of the '70's, Walter Camp had been intensely studying the possibilities of the Rugby type of game in its natural laboratory, the playing field. Here he was confronted with the Rugby "scrum" which gave to neither side the orderly possession, nor the right to put it in play and to execute the ensuing maneuver. With his penetrative mind, keen and powerful notwithstanding his youthful years, he perceived the vast improvement which could be obtained by establishing a method of putting the ball in play which would give to one side its undisturbed possession, thereby permitting a strategic and tactical preparation to advance it. Accordingly he planned a new device, the "scrimmage," and quietly awaited the coming of the next intercollegiate football convention. This eventually convened at Springfield October 12, 1880. It was composed of W. H. Manning and T. C. Thacher of Harvard, Edward Peace and Francis Loney of Princeton, Walter Camp, Robert H. Watson and W. B. Hill of Yale. Mr. Camp as a preliminary renewed his motion to reduce the number of players upon a side from fifteen to eleven, and this time the motion prevailed. Thereupon he suggested the following profound change in the rules, the phrasing of which he personally had penned:

"A scrimmage takes place when the holder of the ball puts it on the ground before him and puts it in play while on-side either by kicking the ball or by snapping it back with his foot. The man who first receives the ball from the snap-back shall be called the quarter-back and shall not rush forward with the ball under penalty of foul." This proposition was accepted unanimously and thus Walter Camp at the outset of his football career became the inventor of the "eleven," the "scrimmage" and the "quarter-back."

The disposition of the eleven players thus provided commanded the immediate attention of the tacticians. Harvard presented an arrangement consisting of seven men upon the line, three at half and one at full, the three halfbacks alternating as quarter-back. Princeton's solution of the problem was the deploying of six men upon the line, one at quarter, two at half and two at full. Walter Camp presented the formation in which seven men stood upon the line, one at quarter, two at half and one at full. This arrangement, as is well known, became the standard formation of the game.

When Walter Camp devised the idea of giving to one side the undisturbed possession of the ball he did not provide for its surrender by limiting the number of the downs. He assumed that the custom of prolific punting which characterized the period would continue and thus would transfer the ball from one side to the other upon every play or two. Strategists at Princeton, however, schemed differently. The wily Edward S. Peace, crafty John S. Harlan and P. T. Bryan planned to hold the ball indefinitely, a policy which in time received the title of the "block game." These tactics attained their most grotesque proportions in the Princeton-Yale game of 1881, in which Princeton retained the ball without scoring throughout the first half and Yale retaliated by keeping it in possession throughout the second half and also did not score. The "block game" precipitated a great outcry of indignation and demands for reform. Again it was Walter Camp who met the crisis by writing another revolutionary innovation into the game:

"If on three consecutive fairs and downs a team shall not have advanced the ball five yards, nor lost ten, they must give up the ball to opponents at the spot of the fourth down."

This was the rule that brought into the sport the familiar "yards to gain," the cross lines of lime and the endeared name of "gridiron."

In the early 80's the old Rugby system of scoring was the source of a number of disputes and quarrels. The system was not a numerical one, but balanced one play against another. Thus a goal from the field was superior to a touchdown, but four touchdowns took precedence over a goal from the field. If the question of victory involved safeties, then the side making four safeties less won the game. Unfortunately, this system was not complete and comprehensive. Hence there came a Harvard-Princeton battle in 1882, bitterly waged, in which Frank A. Mason of Harvard scored a touchdown, missed the try but later kicked a goal from the field. Princeton, in turn, scored a touchdown and a goal on the try through the cleverness of James T. Haxall. Each eleven claimed the victory, contending for the superiority of its particular goal. The referee, Robert W. Watson of Yale, awarded the game to Harvard. Princeton, contending that this award was arbitrary and not in accordance with an existing rule, refused to accept it and informally claimed the game for years. The rancor and disorder was intolerable to the methodical Camp. Therefore, in the convention of October 17, 1883, he introduced another distinctly American institution, numerical scoring. The original values given to the scoring plays were as follows: safety, one point; touchdown, two points; goal from a try, four points; goal from the field, five points.

Five years were now destined to come and go before the fertile Walter Camp was to inject another great basic change into the English inheritances of the Rugby rules, although the pathway of these five years literally is strewn with minor improvements made by him in the game. During these happy years and, indeed from the fall of 1876, tackling had been of the classic Rugby fashion, waist high, with its accompanying technical device known as "held," the latter too intricate for description here. In the convention of March 3, 1888, Mr. Camp introduced a resolution allowing tackles to be made as low as the knees. Prior to that year formations had found the line of scrimmage stretching widely across the field, with the backs far out, the ball being passed to them always by a long pass. This was the beautiful old open game, so loved and lamented by the oldtimers. And now came the low tackle. It apparently was only a slight change in the rule, but a slight change in the rule can make a profound alteration in the practice of play. Against the sure and deadly low tackle the best of backs no longer could gain consistently in an open field. To meet this reinforcement of the defense, the offensive line of scrimmage was contracted until the players stood shoulder to shoulder as they do today. The backs were drawn in and also stationed close to the line. Open field running disappeared and in its place came heavy interference, line bucks and plunges, boxed on the tackle, flying wedges, turtle backs, mass plays, momentum plays, flying interference, revolving wedges, tandems, guards back, tackle tandems and the scores of other ingenious engines of attack which characterized football from 1888 until 1895.

In the invention and creations of these tactical devices Walter Camp was at his best. The extraordinary ingenuity of Lorin F. Deland, who invented for Harvard the flying wedge, the turtle back and other powerful plays, drew from Mr. Camp correspondingly ingenious methods of defense. But Mr. Camp seized the flying principle which Mr. Deland had originated and applied it to almost all of Yale's plays, thus starting the interference before the ball was put in play. In the beginning Walter Camp had opposed all interference. This was one of the few instances in the game in which he opposed progress. This feature of football, called "guarding," was introduced into the sport by Princeton. It originally consisted of a player running at each side of the player carrying the ball to make tackling from the side difficult. As these players began gradually to interfere in advance of the man with the ball, Mr. Camp stoutly resisted the innovation both as an official and as a football legislator, but finally not only succumbed to the custom but in 1890 produced for Yale the most powerful interference the game ever had known and which is still unsurpassed.

So intense and innate was the sense of chivalry and nobleness in Walter Camp that from the very beginning of his athletic career he set forth the standard of athletic morale, and for fifty years incessantly sought to advance it. As early as 1885 he introduced a resolution in the intercollegiate convention establishing a neutral zone between the rival lines in order to lessen the prevalent roughness, but his fellow legislators could not see the merits in this reform and so defeated the resolution. Twenty years were destined to come and go before, in 1905, this rule was adopted. In 1887 he led in obtaining the written pledge of the captains of Harvard, Pennsylvania, Princeton, Wesleyan and Yale, then the components of the Intercollegiate Football Association, to establish the highest possible standards of honorable play. In 1889 he started the stirring revolution that was necessary to establish the principle that only undergraduates should play upon representative college teams. This revolution raged for six years before the principle was accepted. In those six years he also took the lead in abolishing flying wedges, flying interference, momentum mass plays and numerous other dangerous tactical devices. So racking and rending was this revolution that in several instances intercollegiate relations were severed, the old Intercollegiate Football Association went to pieces, two new football tribunals appeared, one composed of Navy, Princeton and Yale, the other of Cornell, Harvard and Pennsylvania, while a most chaotic feature appeared in two different sets of playing rules, widely divergent. In the midst of this turmoil a strong cry came from the public demanding the abolition of the sport. The Army and Navy Departments at Washington promptly responded by erasing football from the regimens at Annapolis and West Point. Football was now in the pillory and facing a fearful crisis.

In this critical juncture, Walter Camp, accompanied by the late Alexander Moffat of Princeton, came forward with the plan for the establishment of a Rules Committee to govern the sport and also with a plan for a series of radical reforms in the game. The Committee was established and at once began a series of sessions that lasted until late in the following summer, but which finally produced a completely reformed game. This revision instantly was accepted by the public and the universities of the country, and the sport swept forward in 1900 into the new century on a great wave of popular favor.

With the marvelous ability with which he could attend to the sport of football in general, and to Yale's game in particular, Walter Camp during the winter months of 1900 was at work upon what was destined to be Yale's most famous tactical device, the "tackle-back." From the earliest days of the game the defensive line had been taught to play low and charge their opponents back at the snap of the ball. Camp's theory was that a play could be devised which would take advantage of this forward plunge by getting a drive into the opening thus made by the defensive lineman and making a substantial gain before that lineman could recover his position. This theory eventually shaped itself into Yale's famous tackle-back formation, which was an adaptation of the "guards-back" formation of George W. Woodruff, also of Yale, but who made that mechanism celebrated while coach at the University of Pennsylvania. For four years this remarkable engine of football warfare ploughed and crashed through Yale's opponents, piling up unprecedented scores.

During these years the Rules Committee consisted of representatives of Cornell, Chicago, Harvard, Navy, Pennsylvania, Princeton and Yale, the legislation of the Committee being accepted by the colleges of the country merely because of its merit and not by any agreement. But a radical revolution was again just over the horizon. Tactics still were designed along the lines of close formations. The public was demanding open play. The colleges of the South and West were demanding representation upon the Rules Committee. In the fall of 1905, Theodore Roosevelt, then President of the United States, summoned to the White House representatives of Harvard, Princeton and Yale and impressed upon them the necessity of meeting the public's objections to the game.

In this juncture, twenty-eight institutions not represented upon the Rules Committee, excepting Harvard, met in New York and established another Rules Committee under the name of "Conference Committee," making its membership equal in number to the older committee, which was known as the "Intercollegiate Committee."

For the second time football was threatened with two governing heads, two different sets of rules, and two fields of playing teams. The leader of the "Conference" group was Captain Palmer E. Pierce of the Army. The leader of the "Intercollegiate Committee" was Walter Camp. Out of the coolness, restraint, wisdom and far vision of these two leaders and their associates on the two committees came a new football tribunal consisting of the members of both committees, each committee preserving its identity but both functioning as a single body under the name of the American Intercollegiate Football Rules Committee.

Procedure in football legislation has been radically different since the establishment of the Rules Committee. The old intercollegiate conventions were typically parliamentary bodies. The Rules Committees have endeavored to act as a unit. Innovations in the sport, therefore, have not been the work of any particular man but have been the products of the Committee as a whole.

The dean in years upon these annual Committees during these past two decades, Mr. Camp, was also dean in fact. His great experience, his keen powers of analysis, his sound, mature judgment and his broad view at all times was a steadying beacon in the deliberations of the various Committees.

There is another great institution in the sport which originated in the genius of Walter Camp in the turbulent period of 1905. That institution is the Central Board on Officials. Mr. Camp first broached the scheme for this useful tribunal at the session of the "old" Committee in 1905 and renewed it in the session of the joint committee in 1906, by whom it was adopted. To Dr. James A. Babbitt, of course, belongs the credit for its subsequent development.

No collegian ever developed greater zeal to his alma mater than Walter Camp gave to Yale, and yet, in his loyalty he was scrupulously fair to Yale's athletic adversaries. There is an incident in his career which vividly illustrates the rugged integrity of his character and the confidence which his opponents reposed in him.

The Princeton-Yale game in 1885 approached in the midst of high feeling between the rival combatants. In the preceding year their struggle had terminated in a dispute which finally resulted in the referee, William H. Appleton of Harvard, the sole official of the game in that period, declaring the contest "no game." As the referee was still the sole official under the rules in 1885, a prolonged deadlock intervened over the selection of this official. Finally Princeton selected Walter Camp, a Yale man, to officiate solely in the game with Yale. The game was fiercely played and its crises placed Walter Camp in one trying position after another. In the first half Harry Beecher of Yale caught a punt and ran sixty-five yards for a touchdown. Mr. Camp nullified the score by ruling that Beecher had stepped out of bounds. Later G. A. Watkinson of Yale kicked a goal from the field which at that time counted five points. The game neared the end with the score Yale 5, Princeton 0. Only a few minutes remained to play. Watkinson sent a long punt twisting down the field. Henry C. Lamar, the glorious "Tilly" of Princeton tradition, caught the ball on the bound and leaped into flight down the left sideline. Beecher and Watkinson ranged into position to tackle Lamar or to force him out of bounds. They collided, went down close to the line, but Lamar, emerging through them and racing on to Yale's goal line, touched down. F. G. Peters, Yale's captain, claimed that Lamar had stepped out of bounds in the collision with Beecher and Watkinson, but Walter Camp, rugged young Roman that he was, ruled against his alma mater, gave Princeton the touchdown, and the score then stood Yale 5, Princeton 4. Richard M. Hodge of Princeton thereupon kicked the goal on the try, and Princeton thus won one of the most famous games in her football history by 6 points to 5.

In 1886 William A. Brooks, captain of Harvard, again signally illustrated the confidence Yale's opponents reposed in the integrity of Walter Camp by selecting him to serve as referee, still the sole official, in the Harvard-Yale game of that year.

Of the side features of American football, none has been more interesting than the selection of the "all-America" teams . . . Mr. Camp's selections, both by his prestige and priority, have been the commanding choices in public imagination. . . .

It has been said that it is as glorious to have written a country's songs as to have fought a country's wars or to have formulated a country's laws. Walter Camp performed an equally large and useful public service by establishing the amateur sports of the country upon a sound and wholesome basis. As the leader of Yale in the years when Yale was the leader of the colleges of the country Walter Camp stood forth so vividly and so correctly for the best in intercollegiate sport that he deeply impressed his ideals upon the outdoor games of the country. His standard, full high advanced, was ever the standard of honor, nobleness and manliness.

In his latter years he enlarged his leadership and his usefulness by advocating the physical well-being of all America. He was one of the pioneers in the municipal playground idea, in the campaigns to improve the health of factory forces. During the war he served his country with his peculiar talents by acting as Chairman of the Athletic Department of the Navy Commission on Training Camp Activities and he also served as physical director of the Air Service. His most direct and widest service to his countrymen, however, was to give the average men and women of the United States a simple and efficient system of exercises widely famous as the "daily dozen."

Is Walter Camp, therefore, not justly characterized as the philanthropist of American sport? He glorified the Homeric thrill of human action, the zest of out-of-doors, the contest of speed, of strength, of skill, of courage and of intelligence. He emphasized the necessity of keeping the human body efficiently fit at all times for strenuous action and taught all how to achieve it. He gave to his country its most complex and one of its two leading games. He so evolved that game—intercollegiate football—that beyond all other games trains its followers, players and spectators in the fundamental qualities of a successful character—knowledge, skill, strength, speed, obedience, initiative, aggressiveness, courage, honor and morale.

Four hundred years ago in England football was called "camp ball." And so today, and for many, many days will the name of Walter Camp be most intimately associated with this game. So wide and deep was the love of the American people for this leader that his memorials will be elaborate and many. They will be wrought in marble, in bronze, upon the painted canvas and upon the printed page. To his name will be dedicated fields and stadia. His most imposing memorial, however, must be the great game which he, more than all others, invented, which for fifty years he spanned and in which from first to last he was the central figure.

Thus, time and time again in the years to come, for the thousands of us who knew him, and for the millions of us who knew of him, as we sit . . . in the towering stands, will the cross lines of lime in fancy leave their places and, reforming in letters of gleaming white against a sward of emerald green, from goal line to goal line, in memory of him, spell the kindly, the mighty, the manly, the noble name of Walter Camp.

The following resolution was adopted by the American Intercollegiate Football Rules Committee on the occasion of Camp's death. The signers of the resolution were Edward K. Hall, chairman; Alonzo Stagg, William S. Langford, William W. Roper, James A. Babbitt, Fred W. Moore, C. W. Savage, M. F. Ahearn, Dana X. Bible, H. J. Stegeman, John J. McEwan, George M. Varnell and C. Henry Smith.

Whereas Death has taken from us our beloved associate, Walter Camp;

Resolved, That we, the members of the American Intercollegiate Football Rules Committee, spread upon our records and publish in the Football Guide for 1925 this acknowledgment of his contribution to the game of American Rugby football.

This contribution covers a period of almost exactly half a century. It began at Yale in the fall of 1876, when he played in the first game of Rugby football ever played by college teams in this country. [This overlooks the game between Harvard and McGill in 1874 at Cambridge and Harvard's two games with Tufts in June and October, 1875.] It ended when he died in his sleep on the night of March 13–14, 1925, during an intermission between sessions of the Rules Committee called together in New York City for the purpose of establishing the playing rules for the season of 1925. . . . From 1879 until 1925 . . . literally up to the hour of his death he was the acknowledged leader in the evolution of the game through the framing of its playing rules.

In the deliberations of this committee his counsel has been always wise and far-seeing; his attitude toward those with whose views he differed has been unfailingly generous and understanding; and his adherence to the highest standards of sportsmanship has been unwavering and inspiring. It is in this last respect that Walter Camp has made his greatest contribution to football. If football is to continue as the greatest of all academic sports, it will be due not alone to the foundations, toward the building of which Walter Camp contributed so generously, but in a far greater measure to the fine standards of American sportsmanship, toward the establishment of which no man in America has contributed more, either by precept or by example.

American Rugby football has lost its founder and its greatest champion, but his influence on the game will endure as long as the game is played.

FOOTBALL IN ITS CRADLE DAYS

The dean of all football coaches, the patriarch of the game, who thought he was too young to retire at the University of Chicago after having served as head coach there for forty-one years; who refused to accept retirement again after fourteen more years at the University of the Pacific, and who finally gave up coaching at the age of 98 only because of the poor health of his wife, AMOS ALONZO STAGG *died in 1965 at the age of 103. In the following article narrated to Wesley Winans Stout and published as "Touchdown" in* The Saturday Evening Post *of October 23, 1926, Stagg portrays what the game was like in its cradle days and the changes that marked its evolution from soccer and rugby into American football.*

THE ARMY AND THE NAVY will play their annual football classic in Chicago this year for the first time. As I write this, more than two months before the game, every seat in the Grant Park Stadium has been sold or allotted and the gate will represent the sum of $700,000, some $200,000 more than the previous record. . . . Our total football receipts our first season of 1892 at Chicago were about one nine hundred and sixtieth of the amount this game is expected to attract. Our books showed $732.92 taken in, $633.33 paid out, and thirteen games played.

For ten years the university's athletics owed me money, a debt that fluctuated around $1,000, until Mrs. Stagg despaired of ever having a bank account of our own. My salary was $2,500 a year. Mr. Rockefeller gave to the new school with unprecedented generosity, but not even a Rockefeller's munificence was equal to the imagination of William Rainey Harper. It was no fresh-water college he envisioned. Doctor Harper was the unusual combination of a sound scholar and a born organizer, promoter and advertiser. In the '80's he had stirred up the whole country to the study of Hebrew. There is the measure of the man. One who could do that could do anything.

Then the panic of '93 tackled us low and accurately, and every dollar in the land hid out in bomb-proof dugouts. I was director of physical culture and athletics without an athletic field. At my urging, Dr. Harper made a request on Marshall Field in the spring of 1893 for the use of a square block of vacant land immediately north of the campus. Mr. Field cabled back on April third from Europe, giving us its use at a rental of one dollar a year.

We passed the hat on the campus then. The faculty and officers of the university contributed $490, the students added $281 and an athletic entertainment raised $95 more. Two lumber companies donated boards and posts. I hired one carpenter to put in the posts and stringers, while the students, headed by me, nailed home the boards and made a lark of it. We graded the uneven pasture, dumping the earth from a mound at the northeast corner into the low spot along Ellis Avenue, then sodded the infield, and I never labored harder on the Newark salt meadows.

Under forced draft, we had the field in reasonably playable condition by middle June, in time to meet the University of Virginia nine in the first game of any kind played on what, since 1914, has been Stagg Field, but was for its first twenty-one years, by an inevitable pun on the donor's name, Marshall Field. I had promoted a college baseball championship series as an adjunct to the World's Fair. Virginia was one of the teams entered, and we beat them 8 to 3. The future Mrs. Stagg, then a freshman of seventeen, attracted from New York State by the fuss being made over this new coeducational university, was in the stands.

The first building on the campus, a contractor's shanty, became our dressing room. I bought it out of my own pocket and moved it on the field, the baseball season having ended with a deficit and left the cupboard bare. We sold advertising space on the inner side of the fence, picking up ten dollars here and there. Our customers had to stand until the spring of 1894, when we built a funny little bleachers that did not accommodate more than 150 persons. In the summer we added a grandstand, seating perhaps 1,200. The gymnasium had been finished the previous winter. It was a one-story brick affair, so bare and graceless that it suggested a machine shop, and it had to serve as library and power plant too.

An Italian squatter had thrown together a shack on the Fifty-Seventh Street side of the block for a lunch counter during the fair and had continued to operate it. I bought the shanty to get rid of him, intending to tear it down, but one of our engineers asked for the stand on behalf of his widowed mother, a Mrs. Ingham. We gave it to her, incorporating it into the fence, and she ran it for many years, making a good bit of money, which she invested shrewdly in real estate. It was the Shanty to the university, and she became such a campus institution that now that it has gone, we reproduce it at each commencement and hold Shanty exercises.

That makeshift student-built fence had to serve for nearly twenty years, until 1913, and we made shift with the old gym until 1903, although the university required ten out of twelve quarters of gym work at a time when not a half dozen other schools enforced even dumb-bell drill. The new gym was worth waiting ten years for. It came as a memorial to Frank Dickinson Bartlett, a Harvard student from Chicago who died in 1900, from his father. There is a mural painting in the entrance hall by Frederic C. Bartlett, a brother of the dead boy, picturing single-stick and two-edged sword contests. Over the front entrance a memorial window depicts the crowning of Ivanhoe by Rowena after his triumphs in the tournament of Ashby-de-la-Zouch, both subjects in harmony with the Gothic architecture of the building and the university.

Lack of money alone did not account for the modesty of our equipment. Low-seating capacity was a settled policy of the university. For all his advanced views on physical training and his keen sense of advertising values, Doctor Harper shared the prevailing faculty fear of over-stressing competitive athletics as a public show.

"It is not the function of the university to provide at great cost spectacular entertainment for enormous crowds of people," he read into the constitution, so to speak, of the school, and there it has remained.

The field had become an eyesore and a constant expense for repairs long before President Judson announced in 1912 the intention of building a permanent wall and grandstand within two years. Almost immediately the city condemned the bleachers, speeding up the program. The new grandstand was occupied partly for the closing game of 1912 with Minnesota, a 7 to 0 victory for us, and the rebuilt field dedicated at the opening game of 1913, which we won from Indiana, 21 to 7. A high stone wall with a round, crenelated tower at either end, suggesting a feudal castle, inclosed the field. The permanent stands seated 8,000 and, with the bleachers and temporary stands, brought our capacity up to about 20,000.

That 1912 capacity has been increased very slowly. We are now rushing a new concrete stand, seating 17,000, to completion, turning the field around and enlarging our capacity to 48,000, but we continue in the rear rank of the conference in accommodations. Ohio State has a great stadium that has held 82,000 spectators. Illinois' new stadium seats 69,000 and will be enlarged. Some 55,000 can watch a game on Minnesota's field. Michigan is increasing its capacity from 46,000 to 70,000, with possibilities of 100,000. Wisconsin already seats 45,000. Northwestern, which has had inferior accommodations, will have a new stadium capable of seating 55,000. Only Iowa, Purdue and Indiana are inferior to our enlarged field. These three and all the others except Northwestern and Minnesota are situated in small cities or country towns.

I confess that I do not subscribe to the wisdom of this university policy. There is no danger at Chicago of athletics getting out of bounds; that was taken care of at the outset by providing rigid faculty control and direction. The absence of a body of alumni was not an unmitigated evil. They were sorely missed in the '90's, but we escaped in our formative years that pressure to win games at any cost that alumni have been known to exert.

On the other hand we are in the midst of a population of upward of 3,000,000, upon virtually all of whom we close our gates. There must be at least 50,000 graduates of other colleges in this great city, a fine body of men and women, most of them trained to enjoy watching college sports. We need their friendship and we need the cooperation of all good citizens, but we have had little room on our field for outsiders.

For thirty-five years I have listened to faculty members argue that a student's choice of college is not governed and infrequently influenced by the athletic prowess of the school—or, if he was so influenced, that he couldn't be much of an addition to the student body.

Yet this is demonstrably not true. We all love a winner. Not even a professional champion of lost causes can work up much enthusiasm over a college team that is trampled upon season after season. So long as a school plays fair in spirit and letter it is entitled to meet this demand. It is not necessary to cheat or to buy players in order to produce a team of which a school may be proud. A college with brains and courage, however small, does not need to hire a squad of mercenaries to wear its uniform.

Henry van Dyke, poet, aesthete, clergyman, diplomat, was not one, I take it, to be accused of gross materialism. I should imagine that most any college could use a young Henry van Dyke in its student body. Doctor van Dyke wrote an introduction to a history of Princeton athletics. In it he testified that he had never heard of Princeton until 1863, when, as a boy in Brooklyn, he saw the

Princeton baseball team wallop the Excelsiors of Brooklyn decisively. From that moment Princeton was his goal.

Big Bill Edwards tells in his book of coming to New York from a little upstate town to attend Horace Mann School, of seeing the drags filling in front of the Fifth Avenue Hotel for the Yale-Princeton Thanksgiving Day game, and of becoming so infected with the spirit of the scene that he walked straight to the nearest Y.M.C.A. and enrolled for a gym course.

When Harvard led the way by building her stadium, followed soon by Syracuse, then Yale and Princeton, there was a revival of faculty alarm, but nothing like the outcry that ensued when the stadium epidemic crossed the Alleghenies, and Ohio State, California, Illinois and others began to bake deep-dish football pies.

As a people we are easily alarmed by mere size. Our excitement over the trusts a generation ago came in part of this distrust of anything larger than we were used to. The sound of 80,000 or more spectators paying $50,000 or more to see twenty-two college boys play a game for an hour was frightening to some minds. That was too much money, too many persons. Such figures are not without precedent, therefore they must be somewhat dangerous.

On the contrary, the results have been uniformly healthy. In those colleges where the faculties had shirked their responsibilities, the great income produced by stadia forced them to intervene and exercise the veto power when necessary. Most of the evils that have beset the game from time to time have been the direct result of student and alumni management, but the blame belongs on the faculty doorstep. The students and alumni ran athletics because the faculties had been too superior to concern themselves with such juvenilia. Their indifference was described, without over-statement at the time, as the crime of the faculties.

Someone has said that college football has become so highly profitable an enterprise financially that it would pay a man, willing to take a chance, to buy a small college outright and operate it as a cloak for his football eleven. With proper management, it has been argued, the promoter might expect to take in enough at the stadium gates on a few fall Saturday afternoons to pay the cost of running the school for nine months, and leave a handsome profit, a successful team, in turn, attracting an influx of new students.

There was a time when an enterprising J. Rufus Wallingford might conceivably have floated such a promotion, for the purposes of fiction at least; but the colleges are so generally organized now from one coast to the other in regional athletic associations, with strictly enforced codes of sportsmanship, eligibility and the like, that the outlaw school is near the end of its tether. Either it must soon join the regional association and obey its laws or it will find itself without respectable athletic opponents. We have seen about the last of an obscure school going to sport-page glory in one season on the tails of a football team of tramp athletes hired in the market place.

We are not a people to sit idly by and see the Jones put anything over on us. If Mugglesdorfer builds a stadium, should Siwash be denied? Not so long as good red American blood runs in Siwash veins, and dollars in the pockets of the Siwash alumni. So the surface of these United States begins to take on a lunar aspect, pock-marked with craters that slumber or smoke lazily ten months of the year, then erupt in concert as Indian summer waxes. Perhaps we approach the saturation point, as they say in Detroit, but I walk warily in the paths of football prophecy.

What happens to the great surpluses rolled up by intercollegiate football? The money is being spent to enlarge the general physical, athletic and welfare programs of the colleges. The soundest criticism made of college athletics in the past was that a hand-picked few played and got the physical benefit of playing, while the bulk of the students sat in the stands and exercised their voices only. Now the intramural games program, taking in the entire student body, has swept the colleges and universities, and I hope soon will become general in the high schools. They cost money and attract no paying spectators. They are possible, except in an occasional exceptionally endowed school, only because of the profits football pays in modern stadia.

An educator of national prominence assured me once that intercollegiate sports at Chicago would end with me. In 1912, President Judson, in opposing a new grandstand that would seat more than 8,000, predicted that five years would see the end of intercollegiate athletics. Doctor Judson, I should add, changed his views radically after the war. On the other hand, there have been instances of college presidents of the newer salesmanship school so intent on booming their institutions that they have overruled faculty boards who were disposed to clean up the school's badly soiled athletics. Students are not fools. The faculty that winks at crooked work by a coach or student manager can save its breath in preaching ideals in the classroom.

I had most of my 1892 football squad back in 1893 and little new material, but I ceased to play. There were not 500 students in all branches of the university; half these were women and half the other half were graduate and special students who had put sports behind them. Some of my recruits sprang from unlikely sources, however. Ruhlkoetter at guard was direct from Germany, with a Weber and Fields accent, and never had seen a football until 1892. We dropped our high-school conditioning games and played Lake Forest, Northwestern three times, Michigan twice, Purdue, Oberlin, Armour Institute and Notre Dame.

The second of the two Michigan games was played on Thanksgiving Day and became the football fixture for that day and our big game, with one interruption, through 1905. Michigan withdrew from the conference after the 1907 season and played a lone hand until 1917, and by the time it returned, the once-incidental game with Illinois had become the high point of our season. We had beaten Michigan in the first game, they won the second. . . .

The third game with Northwestern was Chicago's first indoor football contest, played at night by electric light in Tattersall's Riding Academy at Sixteenth Street and Dearborn Avenue, on a tanbark floor which fell short of the specified regulation length by 60 feet. We won 22 to 14. The contemporary newspaper clippings say that only 300 attended, but it was a sufficiently successful experiment to be repeated several times. . . . The winters in Chicago used to set in earlier and were more severe than now. The severity of the weather hurt attendance and suggested indoor play.

The Notre Dame game was played on New Year's afternoon, also in Tattersall's. The South Benders brought along Lorin F. Deland's new and sensational flying wedge, but we broke it up and beat them, 8 to 0 before a lively crowd of 600. The Deland wedge was the final outgrowth of the original V kick-off formation. The Princeton adaptation, wherein the quarter carried the ball inside a wedge made up of the other ten players, had been copied everywhere and pretty generally stopped in succeeding seasons. The earliest method of breaking it up was to dive under the ponderous slow-moving mass and trip it up. Heffelfinger, of Yale, who was six feet four inches in height, had his own method. He would leap high into the air and come down inside the wedge on the ball carrier. . . .

Deland's contribution was the adding of momentum to the mass play. Parke Davis has written an excellent description of the play and its debut.

Yale opened the Harvard 1892 game in orthodox fashion, with the old Lehigh V. At the opening of the second half the Yale line deployed along the fifty-five-yard line in anticipation of a similar attack by Harvard. To the mystification of Yale and the crowd, Trafford, the Harvard captain and quarter, took position at the center of the Harvard forty-five-yard line, while the remainder of the team divided into two sections of five each and fell back on the twenty-five-yard line on opposite sides of the field. Without putting the ball into play, Trafford waved his hand as a signal, the two sections came swiftly forward in lock step, converged around Trafford, who put the ball into play as they enveloped him, and the mass moved on with high momentum. Yale finally pulled it apart, downed Trafford on their twenty-five-yard line and won the game 6 to 0; but the Deland invention probably was the most spectacular single formation ever opened as a surprise package.

It was a great play when perfectly executed, but, demanding the exact coordination of eleven men, extremely difficult to execute properly. Although Deland failed to beat Yale with it, he changed football history.

By 1893 everybody was using his flying wedge and the mass-momentum principle, and the game so increased in roughness and injuries in consequence that the season ended in an uproar, and the Army and Navy departments abolished the service game. The old Football Association was reduced, by now, to Yale and Princeton and was of little influence. The University Athletic Club of New York stepped into the breach and invited Harvard, Pennsylvania, Princeton and Yale to form a new governing body. All accepted, resulting in the most sweeping rules revision in ten years.

The old Rugby kick-off was brought back from exile, the Lchigh V, the Princeton wedge and Deland's flying wedge were outlawed, and the teeth drawn from all other momentum-mass plays by prohibiting players on offense from grouping more than five yards behind the line. Since 1894 the rules have provided that the ball on kick-off, kick-out (abolished in 1914) or kick from fair catch must travel ten yards unless it is touched by an opponent, or it is not in play. Since 1922 a kick-off or free kick not going ten yards has been a loose ball which the opposition is entitled to recover.

For all the reform, Harvard and Yale split over the bitter roughness of their 1894 game, Cornell restricted its football team to the home grounds, and there was a public clamor for the complete abolition of all mass play. The 1894 rules body having failed to perpetuate itself, Moffat of Princeton and Camp of Yale joined in the spring of 1895 in inviting Penn and Harvard to take a hand in a new effort to save the now seriously threatened sport. The four colleges met and divided, Princeton and Yale for wiping out the mass play utterly, Penn and Harvard for retaining it. Penn, having just landed squarely on the football map by virtue of Woodruff's highly effective mass formations, was in the position of being asked to vote itself back into the minor leagues, or so it was felt at Philadelphia. The split was hopeless, and that season produced two independent sets of rules, one sponsored by Cornell, Princeton and Yale, the other by Harvard and Penn.

United, the Big Four stood; divided, they fell. They had bossed football since 1876, but now the colleges of the country revolted. In our territory, the presidents of Michigan, Wisconsin, Minnesota, Illinois, Chicago, Northwestern and Purdue met at the suggestion of President Smart of Purdue and took the first step in the direction of what now is the Big Ten Conference. The rules upon which this meeting agreed were not uniformly adopted, and a year later, quickened by criticism of Minnesota by Caspar Whitney in Harper's Weekly, Professor McMillan of Minnesota sent out an invitation to the same colleges to confer again.

This time the vaccination took. The conference wove a pattern and blazed a trail that have now been followed by seventy to eighty other regional athletic conferences which now blanket the country and include virtually every American school of collegiate rank, Yale, Harvard and a few others excepted. Iowa and Indiana were admitted to the conference in 1899, and finally Ohio State in 1912 to make it the Big Ten.

Each year since then we have met to modify and enlarge the rules, to the incalculable benefit of the game.

The freshman rule, the three-year playing limitation and the abolition of the training table are among the reforms adopted first by the conference. The first two have become all but universal, but Harvard, Yale, Princeton, Columbia, Penn and Cornell still maintain training tables and some of them training quarters. Faculty control of athletics is complete in the conference and rather general throughout the country, but the old Big Four—Penn, Princeton, Yale and Harvard—still cling to graduate or student management, though with an increasing measure of veto power for the faculty. Where properly managed there can be no objection to a training table, but it is too easy of prostitution into free board and room for athletes. I confess that I was opposed to doing away with the training table, fearing for the physical conditioning of the athletes, but I have changed my mind. Looking back, I cannot see that its abolition has had the least effect on the condition of the men.

The revolt forced the rival rules bodies in the East to bury the hatchet and invite suggestions for reform. Agreement was reached on a new code in midsummer, 1896. The heart of the reform is found in section E, which disposed of the mass play, it was hoped. It did help, but it was inadequate. It reads:

"No player of the side in possession of the ball shall take more than one step toward his opponent's goal before the ball is in play without coming to a full stop. At least five players shall be on the line of scrimmage when the ball is snapped. If six players be behind the line of scrimmage, then two of them must be at least five yeards behind the line, or outside of the players on the end of the line."

This is explicit enough and it has since been strengthened.

In 1903 the experiment was tried of requiring seven men on the offensive line between the two twenty-five yard lines. In 1904 the scrimmage line minimum was raised from five to six for any point on the field, and in 1910 to seven, with the further provision that the one man who can be in motion before the ball is snapped must move only toward his own goal.

Yet the momentum play is a restless shade and stirs in its grave. The joker lies in the phrase "without coming to a full stop." That is a point capable of varied construing, and beating the rules with shift plays based upon momentum has not been unheard of in recent years. . . .

Heisman of Penn reintroduced the momentum principle when coaching Georgia Tech ten to fifteen years back, and the effectiveness of the Yellow Tornadoes was due in part to their emphasis upon shift plays that violated the spirit of the rules. Notre Dame overhurried their shift three or four years ago, to the indignation of Charley Daly, the Army coach. The referee ignoring his protests, Daly adopted the Notre Dame shift into West Point's tactics, which is what usually happens. We have been reemphasizing the rule annually, and there was much less violating last year.

The busiest of all my thirty-nine football seasons was 1894. We played eighteen regular games and four post-season contests —three in California, the first Eastern team to appear on the Pacific slope. . . .

Bucky Vail had come from Pennsylvania to Illinois that season as paid coach, one of the first in the conference. As was customary with coaches at the time, Vail was in uniform. We were leading

Illinois 10 to 6, with only seven minutes to play, when Vail quietly appeared at quarter in place of Tilton. Warhorse Allen let out a vigorous squawk to the referee, to which Vail replied that Tilton had been injured and that he had no substitute for him; furthermore, had I not set the precedent two seasons before of playing on the Chicago teams? No time had been taken out for Tilton's supposed injury and he had been fumbling persistently just before he finished. The coincidence was striking. While we argued about it, the seven minutes elapsed, darkness descended and the game ended in a row.

I originated the tackles-back play that season, and the innovation of having the quarter stand as he received the ball from center. It not only saved the moment lost in rising from a stoop but it minimized fumbles by permitting the quarter to use his body as well as his hands in taking the ball. Credit often went astray in the 90's for new plays, due to the inadequate reporting and the lack of contact between the sport of one region with that of another. For example, the textbooks state that the turtleback play first was used in the 1893 Harvard-Yale game. This was a formation executed by massing the team into a solid oval against the tackle, and at the snap of the ball into the interior of the oval, rolling the mass around an end and unwinding the runner into a clear field. I had used everything but the name at Springfield, working such a revolving mass against both guard and tackle.

Frank Hering, now secretary of the Fraternal Order of Eagles, was my quarter in 1894, and the first man I ever encountered who could throw a football as a baseball is thrown, an ability arising from the unusual size and grip of his hands. I trained Hering, if he got the ball on the kick-off, to pass it out back to an end or a half or to shoot it to a sleeper lying outside.

Our football receipts had grown from $732 in 1892 to $2,792 in 1893, to $5,840 in 1894, but our expenses were keeping step, running to $4,501 in the latter year. The balance was not such as to suggest an excursion to California. Several circumstances combined to take us there.

Leland Stanford Jr. University—opened in 1891 on the former Palo Alto stock farm where Senator Stanford had bred Advertiser, Sunol, Palo Alto, Electioneer, Arion and other great thoroughbreds —and the University of Chicago were the two youngest colleges in the land, only a year apart in nativity. Stanford, coached by my old mentor, Walter Camp, had won the coast championship from California, coached by my old teammate and fellow townsman,

Charley Gill. The two had drawn 11,000 to their game that season, charging $1 and $1.50, where fifty cents was the best we could do even for our Thanksgiving Day game with Michigan. And we could use the advertising.

President Harper was entirely agreeable, as he was toward anything legitimate that put the university's name in print, but he left it to me to find the money. I wrote a letter to the Stanford manager, who wired back an offer of $1,000 guaranty and 75 percent of the net receipts of a Christmas Day game. Nettled at the failure of other coast teams to cooperate in importing us, Stanford stipulated that Chicago should play no other game in San Francisco; but, it appearing that the Reliance Athletic Club of Oakland had an option on the Haight Street ballpark, the only desirable grounds, the Reliance Club was given a New Year's Day game with us. California also yearned for a slice of our carcass. I wired them to fight it out among themselves, and the eventual result was that we played Stanford in San Francisco on Christmas Day, again at Los Angeles in midweek, and the Reliance Club in San Francisco on New Year's, 1895.

The news that the Chicago team would spend the Christmas holidays in California created all the stir that we had hoped. California was several times farther away in 1894, whatever the railway guide may say about it. In the first burst of congratulatory mail came a letter from a strange but well-disposed woman. She would be very happy to let us have the use of her private car, a buffet sleeper at the moment in the process of thorough renovation. The price would be purely nominal—something like $220, which I took to be mere interest on the investment.

I slept restlessly under the financial responsibility of the trip, and when I was not adding figures in my sleep, I was in the thick of scrimmage, for I had played daily in the post-season practice for the California games. Mrs. Stagg was awakened one night by the violent tackle of her head. I had dreamed that I was falling on a fumbled ball on the field. It is not unusual for a player to take the game to bed. Some twenty years later Coleman Clark dreamed that he was kicking off before a cheering throng, and sent his good right foot into the wall alongside his bed with such violence that he was on crutches for days. The oddity of Clark's dream was that the football season had been over four months, and he then was playing on the basketball five.

My knowledge of private cars was wholly academic: but I knew that they were vehicles of princely luxury like steam yachts, and affected only by the greater actresses, touring millionaires and railroad presidents who rode free. I couldn't think of anything pleasanter than riding to California in one any time, but most particularly at this time. I had been married on September 10th, and Mrs. Stagg's honeymoon so far had been spent on the university field. Now I should take my bride to golden California in a palace on wheels. We accepted the offer gratefully. The newspapers dilated on our magnificence, while we stocked the car with sufficient food and drinking water to last the round trip, and found a competent chef.

These details were taken care of by others, and we saw the car for the first time when we boarded it in the yards. I do not remember whether the reporters saw us get away or not; if they did they kept our secret and sent us away in glory. The car looked as though Sherman had just marched through it. It was a show car, a condemned Pullman that had been sold down the river in its old age to limp from siding to siding on the kerosene circuit, housing this carnival troupe and that minstrel company. The wheels were flat, the paint scabrous, the body humped at one spot and sagged at another. Vestiges only remained of the upholstery. The beds were bunks, not berths, and the first night out was explosive with the collapse of the uppers. The team was sleeping double before we passed Cheyenne. Mrs. Stagg and I occupied what was facetiously known as the drawing-room.

The time was mid-December and the weather bitter cold crossing the mountains. In the middle of the night, on the top of the Rockies, I woke to hear that the car was afire. The coal stove at the forward end, becoming red hot, had ignited the woodwork. The train air cord ended with the car ahead of us, the rear flagman was away from his post, and we had no way of signaling the train crew. While the train toiled upgrade, we fought the fire with axes and water and beat it after a blistering fight. Had the flames ever worked through to the outside, where the wind could have got at them, we either should have had to jump for our lives or have been burnt to a crisp, for the car was all wood, sun-dried to tinder.

Quietly, we wired ahead to the Pullman company to provide a standard sleeper at Sacramento and intern our car there until our return, so we rolled into the Oakland Mole in state. Christmas was a very handsome day by Chicago standards, but we were assured that it was unseasonably cold, and only 3,000 sufficiently hardy spectators could be found to see us trim Camp's Stanford eleven handily, 24 to 4. Our share of the net receipts was $1,099.35.

The fence at the Haight Street park was a low one, and the ball bounded over it once. Stanford had a five-yard start, but Ad Ewing, a hurdler on our track team, took the fence in his usual high-hurdle stride and captured the ball. Over the fence was not out in the 90's, and the referee did not bring the ball in when it went out of bounds. Whether it went out at the sidelines or goal lines, it was the property of the first comer. If at the side, it was in touch at the point where it crossed the line. The opposing team surrounded the point and the captain demanded, "What will you do sir? Take it out or touch it in?" To take it out, the player walked in five to fifteen yards and put the ball into play in scrimmage. If he chose to touch it in the two teams lined up at right angles to the sideline. The man with the ball touched it quickly to the sideline, usually after many feints, then passed it to one of his backs or ran with it himself. The in-touch play went out of use long before, but it was not formally abolished by the rules body until 1901.

Three years before I had eliminated it, with much other obsolete stuff, from the conference rules book which we issued, most of the changes being adopted by the Eastern committee.

When the ball was kicked or bounded over a fence, as happened occasionally, ludicrous scenes followed. Georgia and Georgia Tech were playing many years ago on a field surrounded by a perfectly smooth fence fifteen feet high, and not more than twenty feet behind the goal posts. On a try for goal, the ball hit the post, bounded high and dropped out of sight over the fence. Both teams charged for the fence and fought frantically to get over it, but they dragged one another down faster than they could climb. While the fight raged, the referee, with the aid of the spectators, surmounted the fence and found the ball in a weed-grown ditch. He stepped back with a poker face and waited for the first to come over the fence. Hands and an occasional leg appeared and disappeared, but after five minutes a Tech man came over the top with a Georgia man on his heels. Neither could find the ball. The third man over, Red Wilson, of Georgia Tech, discovered its hiding place and fell on it for a touchdown.

That and a game between Gettysburg and Franklin and Marshall, I think it was, where a drop-kicked ball struck on the chest a policeman who had strayed inside the lines and caromed off and over the bar for a clean field goal, take high place in the comedy relief of football.

Stanford gave us a dinner at the hotel Pleasanton after the

game and both teams left for Los Angeles the following night in the hope of getting acclimated, but Stanford, the weather and Warhorse Allen's terrible energy combined to beat us, 12 to 0. The day before the game I was called away from a light practice. Allen asked a native how far it was to the Hotel Westminster, where we were stopping. The native guessed about a mile. "We'll run it, then," said Allen, and led the way. The distance turned out to be three miles, and Allen, a horse for work, killed off the rest of the squad. The day of the game was hot and muggy, with a misty rain falling, which did not help matters.

The Los Angeles Athletic Club had promoted the match, and the receipts had to be split three ways, leaving us only $320 as our share.

We returned to San Francisco to be beaten 6 to 0 on New Year's Day by the Reliance Club, coached by Pringle, of Yale, giving Yale a tight little monopoly of coast coaching. Gale was out of the game, Herschberger folded up early and Ewing did not last out the game. All three were key men and I had to use three of my five subs. Our supply of home-grown water had been exhausted in fighting the fire on our sleeper, and the change of water, as we feared, upset the squad. The San Francisco papers commented unfeelingly that we were not used to water that we did not have to chew. In taking the American Olympic team to Paris in 1924, we were at pains to carry along a barreled supply of our best home water. In Paris, we decided to make a test of the water which the French so carefully avoid using internally. The chemist found that the native water was several degrees purer than that we had painstakingly freighted across the Atlantic.

The greatest handicap an Eastern invader suffers on such a trip is the long lay-off after the regular season's close, with training resumed in mid-December; but all these alibis and new ones are offered periodically by teams that journey 2,000 or 3,000 miles to take a licking on the coast. Syracuse was the victim in 1924, losing to the University of Southern California, 0 to 16 at Pasadena on December 6. The following Christmas at the session of the Football Officials Association in New York, Chick Meehan, the Syracuse coach, spoke, comparing Eastern and coast football and reciting the difficulties of adjusting a team to the long trip, the sharply different climate, and the like.

When he had finished, Coach Zuppke, of Illinois, who was presiding, remarked, "Well, if I was coach of a team going to play in California, I wouldn't get off at any stops on the way to limber

(Left to right) Amos Alonzo Stagg,
Andy Kerr, Glenn (Pop) Warner.

Andy Kerr   Glenn S. "Pop" Warner

the boys up. I'd just get out as fast as I could and take my lickings and come back home right away."

David Starr Jordan had resigned the presidency of the University of Indiana to become head of Stanford when it was opened. At Indiana Doctor Jordan had filled in as professor of Ichthyology. It was his boast there that he knew and invariably greeted by name every student in Bloomington. At Palo Alto it was noticed that although he had been there some three years now, he was content to bow only to the students. Someone commented on the fact.

"I gave it up," Doctor Jordan confessed. "I discovered that every time I remembered the name of a student, I forgot the name of a fish."

Our share of the New Year's Day game was $1,398, and efforts to persuade the Native Sons and Daughters that photographs of the Chicago squad would make a handsome souvenir or den ornament, netted us just $2.35. Faced by a deficit, we were glad to accept a guaranty of $100 to stop off in Salt Lake City and play the Y.M.C.A. The field was aslop with snow and slush, a miserable time was had by all, and the Y lost money. So did we, for our expenses totaled $3,056, our receipts $2,920. The deficit was charged to advertising, and was worth it.

Our sleeper, which we picked up clandestinely at Sacramento on our way home, was seventy feet long. The Southern Pacific snow sheds had not been built to accommodate such ambitious rolling stock, and the car threatened to come apart all the way up the Sierras. The flat wheels grew flatter, until the railroad dropped us off like a load of ballast at Laramie and sent the car to the shops. While new trucks were being run under the senile sleeper, we went skating and jack-rabbit hunting. The silver lining of the trip had been the art of our gifted chef; we had lived high. Returning with a bag of jacks, we handed the game over to him confidently. Unfortunately, neither he nor we were familiar with the high flavor and indestructible fabric of the species. With a splendid flourish he served us with Wyoming jack rabbit a la Macedoine. His culinary French was nothing less than inspired. If the original Macedonians were as hardy as this later species, no wonder Alexander conquered the world at thirty-two.

Clarence Herschberger was the first exceptional back and punter to appear at Chicago. He had made the team with a bang in 1894, his first season, but he was missing in 1895. His mother, alarmed at the injured roll reported by the newspapers, had refused to permit him to play longer. If he could not play, then he would not go to school, and Clarence took a vacation. On a hunting trip that fall he shot himself in the hand by accident. His mother hastened to lift her prohibition and he was back in '96, '97 and '98. Not since the World War have I lost a player or a potential player through parental objection to the sport. Parents do not fear football as they once did; neither, I suspect, do they speak with the old authority. . . .

With a steady rain falling outside, we played Michigan in comfort in the old Coliseum that stood in Sixty-Third Street where the Tower Theatre now is, on Thanksgiving Day, 1896. The papers were flippant, but the results justified us. Thanksgiving Day weather was almost uniformly vile and attendance accordingly reduced, while the Coliseum game drew a gate of $10,812, the largest on record in the West up to then. It was the first big game ever played indoors, with resultant publicity. By three o'clock it was so dark that the lights had to be switched on. The girders interfered with kicking near the sides of the field, the ball lodging in them once. We won, 7 to 6, on a safety and a place-kicked field goal from scrimmage, the first use of the play in the West, at least. I cannot surely claim its invention, but we were among the first to use it. Gordon Clarke held the ball for Herschberger's kick, and the two became the most famous place-kick combination in the game. Herschberger, a good drop kicker, had found that he could kick even more accurately from place. . . .

The group which brought Chicago its first football championship in 1899 arrived on the squad in 1896. We had a trainer and a training table for the first time this season, the latter by arrangement with a boarding house. In 1897 we rented the top floor of an apartment house and opened training quarters.

The group of which I speak was the wildest crew I ever skippered. The animal spirits which later helped to bring home the championship bacon were devoted in quarters to a continuous rough-housing that made life miserable for the other tenants. If you think the family upstairs in your apartment house is noisy, try living beneath a football squad. It was their playful habit to lean out the front windows and drop crockery bombs on the sidewalk behind passers-by to see them jump, what times they were not throwing food at one another. Jonathan Webb, solid, loyal, sober citizen and star tackle, being hit in the ear with a steaming hot potato, the most of which stuck there, refused to dig the potato out, although it was blistering that sensitive organ, as a lesson to his rowdy associates.

These exercises were not conducted in my presence, but I could picture them readily enough. I had a precedent to go by. When I waited tables in a student dining club at Yale, I had seen everything on the table, wet or dry, hot or cold, hurled by the diners at one another out of sheer good feeling. I recall one club member throwing a great dish of apple sauce at a fellow member and getting a large ball of butter, the common supply of the table, squarely on top of the head in rejoinder. Harry Beecher usually started the fight, then ducked under the table when it was thoroughly under way.

Just such horseplay cost us the championship in 1897. We came down to the Wisconsin game undefeated, and would have won it, I am morally certain, but for the usual bantering and coltishness of the training table, over which Trainer Max Bentner presided. Herschberger and Captain Walter Kennedy, close friends, staged a contest to see which could put on the most weight at one sitting. They stripped and weighed in before the meal. Weighing out, Herschberger had gained seven pounds, Kennedy seven and a quarter. Whether piqued at this defeat or merely stimulated into further endeavor, Herschie next ate thirteen eggs at one sitting, was seized with gastritis just before the Wisconsin game, and was lost to the team. He was a key man both offensively and defensively, and I still am convinced that we were beaten 8 to 23 by thirteen eggs rather than eleven Badgers. We played Michigan indoors again on Thanksgiving Day in the old Coliseum and won 21 to 12, but the title had gone a-glimmering.

The fields of football were infested with the boll weevil in 1897, for all the spraying and burning done in 1896. On October thirteenth Vonabalde Gammon of Georgia was injured in the Georgia-Virginia game. He had been a star of Glenn Warner's championship 1896 Georgia eleven. As he was being led off the field by McCarthy, who had succeeded Warner as coach, Kent, the Georgia captain, with no realization of the seriousness of Gammon's hurts, exclaimed, "You aren't going to quit, are you, Von?"

"I've got too much Georgia grit for that," the injured boy answered through clenched teeth, started to turn back and fell unconscious. He never spoke again, dying that night. The South was horrified, and the Georgia legislature, then in session, at once passed an act outlawing the game from the state. Only the personal intercession of the dead boy's mother with Governor Atkinson persuaded him to veto the bill.

The conference season had been marred by no serious injury, but we acted without waiting on the always-tardy East, making our own revision of the rules. We were legislating for ourselves only, but we were accused of usurping the functions of the rules committee. Everts Wrenn—a well-known Western official and a Harvard graduate—and others denounced our "impertinence." Wisconsin, having Eastern games on its 1898 schedule, became alarmed and withdrew its representative, Doctor Elsom, from our committee on revision.

The rules body still was exclusively Eastern in membership, and Walter Camp now suggested that I be elected to the body in recognition of the Mid-West's growing football bulk. I was asked to confer with them at their spring of 1898 session, but baseball and track work kept me in Chicago, and it was not until 1904 that I became a member, the first from a school west of Pennsylvania. I have served continuously since 1904, to become the senior member of the committee, which now is national in its scope.

AMOS ALONZO STAGG, PATRIARCH OF FOOTBALL

The following article was written by the author and was published with deletions in The New York Times *of August 12, 1962, four days before Stagg's one hundredth birthday. Most of it was reprinted in the Yale-Princeton football game program that year.*

IF AMOS ALONZO STAGG is not the man of the century in sports, come August 16 he definitely will become the man of two centuries. On that day football's Grand Old Man will celebrate his hundredth birthday, as will innumerable friends and admirers at testimonial luncheons and dinners across the nation.

Jim Thorpe, the Sac and Fox Indian from Carlisle, was voted the greatest athlete and football player of the century in the national poll of The Associated Press in 1950. He is generally ranked as football's foremost player of all time, and his fame as an Olympic track and field athlete who won both the decathlon and the pentathlon in the 1912 games is legendary too.

Bobby Jones in golf, Babe Ruth and Ty Cobb in baseball, Big Bill Tilden in tennis, Tommy Hitchcock in polo, Willie Hoppe in billiards and Jack Dempsey and Joe Louis in boxing have been acclaimed as the greatest of the century. Golf's Hogan, Palmer and Snead, baseball's Wagner, Mathewson, Johnson, Willie Mays and Joe DiMaggio, tennis' Budge and Gonzales, track's Jesse Owens and football's Red Grange have been in the super class too.

All of these have been as great athletes in their specialties as was Stagg, though none, with the exception of Thorpe, equalled him in his transcendence in more than one sport. An all-America end at Yale in the company of the immortal Pudge Heffelfinger, Stagg also pitched Yale to five baseball championships. He could have had a big-league contract had he not chosen to dedicate his life to the service of youth, with far smaller emoluments.

But it is not because of his prowess as an athlete that Alonzo Stagg is being feted this week as has been no other American in sports. Nor is it because, as a coach, he developed so many fine teams at the University of Chicago and the College (now University) of the Pacific, nor because his was the most fertile and prolific mind football has known in devising and originating plays, formations and techniques that helped to shape the pattern of the American game that evolved from English rugby into the spectacular running, passing test of skill, brains and brawn that attracts millions annually.

It is for his unparalleled service in teaching the young to shoot square, for seventy years; the spartan ruggedness and simplicity of his life in devotion to an ideal, and the granite-like integrity that never compromised for victory and set new standards of sportsmanship in college athletics. It is for these, and a durability surpassing that of Michelangelo and Titian, that Stagg, a throwback to the Spartan mold, who endured semi-starvation to get an education and prized working with youth far above the many opportunities for commercial gain he rejected, has been honored over and over by presidents, his fellow coaches, his athletes, universities, sports-governing and civic bodies and sports writers and broadcasters.

In 1931, on the occasion of the celebration of his fortieth anniversary as head football coach and athletic director at the University of Chicago, his alma mater did Stagg the honor of sending a Yale team beyond the Alleghenies for the first time to play Chicago.

A year later, he coached his last team at Chicago. At the age of seventy his retirement was mandatory under the university rule. Broken-hearted and almost in tears, he rejected the offer of a pension and new post created for him. He was too young to retire, he said. He still had many years of work with youth ahead of him. He chose to go west and accept the coaching portfolio at the College of the Pacific, with an enrollment of 820 students, turning down far more remunerative offers from large universities.

"I am going West and I feel like I am about 21 years old instead of 71," he said, when he accepted the Pacific post in 1933. "I am as happy as a college sophomore with his first varsity football letter. I am too young and too active to give up coaching. . . . I went into athletic work because it offered the largest opportunity for service through contact with young men. No scheme of life which removes that contact would meet my ambition."

For fourteen years Stagg coached at Pacific. There, too, he was retired, and again he refused to be let out to pasture. He joined his son, Paul, at Susquehanna University in Selinsgrove, Pa. From 1947 through 1952 he shared the coaching duties with his son. Then, finally, because of the illness of his wife, Stella, who had a remarkable knowledge of football and gave her husband invaluable assistance throughout his career in scouting teams, keeping records and statistics and advising him on plays and strategy, he gave up formal, full-time coaching.

In August of 1953 he said at his home in Stockton, California, "My wife, the best assistant a coach ever had . . . my buddy, the mainstay and center of my life for 59 years, needs me. I will stay by her in every way."

But football was too much in his blood and the urge to be of service to youth was still too strong within him at the age of 91 for Stagg to retire completely to the armchair and slipper'd pantaloon. He was soon back at work as advisory coach with the Stockton High School team. He continued to assist the team until finally on September 16, 1960, a month after his ninety-eighth birthday, the most remarkable coaching career any game probably has known came to an end.

On the occasion of Stagg's ninety-sixth birthday, President Dwight D. Eisenhower sent him a congratulatory message. He was polishing his car with the help of his wife when he received it at his five-room bungalow in Stockton. Last August 16, President John F. Kennedy telegraphed his greetings to the ninety-ninth birthday party for Stagg at the Lions Club in Stockton.

It would take pages to list all of the honors that have fallen to Stagg. Here are some of them, in chronological order:

In 1889 he was named on the first all-America team to be chosen.

In 1892 he became the first coach to be given faculty status when Dr. William Rainey Harper, the University of Chicago's first president, under whom Stagg had studied at Yale, gave him an associate professorship in appointing him as football coach at a salary of $2,500. He became a full professor in 1901.

In 1904 Stagg was elected a member of the Football Rules Committee. He is the last surviving member of the original committee.

In 1912 he was awarded an honorary master's degree in physical education by Springfield (Mass.) YMCA College, where he had begun his coaching career in 1890 while taking the training course there.

In 1923 he was awarded an honorary Master of Arts degree, by Oberlin College.

In 1929 Princeton University invited Stagg to bring his Chicago team to Osborn Field House and sit down to dinner with the Princeton team the night before their game.

In 1931 Yale sent its team west for the first time to play Chicago in honor of Stagg's fortieth anniversary as Chicago's coach, as mentioned above.

In 1932 Stagg received the medal of the Sportsmanship Brotherhood in New York for his devotion to the highest ideals of good sportsmanship and fair play.

In 1933 the College of Wooster in Ohio conferred an LL.D. degree upon him.

In 1938 Chicago scheduled a home-coming game for Stagg and his College of the Pacific team.

In 1939, his golden anniversary year as a coach, the convention of the American Football Coaches Association was dedicated to Stagg. Herbert Orrin (Fritz) Crisler, who had played football under Stagg and served as his assistant and won renown as coach at Princeton and Michigan, presented him with a bound volume of letters from coaches, university executives, sports writers and others, extolling his contribution to amateur athletics and the pioneer spirit that drove him westward to the College of the Pacific at the age of seventy-one.

Also in 1939, Springfield College presented Stagg with a scroll at his College of the Pacific team's opening game. It read:

"Springfield College pays tribute to Amos Alonzo Stagg, dean of football coaches, who fifty years ago this fall, as a student, organized, coached and captained the first football team at Springfield. Today, after fifty years of continuous contribution, Coach Stagg stands as a symbol of the highest ideals in competitive sport. His name is engraved forever on the rolls of illustrious Springfield alumni who are serving as outstanding leaders for the youth of the world."

In 1940 Stagg received the award of the Touchdown Club of New York City for his unusual service and his contribution to the advancement of football.

In 1943 he was voted football's Coach of the Year by his fellow coaches and honored also by sports writers as football's Man of the Year.

In 1951 Stagg was voted into the National Football Hall of Fame as a player and also as a coach, the only one to be honored in both categories.

In 1958 his neighbors presented him with a power lawn mower

on his ninety-sixth birthday. He declined the gift with thanks. "When I can't cut the grass by hand, I'll have some one else do it," he said.

In 1959 Stagg received the "Greatest Living American" award of the United States Chamber of Commerce.

In 1960 the National Football Foundation and Hall of Fame voted him its Gold Medal Award, an honor he shares with Presidents Kennedy, Eisenhower and Hoover and General of the Army Douglas MacArthur.

In 1962 the University of Chicago established the Amos Alonzo Stagg Scholarship Fund. Also, the Amos Alonzo Stagg Foundation was organized to raise funds for building the Amos Alonzo Stagg Center of Physical Fitness at the University of the Pacific.

These have been some of the rewards for the man who dedicated his life to being of service to others and who for more than three-score years has been sport's shining exemplar of the noble virtues their idealists seek to inculcate.

Stagg was football's original character moulder. Today, in an age of hard-boiled pragmatism that scoffs at such creeds as virtue being its own reward, the term "character moulding" is never used other than facetiously or with an apologetic smile.

Stagg never was facetious or apologized for anything. To this man of ingrained simplicity and honesty, who was intolerant of any sham or trimming at the sacrifice of principles, regardless of the rewards or penalties, there was something more important than victory.

Winning football games was important to him, and he could be a hard taskmaster who gave his players tongue lashings for slip-shod or unworthy performance. Four of his Chicago teams were undefeated and twelve lost only one game, in one of the most rugged conferences. But as much as he prized victory, he attached more importance to his men playing the game honorably and living cleanly. This was a laugh to many of his contemporaries and still is to some coaches active today. That there are so few to whom it now applies is due in part to the example and influence of Stagg in setting higher ethical standards.

The church had a strong influence on Stagg, whose father, a cobbler, was a devout Presbyterian. In his high school days in West Orange, N.J., when he worked at odd jobs to help keep the large family's pot boiling, he decided to become a minister. After taking preparatory work at Phillips Exeter Academy, he chose Yale as his college because it had a divinity school, in preference to Dartmouth, which had offered him what amounted to a baseball scholarship. Yale offered him only the prospect of finding work, and though the sum total of his worldly goods was only $32, he went to Yale, where he lived on twenty cents a day for food. He could not afford an overcoat and so he acquired the hardihood that enabled him to endure the wintry blasts of Chicago's Midway, where, by choice, he wore neither hat nor overcoat and drove an antediluvian flivver.

After matriculating at Yale, Stagg changed his mind about entering the ministry. He came to the conviction that the pulpit was not for him, that he "couldn't preach for sour apples." He decided that he could do a better job, get his message across better, in working with youth on the athletic field. The message was more than how to block, tackle and run with the football or to hit, pitch, catch and slide on the diamond. It was also to live and play by the golden rule, to keep their self-respect, to hit as hard as they knew how, but never below the belt, and to prepare themselves to take their place in society as good citizens.

It was Stagg's custom to lead his teams in prayer before each game, and he said a prayer when he went on the field as an athlete at Yale.

"My prayer has not been for victory," he explained. "It has simply been, 'Let me do my best.'"

That Stagg was more than a character builder is reflected in his record of success as a coach. In addition to the many fine football teams he developed, he was also successful as a coach of track and field. He assisted in preparing four Olympic teams, as well as served on five Olympic Games committees. Along with football, baseball and track, he also coached basketball in his early days. He could have handled tennis and golf too had he the time. He did not take up golf until he was nearly forty years of age and within a year he was shooting in the seventies. He played tennis for half a century and up to the time he was eighty he got in two or three sets each morning as a part of his training to keep himself fit. When he was sixty-eight he played in the Western father-and-son tennis championship with his son Paul and reached the semi-final round.

Fritz Crisler wrote in a letter of Stagg on the football field:

"He was never profane nor a fire-eater but he was the toughest kind of a taskmaster. Chicago teams worked longer hours and harder than any other conference team. He was thoroughly exacting. He was a keen psychologist in handling men. He knew which to be firm with, which to 'gentle' along. No player ever addressed him except as 'Mr. Stagg.' Perhaps no coach was so loved and respected as was Mr. Stagg by those fortunate enough to play for him."

George Varnell, a leading sports writer of Seattle, Wash., who played under Stagg at Chicago and served for years on the Football Rules Committee, cites an incident on the practice field, portraying how tough Stagg could be with his men.

Hugo Bezdek, who was to become one of football's most renowned coaches, was one of the finest halfbacks that Stagg developed. In practice one day Stagg was putting in a new play and became angry at Bezdek. He thought the halfback wasn't rough enough in carrying out his assignment, and in telling him so he addressed him as "Stockyards."

The term was anathema to Bezdek, who came from the Stockyards area of Chicago. He started to walk away and leave the field and told the coach, "You can't call me 'Stockyards.' "

"Listen, Stockyards," Stagg shouted after him, "you know what field this is? This is Stagg Field. [The name had been changed from Marshall Field in Stagg's honor.] I own it. If you go through that gate you won't come back in except by paying to sit in the stands."

Bezdek did not go through the gate. He played through the season as one of the most valuable members of the famous 1905 team, which was unbeaten, administered the first defeat in five years to Michigan's point-a-minute teams, and had the celebrated Walter Eckersall as quarterback. Along with Bezdek and Eckersall, an amazing drop kicker, who was chosen on Walter Camp's first all-America teams of 1904, 1905 and 1906, the outstanding players developed by Stagg included Mark Catlin, 1905 captain; Wally Steffen, another of football's most famous quarterbacks, who was to become a judge; Clarence Herschberger, the first Chicago player honored by Camp, in 1898; Paul DesJardien, Charles Maguire, Pat Page, John Schomer, John Thomas and Five-Yard McCarthy.

Stagg's contributions to the development of the technique of football are innumerable. No other figure in the game's history can compare with him in originality. Born seven years before the first intercollegiate contest was held in this country between Princeton and Rutgers at New Brunswick, N. J., in 1869, he played when the game was evolving from rugby. As a coach he led in the changes that introduced the period of the rough mass-momentum football, and he was a member of the rules committee that, following the fatalities of the 1905 season (when there was a demand that the sport be banned from the campus and President Teddy Roosevelt interceded), saved football by legalizing the forward pass and introducing other changes to make the game less hazardous. He devised no less than sixty-four pass plays in 1906.

The first coach to use a shift, in 1902, Stagg was credited by the renowned Knute Rockne as the source for the shift which Rockne's Notre Dame teams used with spectacular success in the 1920's, until it was hobbled by legislation. And he contributed four fundamental principles to the modern T formation years before it succeeded the Notre Dame system and the single wing of Glenn (Pop) Warner as football's standard modus operandi.

It is remarkable how many plays, devices and techniques Stagg had a hand in, either as the undisputed inventor or as one of the first known to have used them. First of all, he originated in 1890 the first of the mass-momentum formations, the "ends back," which brought linemen into the backfield and embodied the principle of the double wingback formation Warner introduced so successfully many years later. In 1891 he came up with a "turtleback" formation, though Harvard claimed to have had it before him. In 1894 he created the "tackles back" formation.

In 1890 Stagg first used the criss-cross and he incorporated the deception of the hidden-ball play into his attack. That year he invented the "Whoa Back" play and from it he derived the spinner. This was a quarterback whirl and not the fullback spin that came later and for which Hugo Bezdek, Dick Harlow, Carl Snavely and Wally Steffen are credited as the earliest users.

In 1894 he used a backward (lateral) pass on the kick-off, the first "sleeper" play. That year he used the center snap, which John Heisman, inventor at Georgia Tech of the famous shift named after him, claimed to have originated in 1893. Also in 1894 Stagg had the "onside" kick-off and in 1896 the spiral pass. Walter Camp of Yale and George Woodruff of Pennsylvania, inventor of the famous "guards back" formation, are also credited with having it that year, though Bob Zuppke of Illinois maintained that the spiral pass originated with him in 1906.

Also in 1896 Stagg introduced the huddle indoors, long before its first appearance outdoors. He used the quick kick this year and in 1897 the placement kick from scrimmage, a departure from the drop kick. He thought Princeton had it before him and John Minds, Pennsylvania captain, says that he used it first in 1897. In 1899 Stagg showed the sleeper play from scrimmage.

It was in 1894 that Stagg introduced the first of his four

fundamental principles of the modern T formation that George Halas and his staff on the Chicago Bears National Football League club developed with the assistance of Clark Shaughnessy, then the coach of the University of Chicago, in the late 1930's. This formation had a sensational inaugural in 1940, when the Bears massacred the Washington Redskins in a T party, and Stanford University, where Shaughnessy was newly installed, had one of the finest teams the Pacific Coast has known and beat every opponent.

Basically, the T formation the Bears and Stanford used was the same from which Notre Dame had shifted into a box years before. It was football's original formation, dating from 1888, when a change in the rules made it compulsory for linemen to keep their arms at their side. Previously they had extended them wide to protect their backs. The line was spread across the field and the halfbacks were out wide also, as in rugby, to take lateral passes.

With the rule change, the linemen came in close to each other, and so did the backs, for protection. In the positions in which they now lined up, the backs formed a T behind a tight line, with the quarterback under the center and the other three backs in a line some four yards behind him. This was football's regular formation for many years, and the punt, short kick, single wing, box and double wing formations were later developments.

What primarily differentiated the modern T of Halas and Shaughnessy (which was adopted in a stampede after Frank Leahy of Notre Dame and Earl Blaik of Army went over to it in the early 1940's) from the original T was the man in motion. It gave more breadth, scope and speed to the attack and opened up more avenues, putting a greater burden on the defense. The forward pass, of course, was in the game, as it had not been in the early years, and this added all the more to the threat of the modern T.

Stagg was the one who introduced the man in motion. This was the last and most important of the four fundamental principles he contributed to the modern T.

The first, in 1904, changed the posture of the quarterback from a low squatting figure behind the center to the stand-up position in which he receives the snap-back today. From 1899 to 1901 he originated split bucks, preceded by pivots and feints. In 1905 came his third contribution, the quarterback run around end after a pivot and fakes. This was the "keeper" play that figures so importantly in the split-T formation worked out by Don Faurot of Missouri in 1941.

It was in 1927 that Stagg made his fourth contribution, the

"Pedinger" man in motion. Actually, he had used a man in motion as early as 1898. He called him a "flyer." He went laterally or backward to take a pass that could be thrown only to the side or to the rear. In 1906, when the forward pass became legal, he introduced a flanker, stationed out to the side to take a pass. In 1910 he sent his flanker in motion to the inside to block the defensive end, and then, finally, in 1927 came his Pedinger man in motion, who was used, along with a flanker, as targets for the forward passer.

There were many other contributions Stagg made to the technique and pattern of football. In 1908 he established the principle of the Statue of Liberty play and also of the optional pass or run, and he used the fake pass and the double pass between a halfback and an end. With Eddie Cochems of St. Louis and Warner, then at Carlisle, he made more extensive use of the forward pass immediately after it became a part of the game and visualized its great possibilities more probably than did any other coach.

Stagg was original too in his defensive thinking as well as in devising offensive innovations. He pulled his center out of the line and used him as a linebacker in 1898 to stop the feared guards-back formation of Pennsylvania, which had been crushing foes since 1894. In 1890 he departed from the nine-man line which had been commonly used in the days when the team with the ball had to gain five yards in three downs. He switched to a 7–2–2 alignment, known as a "box." In 1898 he used a 7–3–1 when he did not employ his center as a linebacker. In 1932 his team went into a 6–2–1–2 deployment and in 1943, when the T was becoming the vogue, he used a 5–2–1–2–1.

Stagg in 1889 suspended a rolled-up mattress in the gymnasium and used it as a tackling dummy. So far as he knew, this was the first appearance of a tackling dummy, though Warner is credited by some with being the first to use it. Stagg was inventive in baseball too. He designed apparatus for the slide in 1888 and designed a cage in 1893. In 1901 he had lights installed for practice sessions. He is credited with being the first to establish a letter man's club, the Order of the "C," in 1906. Under his direction, Chicago set the example for other colleges in putting its athletics, including the plants, under a department of the university. This made for stricter control and enforcement of regulations and more efficient administration than under the student associations which were in charge at other schools.

Of all Stagg's "firsts," none is more incontestable than his longevity as a coach—full-time from 1890 through 1953 and part-time thereafter until 1960, a span of a full three-score and ten years.

On the occasion of his ninetieth birthday, Stagg said, "I must be going to live forever, because very few die after ninety."

Unlike old soldiers, who never die but only fade away, as General of the Army Douglas MacArthur reminded, football's Grand Old Man refuses to fade out of the picture. His image was never brighter than now, on the eve of his hundredth birthday, which will be celebrated by men of Yale, Springfield, Chicago, Pacific, Susquehanna and Stockton and thousands of others around the country.

THE FIRST HARVARD-YALE GAME, 1875

Because they played football of different styles, Harvard and Yale did not play their first game until 1875, six years after Princeton and Rutgers started the intercollegiate ball rolling at New Brunswick, N. J.

MARTIN L. CATE *was a member of the Harvard team of 1875. His account of the Yale game is taken from the first "H Book of Harvard Athletics" published in 1923.*

IN 1875 THE DESIRE of Harvard and Yale to meet at football became so keen that in October of that year two delegates from Harvard met two from Yale at Springfield and agreed, by making mutual concessions, to a set of "concessionary rules" to govern their first game. . . .

One of the concessions probably made by Yale to Harvard in the rules for this, the first game between the two colleges, was that each team should consist of 15 men, while in return Harvard gave up the right of the side making a touchdown to bring or punt the ball out to be converted into a goal. The No. 6 ball specified in the rules was a leather covered ball 30 inches in circumference and less pointed at the ends than the present Rugby football, which is 27 inches in circumference.

Fairly full descriptions of this first football game between Harvard and Yale were printed in the Advocate of Nov. 19, 1875, and in the Boston daily papers, and the following account has been compiled from these reports and from the personal recollections of some of the Harvard "fifteen."

About 40 students accompanied the Harvard team to New Haven and nearly 100 more arrived on the Saturday morning of the game, "so that there was a large representation of the college at the match."

It was a perfect day with hardly any wind, the sun being obscured by light clouds. An enclosure at Hamilton Park had been roped off, leaving a field of perfect smoothness. The Yale men wore dark trousers, blue shirts and yellow caps; Harvard, the usual crimson shirts and stockings with knee breeches. W. A. Whiting '77, captain of the Harvard team, unable to play because of an injury, acted as umpire for Harvard.

The game began at 2:45 P.M. in the presence of a large number of spectators. Yale kicked off, Harvard having won the toss. The ball was immediately carried in toward the Yale goal, Curtis running with the ball in touch. When he threw it in, it was kicked by Morse over the goal line and, the Yale tenders failing to get it, Leeds, who was on side, rushed in and secured the first touchdown, six minutes after the game began.

A few minutes later, after the ball had again been put in play, Leeds kicked a goal from the field. Yale again took the kick-off and drove the ball toward the Harvard goal, Thompson nearly getting a touchdown. He was stopped by the Harvard goal tenders and the ball was kicked back to the center of the field. Here Seamans got it by a pass from Hall, and, dodging Thompson and the Yale tenders, kicked the second goal.

Bacon led off the second half-hour with a long kick for Harvard. The ball was stopped by Thompson and sent back toward the middle of the field, where it passed between Herrick, Leeds, Curtis and Hall, who got it from Arnold of Yale when the latter attempted to pass to Johnston. Leeds, who kicked it just short of a goal, got a touchdown which was ruled out on a claim of foul. Cushing secured a touchdown immediately afterwards through a kick of Towers', which hit a goal post and just missed a goal.

This was followed directly by Wetherbee's getting the ball as soon as sent in, passing it to Thayer, who, when pressed by the Yale tenders, passed it to Blanchard and the latter kicked a goal. As the second half-hour was not up, Harvard again led off and Cate, getting the ball, started for the Yale goal, but, being headed off, tried for a drop-kick, which fell short. Trumbull secured the ball and got down as far as the middle of the field before he was stopped.

Here ensued a mixup between Hall, Herrick and Wetherbee on the one side and Vaille, Elliot and Thompson on the other, in which the ball was carried in touch, Wetherbee throwing himself on it, and Elliot getting his hands on it under Wetherbee. Both claimed it but the referee decided in favor of Harvard. When the ball was thrown in, it was caught by Worts, who passed it to Thompson; but the latter failed to make any headway, being stopped by three Harvard rushers. The second half-hour was called with the ball toward the Yale end of the field.

In the third half-hour the excitement had grown intense and it was in this part of the game that Yale did her best playing. Thompson of Yale, by fine running, getting up toward the Harvard goal when he was thrown by Hall, and, falling on the ball, burst the wind out of it. It was blown up and thrown in the air by the referee. Curtis got it after it touched the ground, and, dodging two men who collided and knocked each other down, passed it to Blanchard, who secured a touchdown. The fourth and last goal was made by Tower, who kicked it over after a pass from Leeds, the latter nearly getting a touchdown before the goal was kicked. The final point was another touchdown by Blanchard, soon after which time was called, with Harvard the winner by 4 goals and 4 touchdowns to none for Yale.

The accounts of the treasurer of the Harvard University Football Club for the year 1875 show the total expenses of the year to have been $860, including a trip to Montreal and one to New Haven, and uniforms for the team. The total receipts were $705, which included $70 from Yale, Harvard's share of the receipts at New Haven.

The Harvard paper The Crimson *said of the game:*

About 150 Harvard men accompanied the football team to New Haven. Special cars were provided, and arrangements had been made at New Haven so that all found ample accommodations at the New Haven House. The evening train from Boston was delayed at Providence and the time passed most pleasantly by an impromptu game of athletic sports with the Brown men who had gathered at the depot. One-hundred-yard dashes and jumping feats were the order of the day.

Saturday morning the Yale men kindly drove the team about New Haven, showing them the objects of interest, including the college buildings and the new boat-house of the Yale Navy, which is one of the most complete structures of the kind, and one of which Yale may feel justly proud.

The game was called at 2:30 P.M. in the presence of a large number of spectators. . . . The Harvard students formed in a group and encouraged the players, lavishing their applause on Yale or Harvard, as the occasion required it. . . .

The adopted rules were not fully understood by either team, and the Yale men said that they differed from theirs more than from Harvard's. . . .

HARVARD vs. YALE, OLD STYLE

JOHN KIERAN *wrote in his "Sports of The Times" column in* The New York Times *of November 19, 1937:*

WITH HIS BREAKFAST of orange juice in a glass on the table in front of him, Jack Doyle, the Sage of Broadway, said: "Yale vs. Harvard. Or as they always say in Cambridge, Harvard vs. Yale, Harvard being the older, you know. And did you know that I am a veteran of the old Harvard-Yale wars of nearly fifty years ago? Well, sir, I played a part in the game of '89 in my humble New England fashion. I was a messenger boy. Yes, sir, from 1889 until 1894 the games were played in Springfield, Mass., and that's my home town.

"So Harvard and Yale played there in '89 and I was a messenger boy, running newspaper bulletins from where the fellows were writing to another messenger at the outside gate. I don't believe they had a wire in the park—Hampden Park was the name of it. The bleachers were put up especially for the game. Tremendous crowd—15,000. Pudge Heffelfinger played in the Yale line. Old Man Stagg, then a young divinity student, played right end. I remember after the game a woodcut caricature of Stagg handing one of the Harvard fellows a wallop and the caption was 'Stagg's Ministerial Uppercut.' It was in one of the Springfield papers. The players would all get out there and murder one another and after the game they would agree that there had been no slugging by either side.

"I could call off the line-ups of both teams right now. I can see those Traffords in their Harvard uniforms—and what uniforms they had in those days! Cummock was the Harvard captain and Charley Gill was the Yale captain. As I said, Heffelfinger was in there for Yale, which means that Yale won. But it was McClung who scored the touchdown and kicked the goal. In those days you had to kick the goal from a point in front of where the touchdown had gone over the line. The Yale touchdown had been made over at one side of the field and I'm telling you that William Tell couldn't have shot an arrow through the goal posts from that angle, but McClung kicked the goal just the same!

"I'll tell you why the Harvard-Yale game was played at Springfield. In those days the Big Three games were played on neutral grounds. Princeton-Yale was at the Polo Grounds in New York, about half way from each college, you see. Springfield was about seventy-five miles from New Haven and 100 miles from Boston, which made it a good spot for Harvard and Yale to meet.

"Another thing about Springfield was that it was a big railroad junction for New England. That's how the railroad station was wrecked one night. The Williams team and its rooters used to change cars at Springfield going to and from Yale for the annual game. Yale used to slaughter 'em. All the football there was of any class in those days was played by the Big Three. But this year the Williams rooters on the way back from New Haven were wild with delight. For why? Well, Yale won by the usual fifty or a hundred points or whatever it was—but Williams had scored! Yes, sir, Williams had scored on Yale and the Williams crowd on the way back was so exuberant it just about tore down our Springfield railroad station. It was a public benefit at that. We needed a new one.

"Well, Yale won that '89 game from Harvard by 6–0. We will now skip to the '94 battle—and the word 'battle' is used advisedly. The slaughter was so terrific that there was no game for three years after that. Wrightington of Harvard had his collarbone broken. Frank Butterworth of Yale had one eye nearly blinded. Practically all the players were bleeding from cuts or from kicks or smashes in the general mauling. Murphy of Yale was unconscious for five hours afterward in a Springfield hospital.

"I remember when they carried him out of the game. They just dumped him in a pile of blankets, covered him up, and then turned to look at the game again. A bit later, just out of curiosity, I went over and lifted the blankets apart and looked in. There he was, still unconscious—and nobody was paying any attention to him. They were all wrapped up in the game. So I covered him up again and went to have another look at the game myself.

"Hickok, the Yale right guard, was a great shot-put man. Bob Wrenn, later a great tennis champion, was the Harvard quarterback. When Butterworth was hurt, Brink Thorne—the grand guy who died a while back—shifted to fullback in his place. There was a Cabot and a Hallowell playing for Harvard and one Yale end was Lou Hinkey. The other Yale end was The Hinkey! The Hinkey boys were brothers.

"Now, let me tell you something. In those days they didn't have all the special harness that football players wear now. They had some kind of aboriginal helmets and big black rubber noseguards and maybe some old shinguards, but everywhere else they just stuffed their jerseys and pants with cotton and when they trotted on the field they looked—with all that cotton stuffing—like a bloomin' herd of elephants.

"This Hinkey—Frank, I mean—was a little tow-headed runt among those giants—and what did he wear? Nothing! No helmet, no noseguard or shinguard.or padding at all. He just walked in there—or rushed in there—with no protection but what his pants and jersey afforded, and what he did to those upholstered big guys was joyful to behold. He knocked 'em kicking and threw them head over heels.

"They tell me—I didn't see all the Yale games so I wouldn't know myself—that nobody ever made a first down around his end all the time he played for Yale. From the specimen of his playing I saw, I'm ready to believe it. They didn't need to supply me with affidavits. I've seen a lot of fighters, in and out of the ring, and some pretty good ones, but Frank Hinkey of Yale, pound for pound, was the fightingest bird ever I saw.

"They also told me way back in '94 that the Harvard team was sent on the field with only two instructions. The first was to get that Hinkey out of there and the second was to win the ball game.

"I'll say those Harvard birds tried hard and were pretty good men, but they didn't follow instructions. They didn't win the game. Yale won, 12 to 4. As for getting that Hinkey out of there, why, he never had time taken out for him all the while he played for Yale. Never once!

"Well, it's a different game now, and a better game. A much better game. There's an improvement in the rules and an improvement in the general skill of the players. Why wouldn't there be, with expert coaching and the game played from coast to coast? Figures prove that the players, on the average, are bigger now than in the old days. But not tougher! That I'll bet on!"

FRANK HINKEY

In 1935 GRANTLAND RICE, *in his syndicated column, "The Sportlight," quoted Dr. Fred Murphy on his celebrated teammate, Frank Hinkey, the legendary Yale end whose fame is so lasting that even today he is invariably picked first among the ends on the all-time teams. The column follows in part.*

Philadelphia, Pa., Oct. 11—The Blue against the Red and Blue —Yale and Pennsylvania. When they meet at Franklin Field this year of 1935, it is just another football game between two good teams. . . . Few recall that Yale and Pennsylvania were shooting for the football heights forty years ago, when Frank Hinkey was piling up a football name that has outlasted the years—when Brink Thorne was at his height—when George Brooke was the great kicker of his day and one of the best that ever lived—when Fred Murphy was Yale's star tackle—when Knipe and Osgood were around. . . .

It was in this game, around the middle '90's, when Penn got the jump on Yale—leading the Blue, 6 to 0—that Frank Hinkey, "the disembodied spirit," moved from end to halfback to drive his team 60 yards or more to a touchdown with a headlong assault that couldn't be stopped—and Frank Hinkey weighed 155 pounds. But "180" pounds of this was flame and dynamite.

During the recent world series, your correspondent had the pleasure of several visits with Dr. Fred Murphy, one of Yale's famous captains, who played two years with Hinkey—who battled against Penn some forty years ago.

"Those were battles," Dr. Murphy said, "that no one will forget. Yale was around the top in those days, but so was Pennsylvania. But if you pin me down, I'll say that in my opinion Frank Hinkey was the best football player I ever saw. He was undoubtedly the best—pound for pound. He was a great end. He was also a great quarterback and a great halfback. If he had been called on, he would have made a great guard or a great tackle at 155 pounds. . . .

"You'll remember that Hinkey was known as 'the disembodied spirit.' He could sift through any interference—no matter how compact it was—and get his man. He was in no sense a mean or vicious player. But when he tackled a man he seemed to explode. I know of no other word that covers his case. It was something like a grenade or a stick of dynamite hitting a runner. Even a 180-pound back would be flattened out completely.

"Hinkey was a football genius—and no one can explain a genius. His reflexes, mental and physical, were instantaneous. He could sense where every play was going. He made no false moves of any sort. I've seen the parade pass me by for forty years—but I've never seen another Hinkey. I never will. And I am not one of the old-timers who think that all the greatness of football belonged to the past. There are at least 100 fine players to one in my day—maybe 500 to 1, with the growth of the game. But even in the course of forty years you get one Babe Ruth—one Bobby Jones —perhaps one Joe Louis—and certainly one Hinkey. Only those who have played with him can know just what I mean."

In a column a few years later, Rice quoted another teammate of Hinkey's, George T. Adee, on the fabulous Yale end. Mr. Rice wrote:

I ran across my old friend, Colonel George Adee, of football, tennis, golf and war fame. George Adee was quarterback on two of Frank Hinkey's teams at Yale in the early '90s. And he was one of Yale's all-time best. But to Adee there was only one great football player. His name was Hinkey.

"What about Pudge Heffelfinger?" I asked.

"One of the greatest," Adee said. "But Pudge weighed 200 pounds. Hinkey was anywhere from 148 to 152. He was one of the cleanest players I ever saw, but he wrecked more 190-pound giants than any two men who ever played. When he tackled you he simply exploded. No interferer could ever take him out of a play. He sifted through and then struck with the poison of a diamond-back or a cobra. That is why Walter Camp called Frank 'the disembodied spirit.'

"Hinkey was also the smartest player I ever saw, and I've been watching football for over fifty years. He solved the crushing power of the flying wedge. He broke up guards-back. He wrecked the old tandem, within a few minutes after the opening whistle —and we had no scouts then—he told us what to do. And he was never wrong.

"The Disembodied Spirit," Frank Hinkey of Yale, four times all-America end.

"I'll admit he tore big men apart. They said he was too rough. But they could never say he was foul. . . ."

"I have played many games all my life," George Adee went on, "but I have never seen a man with the fiery, flaming spirit of Frank Hinkey, coupled with superb skill. Pudge Heffelfinger was the greatest guard that ever played. In many ways he was the most remarkable of them all. For he is the only man I ever knew who was still a great football player forty years after he left college. He was still playing at the age of sixty-six. He was still a star at the age of fifty-five. Ask Bo McMillin or Chic Harley.

"But to me Frank Hinkey was all that football ever meant. Courage, brains, speed, skill, knowledge, durability, stamina and, above all, the greatest fighting spirit that ever stepped upon any field at any time. . . ."

THE PIONEER YEARS

JOHN W. HEISMAN *was one of the pioneers of football, a man of inventive mind, imagination, and readiness to experiment and reach out for the new. He was advocating the legalization of the forward pass in 1903, three years before it was put into the game. He was the inventor of one of the most famous shifts, named after him—the Heisman shift—and introduced in 1910 when he was the coach at Georgia Tech. It stands with the Minnesota shift, devised by Dr. Harry Williams, and the Notre Dame shift, used by Rockne and Jesse Harper and later coaches at South Bend and deriving from the shift of Alonzo Stagg at Chicago, as the three recognized as basic.*

Heisman, after whom the Heisman Trophy, the most prized individual honor in college football, was named, coached for 36 years after playing football at Brown and Pennsylvania. His Georgia Tech teams were his most renowned. His 1917 eleven, which had a perfect record, was probably his best and his 1915 and 1916 teams also were unbeaten, though tied. He had had great success during his four years at Clemson before serving at Georgia Tech from 1904 to 1919. He also coached at Auburn, Oberlin College, Akron, Clemson, Pennsylvania, Washington and Jefferson, and Rice, retiring in 1927 at the age of sixty.

Heisman was one of the game's elder statesmen and twice served as president of the American Football Coaches Association. He was an organizer and the first president of the Downtown Athletic Club of New York and served as its athletic director. When he died in 1936, the trophy that had been put up in 1935 was named in his honor the Heisman Memorial Trophy. In Frank Menke's Encyclopedia of Sports, *in 1953, he said:*

I PLAYED FOOTBALL first in 1886 on a high school team in Western Pennsylvania. I was at Brown University in '87 and '88, and in '89, '90 and '91 I played at Penn.

The length of the field between goal lines in the old days was 110 yards, not 100, as at present. That made longer runs possible. There were no 5-yard stripe lines running across the field. There were no linesmen, and no line sticks. The referee kept track of distance by just dropping a handkerchief where he guessed the ball was last put into play. The players of both sides would slyly try to move that handkerchief, while some teammate engaged the referee in a discussion of the rules. So we varied action by kicking a handkerchief as well as a football.

We had gotten down to 11 men on a team even so long ago as that, but, as a rule, teams carried only 4 substitutes, even while on a trip, and trips sometimes meant playing two or three games on successive days, so as to be sure to take in enough money at the gate to defray the expenses of the trip.

The time of the playing halves of a game in those days was 45 minutes, not 30 minutes, as now. Furthermore, the game was not divided into quarters, as now, so there is today a rest period we never had in the old days. Players of my time had to be real iron men, because we played two games each week—Wednesdays and Saturdays.

Once a game started, a player could not leave unless he actually was hurt, or, at least, pleaded injury. Accordingly, whenever the captain wanted to put a fresh player into action, he whispered, "Get your arm hurt, or something." In one game my captain whispered to me, "Get your neck broke, Heisman."

We wore jerseys and shorts of great variety. We had no helmets or pads of any kind; in fact, one who wore home-made pads was regarded as a sissy. Hair was the only head protection we knew, and in preparation for football we would let it grow from the first of June. Many college men of that day, especially divinity and medical students, permitted their beards to grow. Often they were referred to as "Gorillas." The divinity students couldn't answer back —I mean, in the right way.

We didn't have many sweaters in those days, but we all wore snug fitting canvas jackets over our jerseys. You see, the tackling in that day wasn't clean-cut and around the legs as it is today. All too often it was wild, haphazard clutching with the hands, and when runners wore loose garments they were often stopped by a defensive player grabbing a handful of loose clothing. Some players wore pants, or jackets, of black horsehair. When you made a fumbling grab, you lost your fingernails.

In those pioneer years, arguments followed most every decision the referee made. The whole team took part, so that half the time the officials scarcely knew who was captain. More than that, every player was privileged to argue as much as he pleased with any and every player of the opposition. The player who was a good linguist always was a priceless asset.

We practiced every afternoon as players do now, but as we had no forward pass in the game then, we put in large chunks of time on sprinting and getting down field under punts. As a result of this, I have no hesitation in saying our punting of those bygone years was decidedly better than what we witness today.

Falling on the ball was also deemed a very important essential of a player's education. We had little concentrated work on practical tackling, or instruction in its technique. That was something we were supposed to figure out for ourselves, as it was much the same when we came to interference. But with or without special instruction, we were past masters at tackling around the neck. There was a rule against it, but that rule was, I am sure, broken oftener than any other in the book.

Line charging? Very little scientific thought had been put on that department of play before the dawn of the present century. Nearly all linemen, as a rule, lined up squarely against those who played the same position on the opposing team. They didn't crouch or squat or play low. They mostly stood bolt upright and fought it out with each other hammer and tongs, tooth and nail, fist and feet. Fact is, you didn't stand much chance of making the line those days unless you were a good wrestler and fair boxer.

Certain ingenious plays featured early-day sport that were quite as startling and unique as is the forward pass of today. There was the flying wedge, invented in 1892 and brought out by Harvard [the outgrowth of Princeton's V Trick]. The play was promptly copied by almost every team in the country.

Today we start the game with a kick-off, but in those days it was a fake kick, the center merely touching the ball to his toe and then tossing it back to a team-mate who ran with it while the rest of the team gave him what interference it could.

In the flying wedge, however, 9 of the players of the team withdrew about 20 yards from mid-field and at a signal those 9, in two lanes, started simultaneously and at full speed, converging on a point indicated by the ball. By the time they arrived at the ball, they had worked up a stupendous mass momentum, and the interference they gave for the runner was something wonderful to behold, and terrible to stop.

In 1893 Coach Woodruff at Penn drafted the principle of the flying wedge for his famous flying interference, which could be put into operation by the team that had the ball in every scrimmage down. This consisted in starting the tackle and end ahead of the snapping of the ball. They swung back together, between their line and the backfield, and then kept on to reinforce the work of their companion tackle and end, on the other side of the ball. Just before they hit the defensive line the ball went into play, and the results were again almost as disastrous to the defense as was the flying wedge. These two plays were quite as spectacular as any that the modern game has produced. So unstoppable were they, however, that the Rules Committee was forced to legislate them out of existence within a few years in order to preserve the proper balance between offense and defense.

One of the greatest drawbacks of the game 50 years ago was the fact that there was no neutral zone between the two scrimmage lines. There was only an imaginary scrimmage line drawn through the center of the ball. Naturally the rush line players of both teams were constantly striving to crowd this imaginary hair line in order to get the jump on their opponents.

This led to endless wrangling between teams and officials as to how many players were a hair's breadth over this hair line on each down. This resulted in so much charging and counter-charging, pushing and wrestling that it often took the quarterback a full minute to get the ball in play.

Bert Walters, a former captain of Harvard, introduced in 1903 the idea of the present neutral zone—a great improvement.

In the old days, players of one side were permitted to grab hold of their runners anywhere they could and push, pull or yank them along in any direction that would make the ball advance. Sometimes two enemy tacklers would be clinging to the runner's legs, and trying to hold him back, while several team-mates of the runner had hold of his arms, head, hair or wherever they could attach themselves, and were pulling him in the other direction. I still wonder how some of the ball carriers escaped dismemberment.

Some backs had leather straps, like valise handles, sewed or riveted on the shoulders of their jackets and on the hips of their trousers, so as to offer good handholds for their team-mates.

Wouldn't it make your eyes pop out if you were attending a football game today and saw the defensive ends going out 30 or 40 feet from their adjacent tackles? Well, that's where defensive ends played in those days. Why? Because a defensive end was not asked, or expected, to do anything much beyond keeping the opposing runner from getting around his end. So they tried to take good care that it didn't happen, by playing so close to the boundary that the runner had to go out of bounds to pass them.

We were allowed only 3 downs in those days but were required to gain only 5 yards on those 3 tries.

Whenever the ball went out of bounds it was not brought in 10 paces and put in play on that spot, as is the case nowadays. Instead, both rush lines faced each other at right angles to the boundary line. The man who had recovered the ball out of bounds brought it to the spot where it went out, and threw it out into the field of play with both sides scrambling to recover it.

FOOTBALL ANCIENT AND MODERN

WILLIAM H. (PA) CORBIN *was captain and center of the Yale team of 1888, which scored 698 points and shut out all of its thirteen opponents. The year was notable for the fact that it marked an important step in the transition from rugby to American football as the game began to take on its close-order formation with the rules changes leading to the introduction of the original T, or regular, formation. Walter Camp, who was to be the guiding hand in the transition, was the coach of the 1888 team, the first Yale coach, and three other Yale immortals were members of the team—Alonzo Stagg, Pudge Heffelfinger, and George Woodruff. Stagg and Woodruff stand with Pop Warner and Bob Zuppke as possibly the most inventive minds football has known.*

Corbin was elected to the National Football Hall of Fame in 1969. In the Yale-Army program of 1939 Corbin wrote:

IT IS A FAR CRY from the football of word and sign signals, snapping the ball by the foot, continuous forty-five-minute halves, one to three games a week, thirteen or fifteen games a season, no substitutions without injury, no neutral zone, free use of the hands and arms, free ball, flying tackles, only one man necessary on scrimmage line, mass plays, "V's," flying wedges, hurling, "guards and tackles back" formations, absolute playing responsibility of captain or quarterback, to this over-legislated, over-restricted, over-supervised, fifteen-minute-quarter pink tea, neutral zone, dead ball, curtailed tackling, hamstrung hands, helmets, armor menace, puppet, sideline managed, commercialized, basketball, Lady Luck spectacle—and few there be that care. "The king is dead! Long live the king!" "On with the dance!" But possibly a few personal incidents from the pages of the past may hold the reader's eye.

Lamar's run is one of Princeton's most prized memories. With a strong, cock-sure veteran team, they came to New Haven to meet a green, inexperienced Yale team, which included six freshmen. To the surprise of all, "hold 'em Yale" worked with that bunch of raw recruits, and five points were finally made by a goal from the field. At that time, the rules provided that in order to retain possession of the ball five yards must be gained or twenty yards lost in three downs. Under this provision Yale had kept the ball nearly all of the last half, and could easily have done so for the few minutes remaining to play. But Peters, one of the greatest of Yale's captains, and a true sport, realizing the monotony of the game, turned to Ray Tompkins, one of the coaches, on the side line, and asked if he should hang on to the ball or kick it.

"Oh, kick it," said Ray, "and have some fun."

The ball, in true spiral form, sailed down the field, was squarely muffed by one of Princeton's halfbacks, and Lamar, who was running up to assist, met it in the air, on the bound from the ground, and continued at full speed until he had crossed the goal line. The previously doleful and suddenly overjubilant Princeton crowd rushed on the field and considerable time was required before play could be resumed. During the interval, the quarterback, Dick Hodge, from Hartford, practiced holding the ball for several tries for the goal. The field was finally cleared, and the tries stood in good stead, for the goal was kicked and the game won, 6 to 5. Captain Peters threw himself on the ground almost heartbroken. But he unknowingly had won a lasting victory for Yale, for, on the foundations laid on that team, were developed Yale's notable victories of more than a decade thereafter.

When George W. Woodruff, at one time U.S. District Judge in Hawaii, formerly attorney general of Pennsylvania and later one of its public utility commissioners, entered Yale, he had a black, full beard. Because of his notable physical development and his natural athletic ability, he at once made the football team, beard and all. He immediately established the high standard of brilliant guard play for which he was noted during his four years on the team.

On a trip to Boston, to play the Institute of Technology, the eleven stopped at the old Tremont House for the night before the game. When Captain Peters was rounding up his men before turning in, he couldn't find the black-bearded freshman and he called out his name quite loudly. A demure, smooth-shaven youth stood up on the far side of the lobby and said, "Here I am, sir!" Then the whole bunch yelled, for, unrecognized by everyone, Woodruff had slid in from the barber shop, minus his whiskers. After graduation he was one of the most successful football coaches in the country, at the University of Pennsylvania, where he originated the "guards back" and many other unique and powerful plays.

Overleaf *Yale's first great football team, which scored 698 points while holding every opponent scoreless. Alonzo Stagg at extreme left and W. W. (Pudge) Heffelfinger behind and to the right of William H. (Pa) Corbin, captain.*

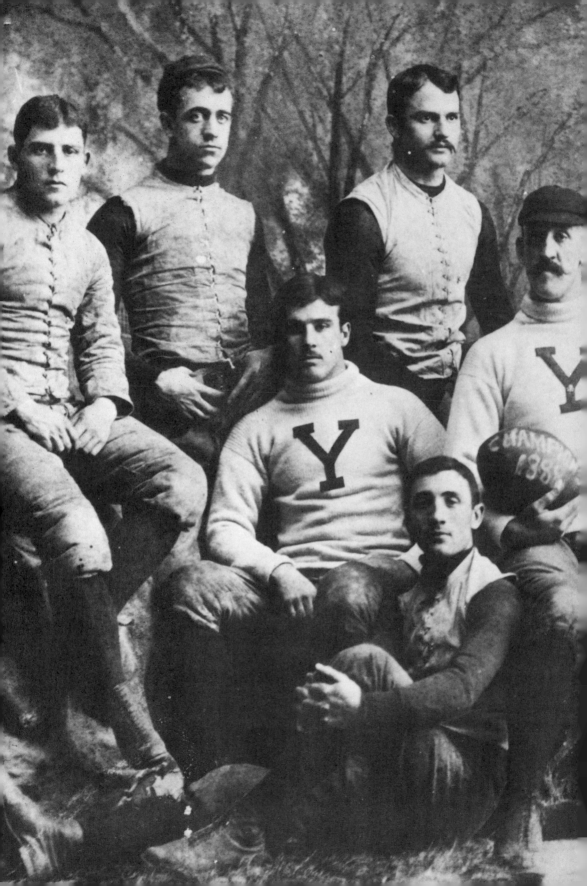

Charles Otis Gill, who was four years on the Yale football team, and a captain, was playing tackle in a game with the University of Pennsylvania at Philadelphia early in the season. He found his opponent very rough and particularly belligerent. Gill was one of the best tackles in the country and could give and take all the law allowed but he thought a line should be drawn somewhere. He called the attention of the umpire to the fisticuffing. The official was a Princeton man who had been noted for "aplenty" along that line when in college, and he was adamant.

At length the U. of P. man drew off and hit Charlie squarely in the mouth and knocked out his two front teeth. Gill immediately picked them up from the ground and held them up in the face of the umpire and said, lispingly, "Now will you put 'im offh?"

This time the umpire had no excuse, and the man went. Gill took the teeth to a dentist at once, who found them whole and the gums in such shape that he put them back in the jaw. In a few weeks they became set and Gill played in the Princeton game and is using the same teeth now so far as I know. Gill later went as a missionary to China and then was pastor of a church in Vermont. In the Princeton game he played opposite tackle Robert E. Speer, who for many years was secretary of the Presbyterian Board of Foreign Missions. Note the demoralizing (?) effect of football!

Frederic W. (Kid) Wallace played five years on the Yale football team, including one as a post-graduate, and was one of the best ends of all time and beloved by everyone. In one of the games with Harvard he played opposite "Vic" Harding, the father of the recent player by the same name. At that time the rules permitted the use of the hands and arms. Kid's reputation as a player was such that Harvard considered it very desirable to eliminate him from the play as much as possible. So during most of the game Kid and Vic would be in a wrestling match over by the side line while the play was going on in other parts of the field. Occasionally, Kid would break away and take part in a play but on the next down the Graeco-Roman exhibition would be resumed. But this unusual divertissement did not prevent a Yale victory.

Amos Alonzo Stagg made his athletic reputation in college as a pitcher, with "Jess" Dann as catcher in that nation-known battery. He did not play on the Yale football team until the year after he was graduated, while a student in the theological seminary, then allowable by the rules. He then very kindly consented to play end on a team which had absolutely no other possible candidate for that position. His legs were so short that he had to take about two strides to every one of "Kid" Wallace, the other end, in running down the field under Billy Bull's long kicks. So in order to develop his wind, his general habit was to run two miles from the field, after practice, while the rest of the team rode in the horse drawn bus, and "Lonny" usually reached the gym first. After playing another year at Yale he entered the YMCA College at Springfield, Mass., where he began his very remarkable career as a football coach, forty-one years of which were at the University of Chicago, where he was professor of the physical department, and since 1933 head football coach at the College of the Pacific.

At Springfield, Stagg immediately showed the foxy, deceptive, strategic plays for which he has been noted during all these years. At that time mass formations were permissible, only one man being required to be on the line of scrimmage to put the ball in play. In the YMCA game with Harvard, ten men formed in a mass, with their bodies bent over each, forming a "turtle back," several yards back of the center of the field. The ball was snapped back and disappeared into the middle of the mass. Soon all but one of the bunch started toward the side of the field in what appeared to be a "flying wedge," then much in vogue, with one man somewhat bent over and apparently carrying the ball, with nearly the entire Harvard team in pursuit. A minute later an unnoticed man on the ground, who all the time had the ball concealed under him, got up and ran down the other side of the field for a touchdown, much to the discomfiture of their opponents.

But while Stagg's deceptive plays, during his whole career, have been almost numberless, and, believing rightly, as he does, that more football games are won with brains than with brawn, he has been a stickler for observing not only the letter but the spirit of the rules. No man who has been connected with athletics has ever been such a force for good on so many boys and men for so long a time as Amos Alonzo Stagg. What a life to be proud of.

When William W. Heffelfinger was a freshman in his first year on the Yale football team, 210 pounds in weight and 6 feet 3 inches in height, he was the most demure, gentle, self-effacing individual that could be imagined. His usual posture was with his head bowed, shoulders stooped, eyes to the ground, with no idea whatever of his nature-given power to strike terror in his opponents.

Howard Knapp, a prominent lawyer, who married a Hartford girl, was one of the graduate coaches. He did everything possible, by word and deeds, to arouse Heff, so that he would give all he had in him for the good of the Yale team. Finally, at his wits' end,

Howard decided that, as a last resort, he would try the sight of blood to stir up his dormant bellicose spirit. So, with a pen dipped in blood which he secured from a slaughter house, he wrote him the sharpest, strongest kind of a letter, using every reasonable form of expression to get him out of his lethargy.

Heff, not knowing the nature of the gore, certainly was stirred, for he played the best game of the season against Princeton and aided materially in the victory. But the climax of his Yale football career was two years after in the 32 to 0 game played at Eastern Park, Brooklyn. While one Yale man would throw himself down in front of Princeton's V's, he would leap into the air and smash in the sides as if they were paper.

This poem, written at the time he left college, is a worthy tribute to Heff as a man and to his almost unequaled football ability and playing:

TO HEFFELFINGER!

Good-bye, Heff! The boys will miss you
And the old men too, and the girls!
You tossed the other side about as if they were ten pins;
You took little Bliss under your wing and he ran with the ball like
 a pilot boat by the Teutonic.
You used eyes, ears, shoulders, legs, arms and head, and took it
 all in.
You're the best football rusher America, or the world, has shown;
And best of all, you never slugged, lost your temper or did anything
 mean.
Oh come, though mighty one, go not away,
The team thou must not fail;
Stay where thou art, please, Heffelfinger, stay
And still be true to Yale—
Linger, yet linger, Heffelfinger!
A truly civil-engineer,
His trust would ne'er surrender.
Unstrap thy trunks—excuse this scalding tear—
Still be Yale's best defender—
Linger, O linger, Heffelfinger
Princeton and Harvard, there is cause to fear,
Will dance joy's double shuffle
When of thy western flight they come to hear.
Stay and their tempers ruffle—
Linger, O linger, Heffelfinger!

Pudge Heffelfinger, Yale's legendary all-time, all-America guard.

When Thomas L. Shevlin, one of the best all-around ends who ever played football, was captain of the Yale team he used to continually talk with "Mike" Murphy, the trainer, about his end work as compared with his eminent predecessor, Frank Hinkey. Mike wouldn't commit himself and Tom would keep pestering him for a definite statement as to which was the better. Finally Mike became disgusted and decided to settle the controversy, so he said, "Tom, if you and Frank were playing at opposite ends of the same Yale team, his playing, as compared with yours, would make you look as if you had sleeping sickness." This settled the argument. For while Tom continued to play his position most brilliantly, he never mentioned the matter to Mike again.

One of the finest instances of Tom Shevlin's skill and almost hypnotic energy as a coach and leader was when he took a discouraged, disheartened Yale team, almost beyond help, with a string of defeats and with a hopeless future, and taught them the Minnesota shift in the week before the Brown and Princeton games. When he disclosed what he had in mind for them, they acted as if he were throwing them a life preserver. They fairly hung on his words and in one day he transformed entirely their spirit, courage and confidence. They went into the Princeton game with their new plays a secret, and with them were able to defeat their surprised, over-confident opponents. It was all Tom Shevlin. Too bad that such a spirit and such pent-up energy should be cut off so soon!

FOOTBALL AT PURDUE
IN THE EARLY YEARS

GEORGE ADE, *Hoosier humorist and playwright, tells what the game of football was like at Purdue University from its inception there in 1887, the year he graduated. In* Liberty *magazine on November 16, 1929 he wrote:*

LET'S SEE, how long did the Children of Israel wander in the wilderness before they came to the Promised Land? A matter of forty years, wasn't it? And yet, all the time, it was a short cut from the east shore of the Red Sea to the most favored spot in Palestine—if there is any favored spot.

All the geography featured in the Scriptures would not make a vestibule for Texas. What ailed the Children? What was the idea of milling around in a circle and coming back to the same old dry hole in the Arabian Desert? All they needed any time was a stronger line, a coach who knew his stuff, and some organized support from the alumni.

Hold on! We are scrambling ancient history. Every time I think of weary pilgrims wandering in a parched desert for forty years, it seems to me that I am talking of dear alma mater instead of the host led by Moses.

At the very beginning of the expedition the sea was divided and the Chosen People crossed over in safety. A happy prelude to forty years of personally conducted non-efficiency. Strangely enough, we had the same experience at Purdue. Soon after the first football was kicked over the Alleghenies and came bounding across the Middle West, the inconspicuous college with which I was hooked up developed a team which proved to be what Corbett was to boxing the very same year, what Man o' War was to racing later on, and what Helen Wills is to tennis now in 1929.

From the time of my graduation (away back yonder, in the dim, prehistoric era of pompadours, polkas, tight trousers, guitars, and Sweet Caporal cigarettes), I have kept up what the efficiency experts call a "contact" with the school which gave me a B.S. From the years in which the first games of modified Rugby were played in the corn belt I have been a consistent football fan, and I never have lost the lust for victory and the various surging impulses which combine to make up the "campus complex"—a form of malady which has attacked many alumni, including some in Iowa.

When I should have been attending to my own business and trying to ornament a profession which will always stand for a little more ornamenting, I was up to my chin in undergraduate activities. Who was it helped put the chimes into the Mechanical Tower? Who rushed in with a check to save the funds for the Memorial Gym? Who wrote the plays for the Harlequin Club, including the Fair Co-Ed, taken over and done professionally by Elsie Janis? Who took the gaff and gave until it hurt when the new frat house was built? Who wrote and sent out, first class, the news bulletins to all Purdue men in service during the World War?

Who fixed up the illustrated lecture for Convocation? Who came through for the Student Union Building? Who trailed along with Dave Ross in securing for the university the neatest boy-size gladiatorial arena in the world called the Ross-Ade Stadium? Who went all the way to Boston to see Purdue defeat Harvard? Pardon these blushes. Modesty compels me to refrain from replying.

All of which is not by way of boasting, mind you, but merely to inform the reader that he is now getting some football talk from one who has been a sophomore for more than forty years.

The first team was organized in 1887. I was across the River, in Lafayette, selling my output of journalism at ten dollars a week. Football was in the air. Evans Woollen, a young aristocrat of Indianapolis who had taken his B.A. at Yale in 1886, had come home and was coaching an eleven at Butler. The newfangled game was simply an unwritten book to that stretch of territory formerly occupied by the Indians and now dominated by the Big Ten.

Young Mr. Woollen knew the tricks already mastered at Yale and he lined up a team at Butler which was probably the class of the prairie regions until about 1890. All of our early ambitions were centered on defeating Butler. You may be interested to know that Mr. Woollen, the voice that cried in the wilderness, is now one of the high-powered bankers of Indiana and will be United States Senator if the Democrats ever get a break.

On the bulletin board of the dormitory appeared a call for volunteers who were willing to lay their young bodies on the altar as a sacrificial offering to dear old Purdue. The school was now over ten years old and the plastering was nearly dry. Any man who wished to play football could make the team by merely signing his name.

Tall, skinny boys who wore spectacles and were bicepped like sandhill cranes put down their names because they had read about Tom Brown at Rugby and wished to get a free railroad ride to Indianapolis.

How about a coach? Someone heard of a deaf-mute over in Lafayette who had returned from an institute in the East at which the game had been investigated. And so a smiling young man who could not speak a word or hear what was said to him came over afternoons to take charge of the lame, the halt, the blind, and the perniciously anaemic and imbue them with stamina, courage and strategy.

The coaching consisted of excited sign language and strange noises coming from the vocal cords. If they could have been translated they would have proved to be profanity. The coach was a deaf-mute, but he could see, and the team must have been something terrible to look at.

For one thing, our athletes, trained to the minute on pie and doughnuts, never could grasp the importance of keeping the center of gravity as near terra firma as possible. When they formed for scrimmage, they stood in a geometrical line, elbow to elbow—not crouching like slaves, but bolt upright, like true sons of freedom. Their fists were clenched. Their chins were tilted and their eyes gleamed determination.

The ball would be snapped into play and the enemy would come into contact with our rush line, whereupon our warriors would fall backward, still with their fists clenched, and lie upon the turf, moaning feebly, while somewhere someone in possession of the ball would carry it to any point which might suit his whim or fancy, because there was none anywhere near him to disarrange his plans.

Those first games with Butler were miniature and low-comedy reproductions of the Custer massacre. We had no coaching and our volunteer players were strangely garbed in bed-ticking material and each wore upon his head a tasseled cap such as a Norwegian puts on when he goes out to attend a ski party. Along about 1890 some of the broken-hearted undergraduates decided that Purdue should no longer be butchered to make an Indianapolis holiday.

We heard of two players who had achieved glory at Princeton and had lately returned to their homes in Chicago. One was Knowlton L. (Snake) Ames, whose spectacular run through the whole Yale team to snatch victory in almost the last minute of play will ever remain one of the hallowed traditions of the game. The other was Ben (Sport) Donnelly, than whom no end player was ever more scrappy, belligerent, resourceful, tricky and versed in all forms of manslaughter which could seldom be detected by the officials.

For we are telling you that football in the '90s bore no resemblance whatever to jackstraws, crokinole, drop-the-handkerchief, or "Heavy, heavy hangs over your head."

Sport Donnelly, one of the most amiable and diverting comrades who ever helped to make the world more interesting, passed beyond the dark goal line a few years ago. Snake lives in Chicago still—owns a newspaper, directs large corporations, and is a gentle-hearted and pugnacious millionaire.

What a piece of luck it was when those two lads consented to come down and take charge of our disorganized and beaten outfit and hammer it into a team! As if by a miracle, there came to the campus from the tall grass and the hickory groves and the quiet Main Streets of our native state a lot of rangy huskies who had the makings.

Maybe it was Paul Anderson, now dean of Engineering Schools at Kentucky, who induced Snake and Sport to come down to our small and struggling school and lead us out of the smoke and gloom. Possibly he was helped by "Russ" Richards, now president of Lehigh and not as keen on football as he used to be since the curriculum became more important to him than the forward pass. Anyhow, we turned over to the Princeton stars a huddle of bewildered bone and muscle and gristle, and before long we had a team that acted like a cageful of Bengal tigers and simply ate up Methodists and Baptists. Sport coached the line and Snake handled the backs and directed general strategy.

Season of 1891: Purdue 44, Wabash 0; Purdue 60, Indiana 0; Purdue 58, Butler 0.

We had arrived, but the fact that we had arrived was local news. Then came the season of 1892. Purdue defeated Wabash, Wisconsin, Michigan, Butler, Indiana, Chicago, and DePauw, scoring a total of 320 points to 24 for all of their opponents. They beat Wisconsin 34 to 6, Michigan 24 to 0, Chicago 38 to 0, and Indiana 68 to 0.

I'll never forget that Chicago game, down on a ragweed gridiron in West Lafayette. Stagg had just taken over the coaching at Chicago. When the slaughter was half over he ran out of substitutes and Purdue gave him permission to play if he would consent to Donnelly going in at end for Purdue. It must have been the last regular college game in which these two celebrities appeared. Stagg fought hard but he had no team as yet, and we howled ourselves hoarse when it became evident that he couldn't do so much with Billy Moore, an unterrified country boy who played opposite Amos Alonzo and who had been eating raw meat and learning the arts of polite murder under the masterful tutelage of Sport.

Those early '90's were the golden age, the Elizabethan era, at our school of technology. Just as football became a big item, we welcomed to the campus a solemn-faced young eccentric from Indianapolis, who was soon known to the whole colony and appraised as a confusing combination of brilliant qualities. Meaning Booth Tarkington. George Barr McCutcheon had already been on the campus. John Tinney McCutcheon, a cartoonist who has made his advertised profession a mere side line to war correspondence, the writing of books, exploration, big-game hunting, and aviation, had finished in 1889.

He and I were doing low-salaried newspaper work in Chicago, but we had our Saturdays off because the Record did not print on Sundays, and we had passes on the Monon, so we were regulars at the fall games.

Snake and Sport stayed only two seasons, but they gave the team a start and planted so much football on the campus that Purdue had winning teams for several years. For instance, take our first seven games with Illinois. Purdue won five and tied two. However, that season of 1892 was the peak.

I can hear some readers say that those heroes at our yap school were great merely by comparison. They were playing with greenhorns who had not learned even the rudiments. Fortunately, some of our stars had a chance to go against the very best teams in the country. William Hale Thompson, of whom you have heard, was managing the team representing the Chicago Athletic Association. He got his players where he could find them. At one time he had a couple of policemen in the line. The hampering conference regulations were not in force, and so he borrowed a few of our players for a tour of the East. "Stevey" Stevenson was a center and Jimmy Studebaker played fullback and Finney was a halfback.

The team went east and played the big varsity teams and the athletic club teams such as the Oranges and Crescents, made up of ex-stars. Stevey was never outplayed at center. No man in the East was better than Studebaker when it came to long and accurate punting. Finney scored against every team which they met.

The other day I had a letter from Snake in which he said: "The Purdue teams for the two years when Donnelly and I were coaching were about the best in the country and had about as good material in them as I ever saw, and you cannot speak too highly of all the boys." So it was over forty years ago that I became an ardent lover of the best of all college games. Ever since then I have been watching football, and no one ever watched it for so long a period and knew so little about it. The first Eastern game I attended was in 1892 between Yale and Princeton in New York City. After nightfall I witnessed the annual college riot at Koster and Bial's Music Hall.

Oh, dear friends, talk about flaming youth. The younger generation of today may be a bit go-ey, but I have never been in a more tumultuous assemblage than that which surged and yipped and fist-fought in the wet and wide-open variety hall there in New York, unless it was the happy mob of ruffians from Oxford and Cambridge who swarmed into Piccadilly one memorable evening after the boat race.

No doubt I am addressing many another football maniac who has always been so interested in the advancement of the ball that he could not find time to analyze the plays and observe the work which was being done by men who were not near the ball. Just the same, I have watched them all from the days of Heffelfinger up to the time of the Four Horsemen of Notre Dame. I saw that quartette in their last game at Pasadena. No big game at Soldier Field in Chicago has escaped me. When the whistle blows and that awkwardly contrived and egg-shaped affair of inflated pigskin goes sailing down the field, the old thrill is in evidence just as it was when Purdue cleaned up on the whole Middle West.

Goodness knows, this piece must not degenerate into a tale of woe regarding the lean years which followed the early triumphs. Right here, and before I forget it, let me say something about the changes that have come about during these years in which I have watched the game so intently without acquiring any knowledge of the technique.

For one thing, the game has been opened up and cleaned up and pretty well purged of professionalism. The most notable change is that regarding sportsmanship. In those old pioneer days a football game was regarded as a battle of extermination. We were such frenzied partisans that probably we did not realize at the time that our boys were playing just as rough as they knew how. Somehow we managed to manufacture a deep and seething hatred of every team playing our team, and of the school which the opposing players represented.

For instance, when Michigan came to Purdue in 1892, the reputed star of the team was a swift and elusive halfback named Jewell. It happened that Mr. Jewell was a Negro. Therefore, the blood-thirsty and oft-repeated chant arising from the Purdue bleachers from the moment the ball went into play, was: "Kill the coon! Kill the coon!" When, early in the first half, the officials unscrambled a high mountain of wriggling players, Mr. Jewell was found underneath the whole mass, flat on his face and dead to the world. He was carried off the field, still unconscious, and all the Purdue rooters stood and cheered wildly. That's pretty hard to believe, isn't it? But I have talked to many of the veterans of the East and they have owned up that in those early days the idea was to cripple permanently and send to the hospital anyone connected with the opposition who was regarded as dangerous.

Nowadays the crowd on one side of the stadium will applaud the songs rendered on the opposite slope of the bowl, and the bands will go over and serenade the enemy, and yells will be exchanged and when any man is hurt there is a merciful silence and when a celebrity limps off the field he gets a hand from every section of the arena. So, no matter how much the world has slid downhill in recent years, football has become more civilized.

And now, if you don't mind, I will do a little weeping on your shoulder. Our team at Purdue struggled through the '90's, winning a good many hard games and also playing close scores with Chicago but never regaining championship form. Early in the present century it looked as if we were to stage a comeback, and then came the appalling tragedy of October 31, 1903.

We were to play Indiana at Indianapolis and a private car containing all of our players and substitutes was on the tail end of a special train standing in the yards at Indianapolis waiting to get up to the station. An engine dashed through an open switch and hit the private car, wrecking it completely. No less than seventeen of our men were killed outright and some twenty more were injured. The team was practically wiped out of existence. One of the players and the captain of the team, with so many broken bones and fractures and ghastly wounds that no one dared to predict his recovery, was Harry (Skillet) Leslie, now governor of Indiana.

It was slow work to rebuild a team, especially in view of the fact that the administration was not keen for football and any school of technology is badly handicapped in intercollegiate sports by the fact that the boys have heavy schedules in the labs and shops and the average hours left for training are much fewer than in any academic school.

Let us not revive bleak and dreary memories by counting scores through the years of disappointment. Let us come to the year of 1913. Elmer Oliphant (Ollie) was one of our backs and we had succeeded in getting Andy Smith of Pennsylvania to coach. Ollie was just as good then as he was when he made the whole country sit up and pay attention to his marvelous performances with Army. Andy knew just as much football as when he made California the best team on the coast and undoubtedly the best in the Western Hemisphere. In 1913 we tied Wisconsin, 7 to 7; tied Bob Zuppke's first Illinois team, 0 to 0; beat Northwestern, 34 to 0, and Indiana, 42 to 7. We were pretty good in 1914, and then another slump and then the war, which put football off the map.

Passing hastily over the period from the armistice to the fall of 1922, we now find Jimmy Phelan on Stuart Field trying to make something out of nothing. About all he could do was to inaugurate the policy to which he had become converted while he was associated with Knute Rockne up at Notre Dame. The first paragraph of the policy was to get the material, and the second was to knock the inferiority complex out of the whole squad, and the third item was to get something we never seemed to have, an abundant supply of eager substitutes who were just about as good as the regulars.

All of which is easy to talk about but involves a program which cannot be put into effect except by years of labor. If we could have put a line in front of Ollie he would have been a real sensation long before he flashed his brilliant record at Army.

While we were still down in the valley and the future looked very bleak, Dave Ross sent for me to come to Lafayette because he had something to show me. Dave is a quiet person and makes steering knuckles for about 75 percent of all the trucks in America and most of the pleasure cars. He did not do much dancing at Purdue and never bothered himself to join a fraternity, but now he is a whale of a fellow and president of the board of trustees.

I went to Purdue and was conducted by Dave and Judge Henry Vinton over to the west side and led up to the top of a high hill, and a temptation was submitted to me. Dave showed me a deep oblong hole away up at the crest of the slope and said, "You are now looking at the ready-made Stadium in which Purdue is going to play football—real football—someday. Our all-wise Creator directed a glacial drift so that it gouged out this large depression so that we could have a concrete bowl without moving several millions of cubic yards of dirt. All we have to do is to buy sixty-five acres of land before the owner finds out that he has a stadium on his premises."

We bought the tract and established the Ross-Ade Foundation, and we knew that some day the stadium would be built, but just then all of us were being bled white for the Student Union Building, so we decided to wait. In a little while Dave came to me again and said, in his low and quiet way (he is a persuasive cuss): "We are a couple of case-hardened and kiln-dried bachelors. We will have no children or grandchildren to sit in any stadium and hear complimentary remarks made about their deceased relatives. I don't seem to derive any great satisfaction from the knowledge that some day a good-looking arena will be constructed on this land that we turned over to the university. My idea would be to build the darn thing so that we can see some of the games played in it."

I followed again and we offered to match up contributions made by alumni who were willing to buy life seats. We made a contract with the athletic association insuring a good rental every year. We went into it and found a contractor, A. E. Kemmer, a Purdue man, who was willing to lose a nice chunk of money in order to carry through the big project, and we built the stadium. By the way, I don't enjoy all of this harping criticism against the alumni who fail to lose interest in their school. It is hard enough to steam them up without throwing any cold water on them.

We dedicated the stadium in the fall of 1924 by defeating Indiana, 26 to 7, just after Indiana had scored a victory over Ohio State. We never have lost a game played in the stadium. There have been two tie games, and all the rest have been satisfactory victories. The new system of coaching worked out.

"Cotton" Wilcox began to prove that he was one of the best halfbacks in the country and then, in the fall of 1927, Ralph ("Pest") Welch appeared and startled the East by doing all of the heavy work when Purdue defeated Harvard, 19 to 0, with Cotton Wilcox crippled and on the sideline. And so we come right up to the present. . . .

After being on the sidelines for quite a spell, I have arrived at certain conclusions regarding football. I don't think it is a curse or a menace. It strikes me as being an annual tonic. It does not begin to flare up until early in October and it is all over before

Thanksgiving. Of course it excites the old grads and the students and is the excuse for raving enthusiasm and great crowds of people, but what of it? We can't keep our students crouched under student lamps all of the time. . . .

Football is all right. I have been so fond of it that repeatedly I have broken into print regarding it. Away back in 1890, while I was still lingering near the campus, I wrote what was intended to be a poem regarding the glorious pastime. Listen to the first verse:

When the crisp autumnal zephyrs whistle through the leafless trees;
    When croquet is a sweet regret and tennis *non est;*
When the baseball player stays indoors for fear that he will freeze,
    And the picnic trousers get a needed rest;
When mackinaws and yellow shoes are packed way with care,
    And the summer sash becomes a muffler gay,
Then the college football specialist emerges from his lair,
    And buckles up his armor for the fray.

This was followed by a verse which described the tortures of training, and then came the following:

But out of these hardships and this abstinence unwilling,
    There comes a day of triumph for the Rugby devotee,
When on the frozen battlefield unheeding winds so chilling,
    He "scrimmages" and "tackles" in the hope of victory.
What though he grinds his features to a pulp so raw and gory,
    While strong and beefy opponents are seated on his frame?
What though he never lives to tell his children of the story?
    Though death come with the victory, his team must win the
        game.
The college yell inspires him still, and though each bone is aching
    And though the hazy landscape swims before his blinded eyes,
The precious spheroid comes his way and through the rush-line
        breaking,
    He's down behind the crossbar and the team has won the prize.
A ton or more of writhing flesh with him is mixed together;
    One leg is wrapped around his neck; four teeth cannot be
        found;
But he has passed beyond the goal and hangs on to "the leather";
    He is the hero of the day—he's carried from the ground.

PRINCETON-YALE, 1889

JOE VILA, *sports editor of* The New York Sun, *who was present at the game between Yale and Princeton in 1889, reviewed it in his column in 1930 as follows:*

PERHAPS THE MOST disagreeable conditions ever provided for a Yale-Princeton football game prevailed when those old rivals lined up on Thanksgiving Day, 1889, at Berkeley Oval, a field owned by an athletic club of that name on Morris Heights [in New York]. Owing to the fact that the new Polo Grounds were not available, Berkeley Oval was selected at short notice. Contracts were let for the building of wooden stands to seat about 15,000 spectators. But the carpenters did not finish their task in time for the game. A heavy rainfall the night before converted the improvised gridiron into a sea of mud. In the center of the field and in front of each goal were pools of water from one to ten inches deep.

At 10 o'clock in the morning, after the gridiron had been covered with sawdust, Pennsylvania and Wesleyan met in their annual combat. Not more than 1,000 persons bought tickets of admission and were compelled to stand around the sidelines because the club managers had not received permission from building inspectors to use the hurriedly constructed bleachers. Wesleyan won, 10 to 2, the players of both teams being drenched to the skin and covered with sticky oil.

At one o'clock the police, commanded by Inspector Conlin, ordered everybody outside of the gates in order to permit the ticket sellers to meet the Yale-Princeton crowd. The Oval was nearly three quarters of a mile from the New York Central Railroad Station, where special trains from the Grand Central Terminal began unloading the fans as early as 12:30 o'clock.

It didn't take long to discover that the gates were too narrow to admit more than two persons at once. Consequently, there was a terrific jam in the mud outside of the entrances, and two ticket booths were overturned.

Meanwhile, tally-ho coaches occupied by Yale and Princeton men were driven onto the soggy field behind the goal posts. Just before the teams made their appearance at 2:15 o'clock, the un-

finished stands were packed, there was a fringe of men and women around the edges of the gridiron and hundreds obtained vantage points in numerous trees.

The reporters, including the writer, did not have a press stand. They were compelled to cover the game from the sidelines, where Police Inspector Conlin provided boards and boxes, on which the scribes squatted while keeping track of the plays. Of course, the players were not numbered and there was no official announcer. Hence the reporters had to get their information under the most trying circumstances.

Princeton won this memorable struggle by a score of 10 to 0. The Tigers were heavier than the Elis and much better mudlarks. Two Harvard men—Saxe and Brooks—officiated as referee and umpire, respectively, and when the battle started the teams lined up as follows:

Princeton—Sport Donnelly, left end; Hector Cowan, left tackle; House Janeway, left guard; William George, center; Captain Jesse Riggs, right guard; Walter (Monte) Cash, right tackle; Ralph Warren, right end; Edgar Allan Poe, quarterback; Roscoe Channing and Jeremiah Black, halfbacks; and Snake Ames, fullback.

Yale—A. A. Stagg, left end; Charley Gill, left tackle; Pudge Heffelfinger, left guard; Bert Hanson, center; Ashbell Newel, right guard; Captain Billy Rhodes, right tackle; Josh Hartwell, right end; Bill Wurtemberg, quarterback; Lee McClung and Perry Harvey, halfbacks; and Herb McBride, fullback.

By game time, late arrivals, unable to pass through the gates, climbed over the fences. In the wild scramble, women were knocked down, hats were lost and umbrellas smashed. Nobody ever will know how many tickets were not collected at the entrances.

Two halves of forty-five minutes each were agreed upon and Princeton, after taking the kick-off, opened with the famous "V trick," a wedge driven through Yale's center, for a material gain. Because of the slippery footing, the game soon developed into a punting duel between Ames and McBride. Princeton's tackles, Cowan and Cash, made short rushes now and then, and so did Gill and Harvey of Yale.

The Tigers' gigantic center, George, soon was put out of commission in a fierce scrimmage. He had to be carried off the field and although he begged to be allowed to watch the fight from the sidelines, he was taken to a hospital suffering with torn ligaments in his right leg. George's place was taken by Jones, and, as a result, Princeton men became apprehensive. Soon Captain Riggs of the

turn-of-the-century twosome.

Tigers was laid out with a sprained ankle, but he wouldn't leave the gridiron. That sort of injury in those days was trivial.

McClung, Yale's great halfback, was knocked out in a head-on collision with Poe, who quickly apologized to him. But McClung was unable to continue, and his place in the backfield was taken by Morison. Near the end of the first half, Poe passed the ball to Ames. Together they sprinted around Yale's left end, Poe interfering beautifully. Ames got in the longest run of the game, covering 45 yards, but was tackled from behind near Yale's goal line. Then Snake missed a drop kick for goal from the 35-yard line just as the half ended.

Another punting duel opened the second half. Cowan soon got through a hole in Yale's rush line and had a clear field, only to slip and fall in the mud. Cash, who was interfering for Cowan, picked up the ball, but it slipped out of his grasp and Princeton lost a chance to score what, momentarily, looked like a sure touchdown. There was rough play on both sides. The tackling was deadly, particularly that of Poe and McBride. Suddenly, Captain Rhodes was disqualified for slugging and Hayworth went in at right tackle for Yale.

Again the gigantic Cowan carried the ball and when he found himself in close quarters he passed it to Ames, who made another dazzling run far into Yale's territory. Snake was tackled by Stagg on the 15-yard line just when he seemed about to score. Yale got the ball on a fumble and McBride's punt was returned by Ames, the ball rolling over Yale's goal line, where three Elis, sliding in the mud, failed to recover it.

Warren and Donnelly of Princeton both fell on the slippery leather for a touchdown, which yielded four points, and Ames followed with a goal from placement, which increased the Tigers' total to six. Not long after that incident, McBride narrowly missed a field goal with a drop-kick from the 40-yard line.

At 4:30 P.M. it was growing dark and many of the spectators were leaving. McBride and Ames exchanged several punts until Cowan, with a minute to play, rushed the ball over Yale's goal line for another touchdown, which made the final score 10 to 0. It was not until 9 o'clock at night that the last special train left Morris Heights for Forty-Second Street. Princeton was the champion that year, having crushed Harvard, 41 to 15 at Jarvis Field, Cambridge, on November 16.

THE FIRST ARMY–NAVY GAME, 1890

GENERAL JOHN MC A. PALMER, *a member of the class of 1892 at the United States Military Academy, wrote an article, "How Football Came to West Point." It was published in the January, 1943, issue of* Assembly. *He said in part:*

IN THE AUTUMN OF 1890 the monotony of cadet life was broken by a revolutionary event. Annapolis challenged West Point to play a game of football. At first, it seemed certain that this challenge must be rejected. We had no football team and very few cadets had ever handled a modern football. The Academic Board would have vetoed such a distracting innovation during the academic year even if the cadets were prepared for such a contest. In the actual circumstances the odds were at least a thousand to one against it.

But these odds were trifling to my classmate, Cadet Dennis Mahan Michie. Dennis had played football at Lawrenceville for several years and was one of the few men in the Corps who had any real knowledge of the game. But even more important, he was the only cadet with any power to influence the academic authorities. He was born at West Point and had spent his childhood there. He knew all the professors and their families intimately. Most of the instructors had chummed and jollied with him when they were cadets and he was an attractive small boy about the post. In fact, Michie's position in the Corps of Cadets was absolutely unique. I was walking with him one day when we met that superb cavalier, Lieutenant Daniel L. Tate of the 3rd Cavalry. As the lieutenant returned our salutes, he said, "Good morning, Denny." When Dennis replied, "Good morning, Danny," I almost expected the skies to fall.

It was something to have intimate friends among the officers on the post. But in those days West Point was dominated by the Academic Board and the Academic Board was dominated by "Old Pete," the professor of Natural and Experimental Philosophy. As the senior professor, Old Pete was known as the Dean of the Board and presided over its meetings. And his official position was fortified by his dominating personality. As a rule, Old Pete was highly conservative and could be counted on to lead resistance against innovation. But when the football challenge came before the Board, his position was weakened by the fact that Cadet Dennis M. Michie was Professor Peter S. Michie's favorite son. When Dennis first told me about the challenge, I inquired, "But how about your father?" To this he replied with a grin: "Old Pete is dead against it now, but I will bring him around." Old Pete finally came around but even he was hard pressed to secure a majority of the Board, and the final approval of Colonel John W. Wilson, the Superintendent of the Military Academy.

Dennis now had his hands full. He was captain, coach, trainer and business manager of the non-existent team that must play a championship game at the end of eight weeks. There was plenty of promising material in the Corps but among those cadets who were physically qualified very few had had any experience. As I recall it, only Michie, Prince and Butler Ames had ever played on an organized team. On the other hand, the midshipmen had been playing for several years. Last year they had defeated Virginia, 26 to 6, and this year they were playing a full schedule of games. Dennis had scant time to teach the simplest fundamentals to his raw recruits. They had no team practice except a few riotous scrimmages against an even more inexperienced second team. And there was not time for coaching except in the brief intervals between military duties. It was only on Saturday afternoons when the weather was too bad for drill and dress parade that Dennis could count on any time for continuous practice. On rainy afternoons he had almost two hours on the tan bark in the riding hall. But that rarely happened. The weather gods up there in the Hudson Highlands are highly militarized. Even after an all-day rain they generally turn off the spigot about 3:50 P.M.—just before first call for drill.

The great day, Saturday, November 29, 1890, finally arrived. A gridiron was laid out at the southeast corner of the Parade Ground. There was plenty of room for the officers and their families and there were not more than a hundred visitors from outside the post. There was no grandstand and no seats except chairs for some of the ladies, borrowed by their escorts from the nearby Academic Building. We cadets had plenty of room along the sidelines. There were so few of us that we could shift freely with the ball from one end of the field to the other.

The West Point band played but we had no football songs. Presently our team ran out on the field and we yelled a welcome, each man yelling for himself. When the Navy team trotted out it was welcomed by an organized cheer from a small group of young Navy officers from some ship down in New York harbor. This was a new one on us. We were surprised to find that a dozen regimented voices could make more effective noise than our whole vocal democracy. . . .

One of the Navy plays was especially effective. Their fullback dropped back to kick and when he got the ball, instead of kicking it as he had clearly promised us, he ran the whole length of the field with it and made a touchdown. We greenhorns on the sidelines were indignant. We expected that the officials would recall the play. It was clearly a false official statement for an officer and gentleman to announce that he was going to kick a ball and then do something else with it. To our surprise and disgust, the officials let the play stand. Instead of protesting the decision, Dennis merely slapped the Navy captain on the shoulder and grinned.

Another play stands out in my memory. One of our husky but inexperienced players grabbed a Middy who was running with the ball and hugged him tight. This strong-arm tackle was hailed by vociferous cheers from the sidelines, but when the tackler heard the demonstration he thought he had made a mistake and that the spectators were voicing their disapproval. He therefore released his captive, who resumed his gallop toward the Army goal line. My memory leaves me uncertain as to the identity of the hero of that play but my impression is that it was "Taurus" Murphy, of the Class of 1891.

The final score was 24 to 0 (in favor of Navy). Dennis had lost the battle but he had won the strategic objective of his campaign. He had started the game of football at West Point AND HE ALONE COULD HAVE DONE IT AT THAT TIME. The Army would not stomach that defeat and there would be at least one more game. In fact, as I recall it, though the first challenge came from Navy, the initiative really came from Michie. There was a slim enough chance that he might be permitted to organize a team to defend a challenge from Annapolis. But even with the influence of "Old Pete" behind him, he would not be permitted to extend a challenge until he had organized his team. My memory is not clear but my impression is that he talked it over with a midshipman friend while he was on furlough. As an informal Ways and Means Committee, these two conspirators decided that in order to start the ball a-rolling, the Navy must send the first challenge.

In the autumn of the following year, we found ourselves in a new West Point. Even the most hidebound conservative conceded that the Army must settle its score with the Navy. Contributions

Overleaf *Army-Navy game at Annapolis in 1891. Army won 32–16, for its first victory in the series.*

came from every regiment in the Army. Dr. H. L. Williams, a former Yale player and future creator of great Minnesota teams, was employed as coach and we had our first series of games with outside teams. We were regimented to practice football yells and to sing paeans of victory in unison with the band. Never had old Cro' Nest echoed such sounds before.

One newspaper account of the game read:

"West Point, New York, November 30—Yesterday afternoon the United States Naval Academy's football team came to West Point, and engaged a team representing the United States Military Academy in the first football contest ever played by the cadets with an outside team. The contest, witnessed by over a hundred officers, their ladies and the Corps of Cadets, ended in a victory for the Midshipmen by the score of 24 to 0.

"Navy's stalwarts, from the kick-off, were too much for the sadly ignorant cadets, and with charges around the ends and center rushes which the West Pointers tried to stop with might and main, succeeded in rolling rough shod over them. Emrich scored most of the touchdowns for Navy, while Michie gave a good account of himself for the Military Academy. He was the only cadet who played football before. After the game the cadets entertained the midshipmen at a dance and the affair ended in an enjoyable day for all."

Said another account:

"Navy's supporters, numbering several hundred, were decorated in colors of red and white, while across the 'Plain' stood the Army's friends in black, gray and orange. It was a cold autumn day, the football field was frozen, but this passed almost unnoticed in the enthusiasm of the spectators. Annapolis came first on the field with red and white stocking caps and red stockings. West Point appeared with black and orange caps, white suits and black stockings. Of this game an old critic writes: 'The Army defeat was the salvation of an athletic development which was just beginning to make itself felt at West Point.' "

A ROUGH GAME IN THE NINETIES

THOMAS (DOGGIE) TRENCHARD *was famous as an end on the Princeton teams of 1892, 1893, and 1894. He was captain in 1893 and 1894 and was named on Walter Camp's all-America team of 1893. In an interview given to Frank Graham of* The New York Sun *in November, 1926, Trenchard said:*

FOOTBALL IN THE NINETIES was a rougher game than it is today, not because of a propensity on the part of individual players to rough their opponents but because the rules were not as tightly drawn then as they are at present and because of great latitude in the method of advancing the ball. Plays outlawed now not only were permissible then but formed the very backbone of the game. As far as cleanness of play is concerned, I dare say the game of thirty years ago compared favorably with that of the present, there having been no great disposition to break the rules and no widespread passes of surreptitious punches.

Force was the thing then and smashing, battering plays were depended upon solely. Deland's flying wedge, Woodruff's mass momentum and guards back plays, roughing the kicker, piling up, hurdling—these were the outstanding weapons of attack and defense. They were rough and dangerous, and protests against football arose periodically. So generally was it regarded as a brutal game that it was forbidden in numerous states. Popular demonstrations against it led ultimately to the refinement of the game, and the bloody gridiron battles such as we knew have been legislated out of existence.

But, as I have said, the play was clean, for all its permissible roughness. When I was at Princeton we didn't play Harvard, and I can speak of the fairness of Harvard's tactics only by hearsay. Of Yale and Pennsylvania, our great rivals then, and of the minor colleges we played, I can speak at first hand and I must say that I never saw an opposing player do an objectionable thing on the field. As I say this, I have in mind particularly Frank Hinkey of Yale. Frank is dead now and yet his reputation as a foul player persists. I would like to do my part to destroy it. I played against him—and directly against him, for we were opposing ends—for three years and I will always cherish a memory of him as a clean, hard player, putting everything he had into every game he played against me and yet never seeking to take the slightest unfair advantage.

The Princeton-Pennsylvania game of 1894, in which I played, has been cited as one of the roughest games in the annals of football and is assigned as the reason for the dropping of Pennsylvania by Princeton the following year. That it was a rough game I will not deny. All games were rough then and this was no exception to the rule, but I must exonerate the Pennsylvania players of any charge of undue roughness. It has been my experience that charges of undue roughness usually are made by spectators, and I have yet to hear a player accuse an opponent of foul tactics. As to the dropping of Pennsylvania by Princeton, I cannot speak authoritatively because I had been graduated before the football season of 1895 began. However, since it was in 1895 that Princeton resumed relations with Harvard, I always have assumed that Pennsylvania was dropped only to make room for Harvard. . . .

We had spring practice in my days as we do now and early fall practice too. A month or so before the fall term opened the football squad would be assembled and training would be begun. We were trained mainly for endurance, for you must remember that we not only had to play a harder game but a longer one than the rules call for today. Instead of playing four periods of fifteen minutes each, with a minute's rest between the first and second, and third and fourth periods, and fifteen between the second and third, we played two halves of forty-five minutes each, with about fifteen minutes between halves. We had a training table and our training was supervised by a professional, who conditioned us as rigorously as though we were professional athletes.

We got up early and retired early. We had a hearty breakfast, light lunch, usually no more than soup and bread, at about 11:30, practiced steadily from 12 to 3, had another bite to eat after practice, went to classes from 4 to 6 and then had a heavy dinner. We were not allowed to smoke or, of course, to drink.

The squads then were much smaller than they are now—smaller by half. The average squad numbered about thirty men and players who failed to make the regular team—as I did in 1891, which was my first year—didn't see much action in games. Substitutions were made only if players were badly hurt or exhausted, and once a man was withdrawn from a game he could not return.

We "pointed" for our big games then, too, though not to the extent that some colleges do now. Our big games were with Yale

*Australia-born Pat O'Dea of Wisconsin,
ranked by some as football's greatest
kicker.*

and Pennsylvania and we always made sure we were on edge when those games rolled around. To do this, we held ourselves in reserve somewhat through the earlier games with weaker teams, but we did not keep the regulars on the sidelines and use mostly substitutes in their places, as so many colleges do at this time.

In the playing of games we had no great strategy to speak of, for Princeton, in my day, had not adopted any of the mass momentum plays, flying wedges and what nots. We relied mainly on being in superb physical condition and getting the jump on our opponents at the outset of the game, and we won many a game in the first few minutes of play. Trained as they were for endurance, many teams found it difficult to get warmed up quickly and such teams were usually at our mercy for the first ten minutes.

Present-day football, I believe, is superior to that of my day. The introduction of the forward pass, which opened up the game, was the greatest single factor in its improvement. It enhanced the attack, developed the defense to combat the attack, created the triple threat man and made the game a much more enjoyable spectacle. In the old days the onlookers seldom knew what was going on beyond being able to follow the movement of the ball up and down the field. Now practically every play is in the open and every point of the game may be grasped. . . .

The modern game is more exacting than the game of my time. While much of the roughness has been eliminated, it is a game that calls for more alertness, physical and mental, than the football in my playing days. Speed is the most important asset now—speed of mind to execute plays on attack or break them up on defense, and speed of foot to supplement the speed of mind. Under the circumstances, the effective player is the one whose brain has not been fogged nor his bodily fitness impaired by the battering of the game. . . .

HOOSIER FOOTBALL IN THE NINETIES

In 1969, in his eighty-seventh year, ZORA G. CLEVENGER was elected to the National Football Hall of Fame in reward for almost half a century of distinguished service as player, coach, and athletic administrator.

Born Dec. 21, 1881, in Muncie, Indiana, he played on Muncie High School's first football team in 1897. Going to Indiana University in 1900, he starred for four years as a 140-pound halfback and also in baseball, and in 1903 was captain of both teams. He coached baseball, basketball, and football for two years after his graduation. After that he successively was athletic director at Nebraska Wesleyan University, played professional baseball, was head coach of football, baseball, and basketball at the University of Tennessee, athletic director and coach of three sports at Kansas State, athletic director at Missouri, and, finally, athletic director for twenty-three years at Indiana, where he brought in Bo McMillin as coach to give the Hoosiers their first Big Ten football title in 1945.

In 1964 Tennessee brought him back to the campus for a fiftieth anniversary with members of his 1914 team, which posted the Volunteers' first undefeated record and beat Vanderbilt for the first time. His own Indiana honored him with the title of Athletic Director Emeritus and conferred upon him the Distinguished Alumnus Award. The "I" Men's Association founded the Clevenger Award. Mr. Clevenger has never lost his interest in football. He traveled in 1968 to Knoxville to see the Tennessee-Georgia game and he never misses an Indiana home game.

The following was written by Mr. Clevenger in February, 1969.

I LIVED IN Muncie, Indiana, and attended the high school there, graduating in the spring of 1900. Life was entirely different then from what it is now. The schools were very different, but the educational processes were exceedingly good. There was no football in the high school when I entered, but it came in before I finished. There were no regulations of any kind covering high school athletics.

A doctor just out of the Chicago Physicians and Surgeons, who had played a little football, volunteered to coach a team. He and the high school principal, who had played a little football at DePauw University, each played a few games with us. There were very few fellows in school who had the desire and ability to play, so a team was scraped up by any and all means possible. This was true for the first year only. The last two years no one was on our team except regular high school students. That was as it should be.

Our uniforms were not much. Pads were home made and sewn on the jerseys. They did not protect too well but did serve. Head-gears were not very good, mostly made in our home town. Most of the time we had only one football, and it was rather elliptical, rather fat. It was leather with a rubber bladder inside. There was a stem for inflation. Then that stem was tucked in and the ball laced over this stem. There were no paid officials, no paid coach. Everything was on a rather informal, voluntary basis.

By my senior year in high school conditions had improved somewhat. The doctor continued to coach us, and, as I said, only pupils were permitted to try for the team. Regulations began to develop. I was out of high school before the state was really organized and the state high school association began to formulate rules and regulations. We did not play too many games, and these were all with nearby towns.

In that day there was no such thing as athletic scholarships. They had not come into existence. One either had enough money to go to college, earn his way, or not go.

The main reason I chose Indiana was because of a high school faculty man and the football captain of the 1900 Indiana team. There was no such rule as the freshman rule. Any student in the university was eligible. The freshman rule had not come into practice yet. It came right after my eligible days.

I think the football captain was such a fine fellow that he is the one who influenced me to go to Indiana. His name was John Foster. He and I remained friends throughout his life. He was one of the finest fellows I ever knew. He came to Muncie and talked with me. He was from the northern part of the state.

I entered Indiana in September of 1900 and played for four years on the team. I was fortunate enough to make the team as left halfback in my freshman year. Indiana was a member of the

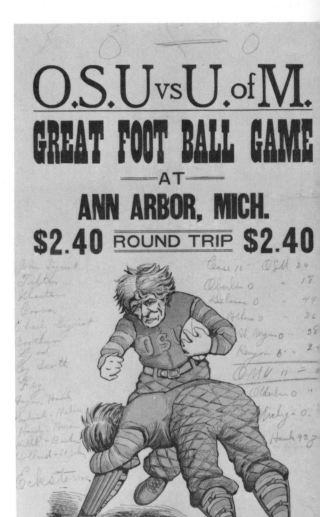

*Ballyhoo for Ohio State. Buckeyes'
invasion of Michigan.*

present Big Ten Conference. It had become a member in the late Nineties. There were not always ten members. When I went to Indiana there were just nine. There were just eight for a while, then nine again, then ten. Everything was under the rules and regulations of the conference. Full schedules were played.

All my playing days were before the forward pass was permitted. There was no such thing as a forward pass, and the first man who received the ball from the center could not run with it. If he passed it forward, or if he crossed the line of scrimmage with the ball, it was illegal. There were three downs to make five yards. It sounds easy to make five yards in three downs, but every defense had ten men right up there to stop the ball carrier. It was practically the same by all teams.

The defensive team had seven men on the line, one man behind each tackle, generally just off his hip; another right behind the center, with just one man back from the line as a safety man. This meant mass football. No one had to be back for a pass, or wonder if the quarterback would run or pass. Such things were illegal.

The result of this mass play was many injuries, and many deaths. It became so bad that many state legislators were introducing bills to regulate or change the game, or abolish it altogether. This agitation became strong throughout all states. It became so intense and pronounced that President Teddy Roosevelt took a hand at it. He wanted the game preserved; called many conferences.

Leaders throughout the country got together and worked out some rules permitting certain types of forward passes and quarterback runs. There were early rules and regulations quite different from those of today. But they opened up the game and changed the defense entirely. It is a much better game now, more interesting for spectators also. Since I am a small fellow, I wish I could have played under the present rules. There was no National Collegiate Athletic Association when I played. That organization came into being after that.

There were no dormitories in my day, no meals served on the campus. Everybody boarded at what we called Boarding Clubs, operated by private individuals in private houses. The fraternities did not serve meals then.

Our uniforms were quite different from today as far as pads are concerned. The pads in my day were sewn on—none of these modern inside shoulder pads, thigh pads inside and such were known then. One thing that made the players' afternoons quite different was a rule that once a fellow was taken out of the game he could not return. He was through for the day. Platoons had not been heard of. Sending a man in for punting, or a try for field goal would end the day for the fellow taken out. There was no such thing as spring practice. Everything was confined to the fall. We did not even report for fall practice before school started.

Some of the famous coaches of my playing days and my own early coaching days were Alonzo Stagg, Fielding Yost, Pop Warner, Robert Zuppke, Knute Rockne. Two of the famous players were Walter Eckersall of Chicago and Willie Heston of Michigan. Pat O'Dea was one of the greatest punters of my day and excellent for any day. He played for Wisconsin. I recall that one day a leading Chicago paper in reporting a game played at Wisconsin had the following headline: Chicago 0; Wisconsin 0; Eckersall 15. In that day a field goal counted 5 points. A famous coach of my coaching years at Tennessee was John Heisman of Georgia Tech; another was Dan McGugin of Vanderbilt. Yost and McGugin were brothers-in-law.

The football in those days was fatter, more rounded, not as pointed as now. My first year at Indiana we had a fine punter, Roy Pike, who punted spirals of considerable distance with that big ball. The present shape helps in forward passing.

When a touchdown was made the ball had to be brought out straight from the point where the carrier was downed. That made a very bad angle to attempt the extra point. However, at one time a fellow could be allowed to punt out to a man for the catch more directly in front of the goal posts. If the other team, which had to remain behind the goal line until the short kick was made, could be kept from interfering, then the point after touchdown could be made from that point.

Also at one time the field proper was longer, there was no end zone, of course, that not being necessary as there was no forward passing. The game was played in halves, not quarters, and the goal posts were on the goal line. There were no hash marks fifteen yards from the sidelines. The ball had to be played from the spot where it was downed. There were no "huddles." The quarterback called signals by numbers.

For a while there was a rule that permitted an onside kick from a punt. The man that could recover the ball must be behind it when it was kicked, and the ball had to hit the ground before he could recover it. The kicker, of course, would punt the ball low and away from the safety man, and it would be a short kick.

PENN'S MIGHTY "GUARDS BACK" JUGGERNAUTS AND GEORGE WOODRUFF

The complete domination of intercollegiate football by Yale, Harvard, and Princeton was challenged by the upsurge of Pennsylvania in 1894. Under coach George Woodruff, who had played at Yale with Stagg, Heffelfinger, and Pa Corbin, Pennsylvania, with Woodruff's dreaded new "guards back" momentum mass formation, put together four of the most remarkable seasons of success in the history of the game.

Up to then, Yale had been the king of the gridiron, but it found itself confronted by a formidable rival as Penn won fifty-five of fifty-six games in 1894, 1895, 1896, and 1897 and added ten more victories in 1898 before losing again. It won thirty-four in succession in the first three years, was beaten 6–4 by Lafayette in 1896, then went on to win thirty-one in succession.

Whereas Penn had placed only two men on the all-America teams from 1889 through 1893, it had three men honored in 1894, four in 1895, three in 1896, and three in 1897. Truxton Hare (1897–1900), one of the few men to make the team four times; Charley Gelbert, thrice honored; George Brooke, one of the greatest kickers of all time, and Buck Wharton were the most famous members of these teams. JOHN H. MINDS, *honored in 1897 and a member of all four teams, furnished the following information about the teams and the "guards back" formation in a letter to the author in 1953.*

THE FOUR YEARS OF 1894 to 1897 constituted the greatest period of continued success in Pennsylvania history. The 1894 team played its home schedule on a field where the dormitories now stand at Thirty-sixth and Spruce Streets [in Philadelphia]. The succeeding three teams played their home games on Franklin Field.

During that period the regular offensive formation was a seven-man line, with the quarterback directly behind center and the

112

other backfield men about 4½ to 5 yards back of the scrimmage line, the fullback being in the center of the trio. It was the **T** formation. Sometimes we used this formation and sometimes we used a formation which became famous as the "guards back." "Guards back" was used for the first time against Princeton in 1894 on the Trenton Fair Grounds.

When we used the "guards back" formation it meant, of course, that only five men were on the scrimmage line. The field captain would call "guards back, right" or "guards back, left" and the guards would take their positions at a convenient distance to the right, or left, of the quarterback and slightly behind him. The tackles and ends would move in to take the vacant places, after which the signal for the play would be given.

But the mere fact that the guards were right or left didn't mean that the play would necessarily go in their direction. It might or it might not. It might even be an end play all the way around the opposite direction, it might go straight through the line, it might go off tackle, a guard might carry the ball, or a back-field man might carry it. We even had an end carry the ball all the way around his opposite end. Where the play went depended entirely on the judgment of the field captain. If he used constant line plunges, it was mass, and if he used the end plays or off-tackle plays, it was open. It just gave two additional men in the inter-ference.

One of our special plays was the quarterback kick. At that time, the man who kicked the ball, or anyone behind him, was eligible to recover it. This was an invention of George Woodruff, who coached "Pass the ball with your foot." That was done beautifully by Carl Williams, who could pass it with his foot any place—short distances or a longer distance—and usually it was recovered for a first down. It was a very effective play, and it was usually mixed in with a variety of other plays. It is my belief that this was the forerunner of the forward pass.

We had another special play, rarely used. It was what we con-sidered our touchdown play. We called it the "delayed pass." The quarterback faked the pass to some member of the backfield, or a guard, and, when the defending team was properly bewildered, passed it to the fullback. It was his job to make a touchdown, and he usually did. We used it only when we absolutely needed it—perhaps two or three times a year. An example of it was in the Harvard game of 1896.

Harvard had us 6 to 2, with not a great deal of time left. The delayed pass signal was given. I went from the center of the field for a touchdown. Unfortunately, the referee was just as much deceived as the Harvard team, and, on the insistence of a Harvard man, erroneously called me out of bounds. The referee had been expecting a play to go in the direction of the guards. He was there waiting for it, so the two teams were between him and the play. But we won that game.

George Woodruff, the coach, had a very strong belief that the strongest defense was a strong offense, but, nevertheless, he had a style of defense. I believe he was the first man to bring the ends in close to the line. In the old days the ends played wide, for the purpose of stopping end runs. He brought them in to a couple of yards outside the tackles. To defend against the end run, it was their duty to shoot right across the line a couple of yards, swing into the interference, strip off the man running with the ball, and it was the duty of the backfield to tackle the runner. That was quite an innovation.

Another part of the defense was for a halfback to stand behind each tackle and, as the opponents snapped the ball, shove the tackle, who, at the same time, jumped across. This, with the end shooting across, was supposed to mess up the play, and it usually did.

As to which of the four teams excelled, I think it was between the '94 and '97 teams, and, since I was captain of the '97 team, of course my chips are on that team, and I think justly so.

There were some great players on the '94 team, particularly in the backfield. The backfield was composed of Carl Williams, quarterback; Arthur Knipe, left halfback; George Brooke, fullback, and Winchester Osgood, right half. Williams was a good field general, Knipe a fast and powerful player off tackle, Brooke a marvelous punter, drop kicker and line plunger, and Osgood, in my opinion, the greatest broken-field runner that I have ever seen, and I don't except Red Grange. He could run full speed and turn any direction on the turn of his foot. My first year, I played right end on the scrub. I believe I was aggressive, but, although in practice Osgood ran against my end constantly, it was one full month before I even put my hands on him. He was unfortunate enough to get killed in the Cuban insurrection.

I placed that quartet well above the Four Horsemen of Notre Dame.

Charlie Gelbert on the '94 team was a great end—none better. He was a marvelous halfback on the '95 team. Wiley Woodruff and Buck Wharton at guard were famous. The tackles and center were light for their positions, but it was a team of substantial weight.

The '97 team was substantially a green team. It didn't start with any big-name players, but it wasn't long until it had plenty of them. No one of that period will ever forget the names of Boyle and Hedges on the ends or Overfield at center, and Hare and McCracken at guards. Some of these players are remembered to the present generation. Woodruff and Wharton, guards on the three preceding teams, had graduated, so Hare and McCracken had their first year. They certainly made good, as did the rest of the team. We still had the same type of offense and defense, and the same coach.

The heaviest man on the team, John Outland, weighed 194 pounds. There wasn't another man on the team within ten pounds of that weight, and I don't believe the team averaged more than about 178 pounds, but it was a fast team and a cohesive team that played together like a machine. I am egotistical enough to believe that the team had faith in its captain. I know the captain had faith in the team. We had no serious trouble winning all of our games except the Cornell game, when the team, having played Harvard on Saturday, played Cornell the following Thursday. That was the last time that the two games were played so close together.

This team ran up the greatest total score made by any Penn team since, 471. We had only 26 points made against us, 10 of which were made by Hudson, the famous drop kicker of the Carlisle Indians, when he drop-kicked two field goals.

The team was quite strong in the kicking department and used the punt as a part of its regular running offensive plays. It kicked from the running formation, as often on first down as on any other down. It was a low, long hard drive to a spot difficult for the defense to reach, and dangerous to handle if reached. It was effective and made much ground. One first-down kick against Harvard, made in the northeast corner of Franklin Field, cleared Harvard's secondary defense and went out of bounds inside the 5-yard line in the southwestern corner of the field. It changed the complexion of the game.

This team had a "first" to its credit. Dr. Randolph Faries, a track man, suggested trying a field goal from the scrimmage forma-

Truxton Hare, Penn's most famous guard, four times all-America.

tion. George Woodruff and I were quite sure it could not be done, but believed that a first-class trick could be developed from it, and, with that in mind, let the newspaper men see us practice it. In a couple of days we found that it could be done—then we were sorry we had let the newspaper men see it, but that worked out beautifully too, so when Harvard was defending the west goal on Franklin Field, we lined up to try that play and the Harvard team, of course, felt sure it was a trick. At any rate, Bill Morice received the ball from the center, placed it on the ground, I kicked it and it went over the goal clear to the gymnasium. That was the first "placement kick."

In the four-year period there were very few substitutes. If a man went off the field he was through for the day, and, since substitutes were so scarce, it was a rare occasion when a regular left the field. In the official photograph of the '97 team there were only eleven players. However, the four teams provided many players for the mythical all-America team, some of them two years, and Hare for four years.

You will note that I referred to mass plays in connection with the "guards back" play. I have done this to show that it wasn't always a mass play, as so frequently charged against it. An open play could always come from it if the field captain so willed. This wasn't true of the old "turtle back" formation or the "revolving wedge" formation, used by teams of other colleges. Open play could not develop from these formations.

TRUXTON HARE, *who is generally named on all-time teams at guard, said that the game he remembered most vividly in his four years was the 1898 meeting with Cornell, won by Penn, 12–6.*

"What a day that was," he wrote. "It started to rain. Then it began to sleet, and finally it snowed. The field was covered with ice and snow. A howling gale was blowing down the field, and the temperature fell far below the freezing point. I was kicking for Penn, and against the gale all I could make was 10 or 15 yards past the scrimmage line. I will never forget the sorry-looking gang we were in the dressing room between the halves. Of course, we all changed our outfits. Jack Outland, captain that year, stood stripped to the waist in front of a blazing stove, yet he shook like a leaf.

It was bitterly cold in the room. The game was marked by a series of breaks, and we took advantage of them and won by 12 to 6. It was a great team that Cornell had that year too (coached by Pop Warner and including Bucky Starbuck, Tar Young, Dan Reed and Ed Sweetland)."

George Trevor wrote of Hare in *The New York Sun*: "As a companion to Yale's Pudge Heffelfinger on the all-time all-America team, Pennsylvania offers that colossus of forwards, Truxton Hare, whose personal popularity equalled his legendary prowess. A soft-spoken gentleman off the field, a devastating berserker on the gridiron—that was Hare. What a figure he made! His clean-cut patrician face radiated the determination which characterized his play. . . . His deep-set, expressive eyes had that 'look of eagles.' . . . Born to the purple, he bested roughnecks at the rugged game of give and take.

"Hare was the nonpareil of linemen, a human juggernaut whose inordinately powerful legs carried him ahead like the driving rods of a locomotive. . . . Hare could drag five tacklers several yards. This wavy-haired behemoth was almost unstoppable running from the guards back formation. He ripped through Harvard's line for 37 yards and a touchdown in 1900, carrying a flock of Crimson tacklers on his back. A beautiful punter too."

The following tribute to George Woodruff was written in the 1934 Football Guide by PARKE H. DAVIS, *noted football historian, who was the coach of the Lafayette team that ended Penn's thirty-four-game winning streak in 1896.*

George Washington Woodruff was the foremost football coach in the United States in the middle nineties. He died at Harrisburg, Pennsylvania, March 23, 1934. No coach in the sixty-five years of American college football has left more lasting impressions upon the game than he. Born Feb. 22, 1864, at Dimmock, Pa., . . . his natal day served to give him his name. In his childhood he was conveyed to Nebraska in a covered wagon by his parent pioneers. Matriculating at Yale in 1885, he instantly became conspicuous as a scholar and an athlete. He was on the crew, played right guard on the eleven, threw the hammer and put the shot, and won his letter in all three sports repeatedly. He was also the college strongman of his time. In his studies he was rewarded by election to Phi Beta Kappa.

After graduating from Yale he taught and coached for a time at the Hill School and Penn Charter. In 1894 he assumed the position of head coach at Pennsylvania, thus becoming one of the pioneer professional coaches. . . . Immediately football became the subject of a revolution in tactics, and simultaneously Pennsylvania football began to achieve a series of unprecedented victories.

For years the tacticians of Harvard, Princeton and Yale had arrayed their ends widely on defense, to await and tackle the carrier in the open. Woodruff moved his ends close to their tackles and required them to charge through with the ball and break the interference before it could form and leap into motion, thus originating the "close" or "smashing" end type of defensive play. For years tactical maxims had approved turning the carriers always inside, to be tackled in the pocket at center. Woodruff reversed this basic rule and turned the opposing carriers always outside, to be tackled by a supporting halfback or forced out of bounds. Shortly afterward he invented the "quarterback" kick, forerunner of the quick kick of today. The three other backs, being on side when the kick was delivered, frequently ran down the field, recovered the ball, and scored.

Next came Woodruff's famous mass play of guards back. . . . The present method of passing the ball from the center to the fullback for a kick also is one of George Woodruff's contributions to the science of the sport. . . .

Before going to Pennsylvania Woodruff had been admitted to the bar, and during his coaching days he practiced law in Philadelphia. Giving up his coaching career in 1901, he plunged wholly into law and politics. In 1903 he was appointed solicitor for the Federal Department of Forestry and soon afterward Assistant Attorney General of the United States, to aid the Department of the Interior. For a time he served as acting Secretary of the Interior. In 1909 he was appointed United States judge for Hawaii. In 1923 he was appointed Attorney General of Pennsylvania and served until 1927. For the past three years he has been the Public Service Commissioner of Pennsylvania.

Woodruff is also credited with introducing the flying principle into all interference in 1893, though Stagg takes issue with this. Heisman says that "no play ever wrought more havoc or stimulated greater football thought." Woodruff is credited, too, with being the first to come out of the line to run interference, in 1886 at Yale. Woodruff used the delayed buck in 1895, and Minds, 1897 captain, claims that he [Minds] kicked the first placement goal from scrimmage, though Stagg says that he used it that same year and believed that Princeton had used it earlier. In 1896, too, Woodruff used the six-man line, with the center backing up.

ARTHUR POE'S DROP-KICK
THAT BEAT YALE

C. EDWARD SPARROW *of the staff of* The Baltimore Sun *received a letter from* ARTHUR POE *clearing up the discrepancies in the numerous accounts of the manner in which Poe had kicked his famous field goal. Sparrow published the letter in* The Sun *on January 29, 1933, and, leading up to it, he wrote:*

AFTER 33 YEARS the experts of the football world still are debating as to how Arthur Poe made the famous drop-kick that carried the day for Princeton against Yale in 1899. Arthur Poe was one of the "Six Little Poes of Baltimore" who made gridiron history for Nassau over a span of approximately 20 years.

Several versions of that kick, which turned the tide of victory, have been written, but none has coincided. None of the authors of the stories sought Arthur Poe's version as to how he accomplished the feat that turned an apparent 10-to-6 defeat into an 11-to-10 victory in the last couple of minutes of play.

Of the several chapters that have appeared in print from time to time, the authors accredited Arthur Poe with drop-kicking the ball on any part of his leg from the ankle to the knee. That is untrue, according to Arthur Poe's version of the kick in a letter to the writer. Anybody who knows anything about drop-kicking realizes that a drop-kick can be made only by the ball coming in contact with the toe or instep as the pigskin touches the ground.

The drop-kick which Arthur Poe made that won for Princeton was booted 35 yards. Gresham S. Poe, his brother, who also starred for the Tiger, was in the stand that day and he remembers the play distinctly and the distance well. But before discussing the drop-kick further, we'll let Arthur Poe himself tell the facts in the celebrated case. His letter follows:

Cedar Rapids, Iowa

Mr. C. Edward Sparrow
The Sun, Baltimore, Md.

Dear Mr. Sparrow—I am in receipt of your letter of the 11th, also the clipping.

(Editor's note—The clipping was from Grantland Rice's column in which Dave Francis of St. Louis went into great detail about Arthur

Poe's drop-kick. Francis played left tackle for Yale and opposite Arthur Poe, who played right end.)

It is surprising after all these years that there is still an interest about this drop-kick. I have never made any statement which I might call official as to this play, as there are so many versions from quite a number of people that I never thought it worth while to get in any controversy over it.

The ball was actually kicked from my instep deliberately, as I was wearing lightweight running shoes in order to increase my speed in getting down the field. It was the first drop-kick that I had attempted in my college career, though I had kicked some in my prep school games and had kicked in practice any number of times. I might add that I am considering writing about some of the controversial points, as I feel after so many years they can be considered rather impersonal.

My knee was so badly injured in my freshman year that I was on crutches for five weeks. In my sophomore year I had an injury to the same knee, which laid me up for the entire season. On account of this I gave up playing in the backfield and shifted to end.

Yours truly,
Arthur Poe.

Following the letter, Sparrow wrote:

In recalling Arthur Poe's drop-kick, Gresham S. Poe, who played on the Princeton varsity as an end at the turn of the century, said that Arthur was one of the best kickers at the university when his leg didn't bother him. It was nothing for him, said Gresham, to boot the ball half the length of the field in those days. The field then was 110 yards long, and under the rules of that time a player could not return to the game once he had been removed. The lineup shows that only Poe, Pell and Captain Big Bill Edwards played the entire game. Hutchinson, quarterback, and Wheeler, fullback, the Princeton kickers, had left the field. So when Arthur Poe, right end, went back into kick formation, the Yale team apparently must have looked for some sort of a fake play and not for a drop-kick.

All of the Poes learned their football fundamentals in Druid Hill Park. They attended a prep school conducted by their uncle, George Carey, Princeton '55, near Richmond Market Armory. The building still stands. . . . Arthur Poe was captain of the Baltimore Athletic

Club team in 1895. Gresham played for the Maryland Athletic Club in 1896 and 1897.

Three of the six Poes played on winning Princeton teams against Yale. Edgar Allan Poe was captain and quarter of the eleven that won in 1889. Neilson Poe was with the second Tiger team that triumphed and Arthur Poe was on two. He beat Old Eli single handed in 1898 by causing Durston, a back, to fumble the ball, and then picking it up and running 100 yards for the only score.

Sparrow then picked up two pieces from The Sun *following the Yale-Princeton game of 1899, one of them a feature article on Arthur Poe and his brothers and the second the news account of the game. The feature piece follows:*

Arthur Poe, Princeton's youngest football hero, is the fifth of the famous Poe brothers of Balitmore who have played on the Princeton varsity. Every one of them so far has won renown on the gridiron, and there is still another Poe, who is expected to do likewise. Last week when the Tigers were having their final touches put on in practice it was Gresham Poe, on the scrubs, who made them play their hardest, and who came very near scoring on the varsity several times by sensational runs.

The famous "Big Six," or should it be "Little Six," for all are short of stature, are:

Class	Weight	Pos.
1. S. Johnson Poe '84	150	R.H.
2. Edgar Allan Poe '91	138	Q.B.
3. John P. Poe Jr. '95	145	F.B.
4. Neilson Poe '97	140	L.H.
5. Arthur Poe '00	145	L.E.
6. Gresham S. Poe '02	140	R.E.

As is well known, these young gladiators of the gridiron are sons of John Prentiss Poe, ex-Attorney General of Maryland, who is himself an alumnus of Princeton of the class of 1854 and who probably would have been on the varsity of that year had the game been in vogue.

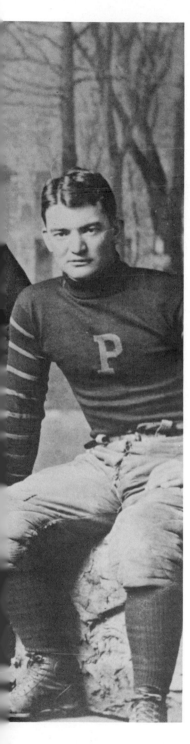

The Poe brothers of Princeton: Arthur '00, S. Johnson '84, Neilson '97 (seated in front), Edgar Allan '91, Gresham '02, and John Jr. '95.

The news report read:

As long as football is played in America the college boys will tell of the marvelous feats of Arthur Poe. For two years in succession have unexpected, sensational, wonderful plays by the little five-foot-six, 145-pound Baltimore boy snatched victory from defeat for the Princeton Tigers against the sturdy giants of Old Yale, which feats, taken together, have never been equalled in the annals of the American game.

Last year, at Princeton, just when it seemed that if either team scored it must be Yale, this swift, little athletic giant, successor on the Princeton varsity of a long line of famous Poes, snatched the ball in a mix-up and, by a run—long, sensational, spectacular— made the only touchdown of the game.

On Saturday, at New Haven, he eclipsed even his feat of 1898. Less than two minutes of play remained in that bruising battle. The score was 10 to 6 in favor of Yale. . . . Every Princeton player, except three, had been replaced by fresher men, in the vain hope that fresher men might batter down that sturdy Blue line. Suddenly, with the ball near Yale's 35-yard line, Arthur Poe fell back, and it was seen that as a last desperate chance the Tigers had determined to place their reliance on the little hero of 1898. Princetonians, as they drew in their breath, murmured that Arthur Poe never had tried a field goal before.

There was a moment of breathless suspense, anxiety, a ray of hope as the ball soared skyward. It seemed to linger in midair, and then, straight and true, dropped over the bar of Yale's goal. The score was 11 to 10 and hardly more than a minute to play was left.

THE FORGOTTEN ROSE BOWL GAME, 1902

According to old record books, the first Rose Bowl game was played January 1, 1916, between Washington State University and Brown.

But fourteen years earlier, Hurry-Up Yost's 1901 Michigan juggernaut, the first of his point-a-minute teams, had crushed Stanford in the first of these post-season games at Pasadena, California, 49–0. GRANTLAND RICE *in 1935 published the following account of the game, dug from the files of* The Michigan Daily News *in Ann Arbor:*

THE GREATEST EVENT of the Michigan vacation period was the football game at Pasadena on January 1st. Michigan defeated Stanford University by a decisive score of 49 to 0. This score is said to be quite in proportion to the general superiority of Michigan over the great team of the Far West, but it does not tell the story of Stanford's desperate but futile effort against defeat.

The game was played under the auspices of the Tournament of Roses Association, and the conservative estimate places the attendance at 8,000. "The enormous crowd sees the Michigan back-breakers make monkeys out of the Stanford footballists," is the significant comment of *The Los Angeles Daily Times.*

Technically speaking, Michigan lost no prestige in the Stanford game. The team successfully kept Stanford out of Michigan territory. Stanford was unable to break the record of 15 yards as the longest gain made against Michigan during the year. None of the Michigan players was compelled to leave the field. Sweeley place-kicked the only goal from field for Michigan, outside of Shorts's successful attempt in the Carlisle game, during the season. Michigan's sacred goal line was never in danger.

In the gathering dusk, with ten minutes yet to play, Captain Fisher [of Stanford] came to Captain White and said, "If you are willing, we are ready to quit," and, at the expense of one or more goals, Michigan granted his request.

The game was called at 2:57 P.M. with Michigan on the south side of the field and Stanford on the north, the former team in possession of the ball. Sweeley kicked 40 yards to McGilvray, who returned the ball 10 yards and fumbled. Herrnstein, Snow and McGugin bucked the line for 11 yards. Snow made two telling straight bucks for 10 yards but on the next play the ball went to Stanford on a foul.

(This, our scout reports, went on for several minutes in which it seemed as if Stanford would be the first to defeat or score on the Michigan team, which had won ten scheduled games, the closest of them being with Ohio State, which was beaten, 21–0.)

But Michigan gained the ball on a fumble and Heston advanced it 30 yards. Stanford recovered the pigskin and terminated a series of small gains with another place kick from Michigan's 45-yard line. It was blocked by Shorts. Sweeley made 10 yards without interference on the following play and then Heston went down the west sideline in a brilliant 35-yard dash. By a series of bucks the ball was carried to Stanford's 5-yard line, where Michigan was held for three downs, but Snow was finally sent through center for a touchdown and Shorts kicked goal. Score—Michigan 6, Stanford 0.

Michigan and Stanford playing in the first Rose Bowl Game, January 1, 1902.

Touchdowns in those days were five points and kicks after were worth one point. A field goal was five points. Sweeley soon executed one from Stanford's 20 and at the end of the half, played in an hour and seventeen minutes, the score was Michigan 17, Stanford 0.

Heston, Herrnstein, Sweeley, Redden, Snow and Weeks plunged and ran back yard after yard, and Michigan scored six touchdowns more in the second half. [The account of the last touchdown reads]:

McFadden kicked off for 25 yards and Sweeley returned the ball on a punt the same distance. McFadden secured the ball and sent it back out of bounds 20 yards. By a fake kick Snow and Herrnstein advanced the ball 9 yards on two plays against the line after Heston's magnificent 45-yard run down the west sideline. Herrnstein secured a touchdown by a 22-yard dash through right tackle. Shorts failed to kick goal. Score—Michigan 49, Stanford 0.

Michigan rushed the ball 503 yards, kicked 881 yards, ran back kicks 127 yards, made twelve first downs and was penalized once. The time of halves was 35 minutes and 27 minutes, the latter shortened at the request of Stanford.

Stanford used substitutes while Michigan went through the game with the original eleven. The officials were David Brown, referee; W. K. Peasley, umpire; Phil Wilson, and C. G. Roe, linesmen; Jack Sheehan and H. K. Crafts, timers.

The lineups:

Michigan		Stanford
Redden	Left End	Clark, Preston
White	Left Tackle	Traegen
McGugin	Left Guard	Roosevelt
Gregory	Center	Lee
Wilson	Right Guard	Thompson
Shorts	Right Tackle	McFadden
Sweeley	Right End	Cooper
Weeks	Quarterback	Tarpay
Heston	Left Halfback	Slaker
Herrnstein	Right Halfback	Fisher
Snow	Fullback	McGilvray

YOST'S POINT-A-MINUTE
MICHIGAN TEAMS

WILLIE HESTON—*Judge Heston—is one of the most glamorous names in college football history, invariably grouped with Thorpe, Mahan, Grange, Coy, Eckersall, Nagurski, Strong, Nevers, Pfann, Friedman among the all-time backs. Heston was the thunderbolt halfback on the point-a-minute Michigan teams of Fielding Harris (Hurry-Up) Yost from 1901 through 1904, which won 43 games, lost none and tied one and scored 2,326 points to 40 for their opponents. Heston, Michigan's initial first-team all-America player, scored 93 touchdowns in the four years. In a letter to the author in 1952, Heston tells about those teams and Coach Yost as follows:*

WILL ENDEAVOR to give you some detailed information of Fielding Harris Yost. . . . As perhaps you know, Mr. Yost was born and raised in West Virginia and possessed that West Virginia accent through his entire life. He always talked slowly and seriously, always meant what he said, had a dull sense of humor, and had no use for liquor, which made it hard for him to tolerate it anywhere or any time. He was a man devoted to his family and very loyal to his friends. He was always truthful and his morals were the best.

As a coach, in my judgment, he was the greatest that ever stepped on a gridiron. The writer makes this statement after playing, coaching and observing football for over fifty years. Yost was a man that thought, talked and illustrated plays continually through every football season, with the exception of a few short hours each night, when he was compelled to give way to sleep. Each player knew that if he met Yost on the campus or on the sidewalk, he would be stopped and that Yost would proceed to instruct him how to block or how to charge. Quite often students would form a ring around them to watch the proceedings.

Fielding Harris Yost would have made a good military general. During World War I, the writer saw him quite frequently in his office. He would have maps and diagrams on the table and would

131

Fielding H. (Hurry-Up) Yost, legendary Michigan coach, in 1901 when his Point-a-Minute teams started on their five-year rampage.

prognosticate the next moves of the opposing armies. Usually he was right.

Coach Yost was a very strong believer in physical condition. Our practice sessions were long and hard, but he always kept in close touch with the trainer to find out if everybody was standing up under the grind.

We used nearly every running play that is being used today. That meant every player must learn at least fifty plays and know what his assignment would be in every play. The coach did not have any time for a player who would not give his all in every play, and would not tolerate a boy who showed any signs of physical fear. I remember one year, during a scrimmage, the fullback was hesitating just before he hit the line, and the coach shouted to the back, "Why if I gave you an axe and put you in a greenhouse, you would not be able to break out."

His pep talks before games were all classics. Ten or fifteen minutes before the kick-off, he would have his squads form a semi-circle in front of him. He would first tell them what he had learned about the team they were to play, their strong points and their weak points. He would then pull from his pocket a list on which he had jotted down mistakes that were made during the week's practice. He would then tell the boys that the entire Michigan alumni, in fact the whole football world, were awaiting the final results of the game. He would finally wind up by telling them to be always alert, be "ball hounds" and would sometimes say, "You know what Willie Heston said: 'Use your searchlights and jump the dead ones' "—an expression the writer made while talking to the team in 1902. As the squad was leaving the dressing room to take the field, he would say, "Who are they to beat a Michigan team? They're only human." By this time every player was in a state of mind to seek raw meat.

To compare the 1901, 1902, 1903 and 1904 teams is rather a difficult task. Naturally, I think they were all strong teams. In the fall of 1901, Coach Yost took over the squad that Biffy Lee had coached in 1900. He very soon shifted the players around. He moved Tug Wilson from center to right guard, placing George Gregory at center. He put Al Herrnstein at right half instead of Arthur Redner, played Neil Snow at right end on defense and fullback on offense, Ev Sweeley at right end on offense and safety man on defense.

He brought to Michigan an entirely new brand of football, not known to the Big Ten nor the Middle West. Particularly that was true of his offense. Speed and more speed was continually emphasized. Boss Weeks was instructed to call his signal for the next play while the team was getting up after the last play. The linesmen would jump into their respective positions, the quarterback would start giving another signal, but the first number was the starting signal. The center would instantly snap the ball, the line would charge and the play was off. This system would usually catch the opposing team flat-footed. During the course of the game, the opposing team would sometimes learn the method being used and would charge at the moment our quarterback gave the starting signal. When this happened, Yost gave us a signal for the quarterback to call in place of the play signal that told every player to hold. The center would not snap the ball immediately, the opposing line would charge over the scrimmage line. The ball would then be snapped, catching the opponents off-side, which would bring a penalty of five yards and a first down.

Yost introduced the old "83" play, which developed from a try at goal from field, a play used very successfully for years. The Statue of Liberty play is the same play but worked from the forward pass formation.

In my judgment, Boss Weeks was the best quarterback and field general during the four years and Neil Snow, I feel, was the best fullback.

On the fact that Michigan was not scored on in 1901, we will have to give it the call. The 1902 team was a powerful team and rolled up the largest score, but it was scored on twice. The 1903 team suffered the only tie game during the four years, accomplished by Minnesota—6 to 6. The 1904 team was the heaviest, but there was a weak spot in the line.

Chicago had a strong team in 1904, and Yost was a little afraid of the outcome. One week before the game, he formulated a play by calling Babe Carter, a 265-pound lineman, out of the line to carry the ball. This was advertised as a touchdown play near the goal line. Coach Yost saw to it that this play was well publicized so that it would reach the ears in the Chicago camp; and this was accomplished. No spectators were allowed on the field Thursday and Friday preceding the game to witness the practice. Yost then revealed his strategy. He never intended to have Carter carry the ball, but to be used as a decoy. During the game, we got within ten yards of the goal line. Carter was called back, the ball was snapped back and the quarterback faked to give the ball to Carter. Carter plunged into the line and every Chicago player went under the play. The ball was slipped to your Uncle Dudley and I ran around the pile of humanity and was across the goal line before a Chicago player ever saw me.

During the four years there were six touchdowns made against Michigan. Only two were made by sustained drives. The other four were the results of fumbles.

You have asked me to express my opinion as to whether the Michigan teams at the turn of the century could have been favorably compared with the best teams of today with the forward pass. As I have already stated, we had fast, powerful teams and, with backs on defense playing back to guard against forward passes, I can see no good reason why we should not have gone to town with running plays. We should have been fairly good in executing the forward pass.

In 1935 GRANTLAND RICE, *most famous, beloved, and widely read sports writer, said of Heston, Yost, Michigan, and football in the early days in his syndicated column, "The Sportlight," as follows:*

Fielding H. (Hurry-Up) Yost crashed upon a startled football world in 1901 under the Maize and Blue banner with Willie Heston, Gregory, Sweeley, Neil Snow, Redden, Boss Weeks and others who ran up something like 600 points in 600 minutes of play. Yost, now athletic director at Michigan, has followed football closer than anyone I know since he played tackle for West Virginia and La-fayette forty years ago.

"Just what is the main difference between the football of 1900–1905 and the football of today?" I asked in talking to Yost.

"In the first place," the Michigan director said, "football 30 years ago was far rougher than it is today. It was a part of football to be rough—to use hands and knees and elbows any way you could—to batter up or batter down the opposition, to rough and knock down the kicker, to do about everything except slug with the closed fist, and even that wasn't always penalized.

"Football in those days was a man-to-man fight on the field. Almost anything went. Today the rules have changed most of this. There are penalties for clipping, for piling up, for roughing the kicker, for striking with the palm of the hand, for anything that looks like intentional roughness. That's one big difference."

"What about the innovations—the spinners and the reverses?" I asked.

"What innovations?" Yost asked in return. "We had spinners

and reverses and double reverses in 1901. We had laterals. We had split bucks. We had everything the game has today except the forward pass.

"There isn't anything new in football. Don't let anybody tell you that. There are fifty good football players today to one in 1901 —fifty good teams and fifty good coaches to one dating back that far. But the outstanding stars of today are no better than the stars of thirty or thirty-five years ago.

"I'll tell you what I mean—I've never seen a running back better than Heston—a 190-pounder who could beat Archie Hahn at 50 yards. I've never seen a surer or fiercer tackler than Neil Snow, 200 pounds of speed and power.

"And take the kickers—you can move from California to Massachusetts, and from Minnesota to Tulane—and you can't even touch that old-time bunch: O'Dea of Wisconsin, Herschberger of Chicago, Sweeley and Garrels of Michigan, George Brooke of Pennsylvania, Eckersall of Chicago, Butterworth of Yale. I could name you a dozen. O'Dea on a drop-kick hit the cross bar at Yale 64 yards away—how many are trying 64-yard drop-kicks today? Brooke of Pennsylvania was one of the greatest kickers I ever saw. He could kick into a bucket at 55 yards.

"In those days there were only a few outstanding teams— three or four in the East, three or four in the Mid-West, none in the South, none on the West Coast. We left a snowstorm in Michigan in 1901, went to California, played 11 men at 90 degrees and beat Stanford, 49 to 0. . . .

"I'll give you just one angle on Heston. He weighed 190 pounds. Playing against Chicago on a field covered with ice and an inch of snow, he reached the open and jumped clean over Walter Eckersall, who dived for his knees. Figure that one out."

As tremendous as were the Michigan teams of 1901 to 1905, Yost rated his 1925 eleven as the best of all he coached. BENNY FRIEDMAN *was quarterback of the 1925 edition and Bennie Oosterbaan was an end, and they rank among football's all-time great.*

In 1931 Grantland Rice quoted Yost as saying, "Those were great teams (1901–1905). With Benny Friedman throwing passes to Heston, I think we would have scored a touchdown on about every other play. But I still think the best team I ever coached was the 1925 bunch. They had everything. Those early teams had speed and power. But the game was simpler then.

"That 1925 bunch could run an end, buck a line, throw passes, kick, block, tackle, think, and do about everything needed on a football field to gain ground and keep the other people from gaining ground. Don't forget about that 1925 team that our opponents had a hard time making first downs, much less winning the game."

The 1925 team lost one game, to Northwestern by 3 to 2 in the mud. Friedman tells about the game, the team, and Yost in the following letter to the author written in 1952.

Yost predicated his coaching philosophy on the theory that football was nothing more than habits of work. It was his philosophy that Saturday afternoon was the testing time, and all you did during the week in the way of practice passed in review Saturday. Therefore it was important to develop the proper habits so that when Saturday afternoon came, you did not have to think, you reacted to a pattern—pattern being a synonym for habit. Apparently we had developed the right habits because we made no mistakes.

Another insight into Yost's unique ability as a coach was his philosophy of offense. He built his entire offensive strategy, from a quarterback's viewpoint, on three principles: first, look the defense over; second, play for position laterally—in those days, remember, we used the whole field; and the third principle was the philosophy that Barnum was right, and you looked for his disciples on the other club.

A bit of explanation on these three principles. First, one had to look the defense over to see if any boys were out of position, or whether certain tendencies showed that they were tending to do certain things that they shouldn't. The second principle had to do with the necessity of acquiring position laterally, because some plays needed a lot of latitude and therefore would have to be used in the middle; other plays, from the psychological viewpoint, needed position to one side or the other of the goal posts. The third one is self-explanatory. One looked for suckers. ·

I think that Yost was a great coach in so many ways that it would take a chapter to write just about that. Suffice it to say that he was not only a great offensive coach but a great defensive coach

Overleaf   *Yost's invincible 1901 Michigan Point-a-Minute team.*

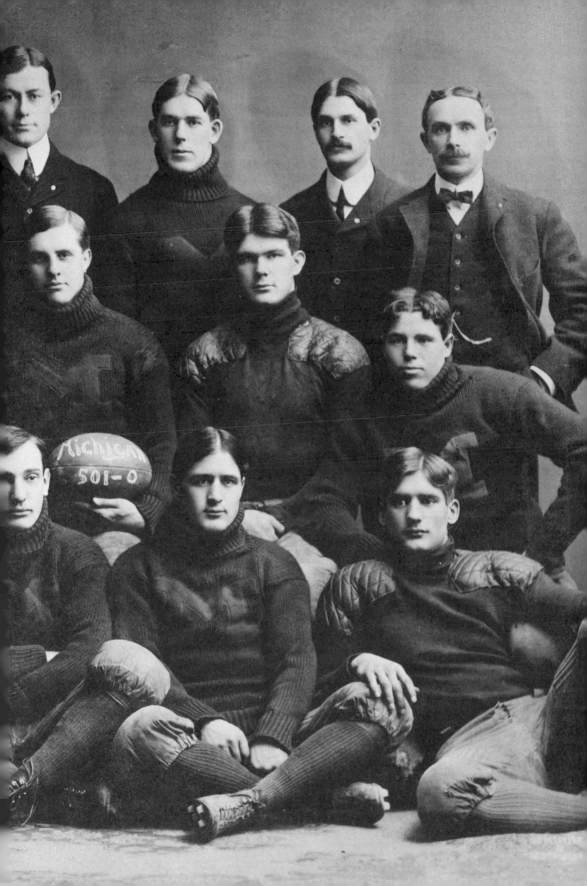

as well, as is evidenced by the record of points scored against us. His ability to pick the right men was an outstanding feature of his work, and I think, also, his ability of making practice interesting. Of course, he had his "homey" way of expressing himself, and that helped too. Our offense was a hodge podge, and was based on our having specialists, and so he took advantage of the peculiar qualities that we had and built his offense accordingly.

Yost considered the 1925 team his best, and it was his best because individually and as a group I would say they were the smartest bunch of boys gathered together in a team. It was a unique team also in that we had no big men. We did not have anyone over 200 pounds, but it was an alert, progressive, well-coordinated unit that made no mistakes.

I think it striking in looking back at the record to think of the scores we ran up that year. My recollection is that we beat Indiana 63–0, Minnesota 3–0, the Naval Academy 54–0, Wisconsin 21–0, Ohio State 10–0, Michigan Aggies 39–0 and Illinois 3–0. We lost to Northwestern 3–2. In looking over that record, you can see that no team crossed our goal line and that we had one field goal scored against us. It's quite a record.

We lost the Northwestern game in the worst day in football history as far as weather was concerned, and besides, we played in Soldier Field, Chicago, the first year of that field. As I recall, the gridiron was nothing but the black muck that had been sucked in from Lake Michigan. There was no grass, and it was raining, hailing and sleeting, with a 55-mile gale blowing in off the lake. When we stepped on the field, we stepped into the muck that was over our shoe tops.

Northwestern won the toss and naturally elected to take the wind. Therefore in the first couple of minutes, after a couple of kicks, they had the ball deep in our territory. They found a fairly hard spot and kicked a field goal. Late in the fourth quarter we got a safety and that was all the scoring of the day. Statistically, there was one first down made and one forward pass attempted in the entire game.

CHICAGO 2, MICHIGAN 0, 1905

In one of the most memorable "naturals" of all time, Chicago ended the fifty-six-game streak of Hurry-Up Yost's point-a-minute Michigan teams in 1905 by the score of 2 to 0. Michigan had won fifty-five games, including the 1902 Rose Bowl contest, and tied one (against Minnesota in 1903) from 1901 through 1905. The defeat came in the final game of the season and cost Michigan the conference championship it had held for four years.

AMOS ALONZO STAGG, the coach of Chicago for forty-one years from 1892 to 1932, sent the following information about the game to the author in 1952.

THE GAME WAS PLAYED November 30, 1905, at Marshall Field (now Stagg Field) in Chicago. There was tremendous interest in the game and the largest crowd in the history of football in the Middle West to that time, 25,791 paid admissions, turned out to see it.

The background of this titanic struggle was that in five years Yost's Michigan teams had rolled up 2,821 points to 40 for the combined foe. In eleven games that season they had not been scored on while making 495 points. Chicago also had a great team. It had played nine games and won them all, scoring 243 points to its opponents' 5.

The enthusiasm of the crowd was unbounded throughout. The field was in perfect condition, protected by many tons of hay. With my approval, after the game the hay was set on fire with a gigantic blaze. Dr. J. E. Raycroft, later of Princeton fame, started the blaze.

The game was played under the old rules, the year before the introduction of the forward pass and the opening up of the game. Five yards had to be gained in three downs. The size of the playing field was 110 yards long, with goal posts on the goal line and no end zones. A ball kicked over the goal line and touched down for a touchback was brought out to the 25-yard line. The length of the game was seventy minutes, divided into halves of thirty-five minutes.

As I wrote in *Touchdown,* Michigan was the heaviest team I had ever seen. Adolph Schulz, the all-America center, weighed 220 pounds. Octopus Graham at one guard weighed 245; Schulte, the other guard, 195, and Captain Curtis at left tackle was a giant from Colorado.

Our team was no featherweight eleven, nor leaden-footed either, and one of the classics of American football ensued. I do not hesitate to name it the greatest game I ever saw played under the 5-yard rule, then in its last season.

The day was Thanksgiving. The weather was clear, and fine for once, and 25,791 spectators paid $35,000 at the gate. The Atlantic Coast had discovered us. Among the Eastern delegation were Walter Camp and Caspar Whitney, the all-America team selectors.

From the start of the game it was shown that the teams were evenly matched. The first half was played almost entirely in the center of the field. Chicago penetrated into Michigan territory three times while Michigan crossed the center of the field once. The nearest we got to the Michigan goal was their 35-yard line; their nearest to ours, the 50-yard line. It was punt, punt, punt, with Garrels, later an Olympic hurdler, holding his own against Eckersall. Both kicked magnificently. The defense was so strong that it looked as though a lucky break or a bad mistake would be the only chance of producing a score. Michigan had a giant line and heavier backs, but Chicago's line held its own. The defense of both teams was deadly.

The play changed somewhat in the second half, for Chicago was six times in possession of the ball in Michigan territory, once on their 32-yard line. Eckersall, who had kicked five goals from the field against Illinois in our preceding game, elected to try a drop kick for a goal from the 37. It was partially blocked.

Once Garrels got off a tremendous punt which Eckersall recovered on Chicago's 15-yard line. We immediately suffered a penalty of half the distance to the goal line, putting the ball on about the 8-yard line. Here Eckersall's clever thinking took Chicago out of immediate danger with the most daring play I ever saw in a championship game. Standing behind the goal line in punt formation, and with Michigan's linemen rushing through to block the punt they expected, Eckersall circled to the right and ran between the goal posts and was run out of bounds at Chicago's 22-yard line while 25,000 hearts palpitated.

This feat heartened Chicago, and it was not long until she was

Adolph (Germany) Schulz of Michigan's all-time, all-America team.

again in Michigan's territory, following a succession of three downs, in which DeTray played a considerable part in spite of his injured eye, which had kept him out of the game until the second half. Michigan fought fiercely and Eckersall punted over their goal line. Denny Clark, instead of touching the ball down and bringing it out to the 25-yard-line, attempted to run it out, circling wide behind the goal posts, and was tackled low by our right tackle, Art Badenoch, just after crossing the goal line. Instantly, right end Mark Catlin tackled him high and they threw him back across the goal line for a safety, under the rules of that period, that won for us, 2 to 0. We had won on an error of judgment and we had been lucky to do it.

Some statistics on the game:

In the first half Chicago punted 12 times; Michigan, 10. In the second half Chicago punted 10 times, Michigan 9. In the first half Tom Hammond of Michigan tried for a place kick with the ball on the Chicago 41; in the second half Eckersall tried for a drop kick with the ball on Michigan's 37. Both attempts failed. On first downs Chicago made 8 in the first half, Michigan, 5; in the second half, Chicago made 11, Michigan, 4.

MY FOOTBALL DAYS AT WESLEYAN, 1901–1905

HENDERSON E. VAN SURDAM *played football for five years at Wesleyan University in Connecticut without any previous experience in high school. He was a skilled musician at an early age, and his professional work in music as a pianist and clarinet soloist with concert bands kept him from going out for football in prep school.*

Music was his chief interest for many years, and in the 1920's he took a symphony orchestra on a world tour, but his love of football has remained with him to this day, and nearing the age of ninety he continues to follow the sport closely, attend games and write articles about it. He was one of the founders of the Touchdown Club in New York and officiated in many games.

Van Surdam played at Wesleyan from 1901 through 1905, the first year on the freshman team and the other four on the varsity. He was eligible as a graduate student in 1905. He was picked as all-New England quarterback in 1903. Following the completion of his graduate work in 1905 he was head coach for two years at Marietta College in Ohio and then went to Sewanee in the South. He sent the following piece to the author in 1969.

IN JUNE, 1901, shortly before graduating from Michigan Military Academy at Orchard Lake, Mich., I was offered a scholarship at the University of Chicago as a clarinetist in the university band. At the same time I was offered a part scholarship at Wesleyan University. Attendance at Chicago meant a continuation of my musical career. At Wesleyan I would be a free lance, and that is where I went.

I was in Detroit for the summer of 1901 as assistant solo clarinetist in the Metropolitan Concert Band. September found me in Buffalo at the Pan American exposition with the Salem Cadet Band. Standing in line September 6 to shake hands with President McKinley, I heard a shot and the President was seen falling into the arms of his aide. He had been shot by Czolgosz, the anarchist.

Through its expert maneuvering the Marine Guard managed to get the assassin away. The mood of the crowd was such that had it been able to lay hands on the assailant he would have been torn to pieces. Vice President Teddy Roosevelt was located in the Adirondacks and, on the death of McKinley, was sworn in as President. He was to be known as the savior of football.

As a freshman at Wesleyan I made my first venture in athletics. Football was my main interest, and I was able to make a creditable showing on the team. I made the varsity in 1902 and was on the team in 1903, 1904 and 1905 also, playing every position behind the line and at both ends. In 1902 I was in the fullback position against Harvard and caught a blocked punt and raced across the goal line for a score. By the late 1903 season I became the regular quarterback.

In those days if you happened to be tackled in a mass play and were being pushed back, you yelled "Down" at the top of your voice to save losing yardage by being pushed back. The ball was dead where you yelled "Down." When you were forced out of bounds, the ball was brought in 5, 10 or 15 yards. It was up to the quarterback to state the distance the ball was to be brought in. When I said 5 yards, or 10, or 15, the number was the signal for the next play.

When a touchdown was made, the ball was brought out on the field of play straight out from where the ball was downed behind the goal line. Or it could be kicked out to a receiver standing 3 to 5 yards in front of the goal posts. The kicker lined up on the goal line where the ball had been carried across.

In the early days of 5 yards to gain in three downs, the Big Three used off-tackle plays, with guards-back and tackle-back mass plays that were bone crushers. They were, of course, the cause of many injuries, with the result that President Roosevelt summoned football people to Washington in 1905 and told them that mass play had to be changed to eliminate so many injuries. The result was the doing away with guards and tackles-back plays.

The forward pass was made legal in 1906 and 10 yards had to be gained in three downs instead of 5 yards. So the game was really opened up. However, the forward pass had to cross the scrimmage line five yards from center, and it was difficult for the quarter to be sure he got the ball across the line correctly.

To get back to Wesleyan, we played Yale every year, Harvard most every year and Dartmouth and Princeton usually in alternate years. Columbia was a fairly regular opponent. Brown was played irregularly.

I was graduated in 1905. I still had a year of eligibility left, so I came back as a post-graduate and acted as a sort of assistant to our coach, Bosey Reiter. This was by far the best Wesleyan team of the four I played on. In our game with Columbia in New York we outplayed them most of the game, but in the second half they began to run our ends.

On one of their wide end runs, I simply ran the back out of bounds and marked the spot where he went out. To my amazement he ran back on the field and started for the goal line. He was tackled by one of our halfbacks. He then started crawling and the fullback ran up and jumped on him, knocking him cold. And then a riot started, with coaches and players slugging it out against each other until the police quieted the ruckus.

So much bad publicity resulted from this game that at the end of the season Columbia banished football—not to be returned until 1915. So you see, my not tackling the runner but forcing him out of bounds was the direct cause of banishing football from Columbia for ten years.

I would say that the greatest team I played against was the 1905 Swarthmore team. And in my book, Tiny Maxwell was without doubt the greatest player I ever played against. His guards-back play was unstoppable, and was used all during our game with devastating effect. Other players that I remember well were Tom Shevlin, Jim Hogan and Foster Rockwell of Yale. Probably the greatest thrill I got playing against Shevlin was in making 7 yards around his end. Hogan and Rockwell also are Yale immortals who were celebrities in my day.

Bullock, Dartmouth Negro end, was also a standout, a man as difficult to run around as Shevlin. His record as a player and as a man was such that he was elected to Dartmouth's exclusive Senior Society.

The guiding genius of Wesleyan teams was Bosey Reiter. He went to Lehigh, where he became the most beloved coach in the history of Lehigh. Vincent Pazzetti, a star at Wesleyan, transferred to Lehigh and under Bosey became a greater star. . . .

In 1906 I began coaching at Marietta College, the first year of the forward pass. In my first game against Ohio Medics at Columbus, the very first play used was a forward pass to the right end. To my chagrin, it was called back, the claim being that it was not thrown 5 yards out. So from then on I began working on a formation that could not possibly be called back by an official. This formation was used with such deadly effect that in our game with Ohio University, Pete Gilman threw that football to halfback Moses for 47 yards and a touchdown, much to the astonishment of Branch Rickey, the umpire. This pass was in the record books for ten years.

Eddie Cochems, coach at St. Louis University, also used the pass that first year. In 1908 when my Sewanee team forward passed for a touchdown (Lanier to Eisele) against St. Louis, the papers gave Sewanee credit for forward passing St. Louis U. to death. Wesleyan University also threw a forward pass of 17 yards, I believe, against Yale in 1906. So there will always be a controversy as to who threw the first forward pass. The record book (Spalding) gives Marietta the first long pass of 47 yards in 1906.*

As I pass down the road of yesterday's greats, may I salute Al Inglis, Wesleyan 1902, the son of Middletown's chief of police. A varsity letter man in three sports—football, track and baseball —and a Phi Beta Kappa, he was Wesleyan's greatest football star. At Harvard there is a chair in education named for Al Inglis. In my years at Sewanee the stars were Lanier, Chigger Brown and Tom Evans, a great center who some years later was killed in Mexico by Pancho Villa.

* Editor's Note: St. Louis University is credited with a pass of 48 yards against Kansas, November 3, 1906.

PRESIDENT THEODORE ROOSEVELT'S
DEFENSE OF FOOTBALL

The year 1905 was a black one for college football. With its mass-momentum, close-order plays, the game had become nothing more than a test of brute force, and there were so many fatalities and serious injuries that there was a swelling public outcry and demands for the abolition of the sport. The Chicago Tribune *reported 18 deaths and 159 more or less serious injuries for the year. At Columbia College, the faculty abolished the game, and it was ten years before it was resumed there. Other colleges suspended play for a year. Stanford and California abandoned football for rugby.*

PRESIDENT THEODORE ROOSEVELT, *a strong believer in the values of football, stepped into the breach. Summoning representatives of Yale, Harvard, and Princeton to the White House, he called on them to save football by removing its brutalizing features. "Brutality and foul play," he declared, "should receive the same summary punishment given to a man who cheats at cards."*

In part as the result of the President's intercession, Chancellor Henry M. McCracken of New York University called a conference in New York on Dec. 28, 1905, attended by representatives of 62 colleges. They appointed a Football Rules Committee, headed by Captain Palmer E. Pierce, and it met with the old rules group headed by Walter Camp on January 12, 1906. The two bodies merged into the American Intercollegiate Football Rules Committee and adopted a reform program that saved the game by opening it up, legalizing the forward pass, banning hazardous features, and instituting other changes.

President Roosevelt, a Harvard graduate, spoke at the Harvard Union in Cambridge, Massachusetts, on Feb. 23, 1907. His remarks in part, as printed in Morris A. Bealle's History of Football at Harvard, *published in 1948, follow.*

IN SPEAKING HERE at the Harvard Union, I wish to say first a special word as one Harvard man to his fellow Harvard men. I feel that we can none of us ever be sufficiently grateful to Major Higginson for having founded this Harvard Union, because each loyal Harvard man should do all he can to foster in Harvard that spirit of real democracy which will make Harvard men feel the vital sense of solidarity so that they can all join to work together in the things that are of most concern to the college.

It is idle to expect, nor indeed would it be desirable, that there should be in Harvard a uniform level of taste and association. Some men will excel in one thing and some in another; some in the things of the body, some in the things of the mind; and when thousands are gathered each will naturally find some group of especially congenial friends with whom he will form ties of peculiar social intimacy.

These groups—athletic, artistic, scientific, social—must inevitably exist. My plea is not for their abolition. My plea is that they shall be got into the right focus in the eyes of college men; that the relative importance of the different groups shall be understood when compared with the infinitely greater life of the college as a whole.

Let each man have his special associates, his special interests, his special studies and pursuits, but let him remember that he cannot get the full benefit of life in college if he does nothing but specialize, and what is even more important, he cannot do full duty by the college unless his first and greatest interest is in the college itself, in his associates taken as a mass, and not in any small group.

One reason why I so thoroughly believe in the athletic spirit at Harvard is because the athletic spirit is essentially democratic. Our chief interest should not lie in the great champions in sport. On the contrary, our concern should be most of all to widen the base, the foundation in athletic sports; to encourage in every way a healthy rivalry which shall give to the largest possible number of students the chance to take part in vigorous outdoor games.

It is of far more importance that a man shall play something himself, even if he does it badly, than that he shall go with hundreds of companions to see someone else play well. And it is not healthy for either students or athletes if the teams are mutually exclusive. But even having this aim especially in view, it seems to me we can best attain it by giving proper encouragement to the

Theodore Roosevelt, twenty-sixth President of the United States

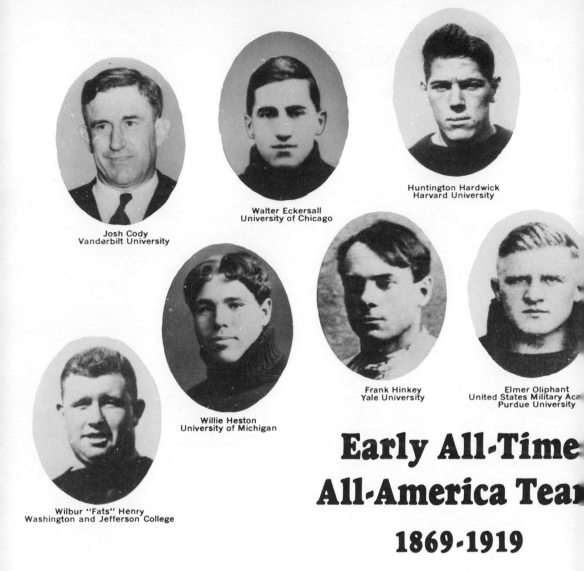

Josh Cody
Vanderbilt University

Walter Eckersall
University of Chicago

Huntington Hardwick
Harvard University

Willie Heston
University of Michigan

Frank Hinkey
Yale University

Elmer Oliphant
United States Military Aca
Purdue University

Wilbur "Fats" Henry
Washington and Jefferson College

Early All-Time
All-America Tear
1869-1919

champion in the sports, and this can only be done by encouraging intercollegiate sport.

As I emphatically disbelieve in seeing Harvard or any other college turn out mollycoddles instead of vigorous men, I may add that I do not in the least object to sport because it is rough. Rowing, baseball, lacrosse, track and field games, hockey, football are all of them good. Moreover, it is to my mind simple nonsense, a mere confession of weakness, to desire to abolish a game because tendencies show themselves, or practices grow up, which prove that the game ought to be reformed. Take football for instance.

Truxton Hare
University of Pennsylvania

W. W. "Pudge" Heffelfinger
Yale University

Adolph "Germany" Schultz
University of Michigan

Jim Thorpe
Carlisle School for Indians

As chosen by the Football Writers Association of America.

The preparatory schools are able to keep football clean and to develop the right spirit in the players without the slightest necessity ever arising as to so much considering the question of abolishing it. There is no excuse whatever for colleges failing to show the same capacity, and there is no real need for considering the question of the abolition of the game.

If necessary, let the college authorities interfere to stop any excess or perversion, making their interference as little officious as possible, and yet as rigorous as is necessary to achieve the end. But there is no justification for stopping a thoroughly manly sport because it is sometimes abused, when the experience of every good preparatory school shows that the abuse is in no shape necessarily attendant upon the game.

We cannot afford to turn out of college men who shrink from physical effort or from a little physical pain. In any republic courage is a prime necessity for the average citizen if he is to be a good citizen, and he needs physical courage no less than moral courage; the courage that dares as well as the courage that endures, the courage that will fight valiantly alike against the foes of the soul and the foes of the body.

Athletics are good, especially in their rougher forms, because they tend to develop such courage. They are good also because they encourage a true democratic spirit, for in the athletic field the man must be judged, not with reference to outside and accidental attributes, but to that combination of bodily vigor and moral quality which go to make up prowess.

Part
Two

THE CARLISLE INDIANS AND JIM THORPE

Among the legendary teams of intercollegiate football were the Carlisle Indians, coached, most successfully by GLENN S. (POP) WARNER, *one of the game's foremost originators and creator of the single wingback and double wingback formations. The tales of their feats, tricks, and prowess are endless, and most famous of them all, if not the greatest college football player of all time, was the Sac and Fox Indian Jim Thorpe, whose phenomenal exploits in track and field at the 1912 Olympic Games in Stockholm added to his worldwide celebrity.*

Winner of both the decathlon and pentathlon with record-breaking performances, Thorpe, who had Irish and Welsh blood in his veins as well as Indian, was honored by King Gustav V of Sweden, Czar Nicholas II of Russia and President Theodore Roosevelt. Said King Gustav as Thorpe stood before the royal box, "Sir, you are the greatest athlete in the world." Later a newspaper man revealed that Thorpe had played semi-pro ball for $25 a week during the summer. Charges of professionalism were filed against him, and the United States Olympic Committee took away his medals and returned them to Stockholm with its apologies.

In football Thorpe, who had a magnificent physique, ran with a speed, elusiveness, and strength equaled by few players in history. He was a kicker of extraordinary ability, both in punting and drop kicking, could pass, and was a deadly blocker and tackler. Even today, he is invariably picked at the top of all-time rankings. He was successively chosen as the No. 1 football player of the age, the No. 1 male athlete of the half century, and the No. 1 football player of the century, and is named on every all-time all-America team.

Warner was the first to receive the award of "Coach Of All The Years." On October 17, 1931 the following article appeared in Collier's Weekly *magazine.*

AFTER THIRTY-SIX YEARS of coaching at such widely separated and differing schools as Iowa State, Cornell University, Georgia, Carlisle, University of Pittsburgh and Stanford, the experiences that stand out most vividly in my memory are those connected with the Indian lads.

Not only were my associations closer, for Carlisle was a small, compact, self-contained school, more like a home than an institution, but the young redskins gave to every one of their football games all the color, dash and drama of a frontier conflict. They tell a story about the great Doctor Harper's first sight of Chicago University back in 1892. He waded through a swamp, walked a wobbly plank to the one and only building, still unfinished, climbed over piles of dirt and brick, and after the tour of inspection had come to an end, turned briskly and said,

"What this institution needs now is tradition."

Like Chicago, Carlisle had no traditions, but what the Indians did have was a very real race pride and a fierce determination to show the palefaces what they could do when the odds were even. It was not that they felt any definite bitterment against the conquering white or against the government for unfair treatment, but contests between red men and white had never been waged on even terms.

"You outnumbered us, and you also had the press agents," a young Sioux once said to me. "When the white man won it was always a battle. When *we* won, it was a massacre."

On the athletic field, where the struggle was man to man, they felt that the Indian had his first even break, and the record proves that they took full advantage of it. For fifteen years little Carlisle took the measure of almost every big university, with student bodies of four and five thousand to draw from, and to this day Jim Thorpe, Bemus Pierce, Frank Hudson, Jimmie Johnson, Mount Pleasant, Exendine, Lone Star and Pete Hauser still rank among the all-time stars of football.

What added to the glory of the record was that Carlisle had only about two hundred and fifty youngsters of football age, and season after season saw us going out to give battle with not more than two or three substitutes. As a consequence, almost every boy could play several positions and thought nothing of being switched around. Lubo was equally good at guard or tackle; Little Boy, a center, could play any line position; Calac went from tackle to fullback; Exendine, a great end, was also a great tackle, and when Jim Thorpe left school Joe Guyon, a tackle, took his place at halfback.

As for kickers, every man knew what to do with his toe. Nowadays, a team is lucky if there's one good leg in the lot, but it was nothing for Carlisle to have a half dozen. There was a season, for instance, when we had Mount Pleasant and Balenti at quarter, Thorpe at half and Pete Hauser at full, every man a deadly kicker from any distance, and just to guard against emergencies, Exendine, Gardner and Wauseka could also boot the ball if anything happened to the others.

Not only did Carlisle lack reserve material but the Indians were invariably outweighed, for I never had a team that averaged over 170 pounds. At that, the fury of their attack tore heavier lines to pieces, and their tackling had the force of a catapult. Trick plays, however, were what the Indians loved best. Nothing delighted them more than to outsmart the palefaces. There was never a time when they wouldn't rather have won by an eyelash with some wily stratagem than by a large score with straight football.

I don't think any one thing ever gave them greater joy than when we worked the "hidden ball" or "hunchback" play on Harvard in 1903. Carlisle's speed scored five points almost at the outset, and it was up to the Crimson to kick off. The ball sailed far and high down the center of the field, and was caught on the five-yard line by Jimmie Johnson, our little quarterback, who was an all-America that year.

The Indians gathered at once in what now would be called a huddle, but facing outward, and Johnson quickly slipped the ball under the back of Charlie Dillon's jersey. Charlie was picked as the "hunchback" because he stood six feet and could do a hundred yards in ten seconds. Besides, being a guard, he was less likely to be suspected of carrying the ball.

"Go!" yelled Johnson. And the Carlisle players scattered and fanned out toward the side lines, each back hugging his helmet to his breast, while Dillon charged straight down the center of the field. Talk about excitement and uproar! The Indian backs were chased and slammed, but when the tacklers saw that it was only headgear they were cuddling, not the ball, they began to leap here and there, yelping like hounds off the scent. Nobody paid any attention to Dillon, for he was running with both arms free, and when he came to Carl Marshall, safety man, the Harvard captain actually sidestepped what he thought was an attempt to block and dash up the field to join the rest of his team in a frantic search for the ball.

The stands were in an uproar, for everybody had seen the big

Glenn S. (Pop) Warner, one of foot-ball's most winning and inventive coaches, who originated the single wingback and double wingback forma-tions.

lump on Dillon's back, but the Harvard players were still scurrying wildly around when Charlie crossed the goal line. One of his mates jerked out the ball and laid it on the turf and, as I had warned the referee that the play might be attempted, he was watching carefully and ruled that the touchdown had been made within the rules.

The trick got columns in the press, being hailed as brand-new. As a matter of fact, it was five years old. While coaching at Cornell in 1898, I had the scrubs work it successfully and later in the season pulled it off on Penn State. The game was not important, however, so it was not until the Harvard game that it won promi-nence. I also used the trick at Carlisle to add interest to the scrim-mage practice, but we never considered it a strictly legitimate play and only employed it against Harvard as a good joke on the haughty Crimson players.

Unhappily, the "hunchback" availed us nothing, for we were beaten 12 to 11. It was not only that the Carlisle boys looked like children against the Harvard giants. That day we went into the game with only two reserves instead of our usual three, while Harvard could pour in a flood of fresh men against the battered Indians. Late in the last half, when every Carlisle player was out on his feet, the Crimson put over two touchdowns. For once, however, there was no mourning over a defeat. Even Nikifer Shouchuk, a sad-faced Eskimo from the Arctic Circle, joined the rest of the team in laughter as the "hunchback" play was gone over again and again.

Carlisle's lack of substitutes was always a handicap, but it never prevented the Indians from taking on all comers, regardless of size. Grantland Rice, in a comparison of early-day football with the modern, recently commented that "the old-timers" had only two or three games a season that called for any worry. Most of the others were "set-ups." Maybe so, but it was the ordinary thing for Carlisle to play hard games on six and eight successive Saturdays, and wind up the season by traveling across the continent to do battle with some California team. I might also mention that when the Indians lost more than one game they felt like painting their faces black and throwing ashes over their heads.

What made the Carlisle showing so amazing was that the little school never saw football until 1894, and did not go in for it seriously until 1896. Vance McCormick, a former Yale quarterback and captain living at Harrisburg, eighteen miles away, gave the Indians their first coaching as an act of friendly interest, and the boys took to the game so quickly that Hickok, another great Yale player, was regularly engaged as coach. He was followed in 1898 by Hall, also of Yale, and the next year saw my employment.

My first view of Carlisle's football material was anything but favorable, for the boys who reported for practice were listless and scrawny, many looking as if they had been drawn through a knot-hole. My heart went down into my shoes, for I was getting $1,200 a year and felt that only an ever-victorious team could possibly justify such a figure.

Major Pratt, superintendent, just smiled when I protested that the squad ought to be trying for beds in a hospital rather than places on the football team.

"They have been on farms all summer," he explained, "and

these Pennsylvania farmers insist on getting their money's worth. The youngsters will soon begin to pick up weight, so don't worry."

A very remarkable man, this Major Pratt. An officer in the Civil War, he had also seen hard service during the Indian uprisings out West, and was in charge of various tribes that the government rounded up and sent to St. Augustine, Fla. In 1878, when the Indians were permitted to go back to their homes, Major Pratt conceived the idea of a school in the East for the growing boys and girls, convinced that it would prove more of a "civilizer" than the reservation affairs.

Powerfully aided by Carl Schurz, then Secretary of the Interior, he induced the Washington authorities to grant him the use of the Carlisle Barracks in Pennsylvania, an old frontier post established for the protection of early settlers against Indian attacks, and used during the Revolutionary War as a prison for captured Hessians. In the fall of 1899, the time of my arrival, there was an enrollment of about a thousand students from seventy different tribes, the ages running from twelve to twenty.

Major Pratt proved a good prophet, for the boys put on flesh quickly, and as practice developed I found that the Indians were not only born lovers of sport but that football came to them almost naturally. In addition to speed and skill in the use of feet and hands, they also had highly developed powers of observation handed down to them through many generations. At the start of every season, boys came out who had never played or even seen a game, but after a week or so of keen-eyed watching, with every movement noted and observed, these beginners would turn in and do the thing as though they had been trained to it all their lives.

One year we played Annapolis, and as Jim Thorpe, who did our kicking, had a bad foot I called on a youngster named Mike Balenti. Mike had never tried for a goal from the field in a game, but four times that day he sent the ball sailing over the Annapolis bar, two kicks being from back of the forty-five-yard line. I asked him afterwards how he did it, and he answered gravely that he had "watched" Thorpe and Mount Pleasant.

Another asset was their amazing perseverance. The white boy usually gets discouraged unless results come quickly, but I have seen an Indian lad keep at the same thing for months, day in day out, in order to become expert. Frank Hudson, a little Pueblo, perhaps the greatest drop-kicker who ever lived, not only worked daily during the season, but when winter came on spent every spare moment in the gymnasium. With the parallel bars as a target, he would kick away, hour after hour, day after day, until he reached a point of accuracy and consistency that enabled him to boot a goal from the fifty-yard line almost every time. And with either foot.

About the only case of paleface pertinacity that I can recall is that of Vic Kennard, whose trained toe won for Harvard over Yale in an historic encounter. All through one summer he practiced drop-kicking day after day, and at night he spent hours letting the ball fall to the floor, studying its rebound and calculating the right distance from his foot. That fall, so Percy Haughton told me, he kicked sixty successive goals in practice from varying distances and angles. Put in against Yale in the last quarter when a field goal was needed to win, Kennard delivered.

My first year at Carlisle proved highly successful, for right at the start we gave Harvard rooters the scare of their lives. The Indians were looked on as a "pushover," but when Redwater, a big Cheyenne, picked up a fumbled punt and ran eighty yards for a touchdown, the Crimson players quit looking bored. Hudson soon followed with a goal from the thirty-five-yard line, and the Harvard captain began to bellow like a bull, clean forgetting his broad A. We went into the second half with a 10-to-0 lead, but Harvard's reserves proved too strong for us and they jammed over two touchdowns near the close of the game.

Nothing daunted, we whipped Pennsylvania, 16 to 5, the first time the Indians had ever won from a "heap big" team, and just to prove to the patronizing sports writers that it wasn't a fluke, we followed it up by a 42–0 victory over Columbia on Thanksgiving Day at the Polo Grounds in New York. At that time Columbia was mighty strong, having defeated Yale, and in addition to a heavy line possessed Harold Weekes, the demon hurdling back. It was confidently expected that Weekes would demolish the Indians, but when the Carlisle line began to rise up and meet his face with the heels of their hands the famous dives became few and far between.

In this game the crouching start was used for the first time in football. Up to then the standard position for the offensive back was to stand with feet well apart, body leaning forward and hands resting on the knees. I figured that if sprinters could get away faster by partly supporting the weight of the body on one or both hands, it was logical to figure that backfield players could obtain the same results. The innovation was a big factor in running up the large score against Columbia, and soon won adoption by other coaches.

The most remarkable thing about the Indians was their receptiveness to new ideas. Your paleface team is usually inclined to stand-patism, but the Carlisle bunch dearly loved to spring surprises and were happiest when I came forward with something different. One year we played a Thanksgiving Day game with Brown at Providence, and featured what I called a "wing shift." A back dashed into the line and on the next play acted as center, snapping back to another player, with the team all lined up on one side of the ball.

On the first attempt the play was stopped for a loss, and Percy Haughton, the Harvard coach, who happened to be on the sideline that day, turned to me and said, "Those series plays are never worth a darn. If they do work, it is only on the first trial, for they depend for success entirely on surprise." Twenty minutes later the same play was called again, and an Indian back ran sixty-five yards for a touchdown. "Well," muttered Haughton, "it did work that time."

That same year we perfected the "wing back," brand-new then but now widely used. For this formation, a back moved up so as to flank the defensive tackle, thus giving us practically an eight-man line. Wanting to be sure it had a fair trial, I sprung it first in a game with West Point, for if there was one team the Indians liked to beat more than another, that team was the Army. The formation proved brilliantly successful, for the flanking back took out the opposing tackle almost every time, and our 27-to-6 victory was largely scored on wide plays.

The cadets could do nothing with the "wing back," utterly failing to fathom it, and an all-America tackle, the best of their line, was actually made to look absurd. He must have felt it himself, for along in the latter part of the game he took a running jump at Joe Guyon, who lay sprawled on the turf. The referee, however, happened to be looking and the raging tackle saw the rest of the struggle from the sideline.

Owing to the speed and daring of the Indians, I was able to work out the "body block," a new idea. Up to that time, all blocking was done with the shoulder, a method that had a good many drawbacks. In the "Indian block," as it came to be called, a man left the ground entirely, half turning as he leaped so as to hit an opponent just above the knees with his hip, and following through with a roll, thus using his entire length. The Indians took to it like ducks to water, and when they blocked a man he *stayed* blocked.

At the close of the 1899 season, Carlisle was invited to play the University of California team in San Francisco on Christmas

Day, and accepted the invitation. I do not know whether the Indians were the first Eastern team to play an intersectional game on the Pacific Coast, but they were at least one of the first. Garry Cochran and Ad Kelly, former Princeton stars, coached California that year and as the team made a good record, beating Stanford 30 to 0, they were anxious to compare strength with a representative Eastern eleven.

On the long trip I had the Indians get off the train for exercise at every stop, and in one Western town an old gentleman asked me who they were and where they were going. When I told him it was the Carlisle Indian football team going to San Francisco to play California, he stroked his whiskers and remarked, "Well, they are going a darned long ways to get the hell kicked out of them." As it happened, he proved a poor prophet, for we won by the narrow margin of 2 to 0.

The game was played upon a field of sand, and as the Indians were much lighter than California and depended mostly on their speed, they were badly handicapped by the slow and insecure footing. Neither team could advance the ball for any large gains, and there was considerable punting in the game, but finally one of California's kicks went wrong and they were forced to touch the ball down behind their goal line for a safety.

This was Carlisle's first long trip, but we soon got to be a regular road team, playing most of our games away from home and earning the title of "Nomads of the Gridiron." Major Pratt, however, held that while the boys lost some time from their regular school work, the education they received from traveling and contact with college men was more than an adequate offset.

No more industrious sightseers ever lived, and when we visited a strange city, it was a general thing for the players to get up at daybreak so as to take in every place of interest. Back at school, the team members always stood up in class and gave accounts of what they had seen and heard, and in this manner the stay-at-homes themselves were instructed and benefited.

At the end of the 1903 season the Indians journeyed to the Pacific Coast again for a meeting with a team of stars called the All-Californians. It was an easy victory, for we won by more than twenty points and the game was remarkable only for the playing of Jimmie Johnson. He was in every play, running kicks back twenty to forty yards regularly, punting and passing superbly, and handling his team flawlessly. Walter Camp had chosen Jimmie for his all-America team that year, and California critics were doubtful about the selection, but after watching him work they agreed that he was "the greatest quarterback ever seen on the Pacific Coast. . . ."

Carlisle played good football from the first, but it was in 1907 that the Indians rounded into true championship form, downing Pennsylvania by a score of 26 to 5, Minnesota by 12 to 0, Harvard by 23 to 15 and Chicago by 18 to 4. With the exception of the unbeaten Pitt team of 1916, it was about as perfect a football machine as I ever sent on the field. Typically Indian, too, for among the first-string men were Little Old Man, Afraid of a Bear, Lubo the Wolf, Little Boy, Wauseka, Mount Pleasant and Balenti. The boys clicked into shape early in the season, and the very first game convinced me that a big year was ahead. Our opponents came from a small college nearby, and later on it was reported to me that the Pennsylvania Dutch coach made this stirring plea to his men:

"Now, poys, I vant you to show dose Indians dat you are yoost as good as dey are. Vatch vat dey do to you and den you do de same ting to dem, only harder."

Despite the poor coach's oratory, Carlisle won by a huge score. Our ends that year were Gardner, a Sioux, and Exendine, an Arapahoe, and I still maintain that they have never been surpassed for sheer brilliance. Pete Hauser, who did the kicking for us, was a big Cheyenne with a powerful toe, his punts averaging 60 yards, and under instructions he always raised them sky high. Gardner and Exendine were off at the swing of his leg, and it was rarely that they failed to keep up with the ball. In the game with Chicago they made life miserable for Wallie Steffen, invariably nailing him in his tracks, although Stagg finally assigned three men to block each end.

Few things have ever given me greater satisfaction than that Chicago victory. Stagg's team, undefeated up to then, was laying claim to the championship and sports writers refused to concede that poor Lo had a chance. The game, in fact, was to be a field day for the great Steffen, famous for his twisting, dodging runs and educated toe, and all Illinois gathered for the spectacle. I remember that Carlisle's share of the gate was $17,000, an almost incredible sum in those days.

Steffen did kick one field goal but that was his only pretense to glory. Gardner and Exendine were on him every time he tried to run back a kick. In selecting his all-America that year, Walter Camp only put Exendine on the second eleven and Hauser on the third, not even mentioning Gardner, and also ignoring Mount

Pleasant, the outstanding quarterback of the season. Wallie Steffen was a true sportsman as well as a very great player, for when I met him some weeks later and asked him what he thought of the all-America selections, he smiled and said, "Well, I certainly would like to see the ends they think better than Gardner and Exendine. And as for Pete Hauser!"

The Carlisle eleven of 1907 was nearly perfect. Jim Thorpe, by the way, made his first appearance that year, subbing now and then for Hendricks.

The forward pass had just been permitted by the new rules and we were about the first to see its value and develop its possibilities to the limit. How the Indians did take to it! Light on their feet as professional dancers, and every one amazingly skillful with his hands, the redskins pirouetted in and out until the receiver was well down the field, and then they shot the ball like a bullet. Poor Pennsylvania, among the first to experience Carlisle's aerial attack, finally reached a point where the players ran in circles, emitting wild yawps. The one defeat of the 1907 season was handed to us by Princeton.

Our 1911 schedule will give you a fair idea of what the Indians went up against regularly. On one Saturday afternoon, for instance, we met Georgetown and won by a score of 28 to 5, although the Catholic boys had a powerful team and were top-heavy favorites in the betting. A week later we whipped the big, fast, well-coached eleven of the University of Pittsburgh by a score of 17 to 0, and on the following Saturday shut out the strong Lafayette team by 19 to 0.

Here were three hard, bruising struggles all in a row, yet on the following Saturday we traveled to Cambridge for a game with Harvard. Percy Haughton started with his second team, just about as good as the first, by the way, and late in the second half when every Carlisle man was out on his feet, sent in his regulars, all fresh and rampant. When I hear people say that Indians can't stand the gaff, I always think of that finish against Harvard. Jim Thorpe, bandaged from head to foot, kicked four field goals, one from the 48-yard line, and his battered, crippled mates, in as fine an exhibition of sheer grit as I have ever seen, not only beat back the rushes of eleven fresh men, but swept them down the field, winning by a score of 18 to 15.

A week later we met Syracuse, and, with four consecutive wins to our credit, all over more powerful teams, we looked on victory as certain. Instead of that, Syracuse trounced us to the queen's taste. Not only was the field a sea of mud, but the Indians, worn out by their series of grueling encounters, played far below their form. By way of proving it, the following year we met Syracuse early in the season and overwhelmed the big Orange team by a score of 33 to 0.

The jinx, however, pursued us through 1912. After smashing Syracuse, we overwhelmed Pittsburgh 45 to 8, hurried up into Canada and defeated Toronto University 49 to 0, and came back to trim Lehigh 34 to 14. Next in order came West Point, and we humbled the cadets by a score of 27 to 6, missing two touchdowns at that. A fifty-yard run by Thorpe was not allowed, and we lost another by a fumble.

Just as we were dreaming of finishing the season unbeaten, Pennsylvania walloped us by a score of 34 to 26, a defeat due entirely to carelessness. It was a game I particularly hated to lose, for Thorpe gave one of his greatest exhibitions that afternoon. Once he took the ball well back in Carlisle territory and raced eighty yards for a touchdown, as beautiful a piece of open field running as I ever expect to see. Twice it seemed they had pulled him down, but each time he shook them off. The last game of the season, however, offered some measure of compensation for the Penn reverse, for we trounced Brown to the tune of 32 to 0 and for the first time overcame Carlisle's bad-weather complex. The ground was covered with snow, an icy wind blew down the field, and the Indians played wretchedly all through the first half, being lucky to hold Brown scoreless.

Talking to the team between halves, a bright idea came to me, and I pointed out to the boys that this was Jim Thorpe's last game and that they owed him a victory in return for the many he had won for them. Before I finished my little talk, I saw the young redskins tightening up, and every man took the field with grim, determined face and set jaw. Brown must have thought a cyclone had blown up, for the Indians swept forward for touchdown after touchdown with resistless fury.

Great teams, those Carlisle elevens that I coached, and what was even finer, sportsmen all. There wasn't an Indian of the lot who didn't love to win and hate to lose, but to a man they were modest in victory and resolute in defeat. They never gloated, they never whined, and no matter how bitter the contest, they played cheerfully, squarely and cleanly.

Whenever I see one of those all-America teams, I cannot help but think what an eleven could have been selected from those *real* Americans who blazed such a trail of glory across the football fields of the country from 1899 to 1914. One might go a long way before he ever found a better line-up than this:

Exendine .... right end
Wauseka .... right tackle
Bemus Pierce .... right guard
Lone Wolf Hunt .... center
Martin Wheelock .... left guard
Hawley Pierce .... left tackle
Ed Rogers .... left end
James Johnson .... quarterback
James Thorpe .... right halfback
Joe Guyon .... left halfback
Pete Hauser .... fullback

A line averaging 190 pounds, and every man with speed. Thorpe, Guyon and Hauser as big and strong as the line, much faster, and each of the three a deadly kicker, a terrific line-bucker and a marvel at passing and receiving. Johnson the only small man, but what a midget! And for substitutes, if substitutes were ever needed for these iron men, how about such players as Bill Gardner, Lone Star Dietz, Lubo, Afraid of a Bear, Little Boy, Seneca, Metoxen, Calac, Hudson, Mount Pleasant and Gus Welch?

In 1928 Warner had written of Thorpe for the Christy Walsh Syndicate:

Jim Thorpe came to Carlisle when he was too young to engage in athletics. He was living in the country under the "outing system" for about a year and when he returned, he had taken on considerable weight and had developed himself to such a degree that he attracted instant attention when he reported for football practice.

Thorpe started his football career during the fall of 1907, when he went in as a substitute. He showed considerable ability on his first try. In the following year he was a regular and began to attract attention as a ball carrier and kicker. At that time he weighed around 178 and was an exceptionally well-built athlete. He had speed as well as strength. He knew how to use his strength and speed as well as any football player or track athlete I have ever known. He was a great competitive athlete and always did much better in actual competition than he did in practice.

In the spring of 1908 Thorpe made the track team for the first time, his specialty being jumping and hurdling. He continued

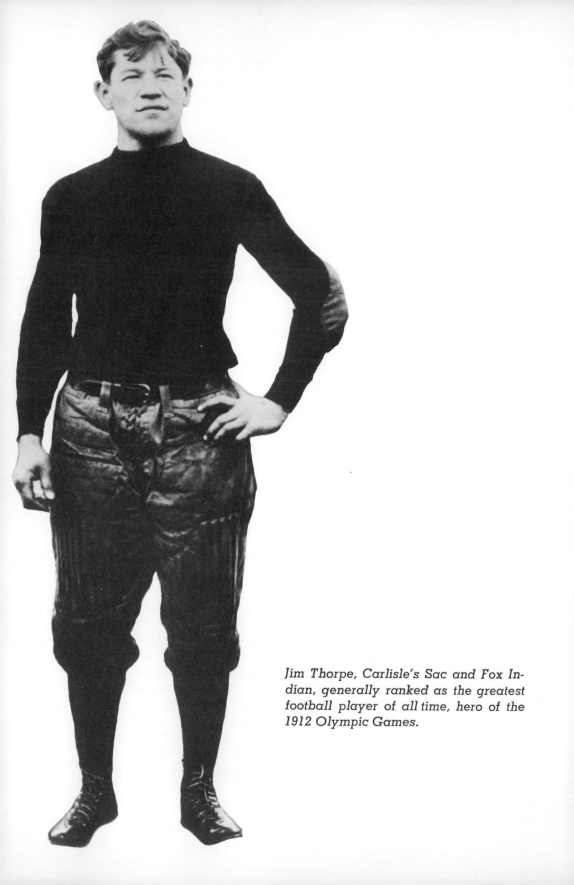

Jim Thorpe, Carlisle's Sac and Fox Indian, generally ranked as the greatest football player of all time, hero of the 1912 Olympic Games.

to improve each year and was a great star when he finished his five-year term in the spring of 1909. As his term of enrollment was concluded Thorpe returned to his home in Oklahoma. I should say the authorities of the school supposed that was where he went. We heard nothing more of Thorpe until the fall of 1911 when the Olympic Games were being discussed. I thought if he would return to the school he would stand a very good chance of making the American Olympic team and wrote him to that effect. He took my advice and, returning to Carlisle, played great football during the 1911 season.

The Carlisle team of that year was one of the best which the school ever turned out, defeating both Harvard and Pennsylvania and losing only one game during the season. Somehow or other the Indians never were able to go through the whole season without at least one defeat, and usually the defeat came at the hands of some team which the Indians should have beaten. As often happened to other excellent teams, the game would be lost by the Indians because they underrated their opponents and lost through overconfidence. . . .

When the football season was over Thorpe was entered in several track meets which were held in the different cities in the East. He won some sensational races and did some marvelous jumping that winter in the indoor meets. Twanima, the Hopi Indian long distance runner, was also going great guns that winter and these two athletes were stars in every meet in which they participated.

When the outdoor season began that spring, they continued to develop and Thorpe started training for the Olympic Games. Up to that time he had confined his efforts to putting the shot, the high and broad jump and the hurdle race, but now he undertook the pole vault, the javelin, the discus, the hammer and the 56-pound weight.

To show how much better Thorpe would do in competition than in practice, before going over to Stockholm for the Olympic Games, he had never vaulted over 9 feet 6 inches in practice. But during the games there in the all-around events he cleared 10 feet 3 inches and then decided that was high enough and quit without missing a jump. He was rather heavy and feared he might break the pole and seriously injure himself. I think he was wise to stop when he did.

While Thorpe was in school I had a tough time keeping him interested in track athletics. He was more interested in baseball and had his mind set on a baseball career. He used to say, "What's the use of bothering with track. There's nothing in it," and I had difficulty in convincing him that it was important to keep up his track training. As a matter of fact, in 1907 and the following year he did play baseball at Carlisle, as well as being a member of the track team.

I recall that on one of our trips after the track season was over, he came through the train smoking a big cigar. When I remonstrated with him for it he said that he was through with track athletics anyway and was going to quit and play baseball. After a great deal of argument I persuaded him to keep up his track activities. It was in that field of athletic competition that he did his best work and earned the reputation of being the greatest all-around athlete in the world. . . .

Early in 1913 after Thorpe's great victories in the Olympic Games, some newspaper man on a paper up in Connecticut came out with a story about Thorpe having played baseball down in North Carolina. By this time Thorpe was a national figure and the newspapers jumped at the story and the possibilities of an athletic scandal.

An immediate investigation proved that the charges were true and that Thorpe had played on a bush league team down in North Carolina after he had severed his connections with the Indian school in 1909. This was news to everyone connected with Carlisle because it was supposed that he had been at his home in Oklahoma from the time he left the school in 1909 until he returned in 1911. These stories created great furor because, if true, they branded Thorpe as a professional at the time he participated in the Olympic Games.

I went to Thorpe with the story and put it up to him cold.

"Yes, Pop," said the Indian, "it's true." He played at Rocky Mount in the North Carolina league one summer. Thorpe named many other athletic stars from other northern colleges who were playing the same league, but they were careful and wise enough to play under assumed names. Their identity was never revealed.

Thorpe was a fellow who always laid his cards on the table face up! He played under his regular name, probably never thinking that he would participate in any amateur sports after that. In a way, the boys at the Indian school were children mentally and did not understand the fine distinctions between amateurism and professionalism, and Thorpe saw no harm in playing baseball and earning a little honest money in the summer. He did not understand why that would prevent him from participating in the Olympic Games on the other side of the world.

The result was that his great collection of medals and trophies was returned and awarded to the athletes who had won second place in all of Thorpe's events abroad. When it became known that Thorpe had played professional baseball and that he was no longer an amateur, he was immediately in great demand by different managers of the big league teams of the country. Several of those clubs sent representatives to Carlisle armed with contracts for Thorpe. They figured that since he was a great athlete he would likely develop into a star baseball player, and this opinion was strengthened when it was proven that he had played some professional baseball in the South. Thorpe was rather unsophisticated in a business way and he asked me to look out for his best interests in dealing with the major league baseball people. I was glad to do so because Thorpe was no longer an amateur and I felt that baseball was the only career in which he might succeed.

I announced to all big league bidders that he would accept the best offer. He was about to sign with the Cincinnati Reds when my old friend John McGraw of the Giants phoned to tell me that if Thorpe was going to play professional baseball, he was in the market. I told him Cincinnati was bidding high and in characteristic McGraw language he offered to double.

The next day I took Thorpe over to the city where he signed with the Giants.

Thorpe's debut in baseball was not very auspicious. McGraw kept him on the bench for a year or two and finally traded him to Boston. I can now see where it was a mistake for Thorpe to go into big league company without spending some time in the minor leagues. He was a competitive athlete and did not like to be idle. Had he joined a team where he would have been in there playing every day I think Thorpe would have developed into a high class big league player. As it turned out his career in professional baseball was short-lived and disappointing. Among other things he did not take the best care of himself and finally drifted down to the minors and into the semipros.

While Thorpe was not a great success as a baseball player, he did do very well at professional football and for many years was an attraction on the gridiron wherever he performed. Thorpe was always a likeable chap and never changed. He has always been popular with his associates, but his one great difficulty was in withstanding the temptation which beset the path of all athletic heroes.

Thorpe will go down in history as having been the greatest all-around athlete of all time—the greatest Indian of them all.

MIKE THOMPSON, *one of football's most famous referees, who officiated in Carlisle games, narrated the following to Wesley Winans Stout in an article called "That's My Story" in* The Saturday Evening Post *of October 24, 1931.*

I told [in a previous issue] about two colorful teams, Centre and Georgia Tech, but the most colorful team of all was the Carlisle Indians. While I'm on superlatives, I'll add that the greatest player in my forty years of football was Jim Thorpe, and the greatest coach, over a period of years, Pop Warner. . . . Some years ago when the country broke out in an all-America rash . . . Tom Kirby, sporting editor of *The Washington Times*, appealed to me. I had consistently avoided such use of my name, but I gave in. After making notes far into the night, I tore them up and wired Kirby, "All-America: Jim Thorpe, Carlisle Indians." He was my team. . . .

I first saw the Indians in 1902, when I refereed their game against Cornell. Bill Warner, Pop's brother, was captain of the Cornell team that year, as Pop had been in 1894. . . . Pop knew his Indians. He walked and acted like one, and came to be a man of few words, mostly grunt, until his boys really believed that he had Indian blood. He knew an Indian's strength and limitations, capitalized on the former and avoided the later. Warner showed each man his job individually, demonstrating it, not talking it. Perhaps he gave his quarter a little theory, but for the most part he depended upon their native cunning, skill and love of the game to do the rest. The Indians loved trick plays. Pop gave them plenty and knew just when to pull his tricks. I doubt that any other coach could have approximated his success at Carlisle. . . .

Warner himself disagreed with me about Thorpe, ranking Ernie Nevers ahead of him. I agree that Nevers was great, but Thorpe, unlike so many later stars, ran alone much of the time, making his own interference and shifting the ball from one arm to the other as he ran. He was both big and lightning fast. He had every threat a backfield man could have, and most of all he loved the game passionately.

He had one trick that was unique in my experience. Tackling in his day demanded hitting your man just above the knees, permitting a clasp around the legs that would insure the runner's coming to earth. Jim had big hips and he had a way of crouching as he ran, scarcely slackening speed, just as the tackler dove at him. Aiming at his knee, the tackler's arms would encircle Thorpe's wide hips instead, and he wrenched loose.

I can see him in a Brown-Carlisle game at Providence one Thanksgiving morning. Brown had a big, powerful eleven, its particular star, Crowther, an all-America quarter, but the Indians outplayed them in the first half. A heavy, wet snow fell between the halves, leaving the field sloppy and the advantage with the heavier team. Brown pounded its way down to Carlisle's 5-yard line, then fumbled in overeagerness, all the backs competing to make the touchdown.

Thorpe was a brilliant punter, of course. When he kicked you thought the ball would never come down, and I can still hear the grunt with which he always accompanied a kick. He dropped back, with the ball on his 5-yard line.

"Watch me, Tommy, watch me!" Jim was one of the few who did not call me Mike.

"Don't try anything foolish on your own goal line," I warned him.

He grinned, called, "Change signals!" and whispered to the quarter. The ball passed from kick formation, but Jim did not kick. Neither did he try an end run. Instead, he lugged the ball right through the center of that powerful Brown eleven for a 110-yard run and a touchdown—and every Brown man got his hands on him. It won the game.

We were all soaked before the game ended. I was sharing a shower with Crowther, and the Brown quarter exclaimed, "Mike, do you think that fellow Thorpe is human? If I hit that Indian once today, I hit him a thousand times, and I haven't got him yet."

They were a temperamental lot. They came to Franklin Field one season with a fine team and a string of victories. Penn kicked off, Thorpe fumbled, recovered the ball and fumbled again, by which time the Penn forwards were on top of him. The Indians might as well have gone home then, for they were done for the day. If Thorpe had led off with his usual brilliance, the team would have played accordingly. But you never knew, from watching them after a game, whether they had won or lost.

They could play everything but "Home, Sweet Home" on the ball when they liked, but they didn't like to go home. Always playing away from home, the referee would consult them first about the length of the playing periods. The Carlisle captain would point

to the other captain and grunt, "No, him." If the other side suggested fifteen or twenty-minute periods, Carlisle invariably ob-
jected. "We play until the dark," their leader would suggest. . . .
Few of Carlisle's opponents could tell one Indian from another,
and Warner used to send in light backs to wind the enemy before
calling on his regulars, with his opponents seldom the wiser.

Even Pop couldn't always control his boys, and when they
didn't like an official they let him know it. They especially despised
timidity or uncertainty. I was more severe on them than any other
official; but an Indian always respects severity if it is just, and I
got along famously with them. . . .

In THE NEW YORK TIMES *report of the Army-Carlisle game of 1912,
in which the Indians scalped the cadets, 27–6, it was said:*

Standing out resplendent in a galaxy of Indian stars was Jim
Thorpe, recently crowned the athletic marvel of the age [in the
Olympics at Stockholm]. The big Indian captain added more lustre
to his already brilliant record, and at times the game itself was
almost forgotten while the spectators gazed on Thorpe, the individual, to wonder at his prowess. . . . He simply ran wild while
the cadets tried in vain to stop his progress. It was like trying to
clutch a shadow. He did not make any of the four touchdowns
credited to his team simply because the brilliant Arcasa was chosen
to carry the ball on three of the four occasions, when a plunge
meant a score [Bergie carried the other time].

Thorpe went through the Army line as if it were an open door.
His defensive play was on a par with his attack. . . . Thorpe tore
off runs of 10 yards or more so often that they became common.
. . . In the third period he made a run which . . . will go down as
one of the greatest ever seen on the Plains. . . . [Catching a punt
on Army's 45-yard line, Thorpe], zigzagging first to one side and
then to the other . . . wormed his way through the entire Army
team. [The run did not score because it was called back owing to
a penalty on Carlisle.]

THE FIRST USE OF THE FORWARD PASS

The forward-passing attack that Notre Dame unsheathed to defeat Army in the first game of their rivalry in 1913, with Gus Dorais throwing to Knute Rockne and others, led many to believe that the Fighting Irish were trail-blazers on this occasion.

The fact is that others had been using the forward pass since 1906, when it was legalized. It had been employed sparingly in the East until the demonstration by Notre Dame awakened coaches and players to its possibilities. But there were Eastern schools that were throwing the ball right from the start, and the claim is made that Wesleyan University was the first to complete a pass in an intercollegiate game, against Yale. On October 3, 1906, Sammy Moore threw to Irvin Van Tassell for a gain of 18 yards. Yale won the game, 21–0.

Henderson E. Van Surdam, who played at Wesleyan from 1902 through 1905 and coached at Marietta College in Ohio, says that his Marietta team in 1906 passed for 47 yards and a touchdown against Ohio University, to the "astonishment of Branch Rickey, the umpire." Two years later, he adds, when he was coaching at Sewanee in the South, his team passed for a touchdown against St. Louis University of Missouri.

St. Louis University claims to have thrown passes in early September, 1906. Its coach, EDDIE COCHEMS, *appears to have been well ahead of other coaches in the importance he attached to the new instrument of attack and in the preparations he took to make his team proficient in its use in the very first year, so that it was throwing spiral passes for long distances in 1906. Knute Rockne credited Cochems, along with Glenn Warner and Alonzo Stagg, as the early leaders in the use of the pass, and Stagg recognized him as a pioneer. Eddie Cochems wrote to Ed Wray, sports editor of* The St. Louis Post-Dispatch, *November 8, 1940:*

O F COURSE we developed the pass first, at St. Louis University.
. . . I first conceived the idea immediately on getting the official
football guide of 1906. . . . In 1905, as coach at Clemson College,
John Heisman (whose place I took when he went to Georgia Tech)
and I talked over the possibility of having the rules committee
permit the use of the forward pass. . . .

I took the team [St. Louis] to Lake Beulah, north of Chicago,
in July, 1906, for the sole purpose of studying and developing the
pass. . . . I studied the proportions of the ball and discovered of
course that it had been designed to fit the instep of the shoe for
kicking and the pit of the arm for carrying. . . . Then I lit on the
seven lacings as the only physical part of the ball for finger pur-
chase in throwing the ball on its long axis.

Just before our first practice, I told the players to put their
fingers between the two lacings nearest the end of the ball where
the diameter was shortest and throw it with a twist of the wrist,
on its long axis. . . . In about half an hour Bradbury Robinson, all
excited, came back and said, "Coach, I can throw the danged thing
40 yards!"

In January, 1954, ED WRAY *wrote the author:*

I was sports editor of *The St. Louis Post-Dispatch* during
Cochems' three-year period as St. Louis University coach . . . and
viewed many of the games. There is no doubt that Cochems was
the first coach to exploit the forward pass thrown overhand, both
long and short, approximating closely the methods used today. I
have a mass of correspondence from Stagg and other old-time
coaches on the subject, letters from Bradbury Robinson and Cochems and other St. Louis University officials, and assure you,
from observation and correspondence, that Cochems was the only
man to effectively use any type of forward pass approaching the
forward pass of today. . . .

Cochems had a powerful team besides having a real secret
weapon. He took his men to Lake Beulah, Wisconsin, in the summer of 1906 and there had a wonderful two months developing
the long-throwing ability of Robinson, with Jack Schneider receiving. . . .

The really wonderful part of the passing lay not only in its being an unknown weapon but in the fact that the team was powerful enough to gain ground by straight football and then shift to the long, long pass (often of 50 or more yards' carry) and then to a fast "bullet" shot just over the forward line. The enemy's ignorance was pitiful, not knowing when to close ranks or spread out its defense. The passing, considering that they used a "blimp" football, not the streamlined, slim one of today, was out of this world. . . . Cochems was really a man of ideas and surely deserves all the credit for first development of the forward pass as used today.

Also in January, 1954, following the death of Gus Dorais, Wray wrote in The Post-Dispatch:

A great football player and coach passed with the death of Charles E. (Gus) Dorais this week. . . . At least one biographer has referred to him as the "discoverer" of the forward pass. The late Knute Rockne and Edward B. Cochems have similarly been characterized. . . .

Two news services of national coverage disagreed in accounts of Dorais' achievements. One hailed him as the "discoverer" of the pass and said that until his advent forward passing had been confined to underhand pitches. Another national news service set forth that Edward B. Cochems of St. Louis University had, during the first three years of the rule legalizing the forward pass, demonstrated the great importance of the long, overhand forward passes by the marvelous success of his teams during 1906–07–08. A motion picture story of Rockne's career left a wide impression that Rockne deserved all the credit. . . .

You can take it from one who was here when Cochems did his stuff that whatever credit attaches to first exploitation of the pass belongs to Cochems. The Rockne-Dorais glamor story had wide circulation. . . . But Cochems' players were throwing 50-yard forward pass strikes when Dorais and Rockne were high school sophomores.

We have heard it said that Cochems' pass plays were primitive. But when we watched his plays run off they had all of the elements of those used today and were achieved under great disadvantages. The ball, for example, was called a "blimp"—so big that only a "ham" could throw it. The passer couldn't legally pass the ball

The 1913 Notre Dame team, which made history in first game against Army with a forward passing attack that overwhelmed the surprised cadets as Gus Dorais threw to Knute Rockne and others.

unless he ran at least five yards to right or left of center before pitching. If the passed ball was touched but not caught, it could be recovered by either team. In spite of these difficulties, Cochems' 1906 players threw both short and long passes. . . .

We have two pictures out of the file in front of us. One shows Bradbury Robinson, St. Louis U. halfback, demonstrating how he threw passes, taken from a book written by Cochems in 1907! The other picture is from the 1907 St. Louis U. Year Book, showing a photo arrangement illustrating Robinson passing to Jack Schneider and captioned "Longest Pass of the Year—48 Yards." And that was from the line of scrimmage. . . . It was all carry and followed a 20-yard or more fadeback by the passer. The date of the game was Nov. 3, 1906; opposing team, Kansas, and the place, Sportsman's Park. [In the 1933 Football Guide this pass was listed by Parke Davis as going 87 yards, but the error was corrected later.]

In a column dated April 10, 1953, following Cochems' death, Wray quoted BRADBURY ROBINSON *as follows:*

"As to who threw the pass first, the first legal forward pass ever thrown, so far as I am concerned, was in a game against Carroll College, Waukesha, Wisconsin, the first or second week of September, 1906."

Wray also said in the column of that date:

"In its first years under the forward pass rule, St. Louis University won all of its games, scoring 402 points and yielding only 11 . . . defeating Iowa, 39–0. It stunned the working officials. Referee Lieutenant Hackett of West Point said, 'I haven't seen anything like this display anywhere.' "

LIEUTENANT HACKETT *was quoted further:*

"What struck me most in the work of the St. Louis eleven this afternoon was the perfection it has attained in the forward pass. It was the most perfect exhibition of the new rules in this respect that I have seen all season and much better than that of Yale and Harvard. The St. Louis style of pass differs entirely from that in use in the East. There the ball is thrown high in the air and the runner who is to catch it is protected by several of his teammates forming an interference for him. The St. Louis players shoot the ball hard and accurately to the man who is to receive it and the latter is not protected. With the high pass, protection is necessary. . . . [because] the ball requires some time to reach its goal, time enough for the defensive side to run in. The fast throw by St. Louis enables the receiving player to dodge the opposing players, and it struck me as being all but perfect."

Knute Rockne disclaimed the credit that many gave Notre Dame as being the first to use the pass following its aerial display in the 1913 Army-Notre Dame game. He cited Cochems, then Warner at Carlisle and Stagg at Chicago as pioneers in the use of the pass and pointed out that the East refused to learn from the West and was satisfied to go along with its old-fashioned line plunges and mass plays instead of taking to the air lanes.

BOB ZUPPKE *agreed that the East lagged behind the West in the use of the forward pass. In a letter to the author, he said:*

"The leaders of the open game as early as 1906 were mostly in the Middle West. The East, as a rule, was slow to follow. Michigan, Wisconsin, Chicago, Purdue, Minnesota, Notre Dame and Illinois —in fact most of the big universities and innumerable high schools—were the leaders. I saw more forward passing in high schools than in college. I took my high school knowledge with me in 1913 to Illinois, and the 1914 team played a more modern game than many today [1952], as Stagg can testify. The Carlisle Indians and Pennsylvania were also leaders in the new game.

"St. Louis under Eddie Cochems received tremendous publicity. Cochems, a great Wisconsin end, went to St. Louis about 1906. He threw the ball all over the lot and immediately began striving for a larger field. That was the basis of my wisecrack to the Rules Committee: 'They want a round field with rubber goal posts.'

"The Rules Committee said you could not throw a pass more than 20 yards. That must have been around 1910 and lasted only a season or two. But they were afraid the pass would open up the game too much and it wouldn't be football any more."

Edwin Pollock, writing in *Franklin Field Illustrated*, said that the coaches at Pennsylvania experimented with the forward pass but were reluctant to employ it as an integral part of the attack until 1916, when Bob Folwell, captain of the 1907 team, became head coach. He had coached at Washington and Jefferson where "he enjoyed a remarkable success, including two consecutive victories over Yale with what was called a 'basketball pass.' His Washington and Jefferson teams attained an amazingly high percentage of completions, and his baseball pass became as consistent a ground-gainer as the controversial end run or off-tackle slant."

PARKE DAVIS *wrote of the reluctance to take up the pass in the 1927 Football Guide:*

"Notwithstanding the great opportunities offered by this new device, the players in the ensuing season [1906] treated this new weapon lightly and made little use of its possibilities. It was not until the Harvard-Yale game that a great forward pass play appeared. P. L. Veeder of Yale flung a pass 30 yards to R. W. Forbes, who was downed on the Harvard 3. H. L. Roome carried it over for the sole and winning touchdown.

"This spectacular victory intensely popularized the pass; but in 1907 there was no conspicuous example of the play until the Yale-Princeton game. Again Yale, starting an attack with 10 points against them, flung two long passes, each placing mighty Ted Coy in position to carry the ball across. The tacticians now awoke to the possibilities of the play, and in 1908 every team carried numerous variations of forward pass plays. But they were employed principally as threats to compel the defense to spread its backfield defenders."

ALONZO STAGG *was quoted by Grantland Rice in January, 1947, as follows:*

"The Middle West took to the pass long before the East ever discovered its value, despite the fact that Yale defeated Harvard, 12–0 in 1907, the game featuring a long pass. After that both Yale and Harvard forgot the pass for several years."

Stagg, a pioneer in blazing so many football trails, did not let any grass grow under his feet in exploiting the pass. He wrote the author in 1952:

"I have seen statements giving credit to certain people as originating the forward pass. The fact is that all coaches were working on it. The first season, 1906, I personally had sixty-four different forward pass patterns. Part of them were duplicated with a six-man line and a seven-man line. Of course, I selected the best ones to use, but since we were winning our games right along in 1906 without the forward pass, I kept them under cover for the Minnesota game on November 10. However, because of the rain on Friday and Saturday . . . the field was a mass of water and mud, and Eckersall did not use any of them. Minnesota won the game, 4 to 2, on a 42-yard place kick by Marshall, her big, colored end. Eckersall used the forward pass patterns the following Saturday, defeating Illinois, 63 to 0. The defeat by Minnesota lost us the Western Conference championship which we had won in 1905. Through the use of the forward pass we won the championship in 1907 and in 1908."

The Associated Press quoted Stagg in 1954 as saying that he saw "Pomeroy Sinnock . . . throwing lots of passes for the University of Illinois in 1906." Grantland Rice quoted him in 1947 as stating, "Fielding Yost used the pass effectively [at Michigan] in 1907 from different puzzling formations."

Just who was the first to throw a spiral pass, delivering the ball overhand instead of underhand, is a matter of dispute. The late General John Reed Kilpatrick was of the belief that he had a good claim to being ahead of all others. He said that while at Andover Academy in 1906, he and a teammate learned by chance how to throw a spiral pass and that he threw a 35-yard pass for a touchdown against Princeton as a Yale freshman in 1907.

But challenging this is the 48-yard pass thrown by Robinson of St. Louis University to Schneider on November 3, 1906. Also there is the 18-yard pass thrown by Wesleyan's Moore to Van Tassell against Yale on October 3, 1906. Howard R. (Bosey) Reiter, the Wesleyan coach, who had played at Princeton, was said to have learned to throw a spiral pass from a former Carlisle Indian player in 1903 when he (Reiter) was coaching and playing on the Philadelphia Football Athletics.

More than a decade before the forward pass was legal, Stagg had a player who could throw a spiral. He told The Associated Press in 1954:

"As far back as 1894 . . . Frank E. Hering at the University of Chicago used to throw the football like a baseball pitcher. I used him to make a long lateral pass to an end on certain plays when he received a kick. . . . Hering was the first man I ever saw throw a football that way. The regular method was to curl the ball against the forearm and throw it out with a sidearm pass."

Another early thrower of the spiral pass was Larry Voorhis of Penn State. Carl Snavely wrote in 1951:

"Larry Voorhis, playing quarterback and shifting to tailback in 1906, was, I believe, the most successful of the early passers that I knew anything about. His principal receiver was an end named Burns, who became outstanding because of the forward pass and was made captain in 1907. They threw a spiral pass."

Zuppke wrote in a letter in 1951:

"The first long pass thrown like a baseball that I ever saw was by Yost's Michigan team against Penn in either 1907 or 1908 at Ann Arbor. I believe Allerdice was the thrower. . . . The ball was thrown like a baseball, but with a flat hand and a loose grip—not as later with a finger grip. . . ."

Pop Warner's early use of the pass, including the spiral, is attested to by numerous coaches and officials. Mike Thompson wrote in *The Saturday Evening Post*:

"Pop Warner said, 'It may be basketball, but it's in the rules, so let's try it,' and he cleaned up with it. Other coaches, hostile or indifferent, were without defense."

Grantland Rice quoted Warner in 1950 as saying:

"I don't think anyone knows who invented or first worked out the spiral pass. . . . It was easy to see from the start that throwing a football end over end was not the best way. Many coaches and passers began experimenting with the spiral early in 1906."

In a letter to the author in 1953, Warner added:

"Frank Mt. Pleasant of Carlisle was using the spiral pass very expertly in 1907. I was coaching at Cornell in 1906 and went back to Carlisle in 1907. And, since the Indian backs were throwing the spiral so well in 1907, it seems reasonable to me that they must have started it the year before. . . ."

William Hollenback, one of Penn's immortals as a player, and famous also as a coach, wrote in 1954:

"The 1907 Carlisle team was a very good one and defeated us. It was only the second year of the forward pass and we had absolutely no defense against it. I give great credit to Pop Warner as one of the pioneers to see the possibilities of the forward pass. We were passing the ball end over end, much as you would flip a basketball; and when the Carlisle Indians came to Franklin Field they were throwing the spiral pass."

In the Southwest, where Ray Morrison was to help make the country pass-conscious with his "aerial circus" in the 1920's, Hugo Bezdek developed a strong passing game at Arkansas. Following the defeat of the Razorbacks in 1908 by Eddie Cochems' St. Louis University team, Bezdek, who had played at Chicago and was to win fame as a coach at Penn State, summoned Stagg, his former coach, to Fayetteville to teach his men to pass. Accompanied by Eckersall, Stagg, according to The United Press, "Went to Fayetteville and Eckersall and Steve Creekmore, the Arkansas quarterback, practiced to perfect a pass that would be accurate and effective. Stagg and Bezdek directed the workouts of the pair. From that time Chicago and Arkansas teams used the forward pass with winning effectiveness against stronger teams that did not employ it."

When the forward pass was legalized in 1906, there were many restrictions put upon it. It had to be thrown from at least 5 yards behind the line of scrimmage. It had to cross the line 5 yards to the right or left of the spot where the ball was put in play. Failure to complete a pass drew a penalty of 15 yards and loss of a down. In 1910 a limitation of 20 yards beyond the line was put upon the distance a pass could be thrown.

In 1907 the 15-yard penalty for an incomplete pass was removed. In 1910 it was no longer necessary for a pass to cross the line 5 yards out and the pass receiver was protected from anyone interfering with him. In 1912 the 20-yard limitation was lifted and, with the reduction of the length of the field from 110 to 100 yards and the establishment of end zones 10 yards deep, it was now legal to complete a pass behind the goal line in the end zone. A fourth down was added in which to make 10 yards and a first down.

In 1914 a 10-yard penalty was imposed for intentionally grounding a pass. In 1916 the quarterback was ruled ineligible to receive a pass unless stationed a yard back, and in 1924 the penalty for intentionally grounding a pass was increased from 10 to 15 yards. In 1926 a loss of 5 yards and a down was imposed on incompleted passes after the first in a series. In 1931 a slight alteration of the ball made it easier to throw and in 1934 it was slenderized an inch more. That year also, the 5-yard penalty for more than one incomplete pass in a series of downs was removed and a first pass to be grounded in the end zone in a series of downs no longer resulted in loss of the ball, except on fourth down.

In 1938 any incomplete pass in the end zone was the same

as any in the field of play, except on fourth down. In 1939 a penalty of 15 yards and loss of down was imposed for a pass hitting an ineligible receiver. In 1940 the penalty was changed to merely loss of down if the player was hit on or behind the line of scrimmage. In 1941 a fourth-down pass incomplete in the end zone no longer resulted in a touchback; instead, the ball went to the opponent where the ball was put in play. In 1945 the 5-yard restriction was removed and the ball could be passed from anywhere behind the line. In 1949 the penalty for intentional grounding was changed from 15 yards from the previous spot to 5 yards from the point of foul, plus loss of down. In 1963 the T-formation quarterback was made an eligible pass receiver.

THE FIRST ARMY–NOTRE DAME GAME AND THE FORWARD PASS

From an article by KNUTE ROCKNE *in* Collier's Weekly, *October 25, 1930.*

THERE HAVE BEEN so much guessing and dispute as to where the aerial game originated, and so many have thought that Notre Dame held and holds the patent, that a little research should settle the question. As with most revolutionary movements in established practice, the forward pass came in quietly, almost obscurely. Eddie Cochems, coach at St. Louis University circa 1907, [1906] enrolled a few boys with hands like steam shovels who could toss a football just as easily and almost as far as they could throw a baseball. St. Louis played and defeated several big teams—using the forward pass. One would have thought that so effective a play would be instantly copied and become the vogue. The East, however, had not learned much or cared much about Mid-West and Western football; indeed, the East hardly realized that football existed beyond the Alleghenies. Old-fashioned line plunges, mass plays and the monotonous kicking game, waiting for a break, were the stock in trade. The pass was a threat which heavy teams disdained. Warner of Carlisle and Stagg of Chicago were just behind Cochems in evolving the open game.

In all, with the pass as a versatile weapon, there are only about ninety possible plays on attack. Since a football team is no stronger than its weakest player, the number of practicable plays mastered by a team is rarely more than twenty. The pass complicated matters too much for old-fashioned technicians, who preferred to rely upon bull strength and Lady Luck. This accounts for the slowness of its general adoption.

We took it up the instant we saw it. Charlie Dorais (our quarterback)—the name, by the way, is pronounced like the first two notes of the tonic sol-fa scale—and I spent a whole summer vacation at Cedar Point on Lake Erie. We worked our way as restaurant checkers and what not, but played our way on the beach with a football, practicing forward passing. There was nothing much else for two young fellows without much pocket money to do, and it made us familiar with the innovation that was to change the entire character of football.

Jack Marks, our coach, had tried a quarterback-to-end pass combination in several games. Against Wabash in 1911, our first year with the pass in full play, Wabash had us beaten on a long and perfectly executed pass from Lambert to Howard. But the officials measured it. It was thrown more than twenty yards beyond the line of scrimmage and therefore was illegal. Wabash was penalized. Also, had that pass been thrown within five yards on either side of center there would have been another penalty. If you can figure out the sense of those rules, you're much better than I.

In football, technically, there are three kinds of forward pass: First, the spot pass, thrown to a spot where the receiver is supposed to be; second, the pass which is thrown to one definite individual; third, the choice pass, in which the passer, dropping back for protection, selects whichever of his eligible receivers is uncovered. This is the best pass in football, but the most difficult to execute.

About the time of which I'm speaking, Wabash had a clever exponent of the choice pass named Skeets Lambert. He was responsible for an extra restriction eventually being put on the forward pass by the rules committee. For instance, when we played Wabash we would rush Lambert and chase him sometimes twenty to twenty-five yards beyond the line of scrimmage and it looked as if we were about to throw him for a big loss. However, he fooled us by purposely grounding the ball when there was no teammate uncovered to whom he could pass. The ball was returned to the spot at which the play had started, with loss of down but not of yardage. Dorais promptly borrowed this trick from Lambert. In turn, Prichard of Army copied it from Dorais, but Prichard got credit as a gridiron fox for this quarterback ruse, which a subsequent rule penalized. Many football tricks of offense and defense have had similar genealogy—the player who performs them before the most newspaper witnesses being usually credited as the originator.

Perfection of the forward pass came to us only through daily, tedious practice. I'd run along the beach, Dorais would throw from all angles. People who didn't know we were two college seniors making painstaking preparations for our final football season probably thought we were crazy. Once a bearded old gentleman took off his shoes to get in the fun, seizing the ball and kicking it merrily, with bare feet, too, until a friendly keeper came along to take him back where he belonged.

But the fruit of our summer work was evidenced in the fall.

In the first three games before meeting the Army for the initial game of a now historic series, Notre Dame piled up 169 points to its opponents' 7, South Dakota being the scoring foe. This was all done on forward passing. Although we were not the first to use the forward pass, it can be truthfully said that we were among the first to learn how it should be used.

In the early days the players threw it and caught it much like a medicine ball. A football weighs fourteen ounces and a medicine ball about fourteen pounds. When you catch the latter it's in a hugging grab. We mastered the technique of catching the football with hands relaxed and tried to master the more difficult feat of catching it with one hand.

Naturally, we had pointed all this aerial practice for the Army game. The West Point boys were the background for Notre Dame's first big Eastern appearance, and while the game was not all-important to them, to us it was the supreme test of our playing careers. The Army had a marvelous line, with two All-America stars, McEwan at center and Merillat at end, while Prichard, at quarterback, also had All-America rating.

The morning we left for West Point the entire student body of the university got up long before breakfast to see us to the day coach that carried the squad to Buffalo—a dreary, all-day trip. From Buffalo we enjoyed the luxury of sleeping-car accommodations—regulars in lowers, substitutes in uppers. There was no pampering in those days. We wanted none of it. We went out to play Army like crusaders, believing that we represented not only our own school, but the whole, aspiring Middle West.

West Point, as always since our meetings have become famous, treated us most hospitably. We were housed in Cullum Hall and given the freedom of the Officers' Club. There was a fair crowd to see the game on the Plains, and the New York newspapers were interested enough to send second-string football reporters.

The cadet body and most of the other spectators seemed to regard the engagement as a quiet, friendly work-out for Army.

For the first part of the first quarter it looked that way. An Army line outweighing ours by about fifteen pounds to the man pushed us all over the place before we overcame the tingling realization that we were actually playing the Army. I recall Merillat shouting:

"Let's lick these Hoosiers!"

So I asked him, in a lull, if he knew how the word Hoosier originated.

"We started it at South Bend," I informed him, John Markoe and what others of the Army team would listen. "After every game the coach goes over the field, picks up what he finds and asks his team: 'Whose ear is this?' Hence, Hoosier."

The gag didn't work so well. Something else did. After we had stood terrific pounding by the Army line, and a trio of backs that charged in like locomotives, we held them on downs. Dorais, in a huddle, said, "Let's open up." It was amusing to see the Army boys huddle after a first, snappy eleven-yard pass had been completed for a first down. Their guards and tackles went tumbling into us to stop line bucks and plunges. Instead, Dorais stepped neatly back and flicked the ball to an uncovered end or halfback. This we did twice in a march up the field, gaining three first downs in almost as many minutes.

Our attack had been well rehearsed. After one fierce scrimmage I emerged limping as if hurt. On the next three plays Dorais threw three successful passes to Pliska, our right halfback, for short gains. On each of these three plays I limped down the field acting as if the thing farthest from my mind was to receive a forward pass. After the third play the Army halfback covering me figured I wasn't worth watching. Even as a decoy he figured I was harmless.

Finally, Dorais called my number, meaning that he was to throw a long forward pass to me as I ran down the field and out towards the side line. I started limping down the field and the Army halfback covering me almost yawned in my face, he was that bored. Suddenly, I put on full speed and left him standing there flat-footed. I raced across the Army goal line as Dorais whipped the ball, and the grandstands roared at the completion of a forty-yard pass. Everybody seemed astonished. There had been no hurdling, no tackling, no plunging, no crushing of fiber and sinew. Just a long-distance touchdown by rapid transit.

At the moment when I touched the ball life for me was complete. We proceeded to make it more than complete. The Army resisted. They charged with devastating power and drove through us for two touchdowns, score at half being Notre Dame 14, Army 13. In the second half Army changed its defense to meet our open game. It didn't work. Dorais, always alert, reversed our tactics sufficiently to take over the Army line-plunging game with Ray Eichenlaub as our spearhead. He ripped the Army line to pieces.

In the last quarter Army closed up to stop Eichenlaub. Dorais instantly switched tactics, opening up with a fresh barrage of passes that completely baffled the cadets.

Fitzgerald, a guard, took special interest in McEwan, Army's great center. Their contest grew personal as Army lost ground and we gained it. Superheated between scrimmages, wild words flew. Fitzgerald closed in on McEwan. He socked McEwan square on the jaw, then instantly yelled as he did so:

"Hey, referee!"

The referee turned round just in time to see McEwan crash home a right to Fitzgerald's nose. McEwan was promptly ordered from the game; but as captain of our team I had to stop and explain that both boys had been too boisterous and so the referee let both of them stay in the game. From then on their decorum was more proper.

Hard-fought to the end, this first Army game, with its score of 35 to 13 in favor of Notre Dame, does not quite represent the difference in playing quality between the two teams. The Army was much better than the score showed. It was, however, the first signal triumph of the new, open game over the old, battering-ram Army game. And the Army was quick to learn.

Press and football public hailed this new game, and Notre Dame received credit as the originator of a style of play that we had simply systematized. Our achievement was that we had demonstrated, by completing fourteen out of seventeen passes in this game against the Army, gaining some two hundred yards thereby, that the forward pass was an integral part of offense and not merely a threat.

GUS DORAIS *gave this account of the 1913 Army-Notre Dame game in his story,* Rock and I. *It was reprinted on the silver anniversary of the Army-Notre Dame game in 1938 by the Notre Dame Club of New York City in a program for a reunion and rally for the benefit of the Rockne Memorial Fund.*

That summer of 1913 at Cedar Point, Rock and I practiced more than we ever had practiced before. Rock perfected his method of catching passes without tenseness in fingers, wrists or arms, and with the hands giving with the ball, just as a baseball should be caught.

He also continued to develop his deceptive, stop-and-go style of going down the field for a pass, a style still used by nearly all good pass receivers.

I worked hard to increase both the accuracy and the length of my passes. A rule change that would become effective that fall had removed all restrictions on the length of a legal forward pass.

When we got back to college, we found that we had a new football coach. He was Jesse C. Harper, who had learned his football from Old Man Stagg at the University of Chicago, and who had coached Wabash for three years. It was Harper who introduced the backfield shift at Notre Dame; in later years Rockne improved and developed it, and made it an important part of the Notre Dame system of play.

Our new coach didn't wait for his team's captain to call on him. He met us at the train. The first thing he said was:

"I've got great news for you fellows. We're going to play Army at West Point on the first of November!"

Believe me, that *was* great news! Army was a power in Eastern football. And this game would be Notre Dame's first real intersectional game. We had played Pittsburgh, of course, but at that time Pittsburgh was considered a Middle Western rather than an Eastern team.

We had a veteran team. Seven of our regulars were seniors who had played on the 1911 team—Rock, Jones, Keefe and Feeney in the line, and Pliska, Eichenlaub and myself in the backfield. The other positions were filled by Fitzgerald, Lathrop, Gushurst and Finegan, all of whom had had a season of varsity experience.

Our first game, against Ohio Northern, was apple pie for us. In the first half, our regulars were neither held for downs nor forced to kick. Then Harper put in the subs to give them some experience. The final score was 87–0.

Our next game was against South Dakota, and that wasn't so easy. In fact, our visitors scored before the contest was three minutes old. But shortly after that, Pliska got loose and ran fifty yards to a touchdown, and a few minutes later I got off a long pass to Nowers, one of our substitute ends, that also was good for a touchdown. The final score was 20–7. A week later we swamped Alma, 62–0.

So we went into our last week of preparation for the all-important Army battle with the comforting knowledge that we had scored 169 points in our first three games, mostly by our air attack and our open running game.

We were confident when we started for West Point, but not overconfident. We weren't at all inclined to underrate Army—not

with a center like McEwan, an end like Merillat, and a back like
Prichard in the Cadets' line-up!

We didn't travel in the style to which later Notre Dame football
teams have become accustomed. We rode a day coach all the way
from South Bend to Buffalo, and thought that we were mighty
lucky because we had sleeper berths the rest of the way to West
Point.

Army regarded Notre Dame as a very minor opponent, but
the West Point authorities couldn't have treated us better if we had
been Yale or Harvard. They put us in Cullum Hall, and gave us
freedom of the Officers' Club.

Through some mistake, our boys entered Cullum Hall through
a side door—and no Notre Dame athletic team that played at West
Point after us would enter Cullum Hall except through that side
door.

Army had no stadium then, and its home football games were
played on a field marked out on the Plains, the Cadets' parade
grounds. There were small wooden stands, but they didn't accommodate more than a fifth of the five thousand spectators. The rest
of them stood along the side lines.

At last, the great moment arrived, and Captain Knute Rockne
led his team out on the field for the game that was to win Notre
Dame a place among the nation's gridiron greats.

There wasn't anything sensational about the first quarter of
that Army-Notre Dame game of 1913. The crowd in the wooden
bleachers and standing along the side lines of the gridiron on
the Plains at West Point saw fifteen minutes of hard, bruising
football, but nearly all of it was played between the forty-yard lines.

Once Merillat of Army carried the ball on an end-around
play, and for a moment it looked as though he would get loose. But
then Captain Rockne tackled him so hard that Merillat was laid
out for a couple of minutes.

Army's big line outweighed ours fifteen pounds to the man, and
we couldn't gain consistently with our running plays. But neither
could Army with theirs. Early in the second quarter, I decided that
the time had come for us to start winning the game.

"Let's open up!" I said to the boys.

We opened up. I threw a short pass to Pliska. It gave us a first
down. Rock went downfield on the play, and the Army secondary-
defense man noticed that he was limping painfully and that his
face looked haggard. That didn't surprise them. They often had

seen opposing players look that way after they had tackled the great Merillat.

Mixing up short passes to Pliska with line plunges by Ray Eichenlaub, we made three first downs in less than three minutes. Rock limped downfield on each pass, but it was obvious to the Army backs that he was just going through the motions of being a decoy—and not going through them any too convincingly either.

Now we had the ball well into Army territory—somewhere in the neighborhood of the thirty-five-yard line. On the next play Pliska and Rockne went downfield as usual as I faded back ten yards or so, Pliska moving like a sprinter and Rock still limping painfully.

The Army players saw that I was going to pass again, and their backs converged on Pliska. Then I got the ball away—toward Rock, who was limping along over near a side line. He lost his woebegone look and his limp as he put on full speed and left the Army back who was covering him flat-footed. A few yards short of the goal line, he reached up and caught the ball without slackening his speed, and then went over for the touchdown without an Army player getting a hand on him. It was a great catch, following a masterly bit of acting.

I kicked the goal after touchdown, and the score was Notre Dame 7, Army 0.

That play disconcerted the Cadets, but it didn't discourage them. There isn't a team in football that is harder to keep beaten than Army.

A few minutes later, the West Pointers showed us that they could play the passing game too. A very nice fling by Prichard, their quarterback, to Jouett, their left end, gave them a first down on our fifteen-yard line. Then Hodgson, their fullback, smashed through our line for a touchdown. They kicked the goal, and the score was 7–7.

Army kept right on going. Before long, another pass by Prichard to Jouett gave them a first down on our five-yard line. We fought with everything we had, and after three line bucks, the ball was still six inches from our goal line. Then we were penalized for holding, giving our opponents a first down. They didn't gain an inch on two more line plunges, but on the next one Prichard went over for a touchdown. They missed the kick for goal, but now the score was Army 13, Notre Dame 7.

That wasn't so good, so we opened up some more. Army kicked off to us. The ball went to Rock, and he was brought down on our fifteen-yard line. I got five yards on a quarterback sneak. Then I passed to Pliska, and it was good for a thirty-yard gain. And then I passed thirty-five yards to Rock. He made one of his perfect catches, and went to the Army five-yard line before he was tackled by the safety man. On the next play, Pliska plowed through the line for a touchdown. I kicked the goal, and we were leading, 14–13.

Our passing attack had the Army players bewildered, so we gave them the works—forward passes, lateral passes, lateral passes that turned into forward passes. Just before the end of the half, when we had the ball near a sideline, I called one of our spread plays. Both of our ends, and all of our backs except me moved over to the other side of the field.

I took the pass from center and faded back as the Army players came rushing at me. Then I passed across the field to Rock. The ball was within inches of his outstretched hands and it looked like a certain touchdown, when Prichard made a spectacular and remarkable flying leap over Rock's head and made the catch. Then the half ended, with us holding a slim one-point lead.

Charles Daly, the Army coach, made some changes in the Cadets' defensive assignments between the halves, strengthening their defense against passes at the cost of weakening their defense against our running plays.

The third quarter was a ding-dong scrap. We couldn't gain consistently, so I tried to drop-kick a field goal from mid-field and missed. Then Army started marching, and Hodgson, Hobbs and Milburn, all good backs, hammered at us until they had a first down on our two-yard line.

Hodgson, the Army fullback, carried the ball on the next play. He tried to go around Rock's end to a touchdown, but Rock picked him up and hurled him back to the five-yard line. Hobbs took a hack at us, and he, too, was thrown for a loss. Then Prichard passed to Merillat behind our goal line, but I intercepted the ball.

A few minutes after that danger was passed, Finegan, our right halfback, made a twenty-five-yard gain on an end run which carried us well into Army's end of the field. Mixing in enough passes to keep the Cadets from strengthening their defense against ground plays, I kept feeding the ball to Eichenlaub, and big Ray kept on going through the Army line until we had another touchdown. I kicked the goal, and the score was Notre Dame 21, Army 13.

Then we started passing again. Heaves to Rock and Pliska soon put the ball on the Army five-yard line. On the next play I passed over the goal line for a touchdown. Then I kicked the goal. That made it 28–13. We had the game sewed up, but we wanted another score. A pass that I threw to Finegan put the ball on the Army thirty-yard line. Then the Cadets drew a fifteen-yard penalty. Eichenlaub went over for a touchdown on a line play. I kicked the goal. The game ended with the score Notre Dame 35, Army 13.

We used only one substitute and we took time out only once— when Pliska broke a shoelace.

That Notre Dame-Army game of 1913 did several things. It inaugurated the annual Notre Dame-Army game that has become one of the classics of college sport. It proved to Eastern fans that Middle Western teams could play top-flight football. It demonstrated to coaches, officials, sports writers and the public the possibilities of the then new forward pass.

It really "sold" the forward pass to "big-time" football, and Army was the first customer. The Cadets used it to beat a fine Navy team that same year. And that first Notre Dame-Army game "made" Notre Dame on the gridiron; after it, no football team ever regarded Notre Dame as a minor opponent!

When we got out of our day coach at the South Bend railroad station, we found most of the town waiting for us. There was a parade with several bands and plenty of red fire, and, of course, Captain Knute Rocke was called on for a speech. He made one, but he was so nervous and embarrassed that he twisted most of the buttons off his coat while he was doing it, and no one in the audience could understand a word of what he said. . . .

I didn't see much of Rock during the five years I was on the Pacific Coast, but I read and heard plenty about him. By the time I came back East in 1925 to become head football coach at the University of Detroit, he had become nationally famous.

But when we met I found that he was the same old Rock, full as ever of sympathy and understanding. The only difference in him that I noticed was that his bald spot was more extensive, and his stock of funny stories considerably larger. The last time I met him was in Detroit at the sales convention of an automobile company with which he had become connected. His sympathy and human understanding made him able to help automobile salesmen to sell more cars, just as it made him able to help football players to make more touchdowns.

We had a long talk. Rock's physicians had given him very bad news. They had told him that he couldn't live more than a year or two at the pace he was going, and not more than two or three years if he slowed down.

"I'm not going to slow down," he told me. "I don't like to take things easy and I want to make all the money I can for my family. So I'm going right ahead!"

Not many weeks after that, he was killed when the air liner in which he was traveling to another sales convention on the Pacific Coast crashed in the Flint Hills country of southeastern Kansas, not so very many miles from Jesse Harper's ranch.

Whenever I go back to Notre Dame, I visit Rock's grave, which lies in the shade of the Old Council Oak, a mighty tree that stands in the cemetery, a few miles from the campus. But I know that Rock isn't dead. He'll never die so long as football is played.

MAL ELWARD, *Rockne's substitute at end on the 1913 team, wrote to the author in October, 1954, as follows:*

This team had a great quarterback in Charles "Gus" Dorais, who died recently. He was a great triple threat man and although that year Notre Dame used the shift for the first time Dorais ran and passed a lot from punt formation. He was also one of the best drop kickers of all time and an excellent punter.

The team had all-around team speed, a great fullback in Ray Eichenlaub, fast halfbacks in Bergman, Berger and Pliska and good receivers in Rockne and Gushurst. Dorais did a lot of passing from punt formation against Army and in 1913 he passed a lot to Joe Pliska, the right half.

Only twelve men played in the 1913 game. "Bunny" Larkin, a sub halfback, got in for two minutes when Pliska broke a shoelace. I was subbing for Rock that year and did not play. About twenty-two men made the trip.

Rock and Gushurst, the ends, were outstanding blockers as well as receivers. Ends then were made blockers first and receivers next.

FOOTBALL NOW AND THEN

HAMILTON FISH *ranks high among Harvard's great football players. He ranks so high among the immortals of the game that he has been chosen as a tackle on many all-time college teams. Walter Camp chose him on his first All-America team in 1908 and again in 1909. He stands with Mahan, Hardwick, Pennock, Newell, Campbell, Wendell, Brickley, and Casey. In* The Spur *magazine of January, 1937, Fish wrote:*

FOOTBALL IS THE greatest American amateur team game and gives every indication of continuing its popularity for years to come. The demand for tickets at the Army-Navy game this year was greater than ever and the final game of the season between the Army and the Navy filled the New Municipal Stadium at Philadelphia with 102,000 shivering fans to witness the second Navy victory in sixteen years. If this new stadium had been twice as big it probably would have been filled at the cost of four dollars and forty cents a ticket.

I am told by old-time players that the Yale-Princeton game this season was one of the most exciting and sensational ever played. I missed that one but saw in all six games this season, three Army defeats—by Colgate, Notre Dame and Navy—and one victory over Columbia; and two Yale victories—one against Navy and the other over Harvard by one point after touchdown. In all these games, except the Army-Navy, both sides scored and generally more than once.

There is now more action, more open play, forward passes, trick plays, long runs and scoring than there were twenty-five or thirty years ago. In that respect the game has improved, but the fundamentals remain the same; teamwork, concentration on signals and assignments, hard charging and blocking on the offense and on the defense, alertness in sizing up the opponents' formations, aggressive line play and sure tackling both by linemen and defensive backs. In spite of vastly improved forward passing, there has been little or no improvement in punting, drop kicking or placement kicks, or in the players themselves.

The main underlying motive that marks football today, as it did over a quarter of a century ago, is that same spirit of the intercollegiate game—that competitive spirit that exemplifies American amateur football. Just so long as that competitive spirit exists, intercollegiate football will endure and remain the greatest of our games.

All life after college is competitive, no matter what profession, business, politics or work graduates of colleges engage in. I sincerely believe that the mental concentration in trying to excel, the physical training, the infusion of self-reliance and the development of the competitive spirit is the best schooling for competition in all walks of life.

Strangely enough, I believe that there is more mental training and development under a good coach than can be had in any college course. The reason for this is that every man on the squad concentrates to perfect himself in his own position, and the devil take the hindmost. If you are a forward passer, punter, drop kicker, receiver of passes, or merely an interferer, blocker or tackler, you aim to excel. In addition, there are the varied signals, trick plays, cross blocking and running interference for the linemen. Unless every man on the team carries out his assignment precisely, the play fails.

I often think, after a team gets running its plays off smoothly and everything is clicking and the players believe their teamwork perfect, that they should be taken to a musical show to watch some well-trained chorus give an exhibition of real teamwork. If one chorus girl misses her step, out she goes, so they all become almost perfect in timing and execution. That, too, is part of the competitive spirit, and I imagine it wages strenuously even among those seeking positions in a first-rate chorus. I am not, however, exactly suggesting that a chorus girl would make a good coach for a Harvard football team, or for any other college.

Before discussing football back in 1907, 1908 and 1909, when I was playing on the Harvard team, I just want to say that I am an ardent football fan and have seen every Harvard-Yale game since 1905. I played in the transitional stage and on the first Harvard team coached by Percy Haughton, and used to catch passes myself when there were no rules to protect you from being knocked down before the ball reached you. I confess I like the modern open game better. Some old-timers sneeringly refer to it as a species of basketball, but as one who played on the Harvard basketball team I know that also is an aggressive and tough game and requires a fighting spirit. No, even with the passing game, football still maintains the same fundamental requirements to excel that it did thirty years ago—speed, strength, a fighting heart and a competitive spirit. What Theodore Roosevelt once said, "Don't flinch, don't foul, but hit the line hard," applies as well to the modernized game of football.

I don't want my readers to think that I believe a football player is a tin god or should be placed on a pedestal. It is true they get quite a lot of publicity and glory in their college days, and immediately afterwards, and receive numerous epistles from female fans, but after you have been married a number of years it does not count for much. Some one asked my wife what position I played on the Harvard football team. She thought a while and finally said, "Oh yes, I remember; he played Captain."

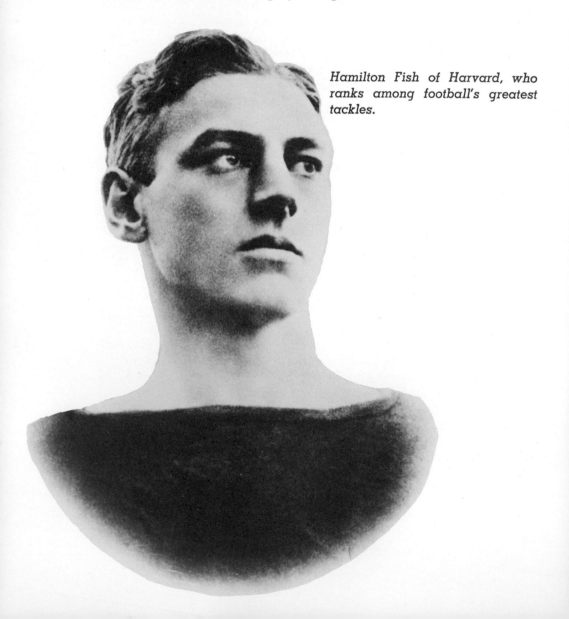

Hamilton Fish of Harvard, who ranks among football's greatest tackles.

Two of my most lasting hobbies for a quarter of a century have been Harvard football and the Republican party, but in recent years I unfortunately haven't been able to say much about either one. Harvard did put up a grand fight this year, however, and deserved at least a tie in the Yale game. I congratulate Dick Harlow, the Harvard coach, and predict a victory for my alma mater next year, but am unwilling to make any predictions about the prospects of the Republican party.

Teams may come and go, but it still takes only eleven players to constitute a team. Give me the best eleven players and with limited coaching I could win the American championship. I admit the need of a good passer, like the new Yale captain, Clinton Frank, and a pass receiver like Larry Kelley, but it also takes a line and two good tackles for offense and defense.

The Yale team of 1909 was a wonder team. In their freshman year they beat the varsity twice decisively. In 1908 we beat them by a field goal, and they returned the compliment in 1909 and beat us by two field goals. On that team were such famous players as Ted Coy, Steve Philbin, John Kilpatrick, Hobbs, Andrus, Cooney, Goebel, Lilley, Howe, Wheaton and Logan. What a galaxy of stars! Walter Camp was compelled to place six of them on his first All-America team and to leave off Goebel, a 215-pound guard who made his first All-America the year before. In 1911 Howe made Camp's first All-America at quarterback, totaling eight players on the Yale 1909 team who were selected between 1908 and 1910 on his All-America. Nowadays Yale qualifies a man like Kelley on the first All-America once in ten years.

Coy and Philbin are still known among Yale's greatest running backs, and Kilpatrick as one of three star ends—Hinkey, Shevlin and Kilpatrick. I once asked Tom Shevlin which he thought was the better end, himself or Kilpatrick, and he replied that Kilpatrick was because he coached him. I don't know whether John Kilpatrick will say he coached Kelley or not.

On the Harvard team, in 1908, Joe Nourse, the center, and I were selected on the All-America and John Cutler and Sam Hoar were on the second and third teams, respectively. In 1909, Wayland Minot, the Harvard fullback, and I were All-America, and Bob McKay, a great tackle, was on the second team. McKay and Bob Fisher at guard the following year made the first team, along with Percy Wendell, halfback, and Bud Smith, end, was on the second. I have always thought that the two most powerful teams that played against each other were the Harvard and Yale teams of

1909. Although we were defeated by field goals, we outgained Yale, three to one, but Coy's punting and drop kicking were extraordinary and turned the tide.

I am repeatedly asked how those teams would stack up against the modern teams. Assuming that Coy, Philbin or Howe were taught to pass and receive passes, it is my opinion that, with ends like Kilpatrick and Logan and a tremendously powerful, fast and experienced line averaging over 200 pounds from end to end, they would easily win the Eastern championship, and Rose Bowl game as well. In 1908, Harvard did not lose a game, and in 1909 lost only to Yale, and Yale neither tied nor lost a game. Teams may come and go, but it takes the same stuff to make the best players —speed, strength, headwork, experience and a fighting spirit. . . .

YALE'S 1909 TEAM AND HOWARD JONES

The Yale team of 1909 is ranked among the strongest in history. Coached by Howard Jones and led by Captain Edward H. (Ted) Coy, who is generally placed at fullback on all-time teams, Yale shut out all of its ten opponents and ran up 209 points. Six members of the eleven were on Camp's first all-America team in 1909 and three others on his second team. The six were JOHN REED KILPATRICK, *end; Coy, fullback; Carroll Cooney, center; Hamlin Andrus, guard; Henry Hobbs, tackle, and Steve Philbin, halfback. William Goebel, guard, who had been picked with Coy on the first team in 1908; Art Howe, quarterback, and Ted Lilley, tackle, were the other three. In an interview with the author in 1953, John Reed Kilpatrick said:*

IT MAY SEEM a strange thing to say of a team that scored more than 200 points and did not give up a single point in ten games, but we never played within forty percent of our potential. We didn't have to. We knew we could lick anybody and we loafed all the time, particularly in our early games.

Defensively, it was the best team I ever saw as a line. They hadn't worked out the refinements of line play in 1909 that are standard now. With the specialized coaching and techniques of today, that Yale team wouldn't have allowed anyone to gain an inch between the tackles.

No one could pass against us. We stopped their passes behind the line of scrimmage. We were on 'em before they had a chance to pass. The jump pass would have bothered us because we were charging so fast. Teams were using the pass very little those days.

Offensively, we had a simple attack. We used a straight buck, a cross buck, an end run, and we kicked. Howe, our quarter, could pass, but we didn't have to. We had so much power and so strong a line that we could make the yardage on the ground. Howard Jones was a fundamentalist. He was terrific in drilling us to block and tackle and achieving precision of execution. He was a very quiet, intense man. All of us liked him no matter how hard and long he worked us in his insistence on fundamentals, which are hardly the most exciting part of football.

Hobbs, Andrus and I had played together at Andover and we worked out our own signals, alongside of each other on the left side of the Yale line. On defense, the three of us would take the ball carrier on a straight buck and murder him. Cooney at center was terrific. He weighed 260 and could run like a deer. Goebel at the other guard was the strongest man I ever saw. Lilley was extremely fast, like the tackle of today, and a hard man to fool. He blocked three kicks in the Princeton game. Harry Vaughn, the other end, was only 165 pounds but a fine defensive player.

Coy was a terrific line smasher. He was a great athlete who could play any position and he was a remarkable kicker. He ran over people, hitting low, with his knees working like pistons and leaving a stream of tacklers behind him on the field. Philbin was a marvelous breakaway runner. Fred Daly was a particularly good interferer and Fred Murphy, who alternated with him at half, was a fine all-round back. Howe was a very heady quarterback. His job was to run the team and he seldom was called on to pass.

I was very fast in my freshman year and ran the hundred and high hurdles. I was big and strong, too, at 195, and I could run away from almost anyone. In my sophomore year I was hurt going down under a kick against Washington and Jefferson. I was too fast in getting down and while waiting for the receiver to catch the punt I was hit by a blocker and my knee was damaged. I had possibly the first cartilage operation in football late in 1908, and my speed was never the same again.

Harvard was by far our toughest opponent. It had fine personnel, particularly in Ham Fish, Bob Fisher and the Withingtons, Paul and Lothrop, in the line, and Percy Haughton, their new coach, was one of the first strategists and a driver on fundamentals. He was about the first to scout opposing teams.

We had trouble running against their line. Coy had been operated on before the season started for appendicitis and wasn't himself, though he was still tough enough to stop. Also Harry Vaughn, our other end, was hurt and Lilley was knocked out on the kick-off, and we had no good subs of experience. So we played a kicking and waiting game, and won, 8–0, Coy booting two field goals. It was Harvard's only defeat of the year.

Haughton used the mouse trap against us, a delayed play straight through our right tackle, and it gained against us. I took it on myself to leave my position at left end (we had no instructions from the bench) and played defensive back behind our right tackle, and we stopped the trap. The Harvard quarter was puzzled and looked around to see who had stopped the play. I did it a second time and he saw me. The third time I turned back and ran to left end before the play started. Frothingham or Leslie circled around my end from halfback. I was going so fast I went right past his interference and hit the carrier the hardest I ever hit anyone in my life for a 22-yard loss.

I believe that I was the first player to use the overhand (spiral) pass. At Andover in 1906 I was a halfback and I was catching punts in practice one day with Upton Favorite, who went from Andover to Pennsylvania. We would throw the ball back to the kicker or punt it back. This day Upton threw the ball overhand and it spiraled.

I said, "What did you do?" and he said, "I don't know." We kept practicing it to find out what he did—we did this only in throwing the ball back to the punter and not in a forward passing drill. Finally we got it.

The next year, 1907, as Yale freshman captain, I worked out the overhand pass as a forward passing play. The rule that year was that a pass going out of bound was like a kick out of bounds: the ball went to the opponent there. So when in the opponent's territory I passed into "coffin corner."

In the Princeton game we were on their 45-yard line and I went back for a fake placement kick. Intead of kicking, I passed to Tony Haines. Tony had been my teammate at Andover. He went all the way down to the goal post and no one covered him. I faked the kick, ran out a bit and threw to Tony for a touchdown.

I believe that was the first touchdown ever scored on an over-hand forward pass. Some one else may have stumbled on the over-hand pass before this, but I doubt it.

The following was written by HOWARD JONES *in 1929, when he was head coach at the University of Southern California.*

From time to time discussion arises as to what was the greatest football team of all gridiron history. Because it is physically impossible for any one man to see all of the great teams of the United States, even in one season, the statement of any coach or critic in this matter is naturally open to dispute.

However, I wish to go on record as casting my vote for the Yale University team of 1909. As far as I can find out, this team had a more impressive record than any eleven prior to or since that time.

No team ever had possession of the ball inside Yale's 28-yard line that season. There was no score of any kind, not even a drop kick or field goal. None of Yale's opponents even seriously threatened the Eli goal. The list of teams played that year included Syracuse, Holy Cross, Colgate, Amherst, Army, Princeton and Harvard. . . .

Of course, the forward pass had only just come into use at that time. Had it been more generally employed, Yale's defensive record might not have been so sensational. The team, in my estimation, was stronger defensively than it was offensively.

There were seven all-America players on this 1909 team and six of them were named that year. Carroll Cooney played center. He could toss the hammer 150 feet and although not the type of a Jeff Cravath covered a lot of ground in the line. With less emphasis on passing, it was not necessary for him to come out of the line on defense as much as is now required of pivot men. Dutch Goebel and Ham Andrus, both 210 pounds, were the all-America guards. The former was related to the famous Goebel of Kentucky. He was Eastern intercollegiate heavyweight wrestling king. Both were tremendously strong men. Heinie Hobbs, 208 pounds, and Ted Lilley, 185 pounds, played the tackle positions. Hobbs was aggressive to the nth degree, was very versatile, knew how to use his hands and was accordingly difficult to handle. He was built much like Jesse Hibbs of the present Southern California team. Lilley was son of the governor of Connecticut. He was tremendously fast and blocked three punts in the Princeton game that year, won by Yale, 17 to 0.

Johnny Kilpatrick, 195, and Harry Vaughn, 165, were the ends. The former was reputed to be the strongest man in Yale. He was a sprinter and high hurdler and a wonderful all-around athlete. An injured knee prevented him from doing much in track athletics. Vaughn, although very light, was a fine defensive player.

Ted Coy, captain and fullback, with 193 pounds of grit and fight, was probably the outstanding star of the team. He was a long kicker, being good for 60 yards consistently. He drop-kicked with phenomenal success despite the fact that he used his instep rather than toe. He could high jump over six feet. Coy was naturally all-American, one of the greatest backs that ever lived.

The seventh all-American was Steve Philbin, 168-pound halfback, who was a wonderful broken-field runner. Art Howe, 155, performed at quarterback and made a capable field general. In those days the quarterback did little other than handle the ball from center. Fred Daly, 170, and Fred Murphy, same weight, alternated at the other halfback position.

Of course, Walter Camp picked most of his all-Americans from Eastern teams in those days, but at that time Western football had hardly started. Michigan was probably the best known of the so-called Western teams. Yost had a great team with Heston, Snow and others back in 1902, '03, '04 and '05, but I doubt if those teams had a defensive record equal to Yale's in 1909 (considering the opposition met).

[Ed. note: Michigan from 1901 through 1905 gave up 42 points —none in 1901 and 2 in 1905.]

When Coy died of pneumonia in 1935 at the age of 47, LOTHROP WITHINGTON, *Harvard captain in 1910, who played against Coy in 1908 and 1909, was quoted by George Carens in* The Boston Transcript *as follows:*

"Whenever the name of Ted Coy is mentioned in connection with football, immediately the vision arises of extreme power. His entire football career consisted of a glorious display of this unusual, natural power. . . . The Yale team he captained was both individually and collectively the most powerful college team I have ever had the good fortune to play against or see in action. In spite of Coy's great strength and intensive competitive instinct, he had an exceedingly good nature and sense of fair play. . . . He will always remain one of football's immortals."

WALTER CAMP, *in picking Coy for his all-time all-America team in 1910, said:*

"Coy of Yale has the most remarkable combination of qualities that have been gathered together in any player on the gridiron. Stripping close to 193 pounds, a remarkably fast runner, and with high-knee action, it was almost impossible to stop him from in front when he had acquired full headway. He had sufficient speed to make his runs from kick formation a very difficult propo-

Overleaf *Steve Philbin of Yale going through Harvard's left tackle, 1907. Score: Yale 12, Harvard 0.*

sition for opponents, whereas when he received the kick and ran it back there was no telling how far he would go.

"In Harvard and Princeton games in his sophomore and junior years it became dangerous for opponents to kick the ball, for Coy, if he had a fair start, would as likely as not run it back the whole length of the kick. As a punter he had tremendous power and with this he combined great accuracy and distance in drop-kicks. . . . As a tackler and defensive player among men of his weight and strength he was exceptional, while his all-round knowledge of the game was such that he could play at end as readily as at full-back. . . ."

Jones coached at Southern California from 1925 until his death of a heart attack on July 27, 1941. His Trojan teams won 121 games, lost 38 and tied 13. Five times they played in the Rose Bowl and won every time, an achievement matched by no other coach. The author wrote in The New York Times *on November 24, 1931:*

Ten years ago a Hawkeye team from Iowa went up against a Notre Dame eleven that had won twenty-two consecutive games. On that Notre Dame team, coached by Knute Rockne, were Eddie Anderson, Paul Castner, Roger Kiley, Harry Mehre, Tom Lieb, Chet Wynne, Glenn Carberry and Johnny Mohardt, all listed on Notre Dame's scroll of honor.

Also playing on the Notre Dame team as one of the best guards of the season was Heartley (Hunk) Anderson. The coach of the Hawkeyes was Howard Jones, and in that game Notre Dame's long winning streak was brought to an end by the score of 10–7, the only defeat suffered by the Ramblers in forty successive games beginning with the last two of 1918.

A few weeks ago a Notre Dame team coached by Heartley Anderson that had gone undefeated in twenty-six consecutive games had its winning streak broken, and again it was an eleven directed by the same Howard Jones that snapped the string, a string that had started after Southern California had vanquished the Ramblers in the last game of 1928.

It is not to be wondered then if Notre Dame men look upon Howard Harding Jones as something of a super coach, a master mind who alone has been able consistently to shatter their ambitions for national dominion, a nemesis whose predilection is for ending their all-conquering rampages.

A year ago the two most celebrated football coaches in the country were Rockne and Glenn Warner of Stanford. When the Wizard of South Bend passed on, Warner was left as the dominating figure in the game, with his wingback formations in vogue at almost every major college save those where the many disciples of Rockne were teaching the Notre Dame shift.

But out on the Pacific Coast, the nursery of great football teams, this categorical reduction of winning football to the systems of two men was not accepted as it has been in other sections of the country. How could it have been when down in Los Angeles there was another coach, with ideas of his own, whose teams were defeating both Stanford and California and annually giving Notre Dame a terrific battle with the exception of 1930?

Howard Jones has probably been the most under-recognized coach, from a national standpoint, the game has had in many years. When one looks back upon his record, takes into consideration the fact that he has been coaching for twenty-four years and the added fact that he played and coached with distinction at Yale, it seems incomprehensible that he should have received so little attention as has been accorded him.

Geographical propinquity has a large bearing on the publicity given to a football coach, but Stanford is 3,000 miles from New York and yet Warner has been publicized more in the Eastern press than has any coach on the Atlantic seaboard.

In the seven years that Jones has been at Southern California, his teams won or tied for the Pacific Coast Conference championship four times, finished second twice and third once—this in his first year at Los Angeles. They have won 61 games to date, tied 2 and lost 10, four of the ten being lost to Notre Dame, and in four instances the defeat was inflicted by a margin of a point after touchdown.

In the last four years Stanford has scored only 12 points against the Trojans, being shut out three times, and in six games California has scored only 15 points, winning by 15–7 from Southern California in 1929 after a scoreless tie in 1928. What other team, with the exception of Notre Dame, can point to as good a record as this, taking the character of the opposition into consideration?

Long before he went to the Pacific Coast Jones had shown his ability as a coach. After graduating from Yale, where he played end on the same teams with his illustrious brother, Tad, who was all-America quarterback in 1907, Howard Jones coached at Syracuse in 1908 and then came back to Yale. His 1909 Eli eleven was one of the greatest defensive combinations ever to step upon a gridiron, worthy of comparison with the famous Michigan point-a-minute teams of a few years before. This Yale team won all of its ten games and not one of its opponents ever had the ball inside the Elis' 28-yard line.

Jones coached four years at Yale, not all of them consecutively, and also served at Ohio State, Duke and Iowa before going to Southern California. His 1921 team at Iowa won the Big Ten championship, the first time the Hawkeyes had taken the title since 1900, and his 1922 team defeated his brother Tad's Yale eleven, 6–0. Aubrey Devine, who is Jones' chief scout; Fred (Duke) Slater, Gordon Locke and Leland Parkins were among the famous players developed by Jones at Iowa.

Much is printed and heard of the personal rivalry between Jones and Warner on the Coast. That rivalry goes back to 1908, when the former was at Syracuse and the Stanford Sachem was coaching the Carlisle Indians. Syracuse and Carlisle met that year and the story is that Jones understood, when the game was arranged, that twenty-minute halves were to be played. Warner, however, said that he knew of no such understanding when the teams came to the field, and so Syracuse had to play thirty-five-minute halves. The rivalry has been going on ever since, though it is not so personal as some of the accounts make out. At least, the coaches always shake hands after the meetings between their teams.

For all of his success, Howard Jones has never had a system named after him, as has Warner and as did Rockne. And yet his is one of the most ingenious and progressive minds in the game. The attack employed by his team against Notre Dame is one of the most complex in the history of the game, entirely individual to Southern California and fabricated by Jones since the close of the 1930 season. While it embraces features of both the Notre Dame and Stanford systems, utilizing the shift, the single and double wing formations, both the balanced and unbalanced lines and spinners, reverses and other plays indigenous to South Bend and Palo Alto, the Trojans' offense has no parallel in the multiple alignments into which Jones deploys his men.

It is the kaleidoscopic change in the pattern of his offense, screening the direction and nature of the thrust, to the confusion of the defense, that makes his attack so difficult to stop, plus the sound principles of line play inculcated and the tremendous power generated by heavy, mercury-footed backs who run with a stark fury that is almost appalling.

It was after his team had suffered its humiliating 27–0 defeat at the hands of Notre Dame last year that Jones decided to experiment anew with his offense, and it was only one of several times during his career that he had shown the same progressiveness in scrapping the old and seeking something better.

After his first two years on the Coast, during which he lost both times to Stanford, Jones changed his defense to smash the wing-back attack, playing his ends in close in a six-man line and sending them in fast to mess up the slow-forming plays behind the line of scrimmage, and also adding to his own offense until it put Warner's "57 varieties" in the shade. The result has been that Stanford has never beaten Southern California since.

Back in 1913, too, Jones showed his ingenuity in devising an offense suited to the needs of the occasion. After serving at Ohio State he went back to Yale in 1913 to find that the situation had changed radically from what it had been in 1909. Under Percy Haughton and with such stars as Brickley, Hardwick and Mahan, Harvard had succeeded to Yale's place at the top of the pack, and the Elis were even finding it difficult to defeat small college teams.

When Maine held Yale to a scoreless tie at the start of the 1913 season, Jones decided that his material was not powerful enough to use the attack it was employing and boldly gambled on changing to a different type of offense. In this new attack, from a balanced line, he spaced his tackles out from the guards, put his ends opposite the defensive ends, his halfbacks four yards back of the offensive tackles, the quarterback behind center and the fullback eight yards back of center. With this new attack, Yale played Princeton to a 3–3 tie and lost to Harvard only through the uncanny kicking skill of Brickley, who made five drop kicks in the game.

Jones is the quiet type of coach who says little and lets his team do his talking for him. Reticent by nature, he finds coaching football teams too taxing a work to permit him to be distracted by anything else and it is only when stung by unjust or unfair criticism that he allows himself the indulgence of a reply. There is one subject, however, on which he has no hesitation in expressing himelf and that is "overemphasis" in football.

"Those who say players spend too much time on football when they should be studying," he remarked recently, "should remember that a student who lets the game come between himself and an education wouldn't study anyway. As far as overemphasis goes, when most teams of today get through practice in the afternoon, they are through. On the other hand, when Tad and I played at Yale, we often were called to the gymnasium at night to run signals."

PERCY HAUGHTON AND
HARVARD'S GOLDEN ERA

Percy Haughton ranks with Stagg, Warner, Rockne, Zuppke, et al among the giants of college football coaching. He brought to Harvard its "Golden Era," from 1908 to 1916. Shut out by Yale for six successive years prior to his taking command in 1908, Harvard lost to its ancient foe only twice during Haughton's tenure, by 8–0 in 1909 and 6–3 in 1916 and inflicted two of the Elis' most crushing defeats in the history of this rivalry—36–0 in 1914 and 41–0 in 1915.

Haughton was an aristocrat, stern of mein, brusque of speech, curt at best to sports reporters on the field and an iron disciplinarian whose men feared, even hated him, in some instances before they got to know him. His fellow coaches respected him as one of the most knowing and ablest men in the profession, a great organizer, a perfectionist in drilling his team and an innovator who introduced much that was new.

His was a new type of offense, with its deception, faking and clever ball handling. He gave Harvard its system of line play. He used the mouse trap as it is run today, if he did not originate it. He came up with a five-man line to stop the lateral passing attack of Frank Hinkey's Yale team, and he was one of the first to emphasize a winning psychology. Also, he was one of those who fought for the elimination of restrictions on the forward pass in the early years when others sought to put more curbs on it, if not do away with it.

EDDIE MAHAN was one of the most celebrated of the galaxy of super-stars developed by Haughton, if not the best back in Harvard history. Tack Hardwick, Charley Brickley, Percy Wendell, Stan Pennock, Mal Logan, Wally Trumbull, Ham Fish, and Sam Felton were others. Mahan, who was captain of the 1915 team, wrote the following letter to the author in 1951.

216

H AUGHTON WAS BORN an aristocrat, yet he could be very rough. He had the qualities that are necessary for a top-flight executive, but I believe his heart was always in sports. He had been a fine athlete and had a highly developed sense of timing. He was good at any game in which a ball was used. He was a great punter, played baseball, tennis, golf and billiards and was national amateur racquets champion. He was a great baseball fan and attended most of the big-league games at home. He was a driver and had a caustic tongue which lashed out at all alike, yet he had a keen sense of humor. He was about six feet two and had the physique of a well trained athlete.

During the first six weeks of the season he was a tyrant and drove, cursed and manhandled players. After this period of rugged work was over he would turn around and become very affable and seem to be everyone's best friend. He was an excellent teacher and never wasted words. He was able to make men play when they were very tired. He would emphasize this point and by his driving methods he would prove to you that you still could play 20 percent better than you thought you could when you were tired. Of course this was under rules when substitutions were restricted. His plan for every game was to wear the other fellow down for three quarters and then win in the last quarter.

In this scheme of play the kick was the basis of play. In our own territory we would kick on first or second down and wait for the breaks. His lines on defense used their hands in charging. The initial charge was with the hands on the head and face of the opponent, thus slowing up his charge. Constant pressure on the opponent's kicker was a must with him. Many breaks were forced by rushing the kicker and either blocking the kick or forcing him to get away a bad kick.

When we received the ball within scoring distance, inside the forty-yard line, then was the time to put on an offensive charge. He used a box formation with an unbalanced line, four linemen on the long side of the center and two on the short side. Our line played straight ahead. The line charged as a cohesive wedge.

In the box formation the quarterback was under center, but down low. He ran almost half his plays from kick formation and the quarterback could be under center or back four yards. Most of the plays from box formation could be run from kick formation without change of assignments.

Haughton was quick to accept the forward pass but used it

more as a means to an end, to help the running attack by keeping the defensive backs from coming up fast. He would try for field goals and take three points rather than gamble for six, especially early in the game. Ground was much harder to gain before the First World War because the defensive play was much better than it is today, and also the forward pass was much restricted and incompleted passes were penalized.

A few players hated Haughton but a big majority liked and respected him. Personally, I hated him at first but got to like him and found him a good friend.

LOTHROP WITHINGTON, *who was captain of the Harvard team in 1910 and a member of Haughton's coaching staff, said in a letter to the author in 1952.*

Percy D. Haughton was a member of the Harvard Class of 1899, which enjoyed the distinction of going through four years of college unbeaten by Yale in football. Haughton played two years as a tackle, one as fullback. In all three years of varsity football he enjoyed unusual success as the team's outstanding punter. In his senior year in the fall of 1898 at New Haven he put on an exhibition of punting that directly led to a 17–0 Harvard victory. He was also an outstanding and versatile baseball player, captaining the nine in his senior year.

After graduation he tried his hand at coaching at Cornell, where he showed unusual drive and resourcefulness.

In the fall of 1907, Francis Burr, captain-elect of the Harvard team, who knew Haughton, insisted upon his appointment as head coach and in the fall of 1908 the so-called Haughton system was installed and carried on until 1917, when the First World War intervened. In that period Harvard won 71 games, lost 7 and tied 5. It was truly the Golden Era of Harvard football. It cannot be said this was because of inferior competition, as Camp was still a power at Yale, Roper at Princeton, Sharp was at his best at Cornell and among opponents were outstanding Dartmouth teams coached by Cavanaugh, Brown teams under Robinson, Roper's Princeton teams, Army, Navy, Michigan, Cornell and Carisle, with Warner coaching and Thorpe playing.

What then, were the oustanding things that Haughton brought to Harvard which created this era of success?

First of all, Haughton was a student of the game. He never hesitated to take what was good from other systems, styles of play or ideas. He recognized the greatness of Camp and the Yale system based on sound fundamentals and superior line play. He did not hesitate to borrow deception from Warner, discipline from the Army, power of the Pennsylvania "guards back," or the passing skills displayed by any opponent.

Coming to Cambridge in the fall of 1908, he installed the so-called "wheel shift" with an unbalanced line to lead a tandem formation attack, which later developed into a single wing attack with unbalanced line, and in his later years a running kick formation with Eddie Mahan as his triple threat that was almost unstoppable, particularly with the development of the hidden ball and Statue of Liberty plays, which were coupled with what is now referred to as mouse-trapping the opposing linemen. These plays were known in those days as "psychologicals," and strange to say the first versions were taken from Groton School plays designed by Dr. Ayrault, who so successfully coached that school for some years.

In his first years at Harvard, Haughton was faced with a dearth of backfield material and with the necessity of making ten yards in three downs, as was then the case. He turned to the development of the kicking game, reserving his offense for the breaks which he felt sure were to come with a perfected kicking game, combined with an outstanding defense.

To this end, he, himself an expert punter, developed an offensive kicking attack, protection for the kicker, expert placing of the kick, good down-the-field coverage and a highly developed system of blocking to permit the returning of the opponent's kicks.

The necessary defensive efficiency came with (1) the obtaining of "Pot" Graves, the famous Army lineman and coach, who knew the Yale system of line play, which was at that time far ahead of any other in the country, as well as knew a great many Army tactics developed by him both as player and coach; (2) the development of at least five (later more) different defenses which coordinated line and backfield deployment commonly used by every team today. So far as the writer knows, Haughton was the first to use a complete set of defensive signals, given by the center both by numbers and by sign, so as to be known to both those in earshot and out, as, for instance, wing halfbacks and the safety man.

Once the break in the game came, Haughton tried either power or surprise, and if these failed he resorted to the drop kick. Kennard's drop kick won the first Harvard-Yale game for a Haughton-coached team, 4–0. Brickley won many Princeton, Dartmouth and Yale games with his educated toe, climaxing his effort with five field goals in the Harvard-Yale game of 1913. Mahan also excelled in the drop kick, though his all-around triple-threat excellence, with the inception of four downs instead of three, and the perfection of the forward pass made these points seem trivial.

Haughton first demolished the prevailing idea that an end should always follow around in back of the play as a safety man. Both Harvard ends were sent through ahead of the runner from the day Haughton took over.

In the early days of the Haughton regime the attack from close formation was made effective by carefully devised and painstakingly taught deception on the part of the quarterback. Most plays went through the quarterback, who stood as in the T formation close to the center but, unlike the T, crouched down for more sure handling of the ball and concealment.

As the offense developed with the elimination of restrictions on the forward pass, and the addition of an extra down, the Harvard quarterback was given freedom to take the ball from center or call for a direct pass, and as time went on engaged with the backs in hidden-ball faking that opened an entirely new type of offense, quick line openings being combined with the power plays.

Haughton never used the huddle. He always employed a starting signal varied so as to fall on the second, third or fourth number of the second series of four numbers called by the quarterback. Haughton used a double series of four numbers, with a break of two beats between the two, always called by the quarterback in a time cadence that had the regularity of a metronome, which, indeed, was employed in teaching quarterbacks. Haughton believed the huddle led to the blind calling of plays and preferred the careful selection of a play by the quarterback after he had called his formation, looked over the other team's defense and found a weakness to play to. His system of numbers was always simple and each number meant a designated point of attack—even numbers to the long side, odd to the short. The holes were 1 and 2 on either side of the center, increasing by one for each position removed from the center. So simple yet complete were his signals that today a Haughton team would remember and respond if a team of old grads were assembled.

Until Haughton had Mahan to kick, run or pass, and Hardwick to interfere, receive or to make a great down-the-field tackle, the Harvard running attack was based mainly upon a powerful drive, either inside or outside tackle (Yale and Princeton called it the "offside tackle play," it came so fast, with the whole team off on a given starting signal), and a power play over the defensive guard, who was drawn away from the hole by a deceptive fake to the No. 1 back (as the first man in the tandem was called). Percy Wendell's fame came from this play, which today would still be good for 4-5 yards if the time could be given to the proper offensive line play which makes it effective.

Haughton's greatest contribution to the modern game of football, however, came with his struggle with Walter Camp for control of the Rules Committee. In the winter of 1909–1910, after Cadet Byrne was killed in the Army game and Wilson, a Navy player, also died as a result of an injury received in a game, there was a great clamor for a reform or radical change from the mass play then prevailing.

The forward pass was little used. It had to be thrown five yards right or left and five yards back of the place the ball was put in play, and, if incomplete, called for a 15-yard penalty. With only three downs to make ten yards, it was small wonder that it was little used. Camp, who incidentally had sponsored the forward pass when it was first permitted in 1906, urged its elimination and the introduction of steps to encourage end runs. Haughton, after experimenting in spring practice, became convinced that defensive steps would make end runs nothing but beautiful lateral sprints and championed the retention of the forward pass and the liberalization of the rules relating to its use.

A bitter fight ensued in which Haughton, E. K. Hall and Bill Roper finally prevailed over Camp and his supporters, and this ended Walter Camp's supremacy on the Rules Committee, which he had ably dominated for many years. From this revolt came noteworthy developments—the elimination of restrictions on the pass, the addition of a down and the rigid protection of the receiver, who hitherto had been a fair target for any defensive man, both before the pass was made and while in flight. It also brought a resumption of the Harvard-Princeton series, which had been interrupted since 1896.

Haughton also sponsored the right to return a player removed from the game at the beginning of a succeeding quarter. Theretofore a player removed was out for the rest of the game, and there were halves, not quarters. The writer believes this rule sound and that if used today it would bring back some of the lost thrill that disappeared with endless substitutions leaving the spectator lost in

the maze of a program rather than intrigued with the battle between recognized gladiators.

After World War I Haughton retired from Harvard football but
was finally induced by Columbia to undertake the renaissance of
football at that institution after it had been discontinued for many
years. He continued at Columbia until his death in the middle of
the 1924 season. For a second time he assembled around him at
Columbia an experienced and fundamentally sound coaching staff.
He brought Dr. Paul Withington from Honolulu not only as his
medical adviser but as head line coach, and Douglas Lawson, an
old Harvard tackle, and Charles Crowley, an old Harvard and Notre
Dame star, as other coaches. Starting from scratch, he soon had
Columbia a worthy opponent for Pennsylvania and Cornell, which
at that time was rolling in high under the able direction of Dobie,
who had perfected the Glenn Warner power plays, with linemen
coming out of the line to lead the interference.

Men who have risen to coaching heights have asked what was
the "Haughton System." It is today somewhat hard to explain that
in 1907 coaching was mostly a one-man job. Except for Yale, where
there were many who thoroughly understood and could teach line,
backfield or end play, good coaches were few and hard to get.
Haughton established the idea of a complete coaching staff—a
backfield, a line and an end coach, all coordinated under the head
coach, with specialists for expert instruction in kicking and passing,
and a scouting system that covered each opponent.

The military precision and discipline which Haughton established in his first years, with Majors Daly and Graves as his backfield and line coaches, were never relaxed throughout his regime.
Each season was regarded as a race against time, each minute of
practice was carefully allotted to individual offensive and defensive
instruction, followed by team evolutions and then scrimmage with
the jayvees or freshmen.

Each season was divided into periods—the first devoted to general instruction of groups in fundamentals and conditioning, the
next to what was called "Fight Week," in which through bitter
scrimmaging Team A backs, behind Team B line, fought Team B
backs behind Team A line. From this week of relentless combat the
wheat was separated from the straw and there followed the selection of "The Varsity" and the moulding of a unit which was taught
to play with a spirit, a bond of sympathy and a growing belief in
themselves as invincible for the final big games.

Haughton, after his first two years, selected and developed his
assistants from his own pupils. His pupils often moved on to coach-

ing jobs of their own, as, for instance, Daly to the Army, Paul Withington to Wisconsin and Columbia, Campbell to North Carolina, Crowley to Columbia, Lawson to Williams and Columbia and Leary, Fisher and Casey as succeeding Harvard head coaches.

The greatest of the Haughton teams was undoubtedly the 1914 team with Mahan, Brickley, Bradlee, Franke, Logan and Watson as the backfield greats, and Hardwick, the Coolidges—Jeff and Charles—as ends, and Pennock, Trumbull, Parsons, Weston, F. B. Withington and Wallace as linemen. This team lost none and could score even with one or more of the stars on the injured list. The peerless Eddie Mahan established beyond question the value of the running pass that left the wing halfback between the deep sea and the devil. In the 1914 Yale game Harvard used a five-man-line defense against Hinkey's lateral pass attack. This was the first five-man-line defense ever used, the writer believes.

However, the outstanding performance of Haughton was the undefeated season of his first Harvard team in 1908. This team had but one star (Ham Fish). Otherwise it was a bunch of men doing two jobs, an offensive halfback played a defensive end, an offensive end played safety man on defense, and one man was first substitute center, guard and tackle. Kennard, a specialist, was inserted to kick the field goal against Yale, and Sprague was inserted to kick from behind his goal line sixty yards to end Yale's gallant second-half rally.

Haughton's greatest disappointment was the 1909 Harvard-Yale game. Ted Coy's great eleven was held to two first downs in the game, but Harvard fumbles of Coy's high punts, and two deep kicks following these fumbles turned the tide. The battle of the two great lines has seldom been equalled, with Yale men General Kilpatrick, Hobbs, Andrus, Cooney, Goebel, Lilley and Savage facing Browne, Fish, Fisher, the Withington brothers, McKay and Bud Smith for Harvard. There are many who still argue that there were never two better college lines facing each other.

Percy Wendell was without question the greatest line breaker of Haughton's regime. Mahan, Brickley and Felton excelled in kicking, and Bud Smith and Hardwick undoubtedly were the outstanding ends. The Haughton quarterbacks, while never outstanding physical specimens, were always clever and brainy. Wigglesworth, Gardner, Logan and Watson carried a reputation for sound strategy coupled with a minimum of errors.

Perhaps one of the most thrilling games of the Haughton regime was the Harvard-Penn State 13–13 tie in 1914. Until the closing minutes of the game it looked as if Harvard would be beaten, 13–6,

Overleaf   *Harvard's golden 1914 champions.*

but, with only minutes to go, Wilcox, a fast quarter-miler, was inserted as a halfback with instructions to use what was referred to as the "99" play, which consisted of a fake buck and a lateral outside of the fast-charging Penn State end. Wilcox ran sixty yards for a touchdown and my brother, Ted Withington, kicked the goal from a very difficult angle, as everybody in the stands suffered from heart failure.

I did not see the Cornell game of 1915 (Harvard's only loss in four years) as I had been sent to scout Yale, but from the reports I received I concluded that the Cornell team as it played on the afternoon it met Harvard was one of the most rugged and powerful that Harvard faced during the entire Haughton regime. It was the only team that made Eddie Mahan look bad and although Barrett, Cornell's outstanding back and captain, was injured early in the game when he tackled Mahan, Fritz Shiverick stepped in and performed as an all-American.

With regard to Haughton's personality, I should perhaps add that except in later years Percy always kept himself quite aloof from any intimacy with the players during the football season. He believed it was necessary to maintain a military discipline and that the slightest let-down would result in a break-down of discipline. He required rigid adherence to his time schedule, both by his coaches and players, and at coaches meetings, which were held in the evening at least once a week, usually at the outset of the week, every coach had to pay strict attention or he would be called to order.

Percy insisted that when a coach was expressing his ideas there should be a complete understanding of the premises before the matter was discussed, as he found all too often that his coaches were not discussing the same situation because of a faulty understanding of the premises. Different colored dominoes were always present at every coaches' meeting in order that the offensive and defensive formations might be set up for all to see and understand. Percy had an uncanny knack of making each coach, and, indeed, toward the end of the season every player, believe that Percy had a particular regard for that person's contribution, and as a result each of the coaches worked his head off for him, contributing his own ideas without the slightest desire for public recognition or credit.

MUSINGS OF AN OLD GRAD

LEVERETT SALTONSTALL, *Governor of Massachusetts and then United States Senator, was a member of the Class of 1914 at Harvard. He was an end on the varsity second team in 1911. In 1915 he coached the Harvard freshman. He was also an oarsman and was captain and bowman on the 1914 junior varsity eight that won the Grand Challenge Cup in the Henley Royal Regatta in England. From the Harvard-Yale program of 1939.*

MY FIRST CONTACT with Harvard football was established right here on Soldiers Field 38 years ago this Saturday. As a very skinny lad of nine, I was permitted by the older members of the family to occupy a 12-inch stretch on the top row of the old wooden stands of that pre-Stadium era. Memory isn't too perfect after the lapse of years, but I have an idea that some member of the party backed out at the last moment, and that the family decided to take little "Levvie" rather than let that precious ticket go to waste.

The date was November 23, 1901. The event was the annual Harvard-Yale game, and the incidents of that memorable day that impressed themselves on the mind of a nine-year-old boy were, in the order of their importance:

1. John the Orangeman, the famous Harvard mascot, parading around the field and selling oranges.

2. The big Harvard flag, which floated in the breeze directly above my head.

3. One of the Yale linemen pushing John the Orangeman when a play came close to the sidelines; and then, when the crowd shouted at him, blowing on his hands and then shaking with John.

4. The score of that game, which was Harvard 22, Yale 0.

Years later I realized that I had sat in on an epochal event in Harvard football. For that was the worst defeat Yale had ever suffered at the hands of Harvard up to that time and it remains the third highest score in Harvard history against Yale [up to 1939]. It was the first time Harvard had beaten Yale on Soldiers Field, which

Major Henry Lee Higginson had presented to the university for its athletic teams a few years earlier.

We were to wait twelve years, or until my senior year in college, before Harvard was to celebrate another Yale victory at home, and fourteen years before Harvard was to score another touchdown against Yale on Soldiers Field.

The Harvard hero that day was "Dave" Campbell, the great captain and end, whose smashing tackles on the Yale runners were still the subject of discussion among the coaches when I was playing football years later. In that day before programs and numbered players, most of the Harvard giants looked alike to a nine-year-old, but I can remember that Carl Marshall was the quarterback and kicked a field goal, and that with him in the backfield were Bob Kernan, Albert Ristine and Tom Graydon. "Pete" Bowditch was the other end; the tackles were the great Crawford Blagden and Oliver Cutts; the guards were William Lee and Charles Barnard, and the center, Elbridge Greene. The substitutes? There were none. That was an "iron man" team, playing through two 35-minute halves without relief.

From that day to this I've been either on the sidelines or in the stands for the opening kick-off of almost every Harvard-Yale game, and I'm perfectly willing to admit that in the course of a year there is no moment more spine-tingling than that which precedes the first play of that game. Harvard and Yale may be drubbed by every team they meet, including colleges that were in the high-school class a generation ago, but on the day of the big game many of us are thinking not so much of the prowess of the teams we are watching as we are of the legends of more than 60 years of keen intercollegiate rivalry.

It has been my good fortune to see many of these legends in the making, and to have known some of the most legendary of the heroes. The first time I went to New Haven was in 1908, the opening of the Haughton era, and the family was excited over the prospect that our cousin, George West, might at least earn his coveted "H." For three years he had been promising varsity material, but in each year he had broken a collarbone. Yet he survived injury in 1908, and I was a proud boy when he trotted out on the field to take his place in the Harvard line to protect the 4–0 lead which Vic Kennard's goal had produced. Kennard was the hero, but my most vivid memory is of "Dutchy" Ver Weibe's smashes through the Yale line.

I saw the great Ted Coy beat us almost single-handed in the

Stadium in 1909. I recall our bitter disappointment in my own first year in college, when underrated Yale teams held two good Haughton teams to scoreless ties. In my freshman year I was a substitute at tackle for Tudor Gardiner, later to be governor of Maine. As a sophomore the best I could do was to make the second team, playing as an end. Dropping back to do the kicking, I was up against the redoubtable Sam Felton in punting duels in our weekday scrimmage with the varsity, and they always ended the same way, with me kicking from behind my own goal line. Tom Hardwick (Tack's older brother, now dead) was the captain of the seconds that year, and our astute quarterback was Bill Blake, now the head of the Veterans Bureau in Boston. Doug Lawson was a teammate. Many years later, when I was chairman of the Community Fund campaign in Boston, Doug and Bill were two of my most loyal associates.

As a junior I quit football to concentrate on rowing, and to be honest, rowing was far more attractive.

But I was not quite through with Harvard football. In my first year in law school I was backfield coach of the freshmen under Dr. Paul Withington, and the next year I was head coach of freshmen. Eddie Casey was one of my protégés. I only succeeded in having him hurt his shoulder when tackling the dummy as I had directed. Unable to tackle any more, he developed into a wizard at putting a man out of play by throwing his body across his path, rather than by tackling. That maneuver was known as "Indianizing." To the end of his football career, Eddie Casey found "Indianizing" was even more effective than tackling, and less wearing on the human frame. Babe Felton, Hank Flower, Morris Phinney, George Batchelder and Rufe Bond were other freshmen who survived my course of instruction and went on to win glory as varsity players.

That season of 1915 was memorable, however, not for what the freshmen did, but for what Eddie Mahan's varsity did to Yale in the final game. That was the 41 to 0 game, the worst defeat Yale ever suffered, and I am inclined to believe that the Eddie Mahan of that November afternoon was the greatest football player I ever saw in action.

These are the musings of an "Old Grad" whose own athletic days, except for occasional tree chopping or an anniversary spin on the river, are over. But we live again the days of our youth as we watch our own boys play the game we loved, which taught us so much in quick thinking, discipline, and self-restraint, and provided us with so many lasting friendships. One of my boys has been on the second freshman squad this year, and I know that he has enjoyed the game under Skip Stahley, and if he wants to try his luck in varsity football next year, here's one father who will have no objection.

THE ORIGIN OF THE NOTRE DAME SHIFT

CHARLES (GUS) DORAIS *is known to fame chiefly as the quarterback of the Notre Dame team that stunned Army and opened the eyes of the East to the potential of the forward pass as he threw strike after strike in the 35–13 victory of the Fighting Irish over the cadets in the first game of this rivalry in 1913 at West Point, New York. Knute Rockne, who was to gain the greatest celebrity of any coach in football history, was captain and an end on the Notre Dame team and was Dorais' target numerous times. Dorais wrote in a letter to the author January 23, 1951:*

YOU'VE GOT QUITE an order if you are going to try and get order out of the chaos existing regarding the evolution of football. A fellow gets a little foggy about things that happened thirty-five or forty years ago. There has even been a lot of differences as to the origin of the Notre Dame shift.

I was there and played on the team during the transition period, 1910 to 1913, and by the way . . . we lost only one game during that period (to Michigan State), to my best recollection. In 1910 Shorty Longman of Michigan was my first coach and we used a T formation (with the quarterback, about a yard back of center, getting the ball on a toss from center) and a good deal of tackle-around-tackle offensive plays. Our T was devised more as a power attack than the deceptive, brush-blocking attack of today.

In 1911 Jack Marks of Dartmouth became our coach. He played at Dartmouth under Major Frank Cavanaugh and he changed our formation to a box (right or left), and to my mind that was the beginning of the Notre Dame style—and it came from Dartmouth.

The next year [Notre Dame records say 1913] Jesse Harper of Chicago was coach and under Stagg he had been taught a shifting style of offense. So he put the shift on from the T to the box either way, and as there was no rule on stopping after the shift we went to town in good shape.

Later Rockne incorporated the ends shifting in unison with the backs, and that was it. Now who started it? Marks, Harper and Rockne all had a piece of it.

Our shift differed from the Minnesota shift in that only the ends shifted with the backs, and Notre Dame stayed in a balanced line. In Dr. Williams' shift at Minnesota all players but the center lined up behind the line and then shifted into an unbalanced line and single wing to either side.

Rockne was the greatest inspirational coach ever in the business. Next to him probably along that line was Bill Roper of Princeton. Rockne got that way by taking an intense personal interest in the players' outside problems—home life, girls, troubles, etc. He was a dean of men to all the athletes, and they would break their necks for him.

Rock was the first end that, to my knowledge, developed the pass lanes as they still are today. All the other ends I threw to and all I saw in those days depended on sheer speed ahead to just get behind the defender. He worked on cuts and angles to get loose, change of pace, and even accidentally developed what is known as the buttonhook pass. On one occasion, going down the field with the defender playing him deep, he fell down. When he got up he was clear and I threw to him and he came back. We decided to put it in the repertoire.

Rock's other great addition to the Notre Dame system was that as a player he learned by feints, head ducks, etc. to tie up a defensive tackle all alone, letting the halfback usually assigned to help the end on his tackle go downfield and get a defensive backer. This single contribution, perfected as he became coach, was responsible for the many breakaway runs that distinguished the Notre Dame attack in those days.

Regarding coaches, I think Rockne and Roper were great inspirational coaches; Percy Haughton, Howard Jones, Andy Smith, Fritz Crisler and Alonzo Stagg were great fundamentalists. Fielding Yost was the greatest exponent of the punting game. Doc Spears, Bob Zuppke, Doc Sutherland and Bernie Bierman were great defensive coaches.

In a letter to the author dated February 10, 1954, at Sitka, Kansas, JESSE HARPER, *who took over as head coach at Notre Dame in 1913, wrote as follows about the shift, the pass, and the Army game of 1913:*

I do not think anyone knows who first used the shift in one form or another. Minnesota used the shift about 1903 or 1904. They shifted the entire line as well as the backfield.

I started the shift at Notre Dame in 1913. Notre Dame was the first team to have a complete offense using a balanced line and shifting only the backfield. In 1914 we started shifting the ends.

I used the forward pass a great deal at Wabash before going to Notre Dame. In fact, Wabash was the first team to use intentional grounding, also throwing the ball out of bounds instead of punting. At that time the ball thrown out of bounds went to the other team at the point it went out of bounds. There was no penalty for intentional grounding a forward pass. It was the same as an incomplete pass.

Dorais was a wonderful passer, as good as you ever saw. In the Army game the ball was thrown to Rockne and Pliska, the right halfback. All the stories you have read about Rock and Dorais at Cedar Point are all bunk. They took a football with them to teach Rock to catch the ball in his hands instead of his stomach the way many coaches taught at that time. If you will check the 1912 team of Notre Dame you will not find anything startling about their forward passes.

The Army game was arranged in a very simple manner. I wrote the Army to see if they had an opening on their schedule, and if so would they give us a game. No outside person knew anything about it until the game was arranged and contracts signed. No time was spent by me or any Notre Dame player instructing the Army coaches about passing. That is another thing that is all bunk.

MAL ELWARD, *Rockne's substitute at end in 1913 and a member of the Notre Dame team also in 1914 and 1915, who coached at Notre Dame, Purdue, and Stanford, wrote in a letter dated October 2, 1954, at Stanford as follows:*

As far as I know Harper first used the Notre Dame shift [in 1913]. Stagg may have used it, but I do not think he ever developed its possibilities. Stagg was at Chicago for many years when I was at Purdue, but he never used the shift.

The end shift started unofficially in 1915. I say unofficially because I shifted against tackles on my own. In 1916 Rock and Harper began shifting both ends, timing it with the backfield shift. . . . In other words, the end shift was not used against Army and was not used as a team maneuver until 1916.

DR. HARRY WILLIAMS' MINNESOTA SHIFT

The Minnesota shift stands with the Notre Dame and Heisman as the three most famous shifts developed in college football. The Minnesota was the first of these, but it may have been preceded by the shift used by Amos Alonzo Stagg at Chicago early in the century. Knute Rockne credited Stagg's Chicago shift as being the fountainhead of the shift he and Jesse Harper, his coach, who played under Stagg at Chicago, employed at Notre Dame. According to Rockne, Notre Dame started to use the shift in 1914; Harper said it was in 1913.

BOB ZUPPKE *believes that Dr. Williams' Minnesota shift was the first. Stagg believes he was the first to shift men, starting with linemen and later backs, "synchronously." Others are uncertain who was first.*

Herewith follow the statements made to the author over the years by Zuppke, Stagg, John McGovern, captain of the Minnesota Big Ten champions of 1909, and Bernie Bierman, who played under Williams and, as coach at Minnesota, developed some of the greatest teams in history, notably in 1934 and 1941. Bob Zuppke wrote the author in 1951:

D R. WILLIAMS was the creator of the shift, and after his team defeated Chicago in '916, 49–0, Stagg became shift crazy. He [Stagg] had the U formation, the shimmy shift and the whirlwind shift. Harper was a Stagg man, but the basis of his shift goes through Stagg to Williams. I do not know whether or not—and never heard of it—all shifts go back to Stagg. I associate his name more with the man-in-motion. It must be remembered that they shifted in the old game. It may be that Stagg was the first. I do not know. But when I first saw Stagg in 1903 and 1904 he was not addicted to shifts as I remember. . . . The Minnesota shift was the greatest ever invented. It had tremendous offensive qualities when the timing was perfect. They only stopped a moment (according to rules), but a moment could be an infinitesimal amount of time. The

235

one-second rule made the shift obsolete because it made the players come to a complete stop.

The principal feature of the Minnesota shift was tackles back, ends and guards wide. The tackles jumped into the line, set for an instant, and they would be gone. The tackles would go into the line at the last moment, on one side or the other, as the ends closed in to their positions. I broke that up in 1916 by using an unorthodox defense. I made my tackles go wide with the Minnesota men, sliding with them, and by lining up my three middle men the same distance back from the line of scrimmage as the Minnesota tackles. My middle men hopped into the line with their tackles, and we had forward momentum. Minnesota was caught flat-footed because of our unorthodox defensive maneuvers. I used an irregular pattern in my defensive secondary for this game. It resolved itself mainly into a seven-diamond.

I don't know whether the Notre Dame shift was derived from the Minnesota. They used to say that the Notre Dame shift was half of the Minnesota (the backfield—both forming a box). Others said it came from Chicago.

JOHN MC GOVERN *and* SIG HARRIS *wrote the following to the author in 1953:*

When the forward pass came into the game, Dr. Williams developed his Minnesota shift. The line was unbalanced, two men on the short side. The tackles lined up behind the center, the quarterback behind the tackles, with the other backs behind the quarterback. Then on a "hep," the shift was made into the line and the backs into whatever position the ensuing play required. On different plays the backfield men ended up in different arrangements after the shift.

Dr. Williams also had a big shift with only one man on the short side, and on some plays there were two shifts before the ball was passed. The theory of the shift was to outflank the defense, or, as I have heard Dr. Williams express it, to get four men against three, or five against four.

The great success of the formation resulted, I believe, in the failure of the defense to shift sufficiently. These shifts were made quite rapidly, just enough of a pause to satisfy the requirements of the rules with respect to a complete stop. Plays were made to the short side, but the full possibilities and effectiveness of the short-side play never reached the perfection to which Bernie Bierman brought it as an integral component of a shift offense.

McGovern and Harris say that Dr. Williams developed his shift when the pass came into the game, 1906. Jesse Harper of Notre Dame put it earlier. In a letter dated February 10, 1954, he wrote:

"I do not think anyone knows who first used the shift in one form or another. Minnesota first used the shift about 1903 or 1904. They shifted the entire line as well as the backfield. I started the shift at Notre Dame in 1913. Notre Dame was the first team to have a complete offense using a balanced line, and shifted only the backfield. In 1914 we started shifting the ends."

BERNIE BIERMAN, *captain of the 1915 Minnesota team, wrote the author in 1951 as follows:*

Dr. Williams started his shift sometime prior to 1910. During the years he used it it was subject to some variation, but the most common, original setup was with the center and the ends on the line of scrimmage, the guards behind the center and splitting him, and the tackles on a line with the guards and just outside of them. The backfield was in one of several formations further back.

On a three-count shift the linemen moved into position on the line, with the ends jockeying either in or out. The line could be unbalanced 4–2 or 5–1, either to the right or left, and the backfield in any one of a number of positions. Frequently there would be a second shift, which usually involved only the backs.

The rules in those days merely required that no one was moving when the ball was snapped. The basic idea, of course, was to make your shift and snap the ball before the defense could get oriented and adjusted. Frequently you could have the defense outflanked even before the ball was passed. When the Rules Committee put in the requirement of the minimum one-second stop, it of course took away much of the advantage of this type of shift.

I believe that about this time, or maybe even before, Stagg put in what later was to be known as the Notre Dame shift. This involved, with the exception of some jockeying of the line, only a shift of the backs from the T formation to some other formation, usually the box. The essential difference between these two was this: In

The Little Brown Jug, one of football's most famous trophies, awarded annually to the winner of the Michigan-Minnesota game.

M	YEAR	M
6	1903	6
15	1909	6
6	1910	0
7	1919	34
3	1920	0
38	1921	0
16	1922	7
10	1923	0
13	1924	0
35	1925	0
20	1926	0
7		6
7	1927	13
7	1929	6
7	1930	0
6	1931	0
3	1932	0
0	1933	0
0	1934	34
0	1935	40
0	1936	26
6	1937	39
6	1938	7
7	1939	20
6	1940	7

Williams' shift the ball could not be put in play until after the shift, while in the other the ball could be put in play without shifting. The Williams shift accomplished this with the double shift.

In 1934 The Associated Press sent out a story in which the claim was made that the Minnesota shift was the same as that used by a Wisconsin high school team in 1900. Police Chief Daniel J. Linehan of River Falls, Wisconsin, was quoted as saying that the River Falls High School team, of which he had been captain in 1900, was the first to use the plays from which the Minnesota shift later was developed. On September 10, 1934, Chief Linehan told The Associated Press:

"There will be a big squawk over our claiming this shift. For years dozens of universities and prep schools have claimed the honor of originating this shift. But I have found no one who ever heard of it or saw it on the field until our 1900 team used it to win the Western Wisconsin High School championship. I say all the credit should go to the late Professor J. W. T. Ames, our principal and coach.

"In 1899 our eleven was defeated, 11–0 by Menomonie (Wisconsin) High School, chiefly because their coach pulled a tackle into the backfield as a battering ram interference leader. Professor Ames, who played center for us, immediately visualized and designed an expansion of that idea. He worked out a series of plays in which power and deception were derived from shifting a guard and tackle from one side of the line to the other. We used this system the following season to win undisputed title to the West State championship."

Red Freeman of the University of Minnesota squad refereed one of the title games, Linehan told the A. P. He said that Freeman had obtained diagrams of the plays from Professor Ames and took them to coach Henry L. Williams and others of the Minnesota staff. Linehan added that he saw the Minnesota team of 1903 come out with the identical shift formations that his own River Falls High School champions had used three years before.

Stagg, in a letter to the author in 1952, wrote:

"At the beginning of the century I was shifting linemen quickly from one side to the other for a quick attack, and in 1904 I sometimes used a backfield shift synchronously."

In 1932 he was quoted in *The New York World-Telegram*:

"This little talk brings me back to 1902, when I upset football defense by taking a tackle from one side of center and placing him on the other side, between tackle and guard. That was the first deviation away from the balanced line and the start of the shift."

In his Scrapbook, Stagg added:

"I started another type of backfield shift in 1910 on which the ball was snapped instantly without delay. This shift later received its most effective demonstration in the Notre Dame system under Harper and Rockne."

In a letter to Sol Metzger in 1931, Stagg said:

"I am enclosing one of Knute Rockne's articles which he wrote in 1929 and in which he quite properly gives me credit for the backfield shift used by Notre Dame. I saw Notre Dame play back in 1922 and again in 1924 . . . when the 'Four Horsemen' were playing, and they were using the backfield shift which I had originated. . . ."

In *The Saturday Evening Post* in 1926, Stagg wrote:

"Dr. Harry Williams' Minnesota shift was the most famous of shift formations. Williams was a graduate of Yale of 1891. When the Minnesota shift was an old story in the West, he offered repeatedly to return to Yale and teach them the play, but Yale was not taking football lessons from a Western state university—an attitude which Harvard and Princeton were able to endorse enthusiastically."

Stagg described the Minnesota shift in a letter to Dr. J. E. Raycroft in 1917:

"The Minnesota shift emphasizes attack on the tackles; and the purpose usually is to get the tackles blocked in and then center two backfield men against the end, while the runner preferably cuts through between the end and tackle and occasionally, when the backs are speedy, goes around end. That is the main essence of the shift as we have met it in the Minnesota play. Of course, the center of the line is attacked; and four times out of five, when the center is attacked, as we know it, it is done through the use of the second man in the tandem. He usually hits on the tackles, which are shifted into line."

Dr. Williams went to Minnesota in 1900 and remained there as head football coach until he was retired at the end of the 1921 season, when he devoted himself to the practice of medicine. His Minnesota teams won 136 games, lost 33 and tied 11. They won

Western Conference championships in 1900, 1904, 1906, 1909, and 1911, and tied for the title with Michigan in 1903 and with Illinois in 1910 and 1915. In his first year, 1900, Dr. Williams took a green team and developed it to win Minnesota's first championship and become known as the "Giants of the North."

In addition to devising the Minnesota shift, Dr. Williams invented the revolving wedge in 1892 and the tackle back formation in 1899. (Stagg originated the tackles back, with both tackles pulled back into the backfield, in 1894.) He was one of those chiefly responsible for persuading the Football Rules Committee to legalize the forward pass and was a member of the committee. Heisman credits him with originating in 1891 crisscross plays in which the halfbacks and ends, while going in opposite directions, passed the ball back to each other, and also, in 1892, the onside quarterback kick. Stagg says that Yale probably was the first to use the crisscross, in 1885, and that he himself devised eight original plays in 1890 or 1891. George Woodruff of Penn also is credited by some with being the first to use the onside quarterback kick. One of Williams' players, John McGovern, says that he used the wide flanker in 1907, but Stagg says that he (Stagg) used a flanker for a forward pass in 1906 and in 1910 established the principle of a flanker end in motion.

John McGovern, a member of the Minnesota teams of 1908, 1909, and 1910 and all-America quarterback in 1909, sent the author the following information, with the assistance of Sig Harris, another famous Minnesota quarterback and assistant coach on Williams' staff:

Henry L. Williams was born at Hartford, Conn., June 26, 1869. His paternal ancestors came from England in 1648, and on his mother's side they reached back to the days of the Salem colony. In the fall of 1887 Williams entered Yale University. He made his letter in football in his freshman year and the three succeeding years, playing with such notables as Pudge Heffelfinger and Alonzo Stagg. He likewise made his track "Y" as a freshman and captained the team as a senior. . . . In his senior year in the Berkeley Oval in New York he ran the hurdles in 15.8 seconds, a new intercollegiate and world record.

After his graduation he took a job teaching at Siglar's Preparatory School, located about ten miles from West Point at Newburgh-on the-Hudson. The Army was not doing so well football-wise. They remembered Williams' performance at Yale and engaged him as coach. He coached by correspondence. In the evening he would diagram plays and tabulate their execution. He would send them to West Point with instructions on offense and defense. Saturday mornings he joined the Army team for further instruction and polishing. Navy had beaten Army the year before, 1890, by 24 to 0. Under Williams' direction in 1891, Army beat Navy, 32 to 16. Williams thus became the first Army coach to beat Navy.

The next year Williams entered the University of Pennsylvania to study medicine. While there he won the D. Hayes Agnew prize for dissection. To help meet expenses he took a job coaching football and track at Penn Charter School in Philadelphia. He coached there for eight years. At that time he turned down an offer from his old Yale teammate, Alonzo Stagg, who had just accepted the position of football coach at the University of Chicago. Stagg wanted Williams to accompany him to Chicago to be his assistant.

Williams, who officiated Saturdays in some of the University of Pennsylvania games, was impressed by the guards back formation used by George Woodruff, Pennsylvania coach . . . Williams then devised a tackle back formation in which one tackle played back of the other—either side. The play worked so well Williams offered it to Yale for use against Harvard and Princeton. However, James Rodgers, the Yale coach in 1899, and Malcolm McBride, the captain, decided they didn't want it. However, Army called Williams to West Point to incorporate the play into Army's offense. They beat Navy with it, 15 to 5.

In the meantime Williams was making notable progress in his medicine. He served a year as a resident physician at Harvard Hospital, followed by two years as instructor in gynecology at the University of Pennsylvania. Parts of each year—1895, 1897, and 1899—were spent abroad in study at medical centers in Berlin and Vienna. Then, in 1900, upon the recommendation of Coach Stagg of Chicago, Williams was hired as football coach at the University of Minnesota at $2,500 a year. The contract was for three years and granted Williams permission to practice medicine. . . .

Williams went from Minnesota as a delegate to the meeting at the College of the City of New York, called at the instigation of of President Theodore Roosevelt when there was the threat to abolish football unless the game were opened up and some of the dangers from injury eliminated. I have heard him tell of the proceedings at that meeting when the forward pass was introduced. He had an important part in devising the changes in the rules which resulted.

Williams never devoted the time to fundamentals—blocking, charging, tackling—to anywhere near the extent Bierman, Rockne and some other coaches did. He was first and foremost a tactician, a deviser of offensive plays, equally expert at setting up a defense for any type of offense. I consider him to be the type of Warner more than any other.

I have such a high regard for Dr. Williams—not only as a great coach but as a fine, scholarly, cultured gentleman—that I get a bit prolix when I start talking about him. I have had many visits with him in his home as well as in his office when the subjects discussed, or rather to which I listened, were not of football. They were interesting recitals of his travels and studies in Europe, of history, the sciences, and literature. He was truly a fine gentleman unfortunately underestimated and unappreciated by many who should have had a better comprehension of his worth and character.

FROM NORWAY TO NOTRE DAME

KNUTE ROCKNE's personal account of his life from the time he arrived in this country as an immigrant boy of five years from Norway until he went to Notre Dame is told in the following article by the most famous of all football coaches. It was published in Collier's Weekly October 18, 1930, some five months before his death in the crash of an airplane.

HOW A YOUNGSTER from Voss, a hamlet in Norway that lies between Bergen and Oslo, could find himself in his midtwenties captain of a typical, mid-Western American football team . . . is a typical American story—in business, athletics, politics. It has occurred so often that it's ordinary. The breaks came my way when I had sense enough to take them; and while that's an unromantic way of explaining a career, it has the advantage of being the truth. . . .

The traditional venturesomeness of the Norsemen, aided by infiltrations of Irish blood acquired when the earlier and hardier Vikings invaded Ireland looking for trouble and returned to Norway with colleens for wives, breaks out at intervals. With my father, it broke out when I was about five. The World's Fair was to be held in Chicago. Dad, by profession a stationary engineer and by avocation a carriage builder, wanted to show his wares at the World's Fair. He went to America. Later he sent for his family. My mother took her three daughters and her only son to New York and we were duly admitted through Castle Garden. My only equipment for life in the new country was a Norwegian vocabulary, a fervent memory of home cooking combined with pleasant recollections of skiing and skating among the Voss Mountains.

How my mother ever managed that tedious voyage, which I still recall with qualms; how she guided us through the intricacies of entry, knowing nothing of English, and took us into the heart of a new, strange and bewildering country without mishap—how, in brief, she achieved the first step in our Americanization unaided by anybody, is one of the millions of minor miracles that are of the stuff and fabric of America. . . .

A Chicago childhood and youth . . . was not unpleasant going.

The new, spacious city, with its endless corner lots and tolerant police, was a great place for a boy to grow up in, in the era B.C.— Before Capone. Our football and baseball games were undisturbed by rifle-fire and the popping of pineapples. At that, there was excitement enough for everybody.

We lived in the Logan Square neighborhood—chiefly inhabited by Irish and Swedes. Chicago's broad ethnology called all Scandinavians "Swedes." The Irish were clubby, so were the Swedes. My lot naturally was with the latter. On a huge vacant corner boys of the two nationalities would meet on Wednesday and Saturday afternoons in impromptu and sometimes violent contests. A husky, middle-aged copper named O'Goole kept a maternal eye on us. When the Irish lads were pounding us "Swedes," O'Goole strode up and down the sidelines grinning. To onlookers who protested that he should stop the free-for-all, he said,

"Nonsense! It's an elegant game, good for the youngsters. Look at Patsy Regan there knock that Swede lad from under a punt." A few of us, dissatisfied with constant lickings at the hands—and feet—of the Irish, scouted other neighborhoods for bigger Swedes. When bigger boys couldn't be found, we enrolled a couple of bruiser-like Italians on our side.

O'Goole strolled by while a bigger and better battle was in progress and the Irishers were getting a free and liberal taste of mud.

"That won't do at all," he said, striding to the midst of the battle and grabbing Swede boys by their necks. "The game is altogether brutal and unfit for small boys."

We could only even matters by appealing to the precinct captain to send us a Swede cop as well as O'Goole to supervise our games. Then mayhem was balanced for both sides.

My first real baptism of mire was received in one of these neighborhood corner-lot games. I was an end on the Tricky Tigers —historic rivals of the Avondales—so-called because we had a wow of a triple pass back of the line when we wanted to impress opponents and onlookers. Our equipment wasn't elaborate. No helmets, one shin guard per player. We tied our ears with elastic tape to prevent spreading.

Many of us graduated to the Barefoot Athletic Club of older boys, mostly Irish. In a crucial game with the Hamburg A.C. for the district championship trouble came in handfuls. Crowds lined the gridless gridiron and broke into it as the game progressed. Irish sympathizers were militant. Only seven policemen were there to hold back the mob. Things grew unpleasant as the more pugnacious spectators slipped away every now and then for refreshments at near-by saloons.

The game was held in a huge lot opposite the White Sox Ball Park. My part in it was not brilliant, but dramatic. In those early days I had spindly legs, which I've retained, and speedy feet, which left me long ago. When the call to carry the ball came, I'd lay back my ears and sprint. That afternoon the ball came. Spurting in an end run, with the Hamburg boys after me, my path to a touchdown was clear. Not a Hamburg player was in front. But Hamburg rooters came to the rescue. They threw me and swiped the ball.

A minor riot ensued, players on both teams being pummeled impartially. There were so many players' noses punched that a police sergeant would only let players with nose-guards wade into the crowd. Most of us returned home that evening with evidence of a strenuous afternoon's sport.

For me this was a serious matter. As a football initiate, I played the game surreptitiously, my parents sharing the general belief that football was a system of modified massacre. My most prized possession, a pair of patched moleskin football pants, had to be smuggled in and out of the house. Scars of battle in the Hamburg game betrayed me. My football career was squelched. As it was nearing winter, this didn't matter much, for when spring arrived with the crack of baseballs on bats, I went out with the rest of the sandlot gang. The family approved baseball. During a vicious, extra-inning game with the Maplewood boys, a hot argument developed. Being blessed or bothered by hidden strains of Irish ancestry, I found myself in the thick of it. Suddenly a bat bent on the bridge of my nose. I went home blinded, but uppermost in my mind was not sorrow, but logic. The family had banned football because it was dangerous.

"And I got this nose from baseball," was my triumphant reply.

With full parental approval, when high school days arrived for me, I went out for football, after making the high school track team as a half-miler. There occurred the inspirational picture of Walter Eckersall in action. Likewise such prodigies of sport as Rube Waddell and Three-Finger Brown took niches in what there was of my mind.

Rube Waddell was a figure to inspire an athletically minded youngster with the easy glory of games. We knew something of his tradition: how he had jogged on to a crowded ball park in Harrisburg, driving a team of mules and a wagon, himself attired like a scarecrow; how, after parking mules and wagon by a players' bench, he took possession of the pitcher's box and struck out twelve men in a row.

The Rube always played up to the youngsters. He'd guide droves of us into the ball park free, and we'd even follow him miles and miles in his eccentricities. He'd take French leave from his club, go to Libertyville or some other town and pitch for a local semi-pro outfit. The man was a great showman. I remember once in a semi-pro game he turned dramatically in the box, waved in all the outfielders, sent them to the bench and struck out every batter.

In those days I yearned to follow in the footsteps of Waddell, or that other fine pitcher, Three-Finger Brown. That meant having exceedingly sizeable feet, which may be one reason why I never became a pitcher, but an outfielder. When the football bug hit me after seeing Eckersall, the diamond's luster dimmed.

The first big thrill of my life came when, at thirteen years of age and weighing 110 pounds, they put me on the scrubs of the Northwest Division High, now Tuley High, in Chicago. In the scrubs we had some slight coaching. Our sandlot football was what the professors called eclectic: We pinched whatever plays we had seen and could remember.

We were keen for signals. Half the fun of the game was the solemnity with which our corner-lot quarterbacks would shout, and we would receive, the long litany of signals. Only colored players excel sandlot boys in love of signals. Two teams of Negro footballers I once umpired for devised a baffling code. Both named their plays after dishes. Pork chops meant a smash through right tackle, pigs' feet a run around right end, fried chicken a split buck, and so on. Very confusing to spectators and hardly less confusing to the players. The only worthwhile thing I recall about that strange game is that one side, led by a quarterback yelling items off a menu, marched down the field and paused on the one-yard line for the team pilot to scream in final challenge: "Now, boys, over that line with the whole blame' dining car."

High school football in those days had all the enthusiasm but none of the finesse of today. Coaches were few. Two professors, Peters and Ellis, volunteered to teach our school squad. They did a good job of it, if only by holding me back and making me realize there was something more to football than the ball. It took me until my senior year to get on the team. Chicago followed our high school games in huge crowds. In those days our team—Northwest Division—beat powerful Marshall High, tied with Crane, and bowed only to North Division High, whose second team licked us. The first-string players, led by Wally Steffen, now Carnegie Tech coach, joshed us from the sidelines.

Then the name of Alonzo Stagg rose on my horizon. Not in connection with football, although I knew something of his fame. It was a favorite trick of the crowd I played with to hook into the Chicago University football field through the motorcar gates, guarded less closely than the turnstiles. We saw Eckersall run his team against squads whose names were almost mythically great to us—teams like Northwestern, Haskell and Michigan. My ambition then was to become a quarterback. When Eckersall wasn't on the field, Wally Steffen or Lee Maxwell directed the Chicago plays; each had a snap to his style that made the quarterback's job the focal point in the football drama. That was right. But a good quarterback needed all of many qualities, only a few of which I had—the principal one being speed.

Coach Stagg supervised an annual series of interscholastic meets around Chicago. The half-mile was my specialty. With the fondness for coincidence that all of us share, many have asked me whether or not Stagg and I met in those days. If we did, it must have been under the stands when I dropped out of long-distance foot races, as invariably occurred. But persistence at track meets won me a small reputation, and when a whimsical switch to pole-vaulting brought me in the news by making an indoor record of 12 feet 4 inches—which today wouldn't qualify a boy to be a mascot—I began to think I'd arrived.

While in high school I got on the Chicago AA junior team, after making the grade in one of the numerous athletic clubs dotted around Chicago. In minor meets the chances to win depended as much on quick wits as stop-watches. Youngsters were quickly initiated into the tricks of the athletic trade. One official timer was known for his distaste for continuous Irish victories. When he was officiating and our teams faced stiff and conquering competition, somebody on our side would always stand near this official and holler of a winning opponent named Schmidt, "Watch that O'Brien come," or of a Thorgensen, "Look at that Reilly jump." But chickens came home to roost. Once when I was bold enough to sub for an absent teammate in an 880-yard sprint for what I thought was record time, some malicious bird yelled, "Come on, Kelly," as I dashed down the lane. The non-Hibernian official overheard: the record was not mine.

The interim between finishing high school and entering college

—four years, to be exact—was the principal period of my not too celebrated career as a track athlete. I carried the colors of Irving Park AC and the Central YMCA . . .

If anybody wonders why it took me so long to get from high school to college, the answer's easy. I was obliged to earn a living. Football, save as a spectator, was neglected, and I relied on track competition to keep in physical shape. I had hoped at high school to make my way in college. To that end, I learned how to earn more money and save it. A Hebrew boy and I got the summer-time job of cleaning our high school windows at good pay. But other boys, possibly jealous over our appointments, would break windows, invade the school, switch door signs with coarsely diabolical wit and commit other sabotage for which the amateur window cleaners were blamed. Naturally, we were fired.

But with an urge for the public weal, I took civil service exams for the mail service and received appointment as a mail dispatcher. At this time I was ambitious to go to the University of Illinois and I set in my mind a goal—to save one thousand dollars and march on Illinois for an education. Athletic fame was secondary, for, to me, college players loomed as supermen to whose heights I could never aspire. It seemed more and more unlikely that any college would have the opportunity to matriculate or reject me, as years of night work ensued, my prep school being the sorting room of the post office. . . .

Notre Dame was hardly a name to me. Football, by that time, had been eclipsed by track and field. Much as I should like to profess being animated by a burning zeal to go out and conquer in the name of pigskin and be acclaimed a mighty player and a coach of massive intellect, the cold, unembellished fact is that a sister of mine was more ambitious for me than I was for myself. She insisted that a college education would mean more to me and the family than anything else. Also, that I'd be able to waste my time to better advantage as a college track athlete than as a part-time wonder of the campus called the Loop. Two friends of mine, Johnny Devine and Johnny Plant, both runners of more than local note, were going to Notre Dame. When we discussed our plans during a Chicago meet, and I told them I was bound for Illinois, they suggested I go along with them to the Indiana school.

"Why," I remember exclaiming, "who ever heard of Notre Dame? They've never won a football game in their lives."

What swung me to go there was the argument that I could probably get a job, and certainly get by cheaper than at Illinois.

So I went down to South Bend with a suitcase and a thousand dollars. I'd hardly seen more than two trees at one time anywhere, so the first impression on me was the sylvan beauty of Notre Dame. The fathers of the Holy Cross who operate the university received a grant of twenty-three hundred acres in the early pre-pioneer days when Indiana was a territory and not a state. By industry and intelligence they made it an ideal site for a university.

Notre Dame University, in 1910, when I felt the strangeness of being a lone Norse Protestant—if the word must be used— invader of a Catholic stronghold, comprised six halls, in one of which, Brownson Dormitory, I was installed. There were 400 under-graduates, physical training was compulsory, and a fellow wasn't thought much of unless he went out to try and make his hall team for football.

Shorty Longman, an end on Michigan's famous point-a-minute teams, was Notre Dame's head coach—the first college coach I ever knew. He was a snappy, belligerent figure who affected a shock of hair after the manner of McCullough, the actor.

The university gave me a chance to work off my room and board as janitor of the chemical laboratory, cleaning out the slop buckets and doing minor chores. Somebody stole a gallon of experimental wine from the pharmacy laboratory. I was blamed and ran risks of expulsion. So my reputation was not glamorous. When, therefore, Joe Collins, a varsity squad man, recommended me for a chance with the big boys, Longman wasn't enthusiastic.

But he gave me the chance. Freshmen were played in those days, and with a small enrollment we needed them. Longman sent me out with the scrubs in a test game with the regulars. He made me fullback. They should have changed my position to drawback. Never on any football field was there so dismal a flop. Trying to spear my first punt, I had frozen fingers and the ball rolled every-where it wasn't wanted.

Longman kept me in that agonizing game. Finally, I tried a punt. Nothing happened. I might have been a statue of a player trying to punt. Nothing was coordinated. I was half paralyzed. A 200-pound tackle smashed into me. My 145 pounds went back for a fifteen-yard loss.

Longman yanked me out of the scrubs and sent me back to Brownson Hall. I was a dub, a washout, not even good enough for the scrubs. But the fact remained that I could run, and running was important to a football player. Perhaps, I reasoned, if I tried for a job at end, my old spot on the sandlot and high school teams,

I'd have better luck. The first step was to get on the varsity track team, which I did. A track letter gave me the prestige to try once more for the football squad.

In the meantime I had sat at the feet of a learned tramp athlete whose name then was Foley, although he had played for many schools under aliases. He was typical of young men who roamed the country, overflowing with college spirit, regardless of the college. His tongue teemed with professional jargon. He knew all of the technique and practiced none of it; yet so glib was he that it invariably took a shrewd coach half a season to get wise to the fact that this tramp athlete had only one principle in football, which he pithily expressed: "Avoid 'em." He opened my eyes to a state of affairs in college football which has since been reformed— of the journeyman players who'd leave new names behind them wherever they went and live to a ripe old age, from foot to mouth, so to speak, taking loyalty and sometimes talent with them to whichever Alma Mater would give them the best break.

We played teams whose purity of enrollment was not quite ninety-nine and three-quarters percent. The Indian schools were careless in that respect, several Indian players changing legal names to Indian names as they switched from one Indian school to another. The famous back, Emil Hauser of Haskell, became Chief Waseka at Carlisle. Another lad I knew named Dietz blossomed into Chief Long Star, and I always called the celebrated back, Pete Hauser, Chief Long Time Eat when I met him playing for his third or fourth alma mater—he shone brightly at training table.

Although a growing youngster, I had the advantage of not being too green when I broke into big football company. I was twenty-three and able to wear a lettered sweater without too much intoxication. There were natural hurdles to be jumped in a social sense, for a lone Norwegian, always mistakenly dubbed a Swede, had difficulties among so many Hibernians. These were largely dissipated when, blushing furiously, I was called on to talk at a football rally and, having heard somebody call somebody else just a dumb Irishman, I had the good fortune to remark, "There's only one thing dumber than a dumb Irishman." Before the bricks could fly, I explained: "A smart Swede."

Notre Dame was struggling to establish itself in football circles. Its schedule was not strong—Ohio Northern, Marquette and Pittsburgh were "big games." Our equipment was poor. In the first game I played in—against Ohio Northern—a guard was so severely injured that we had to use up our lone roll of tape. Later, his substitute in the line cracked up, so we had to take tape off the first boy to bind up the second.

Shorty Longman knew much about football, but he talked much more. Our offense was principally a punt and a prayer—varied with an occasional line plunge. Longman's method was that of the old-fashioned oratorical coach. Before a game, he would enter the dressingroom dramatically, toss back his shock of black hair and burst into rhetoric.

"Boys," he declaimed, "today is the day. The honor of the old school is at stake. Now or never, we must fight the battle of our lives. I don't want any man with a streak of yellow to move from this room. You've all got to be heroes—Heroes—or I never want to see you again. Go out and conquer. It's the crisis of your lives!"

When I heard that for the first time, I was tremendously impressed. The team went out and all but pushed the opposing team —Olivet—over the fence. The next Saturday, as we lay resting in the dressingroom, Coach Longman entered.

"Boys," he detonated, "today is *the* day of days. The honor of the old school is at stake. The eyes of the world are on you. Go out and bleed for the old school, and if anybody has a yellow streak let him—"

I sat there awe-stricken. Then I saw Dorais and Bergman, two veterans, yawn.

"What do you think of the act today?" asked Bergman.

"Not so good," said Dorais. "I thought he was better last week."

One oration a season is quite enough for any football squad. Action brings reaction, and if the coach talks too much, his words lose weight.

From my first coach, Longman, came another valuable lesson. A sturdy man and useful with his fists, he believed that the best way to impress his charges was to demonstrate that he was physically their master. With this in mind, he prescribed boxing lessons which he himself would give, beginning with the lightweights and working his way through to the heavies of the Philbrook displacement.

Respectfully, the squad gathered to see the first demonstration. Several of the less heavy boys, myself included, were to be operated on with boxing gloves. Shorty selected a mild-mannered chap named Matthews, a light end, for the first object lesson. That was a bad break. Matthews stepped out expertly, ducked and weaved and hooked and jabbed. After three minutes Shorty had enough. There were no boxing lessons for the rest of us.

Our next coach was Jack Marks, the Dartmouth back. He made us over from a green, aggressive squad into a slashing, driving outfit. The first time that he looked over Eichenlaub, the Notre Dame 200-pound torpedo, Marks showed he knew his stuff.

"We're playing Wabash this afternoon, Eichenlaub," Marks said. "Jones, Feeney and the rest will make the holes. You tear through them."

"But I'm only a poor high school boy," said Eichenlaub.

Marks turned on his heel. That afternoon Eichenlaub ripped through Wabash for total gains of more than four hundred yards. The Wabash squad piled on a street car for the depot, badly licked. The car stopped for a feeble old lady carrying parcels. She worked her way through the limping Wabash players while a wag cried,

"One side! Here comes Eichenlaub's mother."

Marks was always a quiet mentor, but he liked to pile up scores. Once we led Adrian by 81 to 0, and the Adrian coach said he'd used up all his substitutes and would we agree to let him send men back who had already played. Marks agreed. He returned to the sidelines. Some time later he saw a strange player on the bench.

"You're on the wrong bench," he said.

"I know it," said the lad. "I've been in that scrap four times already, and they're not going to send me back if I can help it. I've had enough."

Marks laughed quietly and let the lad remain. Again, during a game with Butler, a big halfback named Meyers, strong but shy, was missing.

"You've only got ten men on the field," the umpire cried to the Notre Dame coach. Marks looked over the field in anger.

"Where in heck is Meyers?" he demanded.

"Here I am, coach," sang Meyers from his blanket. "I got bumped right on my knee."

Marks smiled quietly, said nothing. But Meyers played no more. That was his method. The team stepped out under his leadership so that gradually we came to be noticed a little beyond the Mid-West. I won a regular berth as end under Marks and had the pleasant surprise of seeing myself discussed as an all-America possibility toward the end of the 1912 season. Almost imperceptibly, it seemed to me, I was established in football. One year, practically abandoning the idea of continuing the game; the next, being talked of—never mind by whom—as an all-America prospect.

Then the end of football and college career impended. My

father died, and it seemed imperative that I quit school, although it's on the record that I passed my special subject, chemistry, cum laude. A wise sister interposed.

"If you quit," she said, "all right. You may earn a living, but it will be as a mail dispatcher."

So I went back, and I had hardly got off the train at South Bend that autumn when I was greeted by a cordial voice.

"You're Rockne?" its owner asked.

"Well," he went on, after having introduced himself as Jesse Harper, Notre Dame's new coach, "I'm grabbing you football men off the trains as fast as I can. We've got to work our heads and legs off."

"What's the excitement?" I said, trying to be calm.

"They're letting us play in the East," he exclaimed. "The Army has agreed to play Notre Dame."

THE FOUR HORSEMEN OF NOTRE DAME

The most glamorous football team in history was the Notre Dame eleven of 1924. It was not the best football team of all time, nor probably the best Notre Dame team ever, nor KNUTE ROCKNE's *best. But no other college eleven has been as publicized or won such national and lasting renown as the "Four Horsemen" team that conquered every foe of the season and beat Stanford and the great Ernie Nevers in the Rose Bowl at Pasadena, California, on New Year's Day, 1925.*

The fame of the team stemmed from the lead paragraph of the report of Notre Dame's game with Army by Grantland Rice. He wrote from the Polo Grounds in New York:

"Outlined against a blue-gray October sky, the Four Horsemen rode again. In dramatic lore they are known as Famine, Pestilence, Destruction and Death. These are only aliases. Their real names are Stuhldreher, Miller, Crowley and Layden. They formed the crest of the South Bend cyclone before which another fighting Army football team was swept over the precipice at the Polo Grounds yesterday afternoon as 55,000 spectators peered down on the bewildering panorama spread on the green plain below."

The name "Four Horsemen" was spread across the sports pages of the nation's press. An enterprising photographer in South Bend, Indiana, flooded the daily papers and magazines across the country with pictures he took of the four backs—Stuhldreher, Miller, Crowley, and Layden—mounted on hastily recruited horses and in football uniforms with a ball tucked under their right arms. Day after day, week after week, and year after year the story of the Four Horsemen, their deeds, exploits, and personalities, was kept alive in word and picture in the press and then on the radio and television. With them rode to immortality their coach, Knute Kenneth Rockne, The Rock, who took his place with Stagg, Warner, Zuppke, Yost among the giants of the coaching ranks.

Other coaches have known phenomenal success since—Leahy,

*Blaik, Wilkinson, Neyland, Wade, Dobie, Jones, Bierman, Crisler,
Sutherland, Royal, Bryant, McKay, Hayes—but none has been put
on quite the pedestal on which Rockne towers, nor has any other
team become the legend that is the Four Horsemen. From* Collier's
magazine November 1, 1930.

A SLEEPY-EYED LAD, who looked as though he were built to be
a tester in an alarm-clock factory, loafed about backfield
in the Notre Dame freshman line-up for practice. With him in the
backfield, his companion halfback, was a youngster who appeared
to be half puzzled by everything going on. Between them was a
smaller and wirier boy with a sharp, handsome face and a clear,
commanding voice. These assets seemed the best the youngster
had, for in his first plays during that practice game he made as
many mistakes as he called signals—and he called a lot. As a rule,
rookie quarterbacks do.

It was not an inspiring practice to watch. Even the likely looking youngster at fullback, who could run like a streak, ran quite
as often into the hands of tackles as through slits in the line. After
watching the backfield performance for an entire quarter, I shook
my head.

"Not so hot," I thought—especially when the entire four were
smeared by a clumsy but willing scrub tackle who weighed about
as much as the entire quartet and pounded through like an ice
wagon to block a kick.

"Not so hot," I repeated, preparing to exercise the virtue of
patience and wait optimistically for the season's developments.
This freshman bunch could be whipped into a combination of
average players. Not much more.

That was the dream I had of them that day. And it didn't
come true.

Three years later, this trio, with another, took the field to the
cheers of fifty thousand people at the Polo Grounds and dazzled
into defeat the strongest Army eleven ever sent against anybody.
The next morning Grantland Rice rose to lyric heights in cele-
brating their speed, rhythm and precision, winding up a litany of
hallelujahs by proclaiming them the "Four Horsemen." Whereupon
an enterprising young gentleman in South Bend perched the returned victors of the backfield on four borrowed steeds and sold
the resultant photographs to the tune of a small fortune.

These accidents will happen in the best of all possible worlds.
Indeed, the football epic of the Four Horsemen is the story of an

accident. How it came to pass that four young men so eminently qualified by temperament, physique and instinctive pacing to complement one another perfectly and thus produce the best coordinated and most picturesque backfield in the recent history of football—how that came about is one of the inscrutable achievements of coincidence, of which I know nothing save it's a rather satisfying mouthful of words.

Harry Stuhldreher, the quarterback, hailed from Massillon, Ohio; Don Miller, halfback, came from Defiance, Ohio; Jimmy Crowley, the other halfback, hailed from Green Bay, Wisconsin, and Elmer Layden, the dashing, slashing fullback, had his home in Davenport, Iowa. The four did not play as a backfield in their freshman year—remember, I had seen them in practice and survived the experience.

These men and the others of the freshmen squad in 1921 were soundly beaten by such teams as Lake Forest Academy and the Michigan State freshmen. Stuhldreher, of the lot, had the most promise. He sounded like a leader on the field. He was a good and fearless blocker and as he gained in football knowledge he showed signs of smartness in emergencies. Layden had speed—he could run a hundred-yard dash in under ten seconds at a track meet. But speed and some kicking ability seemed to be all his football wares. Jimmy Crowley was only less humorous in play than in appearance. He looked dull and always resembled a lad about to get out of or into bed. He showed very little as a freshman— certainly none of the nimble wit that made him as celebrated for repartee as for broken-field running.

Don Miller traveled, that first year, on the reputation and recommendation of his brother, "Red" Miller, the great Notre Dame halfback who made such havoc when his team beat Michigan in 1909. "Red" had sung the praises of another Miller, Jerry, who made a fine high school record but couldn't add to his poundage of one hundred and thirty-five, and, unfortunately, grew quite deaf and so was disqualified for the tough going of big-league football. Don, an also-ran in his freshman year, surprised me when he came out for spring practice and with his fleetness and daring sized up as a halfback to cheer the heart of any coach.

In the fall of 1922, Notre Dame had lost all its veteran backs except Castner at fullback and Thomas at quarterback—one of those decimations by graduation that give coaches gray hair or, as in my case, remove what little hair they have.

This 1922 squad, the first on which the Four Horsemen got their chance, romped through its preliminary games against

Overleaf *They rode to everlasting glory—Notre Dame's legendary Four Horsemen of 1924; (left to right) Don Miller, RH; Elmer Layden, FB; Jim Crowley, LH; and Harry Stuhldreher, QB.*

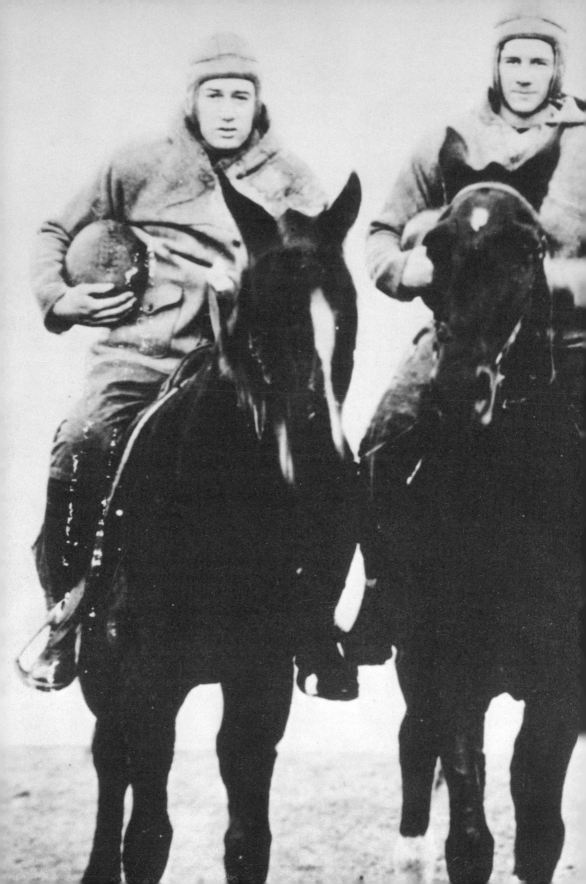

Kalamazoo, St. Louis, Purdue and DePauw. With the first big game looming, against Georgia Tech, Stuhldreher was promoted to alternate as quarterback with Thomas; Crowley and Layden were assigned to alternate as left halfbacks, while Castner, the veteran, remained at fullback and Don Miller received the right halfback berth. Crowley only won his place by a surprising performance against Purdue, when the sleepy one astonished Purdue a great deal and me a great deal more with the liveliest exhibition of cutting, jumping, side-stepping, change of pace and determined ball-toting that I had seen in many a day.

The Georgia Tech game of 1922 found the Four Horsemen ready to demonstrate. The experienced Castner guided them through their green patches, but practice had displayed their unusual gift for synchronization. They showed it against Georgia Tech for the first time and were largely instrumental in turning in a 13–3 victory.

Yet in that same game Stuhldreher, who had appeared most promising of the bunch, made the biggest mistake of his career— one that stamped him still an apprentice quarterback. When our team reached the 5-yard line Stuhldreher passed on second down over the goal line for a touchback and it became Tech's ball on their 20-yard line.

Never again did Stuhldreher make a tactical error while running the team as quarterback. I have in mind the uproar that followed his spectacular or what seemed to be a spectacular error during the Tournament of Roses game against Stanford on New Year's Day in 1925.

Notre Dame was ahead, yet Stuhldreher passed straight into the hands of a Stanford player. The fact is that Stuhldreher had hurt his foot, badly. We didn't know until the game was over that he had broken a bone and was suffering agony throughout the game. Even this circumstance, of course, could not excuse passing on second down with his team leading.

But Hunsinger, our right end, had told Stuhldreher in a huddle that the Stanford halfback who should be covering him, Hunsinger, did not follow him deep into the scoring zone on Notre Dame's offensive plays. Knowing this, Stuhldreher opened up on third down and called for a forward pass from himself to Hunsinger. Sure enough, on the play Hunsinger got clear away from the Stanford halfback, who failed to follow him deep enough. He was clear in the open, ready to race for a touchdown on receipt of the ball. A forty-five-yard pass would have done the trick, and a forty-five-yard pass straight to the target was easy enough for Stuhldreher. But not this time. As the plucky little quarterback squared himself to shoot, bringing down the foot with the broken bone to take his stance, excruciating pain shot through him, so that instead of his usual vigorous throw the ball sailed a feeble twenty yards.

Yet Stuhldreher's tactics were sound—for so good a ball thrower. For even if Hunsinger had failed to catch the ball and it had been intercepted, a forty-five-yard pass would have been as useful as a punt. If Hunsinger had caught it, it was a sure touchdown. The worst thing that could have happened would have been an incompleted pass, which would have cost us a down. As the play took place on third down, an incomplete pass would not have hurt because Layden was there to kick the ball on the next play. And Layden was a kicker!

Stuhldreher was really a master of sound quarterback play. He could read through another team's strategy without a key to the code. Against Army in 1924 Stuhldreher found their ends were smashing in close, with the result that he sent Crowley and Miller circling the ends. In the very next game, against Princeton, he found the tackle and end on each side were very wide, so he confined his tactics all day to sharp thrusts by Layden through the thinned-out line, and cut-backs by Crowley and Miller. In the game following that, against Georgia Tech, he made gains back to our weak side, because Georgia Tech had overshifted to our strong side, thus leaving the weak side unguarded. And in the game against Wisconsin, fairly strong that year, Stuhldreher repeatedly found a gap between tackle and end that netted neat gains. To prove conclusively his versatility, when Nebraska's line, in the next game, was exceedingly tough before a fast, plowing backfield, Stuhldreher wasted little time or strength on line drives. He opened up a passing attack and completed ten before the final whistle, the score being 34 to 7.

This diversity of attack caused a well known football writer to wonder what the Four Horsemen could do with a kicking game. As if in direct response, they put on one in their last appearance for Notre Dame in that Tournament of Roses game against Stanford. The entire team had wilted in the heat. The boys were unable to move. They had to rely on Layden's punting, not their usual game. Layden, however, got off a pair of punts of around eighty yards which were quite useful. Stanford lost the game despite its hard, smashing play, and Pop Warner was disappointed, making much of the fact that Stanford had made more first downs than Notre Dame.

To this comment Crowley, as spontaneous spokesman for the Four Horsemen, pointed out that the score was 27 to 10, adding, "Next year in the major leagues they aren't going to count runs that come over the plate. They'll just count the men left on bases." Pop Warner, like the grand old sport he is, admitted Crowley had the laugh and that the only pay-off in football was the ball over the line and not down close to it.

Crowley was always quick at a comeback. After one big Eastern game an official who had penalized Notre Dame all afternoon, to the neglect of the Eastern team, which he rarely looked at, met Crowley, and they trudged side by side into the dressing room. The official said to Crowley, "You were lucky to win today."

"Yes, Cyclops," said Crowley, "after watching you officiate, you don't even begin to know how lucky we were."

Crowley was the gagman of the outfit, but not at first. You never saw a more serious bunch of football players than the Four Horsemen before they had really made good, or a gayer group afterward.

One afternoon Crowley came from vacation into my office. This was after fame had perched on his sloping shoulders.

"Ran into a grand high-school player in Green Bay, coach," he said.

"You really mean that, Jim?" I said.

"He's awfully good," said Crowley.

"You mean—as good as you?" I asked.

"Well," said Jim, edging toward the door. "Perhaps not that— but awful good." He vanished.

The official debut of Crowley and his other Horsemen as big-leaguers was actually against Carnegie Tech. Castner, the veteran fullback, who had been their bellwether in the early games, was so seriously injured in the game against Butler—a broken hip in a flying fall—that he was out for the season.

I moved Layden from left halfback, where he had been alternating with Crowley, to fullback. These boys surprised the football fans of Pittsburgh with their perfect timing as they functioned for the first time as a unit backfield. Layden amazed me by his terrific speed as fullback. He adopted a straight line drive that made him one of the most unusual fullbacks in football. He pierced a line through sheer speed—cutting it like a knife, although each man in the opposing line outweighed him by twenty pounds.

They won. This victory, however, didn't thrill me as much as the defeat they suffered the very next game—against Nebraska. The Cornhuskers had one of the heaviest teams in their history—

and they are known for very active heft. They pushed the relatively little Four Horsemen team all over the field. At the half the score was 14–0, and it would have been another touchdown if the lightweight boys from South Bend hadn't held the Nebraska heavies on their one-yard line for four straight downs. They emerged from that battering a sadly crumpled team.

But they came out fighting mad for the second half, whacked across a touchdown in the third quarter, and carried the ball to Nebraska's one-yard line toward the end of the final period. Stuhldreher called for a pass, and Layden spurted ahead to a corner of the field, where he was all set to receive and down the ball for six more points. But Stuhldreher, the alert, this time was not alert enough. Weller, the huge 250-pound Nebraska tackle, crashed through the line and smeared the 150-pound Notre Dame quarterback.

Our college alumni in Lincoln had a banquet ready for the Four Horsemen team that night. But Crowley, who came through the drumming bruised and bandaged, put it this way:

"We need a thermometer more than a feed." They went to bed to nurse their sore spots.

The Four Horsemen once were blamed for a breach of football etiquette in which they were no way involved. This was against Wisconsin in 1924. We had the game well in hand, so in the second half the Horsemen were taken out and sent to the showers. In the final two minutes of play a substitute Notre Dame halfback, in for Crowley, strutted his stuff by running for a touchdown. As he crossed the line for the score he thumbed his nose at a Wisconsin player pursuing him. He was instantly yanked from the game. Many thought Crowley had made the vulgar gesture—but that was never Crowley's idea of wit. His style of thought and good-humored balance of character was of the sterling stuff that wears better in adversity than in success. Against Princeton he and his three playmates were at their best. But Crowley faltered once. He had taken the ball, skirted Princeton's shock troops and began one of the rhythmic runs of the Four Horsemen. Slagle of Princeton ripped up the field to meet him. Crowley veered and Slagle nailed him from behind.

In the dressing room between halves sleepy-eyed Jim Crowley was apologetic.

"I made a mistake," he said. "I didn't know Slagle was that fast. I should have cut back."

"That wasn't the mistake you made," I said. "That wasn't it."

"Yes, it was," he said. "I admit it. A mistake."

"No," I said. "Slagle didn't know who you were. If you had shown him those New York clippings you've been saving, telling him how good you were, he wouldn't have dared come near you."

Crowley laughed louder than anybody at this. Perhaps he knew what all the team knew, that the Four Horsemen—great though they were—received a measure of praise that they should have shared with the stalwart linemen—whom we called the Seven Mules.

This caused a few timely prods from some of the Mules. Adam Walsh, our center—a tower of strength for the Horsemen to play behind—watched them try unsuccessfully to get started on one of their famous runs against Lombard, with a second-string line to screen them. There was nothing doing, so I shot in Walsh and the other six Mules.

"What seems to be the matter, boys?" said Walsh, as he took the ball to snap back for the first scrimmage. "It seems you need a little help."

This banter helped to check the rising tide of self-esteem which only the rarest of young athletes can stem in the face of wholesale flattery. One of the Horsemen suffered just a trifle from swelled head. It was cured in short order. This particular Horseman stalked in to the squad manager and asked for a clean pair of stockings and a new belt. The manager said, "O.K., but turn in your old ones."

"What for?" said the Horseman.

Rip Miller, one of the Seven Mules, standing within earshot among five of the other six, rebuked the manager:

"What do you mean," he said, "talking that way? Don't you know who this is? This is one of the Four Horsemen."

"No–o?" said the manager in mock awe.

"Ye–es," said Rip in more mock awe.

As the Horseman walked away, confused, manager and players stood staring, while the players nudged one another, murmuring reverently: "He's one of the Four Horsemen."

The lad was cured. Next morning he went forthwith to the manager and said his old belt and stockings would do.

Those Four Horsemen were pretty good themselves at concerted kidding. Against Army in 1924 they had been warned in practice of the prowess of Garbisch, the great Army all-America center. When they met him he punctuated some of their attempts to get away. They found a neat way to irritate Garbisch. On subsequent plays, when the drive was against him, and he was smeared, one

Horseman would politely inquire of another so that Garbisch, picking himself up from the ground, could overhear:

"Is that the great Mr. Garbisch?"

To which another would solemnly reply:

"Yes, that's the great Mr. Garbisch."

When on another smash the all-America center was floored, Crowley would ask of Miller in amazement:

"You don't mean to say that's the great Mr. Garbisch?"

And Miller would retort, "If the number's correct, it's none other than Mr. Garbisch in person."

It didn't help Garbisch's game much.

Quick to block and banter opponents, the Horsemen, through their most articulate member, did not spare themselves when they failed. I tried to make Jimmy Crowley a triple-threat man. He could pass and run in great shape, but his kicking was good for just about forty yards. This was, perhaps, due to an unusual fault. He would take three steps with the ball—and that made his kicking dangerous as he held the ball too long and there was risk of the defense breaking through and blocking it. He practiced for weeks to kick almost simultaneously with receipt of the ball. So when Layden became slightly injured in the Princeton game Crowley was assigned to do the punting. On the first try his old bad habit returned subconsciously and he took three steps. A fast-charging Princeton tackle broke through and blocked the kick, which rolled over our goal line for a safety and two points for the Tigers.

After the game was over a teammate chided Crowley:

"I see you're a triple-threat man, this year."

"Yes," snapped Crowley. "Trip, stumble or fumble."

While this joshing on the part of their squad-mates lasted, the Horsemen took the best means to offset it by joining in the chorus. On the only day in a great season that they weren't able to shine—against Northwestern at Soldier Field, Chicago—they expected razzing. Northwestern was an inspired team, while the Four Horsemen were off key, off color, stale and plainly unable to get anywhere. We won from Northwestern but only after a heart-catching, nip-and-tuck game.

On the train returning to South Bend a gentleman who had gazed upon rye when it was golden barged into the car containing the squad. The conductor requested his ticket. The drunk brushed him aside.

"Where are you going?" the conductor demanded. "New York, Toledo or Cleveland?"

"I don't know," sighed the inebriate. "I guess I'm not going anywhere."

Jimmy Crowley turned to his teammates and remarked, "Must be one of the Four Horsemen."

Layden, a quiet member of the quartet, was their star on defense. His ability to intercept passes was uncanny and it never had more value than in our Tournament of Roses game with Stanford on New Year's Day, 1925. Pop Warner—greatest originator of smart plays—had a forward pass play that enabled him to win a tie for the Coast championship even without the help of Nevers, his all-America fullback, who had been injured most of the season. Nevers was in the line-up against us—and what a game he played! Twice after Stanford had advanced to about our thirty-yard line they called for this dangerous pass out into the flat zone, and both times Layden, jumping high in the air, tipped and caught the ball and ran for touchdowns.

Each of these Horsemen shone individually on his day. As Layden's was against Stanford, so Miller's was against Princeton. Miller was the most dangerous of the quartet at right half, once in the open field. His long runs for touchdowns were a feature during his three years of play. But he was a much better defensive player than he has been given credit for being.

In this Princeton game of 1923, Miller had just gone off right tackle for what looked like a good gain when he fumbled the ball, which went rolling along the ground. Quick as a flash a Princeton back, trained in the alert Bill Roper way of stooping at full speed and picking up a loose ball, scooped it up. The next thing we saw was this Princeton halfback with two interferers in front, speeding down the field. The goal line was seventy-five yards away—and no one between the runners and that goal line but Don Miller.

Wasting no time after his boner, Miller had recovered poise and was racing across field to cut off the Princeton men. The stands were in an uproar. It seemed impossible that Miller could overtake them, or, if he could, that he could offer much resistance against three men.

Pressing his speed, he ran in front and to one side of the two interferers, crowding them toward the sideline. He feinted in and out to slow up the Princeton cavalcade, and did this so calculatingly that by the time they were within twenty yards or so of the Notre Dame goal line our fastest end, Clem Crowe, had had time to rush up and tackle the ball carrier from behind. The touchdown was not scored, and so Miller redeemed his fumble by as heady a piece of work as any I have ever seen.

Crowley, the sleepy looking wit, was the nerviest back I have known. He would throw himself anywhere. Also, since I'm using superlatives where they belong, he was the greatest interferer for his weight I have ever seen and a particularly effective ball carrier on the critical third down.

Examine their records closely and you'll find the Four Horsemen stand unique as a continuing combination in the backfield. They lost but two games out of thirty—both of these to the heavier Nebraska team—in 1922 and 1923. In the 1923 game their speed was seriously handicapped by the condition of the field. Nebraska had just built a new stadium, and had been unable to grow grass on the gridiron. The clay field was hard baked, so, to prevent unnecessary bruises to the players, this field had been plowed to make it soft. A well-meant procedure, but it applied four-wheel brakes to the Horsemen.

But these lads of the colorful cavalry of Notre Dame need no alibi. The record's good enough. And the same is true of their scholastic records. They retain their interest in football while attaining success in business. All are coaching the game. Stuhl-dreher, the quarterback, coaches Villanova University; Don Miller, the Ohio State backfield; Jimmy Crowley, Michigan State College, and Layden, between spells at the practice of law in Pittsburgh, coaches Duquesne University. Adam Walsh, headman of the Seven Mules that bore the brunt for the charge of the light brigade of the Four Horsemen, is an engineer and coaches the Yale line.

This quartet of backs, destined to be immortal in football, caused me labor, sometimes caused me pain, but mostly brought great joy, not only to their coach but to the spectators. Only their fame was a bit embarrassing. At their heyday I was hounded by newsmen and sob-sisters trying to get collective and individual interviews, genealogies and prophecies with, by and for them. One determined lady pursued them for pieces to appear in an obscure journal by mail, telegraph, telephone and on foot. Finally she caught up with Crowley.

"Who on earth is she?" he was asked.

"Oh," he said blandly, "She's the third Horsewoman."

And biblical students of the Apocalypse will recall that the third horseman personified pestilence.

An accident of Blasco Ibáñez's best-selling popularity inspired their name; by accident they were brought together. But it was no accident that made them collectively and individually fine players. That was design and hard work. The Four Horsemen have the right to ride with the gridiron great.

KNUTE ROCKNE

GLENN S. (POP) WARNER was Rockne's greatest rival for pre-eminence in the coaching ranks. His Stanford team of 1928 caused a stampede from the Notre Dame shifting box formation to the Warner double wingback with the tremendously convincing display it put on against Army at the Polo Grounds. Warner's remarks originally appeared in The Saturday Evening Post, *October 6, 1934 in a story called "Is the Notre Dame System Slipping?"*

NO ONE EVER ASKED ME to pick the greatest football coach of all time, but if I were asked I would unhesitatingly name Rockne. No man ever had a stronger or more magnetic personality. No man has ever had a greater ability to transform that magnetism into football results. It is my contention that, with such power as a coach and such personality, Knute Rockne would have been just as successful with the punt formation system, the single wingback system, or the tiddlywinks system as he was with the Notre Dame system.

It was Rockne's personality and ability as a coach, together with his willingness to depart from the merely orthodox and traditional, that gave Notre Dame successful football seasons. Because Rockne made it successful it attracted the cream of the raw football material of the country. . . . At one time Rockne had more than thirty high school captains on his freshmen squad alone. He never had to look for replacements. His reputation drew them in ever-increasing numbers. Because Rockne was successful, because his team put on a good show, his team was in demand all over the country. It was a sure sellout wherever it played. It became every man's alma mater whether he had been to college or not. . . . The name Rockne's Ramblers was a magnet.

Because Rockne made the Notre Dame system a byword, the demand for Notre Dame players as coaches grew and became a national clamor. . . . And the snowball rolled on. On and on, to national championships and undefeated seasons and fifty or seventy-five Rockne graduates coaching all over the country. It rolled over Pittsburgh and Carnegie Tech and Army and Southern California and Pennsylvania and Navy. And scores of others. Its

Knute Rockne as coach at Notre Dame in 1925.

list of victims reads like a football Blue Book. It rolled through the hardest, most colorful, and most exciting schedules. . . .

Rockne was his own graduate manager. He helped plan the schedules. He helped build the Notre Dame stadium. He designed his own team's uniforms. He improved on football equipment when it was necessary. He worked out the Notre Dame shift for his men after seeing a chorus in action. He perfected their plays, worked tricks of psychology on his men as only Rockne could. He tried to pass the honor and glory on to his boys. But in the final analysis Notre Dame football was Rockne. And so it is my feeling that the spirit, the personality that was Rockne was a very important part of the success of the Notre Dame system.

And I am not alone in thinking that Rockne was the sparkplug of the Notre Dame system, that he personally dominated it more than Percy Haughton ever dominated the Haughton system, more than Woodruff ever dominated the guards back system, more than Heisman ever dominated at Georgia Tech with his shift.

My opponent in this friendly debate, Harry Stuhldreher, proved my contention beyond the shadow of a doubt in his book, *Knute Rockne, Man Builder*. Let me quote a few passages. . . . One describes an afternoon practice session. Rockne has just shouted the words, 'Everybody up,' which brings the squad together for the start of practice:

"But now they [the squad] experience that crystallization of emotion. They have experienced it before. Every day at quarter to four it gets them. It sets their jaws a little firmer; it flexes their muscles and stiffens their backbones; it makes the blood run faster in their veins. SUBJECTED TO THE ELECTRIC FLOW OF HIS PERSONALITY, THEY BECOME AS SUPERMEN (The caps are mine)."

Again I quote: "The progress of those blue-clad legs down the field is a progress born of infinite pains, of almost unbelievable attention to detail, of sweat, of harder-than-hard work—in short, of the thing that Rockne, and Rockne alone, seemed to be able to put to the nth degree into the molding of a team."

The author wrote of Rockne in The New York Times, *December 10, 1929.*

From Norway, the land of sagas, there came to America shortly after the turn of the century an immigrant boy who was, in the course of time, to write a saga of success as vivid in its appeal to the youth of today as the Icelandic exploits of Leif, the son of Eric the Red.

Knute Rockne is the name of this carrier-forward of Scandinavian traditions, and wherever football is played or discussed in the United States no figure is held in higher esteem.

The boy of tender age who was thrown upon his own resources before he went to high school, who worked to pay his college tuition, has contributed a chapter to football history which marks him as one of the game's real geniuses and assures him of a fixed place as part and parcel of its traditions. He is, of course, one of its transcendently successful coaches.

Today, in South Bend, Ind., Knute Rockne sits in his wheelchair with a crippled leg, planning for the year ahead, while telegrams and letters of congratulation still pour in upon him following Notre Dame's successful completion of probably the most exacting schedule ever undertaken by an eleven. . . .

This is not the first time that Rockne has brought a team through an arduous schedule undefeated. In the twelve years that he has been at the helm since he succeeded Jesse Harper as coach in 1918, he has had four unbeaten teams, in 1919, 1920, 1924 and 1929. In only two of those twelve years has his team lost more than one game. The total reckoning for the period is 95 games games won, 12 lost and 5 tied, while Notre Dame has piled up 2,582 points to 593 for its 112 opponents. . . .

But Rockne's fame does not rest solely upon the victories turned in by his teams. . . . His formations and plays have been copied as much as those of almost any coach that can be named. His pupils have been more in demand as coaches than those from any other college. His coaching schools have been the mecca of college and high school coaches; his books on the game have circulated widely; and there has been no other coach who has been so much in demand both as a lecturer on the technique and strategy of football and as a raconteur with an inexhaustible mine of amusing stories about the game.

Wherever football men assemble, if the thick-set, bald-headed, flat-nosed Rockne is present, he is certain to be the center of the group. To see him stand in front of a blackboard before a gathering of his colleagues and diagram his plays, often for the edification, he announces drily, of a rival in the group, is an entertaining and profitable experience that is not soon forgotten.

Although he has been heard to remark, "They call me a rough-neck," Rockne has an erudition and culture that make him equally at home whether he is speaking in the vernacular of the football field, addressing a Back Bay gathering in Boston, or engaging in a learned discourse on eurythmics with Bob Zuppke, the poet-painter of Champaign, Illinois. As an undergraduate he took honors in chemistry, of which he is an instructor at Notre Dame.

There is never anything half-hearted or faint-hearted about what Rockne says. He is a man with intense convictions and the courage of those convictions, who speaks forcibly and fearlessly. Football is of his very fiber and being. Both as a player (he was one of the best ends turned out at Notre Dame) and as a coach, he has acquired a deep and abiding affection for the game; and he has emphatic ideas of its worth as a school of training for shaping the character of the boys under him.

"Football," he said on one occasion, "teaches a boy a sense of responsibility—responsibility as a representative of his college, responsibility to his teammates, responsibility in controlling his passions—fear, hatred, jealousy, and rashness. Football brings out the best in everyone."

As intense as is his devotion to the game, just as fierce is his hostility to those who seek to disparage its benefits, while withering is his scorn for a certain type of collegian whom he terms "powder puff youths," "rumble seat cowboys" and "mezzanine floor hurdlers." Fraternities and coeds have also drawn his ire. He has no objection to them academically, but both of them he regards as nuisances around a football camp. . . . It is to the fact that Notre Dame neither is coeducational nor allows fraternities, with their athletic politics, that Rockne attributes in part the success of his teams. Another factor, he states, is the isolation and cohesiveness of the university; still another is the system of mass athletics that he, as athletic director, has built up at South Bend.

"If football is a good sport for the varsity players," he argues, "why isn't it a good sport for the entire undergraduate body? Granted that it is, I want every boy at Notre Dame who cares to kick a football to have some place in which to kick it."

Rockne teams have always been noted for their speed, alertness and intelligence, the chief reason being that he is so careful in choosing the right type of youth to fit his system. There are six cardinal points he keeps before him in selecting his material and in molding it. They are:

(1) Brains—"resiliency of mind, resourcefulness, power of analysis."

(2) Spark—"the emotional urge that lifts a man out of the commonplace."

(3) Hard work—"no one has ever succeeded without it."

(4) Sense of responsibility—"chores pay dividends, and clearing the path for a teammate comes under the heading of chores."

(5) Proper point of view—"to play fairly, to respect the rights of opponents and the rules of the game."

(6) Mental and moral courage.

Rockne, born in Voss, Norway, March 4, 1888, started his coaching career at Notre Dame as assistant to Jesse Harper in 1914. He had played end on the varsity under Harper and was captain of the 1913 team, on which he and Gus Dorais, the quarterback, made history as a passing combination in the victory over Army at West Point. From 1914 to 1916 he was assistant track and football coach and in 1918 he succeeded Harper as head coach of football, a portfolio he held until his shocking death in an airplane crash early in 1931, which left the nation stunned and saddened millions of sports followers.

FRANK LEAHY, *who played under Rockne and went on to phenomenal success as a coach at Boston College and Notre Dame, said in a letter to the author:*

"In my opinion the most important feature about Rockne that has been overlooked is the fact that he was a defensive genius. Everyone will admit that he was one of football's great offensive men, but a look at the record will show that in his most important games he held the enemy scoreless. In the real tough ones he stopped the opponents and they could not stop him."

Among the things Rockne told Leahy when they were lying in adjoining beds at Mayo's Hospital during the Christmas vacation of 1930 were:

(1) "Football coaching is no profession for a lazy man."

(2) "Don't be as mild while coaching as you are off the field."

(3) "A football coach must pay the price for victory—that price is work and perspiration."

ADAM WALSH *is one of football's legendary figures. He rose to towering fame in sports' golden age—the 1920's—when more immortals of the game were established than in any other decade of a century of intercollegiate competition.*

In a period of so many transcendent figures, Adam Walsh was a celebrity of the first magnitude. Playing on a team that had the most glamour and publicity of any in all football history, it called for extraordinary talents and ability to escape total eclipse in the effulgence of their everlasting fame. This strikingly handsome, superbly proportioned and magnetically likeable, athletic Apollo was the one member of the "Seven Mules," as the line was called, who could challenge the Four Horsemen in the backfield for pre-eminence. He was the captain of the team, the apple of Rockne's eye, and his exploit in playing almost the entire game against a powerful 1924 Army team with both hands broken and passing the ball back from center unerringly is one of the great legends of the gridiron.

President John F. Kennedy knew the measure of this man from their acquaintance when Walsh was coaching at Harvard, and appointed him when he was at the age of 60 a United States Marshal for the State of Maine. Along with Harry Stuhldreher, Jim Crowley, Elmer Layden, and Don Miller, the Four Horsemen, and Rip Miller, a Mule, Adam Walsh is enshrined in the National Football Hall of Fame.

The following was written to the author by Walsh in 1968:

THIS IS THE TALE of a lucky Irishman born in Iowa who made his way to Notre Dame by way of California, where, in Hollywood, he played high school football as a runt of 132 pounds. The odds had to be a hundred to one that Rockne, the Four Horsemen and South Bend, Indiana, never would set eyes on me.

My father, an Irish Catholic born in Iowa of parents who came over from Counties Cork and Mayo during the Potato Famine of 1846–1848, was not enthusiastic about my playing football. Unknown to me (until he told me at the time of the Rose Bowl Notre Dame-Stanford game of 1925—the only game he ever saw me play) Dad had played football at Drake until someone jumped on his chest out of bounds and tore his sternum. Because of his experience I had to continually bug him before he would finally agree to letting me play one game for Hollywood High.

I would never be where I am today except for my mother, a Presbyterian who was converted to Catholicism when she married, and my two sisters and the principal of Hollywood High, Dr. William H. Snyder, a graduate of Amherst College with a master's and Ph.D. from Harvard, who corresponded with me until his 87th year. Thanks to my mother, I was able to play football and become team captain in 1919, as well as win letters in baseball, basketball and track.

We were a family of little money to feed six growing children. All of us had to work. Dad was a clerk in a grocery store. He saved enough to buy the store when I was a junior in high school. I delivered groceries Saturdays to movie stars—Mary Pickford, William S. Hart, Will Rogers, Charlie Chaplin—making my rounds with a horse and buggy. In the summertime I worked full time and received seventy-five cents a week. I also delivered papers and worked in a confectionery store nights.

I finished grammar school at the age of 11 and could have graduated from high school at 15, but my parents wanted me to go to college. I went back to Churchville, Iowa, where I was born, for eighteen months and when I returned to Hollywood my progress in high school was held up by the flu and by my being kicked out, so that I missed almost two years more.

When I was readmitted, Dr. Snyder told me to bring my mother to him. He said that if I took the courses he prescribed I could get into any college in the country. So I took college algebra, advanced physics, chemistry, English and Spanish. When the teacher was taken sick, I was allowed to instruct the algebra class.

A spiral break of the leg above the ankle on the football field (I was clipped from behind) set me back again, and I was frustrated further in my efforts to join the Army, the Air Corps and the Marines, which turned me down because of my age. The war (World War I) was over before I was 17.

When I broke my leg I needed only half a credit to graduate from high school. I was out of school six weeks, and though I had all A's and B's all the way through, the teacher wouldn't pass me. So I went to work to earn money to go to college. I drove a

10-ton truck, working 10½ hours a day seven days a week for $15. During this time I was lifting pigs of lead weighing 105 pounds twenty-five times every morning, and this helped to develop my physique.

I had my heart set on going to Stanford University but my mother wanted me to go to a Catholic college. My sister Maude was being squired around by a red-headed Irishman, Leo Ward, who had just graduated from Notre Dame law school. He kept singing the praises of Notre Dame to my mother, my sisters and me. To him it was Utopia and to Mother it was just one short step from heaven, and that was the place for her oldest son.

Still I wanted Stanford and I was all set to go, over strong protests and sales talks from the University of Southern California. I had the credits to be accepted any place—all A's and B's in college preparatory courses. I had the works, thanks to "Doc" Snyder.

Why Stanford? It was a fine school, some of my pals were going there, and a wealthy alumnus wrote me a letter telling me I would be loaned $3,000 a year so long as I kept up in my studies and would have ten years after graduation to repay. That was quite an inducement, especially in the depression days of 1921.

Now a second Notre Dame graduate enters the picture. That summer, after I got my diploma in June, Stanley Cofall, fullback and captain of the 1916 Notre Dame team and a great friend of Leo Ward, as well as Rockne, was brought over by Ward to talk to me about Notre Dame, the Virgin Mary and the Golden Dome. Mother is gaining ground fast while I get the double teaming despite all the stories of man-for-man blocking and man-for-man defense at Notre Dame. These artists painted such a glowing picture that they soon had me on cloud nine—right in the center of the picture up and above the famous Golden Dome.

Everything looks easy now. No problems. Just money for transportation, books, laundry, fees, etc. Cofall got hold of Rockne and he told Stanley that he would give me a partial scholarship if I could keep up in my academic work, get me a campus job to help defray room, board and tuition, and another job in South Bend, and if I was willing to work I could make it. I was to report to his office September 8, 1921.

Mother is happy. My two older sisters are happy and Dad says nothing because of mother's glee. My pals are disturbed and I'm scared stiff. But off I go in a tourist sleeper (upper berth). Not knowing a single person at Notre Dame didn't ease the situation while en route. The long ride added to my worries and tension. I

Adam Walsh, captain and center of Notre Dame's Four Horsemen team, played against Army with both hands broken, now in the football Hall of Fame along with the Four Horsemen.

wondered if I had made a big mistake. I might be in over my head. I was torn between engineering, law and medicine, not knowing what to take (I took mechanical engineering).

I met Rockne for the first time. I cannot recall the details of the meeting and my first few days on the campus, I was so scared and bewildered. The varsity squad reported the same day and Rockne turned me over to them to take me to my room and register. I lived in Corby Hall Subway the first two years in the room known as the "Ice Box," it was that cold and small. It had army steel double-decker bunks, a wood wardrobe, two wooden tables for desks and two wooden straight back chairs, on a bare wood floor—for two people. Rats ran up and down the corridor, close by where waste paper was dumped, and we popped them with bats.

There was no training table in those days at Notre Dame. All students ate the same food, eight to a table. Meat was down one side and vegetables down the other. There were no fancy dishes—eggs, milk, buns, pork, beef.

My classes in engineering started at 8 A.M. and labs ended at 4. Football practice began at 3 and I had to make up the hour of lab in the evening. The freshmen had no schedule of games. We scrimmaged the varsity five days a week, running opponents' plays and defenses and acting as live tackling and blocking dummies. Rock had little use for dummies, preferring live practice. He had a heavy seven-man sled built, used to develop leg drive, as well as to get body position and to get off together both on offense and defense.

I broke my arm and dislocated my collarbone September 30. I was back on the field in late October and scrimmaged in November. I feel I really got to know Rock after this accident happened. He knew what I had been through and took me under his wing and was as much of a father to me as my own dad could have been.

During the second semester Rock got me a job with the Northern Indiana Gas and Electric Company. I worked from 6 P.M. to 11:20 seven nights a week, 365 days a year. I serviced Ford pickups, put oil in 'em, blew up the tires, filled 'em with water and washed the windshields and I also fired the big coal furnace. I was paid $65 a month.

In my sophomore year I got an additional job with Liggett & Myers Tobacco Company. It paid $60 a month, and I was earning $125. In my junior year Rock gave me and three others the parking concession. There was no charge for parking. They gave anything they wished—from 25 cents to a $10 bill—not only for the four of us but for any student that needed help. We varsity men took a much smaller percentage than the students we hired.

In my senior year Rock gave the four backs (Horsemen) and myself the program concession for home games. We gave 20 percent of the profits to the university. The balance was for us. We put out a 72-page program on the finest paper, and we solicited ads. We split $1,500 each before we sold a program and we worked like heck getting ads. I remained at South Bend all summer and the backs reported back early and I demonstrated at Rock's coaching schools.

I started college with 30 bucks and for months had only pennies. When I left Notre Dame I had a wife, a baby on the way and a master Buick convertible with wire wheels, given to us by my wife's mother.

In my junior year I came down with a strep throat and Rock advised me to drop out at the end of the first semester and go home. In nine days I lost 33 pounds. I went home for a semester and then returned to summer school. My brother and I drove a Model T touring car from California to South Bend and in September of that year, 1924, came that glorious last season for this lucky Irishman.

The Army game was the high spot of the season. This rivalry, which began with the historic passing exhibition by Gus Dorais and Rockne at West Point in 1913, generated tremendous national interest yearly until it was broken off as an annual fixture following the 1947 game. It also was a gold mine. In 1921, my freshman year, Notre Dame was guaranteed $1,000, and after the Irish won, 28–0, General Douglas MacArthur, the superintendent of the U.S. Military Academy, wanted to hire Rockne as coach. In 1922, the teams met for the last time on the parade grounds at West Point before a crowd of probably 20,000. In 1923 the game was brought to greater New York, to Ebbets Field in Brooklyn. This was the first game in the series in which Notre Dame got a percentage, 33 percent of the net gate. It received $23,500, its largest take by far for any game away from home. My mother and sister saw the play from the sideline.

Then came the 1924 game at the Polo Grounds in New York. I suffered a broken hand against Indiana the week before and the other was fractured against the cadets. There was always a lot of patter back and forth between the teams, and Ed Garbisch, Army's captain and great all-America center, was the particular target for our kidding this time. Army tried a six-man line against us, with Garbisch dropping out as a line backer. Some one shouted, "Hey, Ed, we're going right through the middle. Better get back where you belong." Noble Kizer, one of our Mules, added, "Where's Garbisch, that all-America center? Has anyone seen him?" Garbisch kicked four field goals to beat Navy, 12–0, that year.

For the first and only time, Notre Dame played in a bowl game following the 1924 season. Stanford was the opponent in the Rose Bowl at Pasadena, Calif., and we came off the winner, 27–10, thanks in part to our defense, which stopped the mighty Ernie Nevers on four tries from our 1-yard line. Nevers was tremendous and gained enough ground to win ten ball games, but it was between the 20-yard lines. I was black and blue for ten days from contact with him. Most of the Stanford players had been my teammates at Hollywood High.

Yes, I was a lucky Irishman that I went to Notre Dame and not to Stanford, the school of my choice, great university though it be. I can't imagine anything luckier for me than that Knute Rockne was my coach. He was a great coach, but much more than that, he was a great person—honest, modest and humble, always sincere and real. Also, he was highly intelligent and so widely read and informed that he could talk readily with doctors, lawyers, financiers and engineers. He took chemical engineering, about as tough as anything you can take in college, and he got all 90's and graduated "cum laude." He wanted to be a doctor and was accepted by medical schools, but they turned him down as a coach and he stayed at Notre Dame as an instructor in chemistry when he was offered the job as track coach and assistant to Jesse Harper, the football coach.

As a coach Rockne was tough as hell—a real taskmaster, but he was a perfectionist as tough on himself as on his men. He was devoted to his men and had their confidence and respect, their affection. They went to him with their problems, things you wouldn't go to your parents about. He gave them hell if they did not go to communion every morning and he checked with their profs on their school work.

"If you don't believe in it, give it up," he ordered. He required them to maintain roughly a 5 percent better average than the school required. He would not tolerate dirty football.

"Foul and dirty play," he told them, "is only an honest admission that your opponent is a better man than you."

We had such respect for him that when George Halas and the

Chicago Bears offered the Four Horsemen and myself $35 a week and living expenses, plus 50 percent of the net gate to split among us, we did not take it because Rock didn't want us to. Because I knew how he felt, I did not play any pro football.

Rockne was an ingenious coach like Stagg, Warner, Zuppke, and he was a master psychologist. He was years ahead of others. His double shift—the backs from the T to a box and the ends flexing out—is now the split-end flanker setup. He used slants and loops on defense before others who were credited with originating them. He was running plays from the T formation before the modern revival of the ancient T (with additions in part stemming from Stagg) by George Halas and his staff and Clark Shaughnessy in the late 1930's, though Rock used it only inside the opponent's 20-yard line, and he would have had no part of the brush block. When his men blocked it was for keeps. He employed the double-digits signals. Incidentally, the modern T would have been duck soup for our 1924 team with our size, speed and quick starters. We had good blockers, good passers and good receivers. All our backs except Miller could run the option or anything.

Fritz Crisler started the use of platoons in 1945 when his Michigan team, feeling the pinch of the wartime shortage of experienced manpower, used offensive and defensive lines. In 1947 Crisler substituted entire teams for offense and defense. But when you get right down to it, Rock's use of shock troops, preparatory to sending out the regulars, was the beginning of platoons.

In Rock's day there was no free substitution rule and a player had to be able to go both ways, on both offense and defense. But he was no advocate of the 60-minute player. In my years Rip Miller, Joe Bach and myself were the only ones he let stay in the game all the way.

One of the big reasons for the success of his teams was their solid grounding in the fundamentals and their absolute precision in execution. He spent hours and hours to get precision timing, blocking and tackling. I worked continuously in passing the ball back, along with blocking and tackling. In those days you had to pass the ball directly to the carrier or passer in the box formation (except when we stayed in the T inside the opponent's 20). In the modern T, of course, the center has only to lift the ball up to the hands of the quarterback bending over him.

In a period when many coaches scrimmaged their teams continually, some of them three days a week, Rock had little or no scrimmage after the first game. The men who played regularly seldom got any contact. Their time was devoted to perfecting themselves. Rock was the great perfectionist both in the standard he set for his team and for himself. He was about as close to the perfect man as anyone I have known in his philosophy, principles and actions as a coach and as one of God's human creatures. Lucky the one who knew him and came under his influence as a team disciple or fellow coach.

In 1931, following the tragic death of Rockne in a plane crash, Adam Walsh wrote the following tribute to his former coach for publication in Robert Harron's book, Rockne.

It is often that the sinister hand of Death reaches out and takes a life away, but none more dramatic than the death of Knute Rockne. At the height of his career he was taken from us, and the sudden end made the nation realize the immensity of its loss. His deep understanding of human nature caused his great spirit to be radiated to thousands who never knew or even saw the man.

To the boys who knew him well, he was an even greater man. His courage, infectious spirit of camaraderie and sparkling humor, coupled with modesty, made him the man we loved. Yes, we loved him as a father, and to this genius we would take all our troubles, no matter how great or how small. These attributes, rather than the mastery of football technique, carried "Rock" to the heights of sportsmanship that few have ever reached, or may ever reach again. Always that wholesome respect for the other fellow's point of view, always that great understanding that made him stand above the horde.

He knew football probably as no one else knew it, but I am convinced that this was a mere incident. He succeeded as he did because he so endeared himself to his boys, inspired them, loved them. Few of us realized at the time that he was transplanting his spirit, his very soul into each of us. WORK, WORK HARD, PRE-PARE YOURSELF, THEN GO!

Loyalty and tradition, a combination of reverence, spirit and unselfish service, typified our "Rock" of Notre Dame. When the years, the great healer of grief, have rolled by and the football tricks of the great master are history, all of us who played under him, loved him, fought for him and Notre Dame will not think of his football. We will think of his great understanding and of his humor and of his big heart. Every one of us will carry on with his great teachings, spreading his spirit in our own smaller way, because we knew "Rock," and knew we were one of his boys.

HARRY STUHLDREHER, *the quarterback of the Four Horsemen, wrote in a letter to the author in 1953:*

Although not named until 1924, the Four Horsemen backfield was first formed after the Butler game in Indianapolis in 1922. Our senior fullback, Paul Castner, had broken his hip, which prompted Rockne to shift Layden into the middle spot. In the two remaining games against Carnegie Tech and Nebraska, as well as during the seasons of 1923 and 1924, Layden did a great job as fullback.

Overenthusiastic fans stated that in 1924 the Seven Mules were jealous of the Four Horsemen because the latter were getting all the publicity. That was a silly notion because anyone with common sense would know that you couldn't have had the record we attained without complete harmony. But still we heard the story, "The line hates the backfield." So we decided to take a vote as to which was the more important—the line or the backfield. The line won, seven votes to four. . . .

It is interesting to note that Rock, back in 1924, originated what was later to become the much-maligned free substitution rule when he employed the use of shock troops. He knew that our outfit wasn't big enough to stand the pace of that heavy ten-game schedule, so he introduced this heavier, though not as active, team to play the first five minutes or so of the first and third quarters. . . . The idea, as you know, worked well, and I would have to say there would never have been any Four Horsemen or national championship had it not been for the two-team idea and the help we got from the shock troops.

The following piece was written by CHARLES (GUS) DORAIS *for The Associated Press on April 2, 1931, two days after the death of Knute Rockne.*

(AP)—I want to say a word about my Rock, my friend, my roommate, in the hope that I may in a way give thousands as good a picture as I can of Rock as I knew him intimately. I would like to show the humanness, the kindness, the sympathy, the lovableness that was his. To me he was not the great international figure that thousands mourn today, but my best remembrance is as an ambitious poor boy who dreamed dreams and made them come true.

It was in 1910 that I came to Notre Dame from Chippewa Falls, Wis. I registered and was assigned my room. I found it in Sorin Hall a little later and found another already there, making himself at home, a chunky, tow-headed fellow with keen blue eyes and a ready smile. He looked me over and I looked him over. He said, "My name is K. K. Rockne, Chicago." I told him mine. We shook hands, and that was the beginning of one of the finest friendships of my life.

We roomed together during the rest of our school careers and spent the summers together working at Cedar Point. When we were getting located Rock said, "Where will we put your trunk?" I replied, "Never mind about my trunk, I didn't bring one."

"Shake on that," said Rock. "I guess we're about even on this world's goods."

We played around together a good deal, and many was the time we walked the two miles to South Bend and back to save the precious nickels that were so scarce for him and for me.

Those walks were always interesting because Rock was one of the most entertaining talkers I ever had listened to. I can recall a remark of his that shows well his thirst for knowledge even back in those days.

"Folks wanting to learn something should talk about things, not people." That statement has always stayed with me.

Rock was always doping out new ways to fatten our slim treasury. Every once in a while we would sneak away from the campus and take part in club smokers in the near vicinity, Rock as the fighter and I as his second. It is good to remember that on no occasion of this kind was he ever returned anything but winner of both the meager purse and the bout.

Another time during our first year Rock heard that the players in the band and the orchestra received a small stipend for their services, so he sent home for his flute. And for a while after the arrival of the famous instrument the days and evenings were made hideous in our room by a serious Norwegian preparing to make the orchestra and the band.

Soon thereafter his efforts were rewarded and he was accepted by both the band and the orchestra. At times, in desperation, I used to take that terrible flute apart and hide the various pieces in different places, but his ingenuity was enough for the test and the dulcet notes of the flute went on and on.

Our condition was well expressed by Rock one day when we met after we had both gone our way.

"Gus," said he, "I came to Notre Dame with a collar button. I built around it and I can see the time coming when I'll have the whole wardrobe assembled."

As his close friend of college days I listened often to Rock's ambitions and hopes. First I remember vividly his oft-expressed idea that at the end of his pharmacy course he would get a good break so that some day he would be a druggist with a nice little drug store of his own.

Evidently he developed a fondness for chemistry during his first year in pharmacy, because after that his horizon broadened a bit. He now wanted to be a professor of chemistry. He therefore changed his course to pharmaceutical chemistry and achieved this ambition before graduation, for due to his excellence in chemistry he was engaged as an instructor. He continued teaching chemistry for several years after taking the job as football coach.

His objective again changed during his student days and his latest ambition was to be a chemist. In my later conversations with him after he had achieved fame as a football coach I have formed the idea that he still had a secret hope that some day he might yet go back to that which was at one time his greatest interest—chemistry.

At no time did I ever hear old Rock voice a desire to be an athletic instructor. Fate sort of threw him into the work. For the summer after his graduation he met and married Bonnie Skiles from Tiffin, Ohio. He then had to have something to make ends meet right away and the assistant coach job offered by Jesse Harper was the solution.

Rock as a student was the some forceful character that he was later on. He went into campus activities with a vim and was a campus leader. He was a good singer, played in the band, the orchestra, on the track, the football field, a leader in dramatics. In dramatics his role was that of a Negro mammy in one of the plays, which was the hit of the year.

What Rock was not good at he worked at until he won. He had a wonderful persistence. I remember his first talks in public, when he was head coach and I his assistant. He was bad. He didn't know what to do with his hands. He was nervous and his words were

halting and anything but fluent. Now thousands can testify to the fact that Rock overcame that difficulty, as he had many others. In the last few years I have heard him at several important functions, and he certainly was a fluent and convincing speaker.

As a fellow football player, the thing that impressed me early about Rock was the fact that he refused to accept traditional methods in playing the position. The method that he invented to use on both offense and defense was the beginning, as far as I know, of the intelligent end play of today. In the early days of the past, at which we later were to excel, Rock used to say to me, "Gus, I'm supposed to get away from those defensive backs by speed. But some of them are faster than me. I'm going to fake injury and break fast when they are lulled into security, or I'll fake out and cut in fast, or I'll loaf down and break fast. I'll tip you off what I'll do and you whip it to me when I break loose."

That, to my knowledge, was the beginning of smart maneuvering by pass receivers, and the results of his ideas were shown in our record. We didn't lose a game during the three years we played together, and the pass to him played an important part in all these victories. His ideas on the other phases of end play were equally radical, and the fact that he started as a mediocre performer and finished his career by being selected as all-Western end justified his ideas.

The thing that was indicative of the Rockne that I knew was well exemplified in his latest gesture of defiance to death. When he was told that he had three years to live, maybe two, did he think of himself or the pleasure he might grasp during this time? Not Rock. He said, in effect, "Well, I'll have to hustle then, to get all the money I can get together for the family. My time is short, so here goes."

Rock is not dead to me, any more than any great man really dies. The imprint of his charming, wonderful personality that he planted in the hearts of his boys will carry his gospel of clean living and fair play on and on after we all are gone.

'otre Dame's Stuhldreher runs for a twenty-yard gain ʒainst Princeton in 1923.

DWIGHT EISENHOWER: MY FOOTBALL DAYS AT WEST POINT

GENERAL DWIGHT D. EISENHOWER *reminisces in an interview with the author at Palm Desert, California in 1968.*

WHEN I FIRST played football I was in high school. I was 15 years old and that was in 1905, and that was the last year that they did not have the forward pass.

At that time we had to make five yards in three downs, and it was pretty much of a mass game—mass pushing and hauling—though there were exceedingly fast men, and you could get some interference on the side. The long run was not unknown. You could go around the end and sometimes, of course, succeeded in breaking through and making a long run.

In 1906 the pass came in, but no one knew much about it. From then on we began to use the pass in central Kansas, but in a very funny way, and the rules were not yet established as they are today. For example, the pass had to cross the line five yards out to either side of the center, and a pass caught behind the goal line was a touchback—not a touchdown. I think that on fourth down if you didn't complete the pass you could use it as a punt.

We had one man who could throw the ball end over end a very tremendous distance, and so we had all sorts of things we tried to use. But it was used as a desperation play, and it was not really understood. As a matter of fact, six years later, in 1912, I was playing football at West Point and we didn't really use the forward pass then.

Now we did have at this time some innovations. For example, in 1912 we were using a formation that was a single wing, we would call it now. We used a quarterback, either under the center, or back as one of the runners, and the ball would be passed directly. But we nearly always had an unbalanced line, and of course we had our short-side plays. And we had a wingback out just beyond the end, so as to help the end on the big defensive tackle just coming in.

Our best scoring play was what we called a split tackle, which hit between the tackle and the end, and we would put our entire power there. And that was our scoring play, you know, from two to

288

Cadet Dwight D. Eisenhower, member of Army's 1912 varsity backfie wearing his football "A."

three yards out. But in that year we played Carlisle, and again, while the forward pass was used as a sort of feeble attempt to loosen up the defense a bit, the fact is it was not yet a real tool for the offensive side.

It wasn't until 1913 that the pass caught on. We had a game with Notre Dame. Dorais was their quarterback and Rockne was an end, and they used what they call now the option play. They used that a great deal, and most of their forward play was from a running formation of some kind, and it was very baffling to someone who had never played it. I forget how badly they beat us that day—but from that moment the pass took hold at West Point.

At that time we had a coach named Charlie Daly who had been a great open-field runner in his day. As a matter of fact, he was an all-America from Harvard, and I think later from West Point. He was quick enough to pick up and see the capabilities of this forward pass used in that fashion, and in that year we went into the Navy game as underdogs, and we began to use this pass from Prichard to Merillat.

Merillat was a rather short man but very fast. He was our best sprinter in the school at the time, and Prichard had a very fine arm. He was shortstop on the baseball team. He threw the ball way down there. I never saw anyone else do it. He had a small hand and he didn't grasp it. He just threw it with the flat of his hand, just like a shortstop throwing to first base. There was no question about it—it was a very fine spiral pass. We beat the Navy, 22 to 9, that year.

Now from that time on, West Point became much more interested in the forward pass and opening up the game, and they began to emerge really into modern football.

I was a plebe in '11, and in '12 I played until I got hurt in the Tufts game and I never again got to play football. As a matter of fact, even today my leg is just as bad.

The most notable game we had that year was with Carlisle. They had some very good players besides Thorpe. It didn't take more than about two minutes to realize that Thorpe had to be stopped. So we changed our defensive formation quite a bit, and they didn't throw much. A fellow named Benedict and I were the linebackers. So we just decided one thing: Wherever Thorpe went, we went, whether he had the ball or not. All the rest could take care of that Indian team.

For a quarter, after we finally got to him, we could stop Thorpe. He'd make gains all right, but nothing like some of the others he'd been making at the start. The first half ended 14–13 in their favor.

Early in the third quarter Benedict and I, hitting Thorpe, were momentarily dizzy—that's all. The coach saw us get up and start to stagger a bit and he took us out and called us over. We protested to the coach—he was a man named Graves, Captain Graves— saying we now had this man figured out and were doing all right, and please let us alone. So he said, "Go on out, you can go back in the next quarter." You could do that in those days.

But in the meantime our biggest defensive tackle came out, just about this same time. He was a man named Devore, who had been named all-America the year before. That was three of us who had now gotten some experience. By the end of the third quarter I think it was 28–13, and the coach just told us to go to the showers. Then they made another touchdown when one of our substitutes kicked the ball behind our goal line, kicked it into the goal post and they fell on it for the touchdown. That's the way it ended.

Now, personally, I think that if we'd all been let alone, we'd have really been closer, but Carlisle should have won because Thorpe was really terrific. He could throw the ball I don't know how far—sixty yards—without any trouble. He kicked the same way. He never bothered about form. He just put his foot on that football, and it would just soar. No spiral, it just floated down fifty yards— something like that, you know.

Running—he would run along behind his interference, his knees coming way up to his chin, and then he'd suddenly put on a burst of speed. He was very fast and a big man. He weighed about 190, 195. He was certainly up to that time the finest player I ever saw on a football field.

I think of all the sports I know—team sports—football develops a great leadership and a great team spirit. I liked it and I often have said that I cannot recall during World War II of ever having to relieve an ex-football player for lack of aggressive leadership, in whatever level of command. It develops, I think, a loyalty to an idea, a team, and I think minimizes the selfish attitudes in athletics, of making a name for yourself. I think it's a fine sport.

Now, there's only one thing about it, and this probably I emphasize because of my own experience. The knee is really the vulnerable spot of a man in football, and it can happen in so many ways. Once the knee is really injured, it's the weakest joint in the body. No question. In my day they didn't dare operate, if they could avoid it, because they had no antibiotics. They were frightened to death of infection—give you a stiff knee—things like that. So, two or three times they took me to the operating room, but they couldn't find some of the loose cartilage, and they didn't really have all of the techniques, facilities that they have now.

I imagine, particularly on my first injury, I probably could have been operated on, waited a year and been all right. As it was, the doctors didn't even tell me it was a serious injury, and after this first one my knee swelled a little bit and then went down. I went to riding and I belonged to a monkey drill crowd and we liked to jump off a horse. I jumped off a horse to vault over him. My leg just went crashing all to pieces, and they said tendons on both sides were gone and I had broken cartilage all over. So that's the way my knee still is.

Every team gets it. Only thing, I don't know if there's anything anybody can do about it. I would hate to see football eliminated because of that knee problem. I would like to find out some way in which they could do something about it.

I think football is very much worthwhile. I think even a fan gets something from it. He develops a tremendous enthusiasm for a school or what he thinks at the moment is the most important thing in the world. For the players and the people who try to play it—and this goes to the scrubs right on down to the last man, the last plebe, the last freshman in college—I think they learn a lot about cooperation with others.

A man learns to be less fearful of body contacts and tough jolts that he has to encounter. He learns something of leadership. And I think it's a darn good game and has a very fine effect on a man's morale in later life. But, as I say, I do deplore this trouble on the knee, because right now if I should step on my left foot and turn rapidly with my foot flat, I'd probably be in the hospital. It's just that bad.

UPSET OF THE EARLY AGES,
ILLINOIS–MINNESOTA

"I am Louis XV and you are my court—after us the deluge." So said BOB ZUPPKE *in the dressing room to his Illinois team of 1916 before sending it out to defeat Minnesota, 14–9 in what was termed the "greatest upset of all time."*

Dr. Harry Williams' Gophers were called "the perfect team of history" by Walter Camp. In their first four games they scored 236 points. They beat Stagg's Chicago eleven, 49–0. This great ensemble, led by Bert Baston, two-time all-America end, was expected to murder Illinois, which had been beaten by Ohio State and Colgate and whose coach was a little Dutchman who had been a scrub in his playing days at Wisconsin and had been looked upon as an upstart when he went to Illinois from Oak Park High in Chicago.

Such was the renown of Minnesota that Camp went out to have a look at the team in this game, and the talk was that as many as seven of its members would be chosen for his all-America teams. In honor of the occasion, a special box was built from which the great father of American football could view the butchery that was expected to be perpetrated on Zuppke's Illini.

The following account of what happened was written by Zuppke in a letter to the author in 1951.

MINNESOTA HAD THE perfect team. Its scores ranged from 49 to 83, except against Illinois, which was 9 to 14 for Illinois. We were expected to lose by 40 points. In fact, Williams called on me Friday when we arrived in Minneapolis and asked me what I had up my sleeve. I wise-cracked, "Just the hair on my forearm."

I planned to keep my team keyed at its highest pitch. Instead of resting them, I scrimmaged the boys Friday afternoon, telling them that everybody would be on crutches after the game and I wanted them to have their last healthy scrimmage. Kline was on crutches. He was a regular end. And George Halas, the present Chicago Bears coach and owner, had a broken jaw.

The next day Joe Sternaman, my excellent back, asked for a stirring talk during the dressing period. I responded that this was the chance of a lifetime and among other things I said that I felt like Louis XV talking to his court . . . and after us the deluge.

My watch was out of kilter and wrong. So as a result we got onto the field much too soon. They claimed I was practicing some kind of psychology, but that is not true.

As we waited, I noticed a little stand on which sat Walter Camp, Withington of Harvard and a famous *Collier's Weekly* writer by the name of Patterson, if my memory is correct.

Finally, the game started and we kicked off—a flat ball lying on the ground, points to the sidelines. It scooted crazily along the ground, where it was picked up and fumbled long enough for our linemen to get to the receiver on the 5-yard line.

I knew that Minnesota always opened their play, because of superstition, with the same three backs in succession. We had the names of those backs in order—Sprafka, Wyman, Long—and I asked my men to tackle them in that order. If they tackled the wrong man, and the right one got away, then I would be responsible.

It happened in that order, as we anticipated, and after three tries Minnesota was still on the 5-yard line and forced to punt. As soon as we got the ball, on about the 50, the Illinois team spread out from sideline to sideline with no back showing.

On a given signal two backs were dropped back. Hanson, the Minnesota center, thought we were confused and he expected us to kick off. While he was thinking, we snapped the ball, and in this way we made big gains. We employed the punt formation and spread alternately. Bart Macomber sneaked over from the quarterback position of the T formation for the first tally. Walter Camp picked Macomber on his all-America team. Later he retracted this, although admitting that Macomber was the outstanding player on the field.

Illinois' Ren Kraft, an end, intercepted a pass from Minnesota's Wyman and ran 55 yards for the second touchdown. Minnesota was the confused team now.

After the game the deluge did come, and I never saw it rain harder.

The spectators could not believe the score—Illinois 14, Minnesota 9. And the next day *The Chicago Tribune* came out with a big headline: HOLD ON TIGHT WHEN YOU READ THIS.

Our defense was also unorthodox in this game. We used a seven-man line with the three middle men lined up two yards back of the line of scrimmage.

By the author.

Robert C. Zuppke is one of the giants of American football as one of its most successful, creative teachers and vital characters for more than a quarter of a century. The stocky, shock-haired little Dutchman with the dynamic personality and lively wit achieved his success through his ingenuity in devising plays, his astuteness as a strategist and his compelling power in "firing up" a team. His twenty-nine-year tenure at Illinois was exceeded when he resigned in November, 1941, only by Stagg's forty-one-year dynasty at Chicago, and surpassed Yost's twenty-five-year regime at Michigan. Four of his teams were designated as national champions, in 1914, 1919, 1923, and 1927, though he never made any such claims for them. His all-time record at Illinois shows his teams won 132 games, lost 79, and tied 12.

Zuppke never took any credit to himself for the success of his teams. He scoffed at systems and plays. "Plays don't win," he said. "It's the men who carry out the plays."

"Zup," as he was called by everyone on the campus at Champaign, was a philosopher and a painter, with a strong streak of the artist. He had considerable talent with the brush and was happiest when he was painting marinescapes and landscapes. Annually he spent a few weeks painting in the Arizona desert. His talent probably was derived from his father, a designer of jewelry for Tiffany's in New York.

Zuppke was one of the most successful after-dinner speakers football has known. He had a facile tongue and a keen sense of humor. He was blunt and reveled in trading barbs and jests with the best of them, including Rockne, a master of forensics.

The little Dutchman was at his best in presiding over the annual dinner of the football coaches with his Napoleonic stance, and there was a keen rivalry between him and Rockne in the story-telling contests at the banquets. He talked with a German accent that became more pronounced when he was excited, and he was practically always excited in the jousts of jokes and personalities. As sharp and sarcastic as his remarks might be, Zup spoke in a spirit of levity and without rancor. But he was a fighter and he never backed water or minced words for anyone, regardless of how big and important he might be.

Chic Harley, most famous Ohio player of football's first half-century.

CHIC HARLEY

By JAMES THURBER *in* PM, *October 22, 1940.*

OUT IN COLUMBUS, O., today there is no joy. On top of North-western's victory came Ohio State's humbling by Minnesota last Saturday, in the rain. It is still raining in Columbus. If they couldn't win for God, for country, or for Ohio, the people of Columbus will be saying, they should have won for Harley. And eyes will light up at the name, and the people will fall silent.

As all sports writers know, Columbus, O., is the most feverish and intense of all towns where football, or, for that matter, anything else, is played. I watched the growth of this remarkable spirit. It makes a remarkable story; it is, in fact, one of the great sagas of American sport.

Away back in 1905, when I was not yet in my teens, Ohio State was a small university, unfamed on the gridiron. Once every November for many Novembers the Scarlet and Gray was soundly trounced by Michigan. A fullback in those days named Millard Gibson was famous for having scored on Michigan; that was something. For the rest, Ohio State played Wooster, Oberlin, Case, Western Reserve, Otterbein, and, on Thanksgiving Day, Kenyon. The Kenyon game frequently ended in a pitched battle in which spectators and players took part; now and then even the ladies would wham somebody over the head with an umbrella. Thus it went, Ohio State's obscure little part in the American football scene, up to 1916. In that year Ohio was admitted to the Western Conference, which was one step above being admitted to the Union.

On the Ohio team that year was a young man named Charles W. Harley, from Chicago. Chic (you must not add the "k") was not very tall and weighed only 164 pounds, but he was the greatest football player we Ohioans had ever seen and, we like to add, belligerently, we have seen them all. A certain red-headed youngster watched him play and it inspired him; it inspired him, I might say plenty, for the red head grew up to wear a 77 on the back of his jersey for Illinois. Once, a few years ago, when Grange and Harley were in Columbus at the same time, Grange was asked if he would pose for a picture with Chic.

297

"I would consider it an honor," he said, with something of his old awe for the Only One.

If you never saw Chic Harley run with a football, we Ohioans could not describe it for you. It wasn't like Grange or Harmon or anybody else. It was a kind of cross between music and cannon fire, and it brought your heart up under your ears. He could pass and punt and place kick and block and tackle, but it was his running that got you. Usually in the last few minutes or seconds of a game he would get away like a flame and score the winning touchdown. He was closer to the Merriwells than any player in history, for that reason. He won the Conference championship in Ohio's maiden year in the Big Ten. He beat Michigan to avenge a quarter century of defeats. Camp put him on his all-America. Columbus went raving crazy.

The only game he lost was his last one against Illinois in his senior year. It broke the city's heart. I ran into a Columbus friend out there a year ago who began, just after we had greeted each other, "I can see him now, the tears in his eyes and everybody crying, and the team crying, and everybody in the stands crying." The name of Chic Harley is still on the tip of everybody's tongue in Columbus, Ohio.

Mr. Joe Williams of this city was in Columbus recently and he looked up L. W. St. John, Ohio State's director of athletics. After they had shaken hands, St. John began, "Harmon of Michigan and Scott of Ohio State are good—as standards are measured today, probably great, but they can't class with Chic Harley. He could do anything that Harmon and Scott can do and do it better. He was the biggest footballer that ever lived." You tell 'em, Saint, I'm right here behind you.

Mr. Williams points out that Harley's dazzling exploits gave Ohio State football fame and that he was the impetus behind the stadium that seats 75,000. He is still the impetus behind the excitement, the hopes and the tears. Twenty-five years ago, Columbus was fed miracles and she still hungers for them. They (I might say we) who have seen the greatest man in the world run with a ball have since that day seen only the halt, the hobbled, and the Harmon. *Sic transit gloria* Saturday.

DR. JOHN W. WILCE *was coach of Ohio State from 1913, the first year the Buckeyes played in the Western Conference, to 1928. His*

*1916 team was the first Ohio State eleven to win every game on its
schedule, scoring 266 points to 29 for its seven opponents, and
also the first to win the conference title. His 1917 team repeated
as champions and was unbeaten. The 1919 eleven lost only to
Illinois, in the last few minutes of play, and was the first Ohio
State team to beat Michigan.*

*Harley was the standout on all three of these teams. Dr. Wilce
tells about his deeds in this letter to the author written in 1954.*

The greatest all-around player in Ohio State's football history,
Charles W. (Chic) Harley, 157 pounds, was the star of the 1916,
1917 and 1919 teams. This man brought the first national recognition to Ohio State's teams. He could do everything in football
in an outstanding way, and the three teams were built offensively
around his threat of running, passing, punting, drop and place
kicking. He also blocked and defended excellently, and his fascinat-
ing personality was a morale factor of great value. We know him
as Ohio State's football immortal.

In 1916 Chic returned two punts for a touchdown against
Wisconsin in a 14–13 victory. He ran for a touchdown after a
faked pass against Illinois on a muddy field, changed his shoes
and dramatically place kicked the winning point after touchdown
from near the sideline 24 yards out, to win, 7–6. The season was
concluded and the championship decided against the great Paddy
Driscoll's Northwestern team in a 23–3 victory. The defense char-
acteristically held this team to 3 points. Chic's most spectacular
play in the game was another fake pass-run from the same passing
formation on the other side, using an official as interference part
of the way.

Harley was chosen as an all-American in 1916 and 1919, and in
1917 the team was given national rating with Warner's Pittsburgh and Heisman's Georgia Tech teams after scoring 292 points
in nine games to 6 for the opponents. The 1919 team, captained
by Harley, scored 176 points to its opponents' 12, 9 of which came
in the victory of Illinois in the last few minutes—Chic's only
defeat in three years of play.

Harley's run for the first touchdown ever scored by Ohio State
against Michigan was, to me, his greatest piece of individual play.
He broke off left tackle from left wingback formation against a
diamond defense, ran through the defensive fullback, stiff-armed

Overleaf *Buckeyes, Chicago-bound.*

the defensive right half and left the safety man standing, to score standing up. Against Wisconsin, after being held by a spread line for three-quarters of the game, he finally ran 40 yards from fake punt and won the game, 3–0, with a drop kick on fourth down from 30 yards out.

PROFESSIONAL FOOTBALL'S EARLY DAYS

GEORGE HALAS *was one of the pioneers of professional football in the United States. For half a century he has been connected with the Chicago Bears, which he organized in 1920 as the Decatur (Ill.) Staleys and moved to Chicago a year later to become a charter member of the National Football League. A playing member of the team until 1929, he was also the coach, captain, and owner at the same time. He has remained the owner ever since and the coach almost continuously until he gave up the reins in May, 1968. He had resigned in 1929, again in 1942 (to enter military service), and once more in 1955, only to find each time that he had to get back into harness.*

The Bears, known as the Monsters of the Midway, came to their greatest fame in 1940 when they crushed the Washington Redskins by the score of 73–0 in the championship play-off game. They used the T formation, and there was a rush by coaches to switch to that formation. Halas and his staff of coaches, along with Clark Shaughnessy, then coach of the University of Chicago, worked out the modern T formation in the late 1930's, and in 1940 Stanford University, coached by Shaughnessy, won every game on its schedule and the Rose Bowl game with the T.

Halas, who played at the University of Illinois under Bob Zuppke and is a charter member of the Professional Football Hall of Fame at Canton, Ohio, led the Bears to 321 victories in 39 seasons, as against 142 defeats, with 31 games ending in a tie. The Bears won six league championships and captured honors in their division ten times. Red Grange, Bronko Nagurski, and Sid Luckman were among the most famous members of Halas' teams, and his signing of Grange, at the height of his glory in 1925, after his sensational day against Michigan in 1924, was one of the turning points in professional football's climb from penury to riches undreamed of by Halas and the other pioneers fifty years ago. From The Saturday Evening Post, *November 23, 1957.*

MY WIFE, MIN, may lose her car keys occasionally, and she has trouble locating gloves and earrings, but she's the most careful woman in the world about one thing—reading the sports pages of the newspapers. When Min spots a story about the Bears, she tears it out and drops it into an old breadbox we've had around the kitchen ever since she started keeping house. When the breadbox is filled, Min pastes the clippings into a scrapbook.

Over the years, Min has put together thirty-eight scrapbooks—one for each season since 1919, when I broke into professional football playing right end for the Hammond Pros against Jim Thorpe and the Canton Bulldogs. Naturally, I get a big kick out of skimming through Min's scrapbooks. They stir up a lot of memories.

That first game against Canton, for example, was a pretty rugged initiation. Early in the first quarter, our big fullback, Gil Falcon, tripped Thorpe with an ankle tackle and bounced him across the sideline into our bench. The collision dazed Thorpe. Blood trickled from a cut over his right eye. He took time out while somebody slapped a piece of tape over the cut, then went back to work at left half.

On the next play Thorpe smashed through our line and powered straight for Falcon. This time Thorpe lowered his left shoulder and drove under Falcon, knocking him about three feet into the air. Gil landed with a Whoos-sh-h-h flat on his back—and we took another time out while the trainer pumped some air into him. That's the way Thorpe played ball. Every tackle was a challenge. Jim had a fierce pride in his own strength. No matter how hard you hit him, he came right back and hit you just as hard or harder.

Thorpe's club beat us, 7 to 0. Jim scored the touchdown, bulling over from the four-yard line. Our only scoring opportunity came late in the final period when we reached Canton's one-yard line on fourth down. I put a solid block on the left tackle and Falcon churned into the hole for what looked like a sure touchdown. But Thorpe sensed the play. Charging up from his defensive halfback post, he hit Falcon with a tremendous body block and Falcon bounced back to the two-yard line.

That defensive body block, delivered at top speed, was Thorpe's trade-mark. Jim never used his arms in orthodox tackling style. Instead, he hunched his shoulders and rammed his 210 pounds into the ball carrier. Jim racked up an awful lot of ball carriers that way, particularly when he happened to be wearing his "special" shoulder pads, which were reinforced with a stiffening layer of sheet metal. The use of sheet metal in shoulder pads wasn't quite legal, of course, but in those days Thorpe was playing two or three games a week, barnstorming around the country, and he occasionally needed some extra padding.

Anyway, in addition to enjoying the artistic satisfaction of playing against Thorpe—then the greatest name in football—I collected $100 from the Hammond management for my professional services. Naturally, I was impressed. That was almost twice as much money as I made in a week working in the bridge department for the Chicago, Burlington & Quincy Railroad.

I played half a dozen games for Hammond that fall, and those games sold me on pro football. Our line-up was packed with former Midwest college players, including such nationally known stars as Bert Baston of Minnesota, at end, and Paddy Driscoll of Northwestern, at halfback. Driscoll, only 158 pounds, was an elusive runner and tough as a keg of nails. Paddy could drop-kick accurately up to fifty yards and was a tremendous punter.

I figured that any sport that could attract great players like Baston and Driscoll had a real future. Consequently, I could hardly say "yes" fast enough in March of 1920 when Mr. A. E. Staley offered me the job of organizing a new pro football team to represent his company. Mr. Staley, an enthusiastic sports fan, owned a prosperous corn-products business in Decatur, Illinois. His firm already supported a strong semipro baseball team managed by a famous ex-big-league pitcher, Joe (Iron Man) McGinnity, and Mr. Staley wanted to sponsor an equally strong football team to be named the Staley Starchmakers.

"We'll keep you busy, Halas," he promised. "You can play ball for McGinnity during the summer, run the football team, be athletic director and spend the rest of your time learning how to make starch."

That sounded good to me—particularly the part about playing ball for McGinnity. Actually, baseball always had been my favorite sport. I'd made a lot more base hits than tackles during my college days at Illinois. In fact, I played practically no football at all until I made the varsity at right end as a senior in 1917. A fractured jaw had ruined my sophomore season, and I was side-lined by a broken leg most of my junior year.

But I had better luck in college baseball. Over three seasons I batted .350 for the Illini, and a scout named Bob Connery recommended me to the New York Yankees for a tryout. However, the war was on and I served a fourteen-month hitch in the Navy at Great Lakes before finally reporting to the Yankees at their spring training camp at Jacksonville, Florida, in March, 1919.

I got off to a good start with the bat. Manager Miller Huggins put me in right field for an exhibition game against the Brooklyn Dodgers at Jacksonville. Rube Marquard, the great southpaw who set the modern major-league record of nineteen consecutive victories, hurled for the Dodgers. On my first time at bat, Rube came right down the middle with a fast one, and I banged a line drive into left center. The ball rolled to the fence, and I stretched the drive into a triple with a bouncing slide.

I didn't realize it at the time but I was sliding right out of major-league baseball. The jar of hitting the hard dirt at third base injured my right hip. Eventually the soreness disappeared, but so did some of my speed. I opened the season with the Yanks, but they released me about a month later. I finished the season with St. Paul in the American Association, then returned home to Chicago and went to work for the railroad.

Looking back now, I have a hunch that the hip injury which knocked me out of baseball and into pro football was just about the luckiest break of my life. At least one thing's sure. I wouldn't have enjoyed an extended career as the Yanks' right fielder. Just about the time I started in at the Staley Starchworks, the Yankees bought a pretty fair right fielder from the Boston Red Sox. Fellow named Babe Ruth.

Occasionally a banquet toastmaster will introduce me as "the man who has been in pro football since its very beginning, George Halas." Of course that's an exaggeration. The first professional football game took place at Latrobe, Pennsylvania on August 31, 1895, between the local YMCA and a team from nearby Jeannette. Contrary to a story given wide circulation by my favorite gin rummy pigeon, Jim Conzelman, during his tenure as head coach of the Chicago Cardinals, I did *not* play for Latrobe under an alias in that inaugural contest. As a matter of fact, I was six years old at the time. Just the same, I was relieved when Conzelman gave up working to become an advertising agency executive. Jim had too many people believing his story.

Although pro football flourished in Pennsylvania and Ohio for many years, it still was a small-town sport when I started lining up players for the Staleys in the spring of 1920. The strongest clubs were concentrated in the Akron-Massillon-Canton area. Over the years their lineups had boasted many great players who became outstanding coaches—fellows like Knute Rockne, Jock Sutherland, Gus Dorais, Tuss McLaughry, Lou Little and Earle (Greasy) Neale.

In order to compete with established clubs like the Canton Bulldogs for players, the Staleys offered a package deal which included a year-round job with the starch company and a share of the profits from the gate receipts. And the real clincher—at least from my viewpoint—was Staley's decision that the players could practice two hours a day on company time. So far as I know, we were the first pro team that ever held organized daily practice drills.

With an attractive deal like that, I didn't have much trouble recruiting some outstanding ball players. Dutch Sternaman, the star back of Illinois' Big Ten champs, signed up. So did Walter (Pard) Pearce of Penn, Jerry Jones and George Trafton of Notre Dame, Hugh Blacklock of Michigan State, Bob Koehler of Northwestern and Guy Chamberlin of Nebraska.

While the ball club was taking shape, I still had the problem of arranging a schedule. There was no organized professional league. If you wanted to play a club you wrote a letter to the manager and proposed a date. In corresponding with Ralph Hay, who ran the Canton Bulldogs, I suggested that it might be a good idea if some of the best teams got together and formed a league. Hay liked the idea and talked it over with Stan Cofall, manager of the Massillon Tigers. They decided to call a meeting, and the managers of the eleven pro clubs got together in Hay's automobile agency at Canton on September 17, 1920. I'll never forget the date, because it marked the beginning of the National Football League.

That meeting in Hay's showroom must have been the most informal on record. There were no chairs. We lounged around on fenders and running boards and talked things over. We finally agreed on a name for the organization—it was the American Professional Football Association for the first two years—and elected Jim Thorpe president.

To give the new organization an appearance of financial stability, we announced that the membership fee for individual clubs had been set at $100. However, I can testify that no money changed hands. I doubt if there was a hundred bucks in the whole room. We awarded a total of eleven franchises: Canton Bulldogs, Cleveland Indians, Dayton Triangles, Akron Professionals, Massillon Tigers, Rochester All-Stars, Rock Island Independents, Muncie Tigers, Hammond Pros, Chicago Cardinals and Decatur Staleys.

That list pretty well illustrates the financial hazards of those early days. Only two of those original eleven members—the Chicago Cardinals and the Staleys, who later became the Chicago Bears—are still playing in the National Football League. Come to think of it, only one of the men who attended that meeting is still active in pro football. I hope he stays that way for quite a while.

The value of our daily practice sessions quickly showed up when the season started. We were easily the best conditioned team in the circuit, and probably the best organized. League records were so loosely kept that the National Football League today does not officially recognize that 1920 season. However, we lost only one of thirteen games, and laid claim to the title. Our lone defeat came at the hands of the Cardinals, 7 to 6, and we whipped them in a return match four days later, 10 to 0. At the end of the season we split the gate receipts, and each player's share came to $1,900. All in all, it was a most successful season.

Looking back now, one game stands out almost as vividly as that check for $1,900. That was our midseason battle with the Rock Island Independents. In the fourth quarter, our big center, George Trafton, tackled a fast Rock Island halfback named Chicken —and Chicken flew up against the low wooden fence bordering the field and broke his leg. Then the game got a little rough. In the next twelve plays, three other Rock Island players were knocked out of action. Since the game was being contested in Rock Island, the home town fans became a bit restless. There were numerous predictions from the stands about what was going to happen to Trafton in particular and the Staleys in general when the game was over.

"This is getting serious, Halas," Trafton complained during a time-out. "We may have trouble getting out of here."

"Head for the bench when the gun goes off," I said. "We'll cover you."

When the gun sounded, Trafton raced for the bench, and trainer Andy Lotshaw handed him a sweatshirt. "Put it on," Andy urged. "Cover up that number."

Trafton required no urging. As an extra precaution, he grabbed an empty milk bottle from the water bucket, then sprinted for the exit behind our bench, where a cab was waiting. As Trafton leaped inside, large quantities of rock crashed through the windows, so George jumped right out the other door and started running down the road in the general direction of the state line. He had proceeded about 200 yards when a shiny blue Mercer pulled alongside, and the driver asked, "Where you goin', kid?"

"Davenport," puffed Trafton; "in a helluva hurry."

"Jump in," said the driver. Trafton jumped.

At the end of the 1920 season things looked awfully good. I was in line for a promotion in the glucose department at the starch works, and I had become engaged to Min. Then the first shock of the 1921 depression hit the Staley Company. Reluctantly, Mr. Staley decided he would have to curtail his athletic program, so he called me into his office.

"George," he said, "I know you're more interested in football than the starch business, but we simply can't underwrite the team's expenses any longer. Why don't you move the boys up to Chicago? I think pro football can go over in a big way there—and I'll give you five thousand to help you get started. All I ask is that you continue to call the team 'The Staleys' for one season."

It was an overwhelmingly generous offer, entirely characteristic of Mr. Staley. I can't remember what words I used to thank him, but I'm sure they couldn't have been adequate. We shook hands on the deal, and the next morning I hustled off to Chicago to sound out Bill Veeck, Sr., the boss of the Chicago Cubs, on the possibility of our playing our games in Wrigley Field.

Veeck, whose son was later to operate the Cleveland Indians and the St. Louis Browns, was an ex-sports writer with a flair for promotion. He was positive that Chicago had more than enough football fans to support a pro team. "Think of all the people who work on Saturdays and can't attend college games," he enthused. "They'll jump at the chance to see pro games if you play on Sunday afternoon."

"How much would it cost to rent your park?" I asked.

"Fifteen percent of the gross gate receipts," Veeck replied, "and we keep the profits from the concessions."

"That sounds fair," I countered, "if we keep the profits from the score cards." We had charged ten cents apiece for score cards at Decatur, netting almost $300 for the season, and I didn't want to let that plum fall into Veeck's hands. Besides, there was a business expression I had read somewhere—"Never pay the first price" —and I didn't want to appear over-anxious. Certainly I didn't want Veeck to think this was my first experience in a business deal, even though it was.

"Good enough," said Veeck. "You sell the score cards."

Our negotiations took all of seventy-five seconds, and we must have worked out a pretty fair deal, because we're still renting Wrigley Field on the same terms thirty-six years later.

Riding back to Decatur on the train, I settled down to some serious thinking. In less than twenty-four hours I had acquired a football team, $5,000 working capital and a lease to play in one of the country's finest parks on a percentage rental. That was all to the good, but there were some serious problems.

First and foremost, I had to get a job in Chicago to support myself until the team started making money, whenever that might be. Also, while supporting myself, I had to find time to sign the players, coach the club, write the publicity, distribute tickets, arrange the schedule and handle half a dozen other chores.

What I needed, I finally decided, was a partner. Our Staley halfback, Dutch Sternaman, seemed like an ideal choice. He was from Springfield, Illinois, and a topnotch ballplayer. By inducing Dutch to join the firm, I would reduce the administrative work load by 50 percent and also lighten the payroll by $100 a game. Happily, the idea appealed to Dutch, so we joined forces.

As I recall, Dutch landed a job in a gasoline station, and I went to work selling automobiles. Lacking an office, we held our daily business meetings in the rear of the lobby of the Planters Hotel. In fact, we even signed our players at the Planters. The lobby was a bit crowded, I remember, the afternoon we signed three members of Ohio State's Big Ten champions—Chic Harley, Pete Stinchcomb and John L. (Tarzan) Taylor. Harley and Stinchcomb were all-America backs and Taylor a fiercely aggressive guard.

The new men from Ohio State—plus the nucleus we brought along from Decatur—added up to a sixteen-man squad, which included Sternaman at halfback and Halas at end. We had only one substitute lineman, Lou Usher, an all-America from Syracuse. Lou played every position in the line.

Our opening game against Rochester attracted 8,000 fans to Wrigley Field and we rallied from a 10-point deficit to win, 16 to 13. None of the Chicago papers assigned staff writers to the game. Consequently, we paid a press agent ten dollars to prepare an account of the action, and immediately after the game, Dutch and I hustled downtown to distribute the press agent's piece to the papers. Most of them rewrote our handout and devoted about half a column to the contest.

That close victory over Rochester enabled us to run up a seven-game winning streak which lasted until mid-November, when we took on the Buffalo All-Stars in Wrigley Field. Buffalo, also undefeated, had been tied twice. As a promotional stimulus, we billed the clash as a battle for the "world championship," disregarding the fact that the regular season would not be over for at least two weeks. Buffalo won, 7 to 6, but fortunately for us, schedule commitments were decidedly elastic in those days. I immediately carded a return match to be played two Sundays later. We warmed up for this second "world championship" by whipping the Green Bay Packers, 20 to 0, in the inaugural of what was to become the longest and most fierce rivalry in pro football.

Upwards of 12,000 fans—our largest crowd of the season—came out for our title encore with Buffalo, and they watched our big right end from Nebraska, Guy Chamberlin, turn in a tremendous individual performance. At six-two and 210 pounds, Chamberlin was the best two-way end I've ever seen. He was a tremendous tackler on defense, and a triple-threat performer on offense. He was the star of the day against Buffalo, running seventy yards with an intercepted pass to score our only touchdown in a 10-to-7 victory.

Over thirty years of coaching I've made my share of mistakes, but one of the biggest was my failure to sign Chamberlin again for the 1922 season. Instead, Guy went to Canton as player-coach, and led the Bulldogs through two undefeated championship seasons. In '24 Guy moved to Cleveland, taking most of the Canton players with him, and won the pro title again. Then in '25, Guy took over as coach of the Frankford Yellowjackets in Philadelphia, and won the championship for that club in '26. Over five years, Chamberlin won four championships with three different teams—a coaching record without parallel in National Football League history. He retired after coaching the Chicago Cardinals in 1928.

Getting back to that 1921 payoff game with Buffalo, not only did it decide the pro title but also it almost put us in the black financially. We concluded the season with a loss of only $71.63.

This appeared fairly promising to me, but my mother wasn't impressed. She advised me to put the civil engineering degree I'd acquired at Illinois to work immediately. "Go back to the railroad, George," she urged. "It's a steady job."

Mother and Dad were immigrants from Pilsen, in what now is Czechoslovakia. They grew up in the Bohemian neighborhood around 18th Street and Ashland Avenue on the West Side of Chicago. Dad was a tailor, and mother helped increase the family income by operating a grocery counter in the front end of the shop. They worked hard and used their savings to buy an apartment building near the store. Dad died in 1910, when I was fifteen. Mother held the family together after that by managing the building. It contained eighteen small apartments as I very well remember. Every day after school my brothers, Frank and Walter, and I performed the janitor chores for those eighteen apartments while our sister, Lillian, helped Mother at the store.

That didn't leave much time for day-time sports like baseball and football, but we managed to play a few innings of softball—known then as "indoor baseball"—almost every night. We played under the street light on the corner outside our store. On summer evenings Mother liked to sit in front of the store, visiting with the neighbors, and gradually she developed a real interest in our ball games. Frank and Walter turned out to be star pitchers in the Knights of Columbus indoor baseball league, and she often went to watch them play. But football was something else entirely. Mother's suspicions were aroused when I incurred my broken jaw and fractured leg in successive seasons at Illinois, and she never really reconciled herself to the physical hazards which she felt were involved in my playing pro football—particularly after I had made the mistake of bringing Ed Healey home to dinner one evening.

Healey was a big, rugged Irishman, about six-two and 220 pounds. I weighed only about 178. Mother just looked at us and shook her head. "Don't worry," I assured her. "He's on our side."

When Walter Camp, the famed all-America selector, watched Healey play against the Chicago Cardinals in 1923, he asked, "Who's that magnificent tackle?"

"Healey," Camp was told. "Ed Healey of Dartmouth."

"H'm-m-m," commented Camp. "I wonder how I overlooked him. He's the best I ever saw."

There was a good reason why Camp overlooked Healey as an all-America candidate. Ed was a lanky 190-pound end of only average ability at Dartmouth. As often happens with college athletes, he didn't really mature until he filled out to 220 pounds in pro football, where he shifted to tackle.

How Healey came to the Bears is one of my favorite stories. He broke in with the Rock Island club at left tackle. He lined up directly opposite me at right end for the Staleys. Ed was just too big and strong for me to block, so I finally decided to try a slightly unorthodox technique which involved a bit of holding—not much—just a quick grab at Healey's pants.

My first grab tripped Healey, and our halfback, Dutch Sternaman, popped through the hole for seven yards. Healey was furious.

"Holding!" he bellowed. "Holding! You do that again, Halas, and I'll—" He then proceeded to tell me explicitly what he had in mind.

Unfortunately, our quarterback decided to repeat that off-tackle play which had worked so successfully. I was forced to grab Healey's pants again, and again Sternaman popped through the hole for a substantial gain.

I was still down on my hands and knees when a sixth sense warned me to duck, and it's a darn good thing I did. Just as I jerked my head back, Healey's big fist whistled past my chin and buried itself in the mud, up to the wrist.

I jumped up and ran to the referee. "Healey punched me!" I yelled. "He's slugging! Put him out of the game!"

By this time Healey was up on his feet. "Holding!" he bellowed. "Halas held me!"

The referee paid no attention to us. Play resumed and I made no further grabs at Healey's pants. But I decided then and there I'd much rather have Healey playing on our side than against us. At the end of the 1922 season, we finally nailed him by canceling a $100 debt Rock Island owed us and paying an additional $100 for Healey's contract. No club ever got a bigger bargain.

Despite the acquisition of Healey and such other outstanding players as end Duke Hanny, from Indiana; guard Hunk Anderson, from Notre Dame, and fullback Oscar Knop, from Illinois, the Bears could not quite repeat their '21 title success. We finished second three straight years, from 1922 through 1924. Financially, we just about broke even.

Something had to be done to attract more customers. I decided what the Bears needed was a big-name star. The man we wanted was Harold (Red) Grange of Illinois, who took the country by storm by making four touchdowns in twelve minutes against Michigan. I doubt if any other football player ever received the adulation showered on Grange—"The Galloping Ghost," as Granny Rice dubbed him. Red was almost as famous as Babe Ruth.

But signing Grange turned out to be quite an assignment. Red still had the 1925 season to play at Illinois, and he refused to endanger his eligibility by talking to pro football representatives. Dutch and I wrote several letters to Grange that summer but received no reply.

Luckily, while we were attempting to contact Grange, an enterprising gentleman named Charles C. Pyle, who then managed a movie theatre near the Illinois campus, also was weighing Grange's box office potential. One day that fall, Pyle paid a call on Dutch Sternaman and me in Chicago.

"Grange is ready to turn pro," Pyle assured us. "He'll join the

Bears immediately after his final college game against Ohio State, and finish the season with your club. Then we'll go on tour for a couple of months—schedule a string of exhibition games down through Florida and out to the West Coast."

I didn't know quite what to make of Pyle, but certainly we couldn't lose anything by negotiating with him. He was about forty years old, I judged—a smiling, dapper man with a neatly trimmed black mustache. He wore an elegantly tailored gray flannel suit and gray spats with fashionable pearl buttons.

Frankly, Dutch and I figured that a middle-aged, small-town theatre owner who wore spats might not prove too tough an opponent in financial negotiations for a couple of smart young men from Chicago. But we considerably underestimated Mr. C. C. Pyle.

When we finally met with Pyle in a suite at the Morrison Hotel to thrash out final details, Dutch and I were prepared to offer Pyle a flat third of our net profits for Grange's services. It developed that C. C.—soon to be internationally known by his richly deserved nickname of "Cash and Carry"—also thought a one-third split of the profits was fair. However, Charley's proposition differed from ours in one rather important respect. He figured the Bears should retain the one third, leaving two thirds for Grange and Pyle.

At ten o'clock on a Saturday morning we settled down to negotiations which continued all day, through the night and up until noon on Sunday. After twenty-six hours, Dutch and I emerged with a deal permitting us to retain one half of the net profits.

Pyle was just about the greatest talker I ever met. My only regret is that Charley didn't stay in pro football long enough to take on my old pal, George Preston Marshall, owner of the Washington Redskins. That would have been quite a match.

At any rate, Grange signed with the Chicago Bears. Well, Wrigley Field wasn't big enough to hold all the fans who wanted to watch Red's pro debut against the Chicago Cardinals on Thanksgiving Day.

DARTMOUTH-COLGATE DONNYBROOK

In 1919 veterans of the First World War swarmed back to the campus, and college football teams were reinforced by a massive inflow of manpower. Dartmouth and Colgate each came up with one of its best teams in history. They met in the mud of Hanover with unbeaten records. This battle between hard-bitten, hard-boiled war veterans, to whom the savage conflict of the gridiron was a relief after their experiences in trench warfare on the Western Front at Château-Thierry and in the Argonne, can be described only as titanic. It was one of the most memorable football games of all time. It ended in a 7–7 tie.

Playing for Colgate were Belf West, twice all-America and ranked among the greatest tackles the game has known; Oc Anderson, the most renowned quarterback to wear the Maroon; Hank Gillo, Watkins and Laird. Dartmouth sent out Swede Youngstrom, who blocked three kicks in the game; "Dynamite Gus" Sonnenberg, famed afterward as a wrestler; Cuddy Murphy, Bill Cunningham, Jackson Cannell, Zack Jordan, Pat Holbrook, Jim Robertson and Norman Crisp. Larry Bankart, one of Dartmouth's heroes as a player, coached Colgate, and the Hanoverians were directed by Fut Spears, famed as a player and as a coach at Minnesota and Oregon as well as at Dartmouth.

BILL CUNNINGHAM, who was honored by Camp on his second all-America team in 1920, reviewed the game in the following article in The Boston Herald *in 1942.*

SOME OF THE OLDER and more sentimental historians have been hearkening back to that still historical battle on Hanover Plain, and since there's hearkening going on—move over.

Larry Bankart, one of the three famous Bankart brothers of Dartmouth lore and legend, was the coach of that magnificent postwar Colgate team. The immortal Dr. Clarence W. (King Kong) Spears was the teacher of our Sunday school class. Both teams were composed entirely of war veterans and richly studded with all-

A nerica and lesser team holdovers. With certain refinements, it was practically the Chicago Bears against the Green Bay Packers. The Colgate ends, Cottrell and Harris, I don't remember much about. The right tackle, Wooster, was a powerhouse, but the left tackle, Belford West, was Walter Camp's all-America and every inch deserving of it. He was the captain of the invaders. Barton, the right guard, I'd soldiered with at Devens and in France. . . . Martin, the other guard, I have no memory of, but Woodnam, the center, was a blocky bearcat and plenty of man.

Colgate had practically an all-America backfield. The brilliant all-America Anderson was at quarterback. Laird and Watkins were the halves and the fullback was Camp's all-America Hank Gillo.

Squatting like the British on the bitter *qui vive* against this invasion, we waited with a lot of guys playing end: Guy Cogswell, Eddie Lynch, Phil Threshie, Bill Streng, etc. . . . The tackles were Gus Sonnenberg, who later metamorphosed into a world champion wrestler, and the powerful Cuddy Murphy, now gone to his reward, which was rich if it measured the size of his heart. Guards were the mighty Swede Youngstrom, Camp's all-America that year, and the quiet but deadly little Normie Crisp, long a fine coach afterward and now a distinguished medico in New Hampshire. I was vice president in charge of centering and incidental oratory.

Jack Cannell, later and for many years the Dartmouth head coach, was captain and quarterback. Big Jim Robertson was the powerful, triple-threat star. Then we had a bunch of what might be called "scat" backs, fast as lightning . . . Zack Jordan, Pat Holbrook . . . a Minnesota Swede named Bert Eckberg, and so it went.

It had rained for three days . . . and we mudhooked it before a damp throng of 6,000. An emotional touch was added by the Colgate coach, Bankart, who remained in retirement at White River Junction . . . because he couldn't personally drive a team against the colors he himself once wore. . . .

It was a terrific game of football from the kick-off to curfew. Colgate scored in the first period with a little over-the-line forward from Anderson to the mighty Gillo. It was a tricky stratagem . . . (and we were behind 7–0).

At long last there were less than two minutes to play. Colgate was kicking from about the 20-yard line. One last time the mighty Swede Youngstrom tore successfully through and hurled his powerful body in the path of the boot. Only this time he didn't lose his feet, and as the missile bounded back toward the Colgate goal he was after it, yards ahead of anybody else. He managed to pick it up on the dead run on the 5-yard line and dive into the ooze for a touchdown as the whole world went crazy.

It was the tying point that nobody in Hanover will ever forget. The angle was bad. . . . The field was marmalade, and the ball was heavy as brick. Jim Robertson kicked it from Jack Cannell's hands. The ball went straight enough but it was slightly off line. Striking the right upright, it bounced back upon the cross bar, teetered there for an endless second, then dropped over the back-side for the game-locking point!

THE CALIFORNIA WONDER TEAMS
AND ANDY SMITH

Among the legendary teams of football were the "Wonder Teams"
of Andy Smith at the University of California. They are invested
with the aura of immortality that glorifies Yost's Point-a-Minute
Michigan teams, Woodruff's "Guards Back" elevens at Penn,
Rockne's "Four Horsemen" team of Notre Dame, Bill Roper's Prince-
ton "Team of Destiny," Haughton's masterpieces at Harvard, Gil
Dobie's steam-rollers at Cornell and Washington, Tad Jones' Yale
invincibles of 1923 and his brother, Howard's, 1909 Yale cham-
pions, and Andy Kerr's "unbeaten, untied, unscored on—and unin-
vited" Colgate team.

For five years, from 1920 through 1924, the California Bears
were unbeaten, winning 44 games and tying 4. The most famous
player on these teams was Harold (Brick) Muller, one of football's
all-time ends. He is particularly famed for the pass he threw to
Brodie Stephens in the Rose Bowl game January 1, 1921. The length
of the pass was a matter of controversy for years. Some put it at
70 yards but the figure generally accepted is 50, or more.

LEE CRANMER *played on the 1919 team at tackle and was a guard*
on the 1920 and 1921 teams. He gave the following account of
the Wonder Teams in 1928 to L. H. Gregory of Portland, Oregon,
one of the foremost authorities on the West Coast.

O UR 1920 TEAM was the best of all the California Wonder
Teams. I played in 1921 also and we had as good a year as in
1920, and with few changes in the lineup. But good as was the
1921 team, and its successors, to my mind none of them quite came
up to the 1920 eleven.

What made the 1920 team so great was the fire and inspiration
of youth, plus fine material and the most wonderful collective team
spirit, I believe, that ever existed on a football eleven. Most of the
players were juniors in college. We were all for one and one for all

while we were playing football. We had the best quarterback and field general in Pacific Coast history in Charley Erb.

The difference between that team and the one of 1921 was that in 1920 we knew we were good, that we had the stuff, and we were out to demonstrate it. In 1921 we knew we were good, and pretty darn good—so good that we sometimes felt we didn't have to prove it. The 1921 team felt its oats at times and was hard to handle. We were all veterans then and felt we knew about everything there was to know in football. We got away with it too—but the 1920 team was better.

One thing that made Andy Smith so great a coach was his ability to inspire a team in a few words, but that was not all. Andy knew football so thoroughly and his rival coaches so completely that in his blackboard talks and lectures before any specific game he would tell us just what to expect. He never missed. Andy sized up everything that was ever sprung on us by another team, and warned us about it in advance. He seemed to have analyzed the character of the other coach and to know exactly how much and what kind of football he would use. In 1920 we listened to everything Andy told us. In 1921 we were so good and knew we were so good that Andy had his troubles.

For years the story was heard that Andy in the tough spots would signal his team from the bench: that in the nervous excitement of a game he drank so copiously of water that he kept a tin dipper in almost continuous motion, ladling up sips from the water buckets, and had an elaborate system of signs, depending on what bucket he dipped water from.

Nothing to it at all. In the three years I played under Andy I never once knew him to signal from the bench. The water drinking was merely an expression of Andy's nervousness during a game.

Andy was too smart a coach to signal. Signaling from the bench might win one game in the pinch, but in the long run it is mighty poor coaching policy. If a quarterback is taught to look to the bench for help, how can he possibly become a real quarterback and field general? He'd never have any confidence in himself.

When the Bears went on the field, running the team was in the hands of Charley Erb, and it was Charley who called every play. One reason Erb was such a great quarterback was that Andy Smith, after the game started, left him absolutely alone. It was up to Charley to handle the team by himself.

Overleaf *California's 1920 Wonder Team with Brick Muller (left).*

L. H. GREGORY *agreed with Cranmer that the 1920 varsity was the best of the Wonder Teams. He wrote:*

All these five "Wonder Teams" were great football aggregations, but, of them all, which was best?

This writer saw the first of them rise to its stride on an October afternoon in 1920 when it opened the long string of California victories by defeating Oregon Agricultural College at Corvallis, 17 to 7. He has always felt that this 1920 team had just a little more behind it, a little more inspiration, a little more dash than any of its successors. And now comes Lee Cranmer, one of the California football immortals of the "Wonder Team" era, to confirm the belief. . . .

The remarkable power and speed of the 1920 aggregation you may judge from the fact that Cranmer weighed 193 pounds, yet as running guard was in most of the interference.

DR. JOHN W. WILCE, *coach of the Ohio State team that lost to California in the Rose Bowl January 1, 1921, after winning the Big Ten championship, wrote to the author in 1954 as follows:*

This was indeed the first of the California "Wonder Teams." As with most great teams, success was primarily in an outstandingly strong, balanced line: Captain Cort Majors, a real leader; Cranmer, a solid guard; the tall, powerful Dan McMillan and spirited Barnes as tackles, and the football immortal, Brick Muller, great all-around athlete, and Brodie Stephens, smaller, fast-catching, brilliant speed merchant, at the ends. Pesky Sprott, the power speed back; Morrison, the plunging, punting fullback, and Erb, the pepper pot quarter, furnished backfield brilliance.

Muller was the talked-of star. He seemed to be passing 75 yards or more before the game. His then record 57-yard-line forward pass to Stephens from a complicated series play, aced Ohio State and is among the most famous in passing annals. Muller's passing reputation overshadowed his outstanding greatness as a pass catcher and all-around end player.

This squad was deep in talent. Coach Andy Smith brought to a rugby-steeped West Coast, then relatively backward in football, a brilliance of all-around coaching know-how, which, combined with the great coast material, left an indelible record in the total annals of football.

California first came to national fame by defeating Ohio State in the Rose Bowl game, 28–0. After three brilliant, sustained, short-gain drives to near touchdowns in a temperature of 88 degrees in the first quarter and early second quarter, Ohio State's light, single-platoon squad of 21 was unable to get the championship long-and-short passing combination, particularly Workman to Stinchcomb, working against the all-around potency of the "Wonder Team."

GRANTLAND RICE *wrote of Muller on December 30, 1949 from California:*

Twenty-nine years ago, on January 1, 1921, a young California giant led an assault that wrecked Ohio State, 28–0. The young giant was a fellow named Brick Muller. Brick Muller was then 6 feet 2, weighing 215 pounds. He was also a track star, high jumping 6 feet, 5 inches; a sprinter, an all-around athlete. He was the one who threw the famous pass, rated 50 yards. It was thrown in a diagonal course and, while it actually carried 63 yards through the air, it covered only 50 yards down the field. This, at least, is the best estimate I can get from old-timers who saw Andy Smith's "Wonder Team" mop up the prides of the Mid-West.

Muller had big powerful hands. Dr. Wilce tells me he was about the greatest end he ever saw. They'll all tell you out here that Muller was the greatest end the Pacific Coast ever knew.

JOE WILLIAMS *wrote in 1930 in* The New York World-Telegram:

A player of comparatively recent vintage who seems destined to rank consistently with the greats of all time is Brick Muller, the California end. . . . The late Andy Smith used to say he was the greatest player he ever saw on either end of a forward pass—throwing or receiving. It is probably true that he could throw a football farther and with a flatter trajectory than any other player the game has ever seen.

THE STORY OF CENTRE COLLEGE

In 1921 Centre College, a little, unknown school in Danville, Kentucky, stunned the football world by defeating mighty Harvard in the Stadium, 6–0. The feats of Texan ALVIN (BO) MC MILLIN, *the shaggy-haired quarterback leader of the Praying Colonels, and the mighty Red Roberts, the Kentucky-reared end, became legendary, and Coach Uncle Charley Moran, a baseball umpire, was also projected into fame. In an Associated Press poll taken 29 years later, the victory was voted the biggest upset of half a century.*

For years Grantland Rice and the other top sports writers of the country recounted the remarkable success story of McMillin, Roberts, and Red Weaver over and over. When in 1945 McMillin as coach at Indiana led the Hoosiers to their first Big Ten championship in 46 years, there was a new flood of stories about the Praying Colonels. Today, a quarter of a century still later, the memory of the Praying Colonels and their triumph over a team that hadn't lost a game since 1916 and that stood with Yale for years from the game's infancy as the most prestigious powers of the gridiron, is still kept alive in the press. From the 1941 Football Guide.

I AM GLAD TO comply with Walter Okeson's invitation to write about Centre College and her colorful football team of twenty years ago.

A number of stories have been written about Centre and the boys who played football for her between 1917 and 1921. Some of them are somewhat distorted. I am happy to recount the story here briefly, first, because the true story has never been told before, and second, because I think it vividly relates how football, as only football can, awakens in boys the necessity for a well-grounded background with which they can leave college and football and go out and meet successfully the competition of the market place in later life. As I tell it, I hope you will pardon the personal reference as I am merely trying to tell the story as it happened.

It is the simple story not only of a group of young men who

Bo McMillin, celebrated quarterback of the Centre College Pray Colonels, who defeated Harvard in 1921.

came off the campus of a small American college to conquer major football foes and win national acclaim, but it's also the story of a man who became great in his spirit of self-sacrifice, and the story of a set of men whose lives were moulded during that period of life in which they learned the lessons of football and the lessons of life as they were taught by that fine gentleman, Robert L. "Chief" Myers.

Back in 1911 and 1912, a number of the boys who were later to enact this story were pestiferous brats hanging around the football field at North Side High School in Fort Worth, Texas, where Chief Myers was head football coach. Because our gang loved football so much—and because Chief Myers was fully aware of it—he refrained from giving us the bum's rush, despite the fact that most of us were constantly getting in his hair. Some of us were sadly lacking in what we know now as social background. But, realizing as he did our love for the game of football, Chief Myers knew it was the means by which he could—and did—induce us to cultivate the more precious things in life. For a bunch of boys who had been "on the loose" most of their boyhood, without being conscious—even somewhat scornful—of the need of academic achievement and better training in social, religious and cultural values, football was the one thing around which Chief Myers rallied us. Because of our love for the game—and only because of it—we boys were able and willing to devote ourselves to our academic work and to the development of these values until our efforts had ripened into a genuine appreciation of these other things that are so essential in everyday life.

During the days we later spent playing for him at North Side High School, Chief painted word pictures for us about Centre College, located in the beautiful blue grass section of Kentucky. Himself a graduate of Centre, he told us he hoped to go back there some day as coach and that we would go with him. He used to talk to us by the hour about the school, the faculty, its alumni and the great men Centre had produced. He pictured the great record we could make in football, if we would do our class work and make the sacrifices that he asked of us for the good of ourselves as well as for football. He said that we would have a fine schedule and, "Bo, you'll be the All-America quarterback, and Red Weaver, you'll make All-America center, and in spite of your size, Matty Bell, you'll be one of America's greatest ends." He told us we would have a game with Yale or Harvard, that we would not only play them, but that we would win from them and from all the others too. He pictured that we would win the Kentucky, the Southern and even the national championship.

Finally, in the fall of 1917 the word picture he had been painting for so many years started to unfold. Chief was appointed head football coach at Centre, and all the North Side boys who could meet the entrance requirements followed him there. We had been practicing only a few weeks when Chief called in several of us whom he knew best, and said, "Boys, I'm going to get somebody who knows more about football than I do to come in and coach the team." We begged him not to do it, but he wouldn't listen to us.

Picture, if you will, a man who has been thinking about becoming head coach at his alma mater for years—a man who had been talking to his high school players about it, and then when he was appointed, when his ambitions had been realized, to say, "I'm going to get somebody to come in and take my place." That is truly the spirit of self-sacrifice. That same spirit won more than one game for Centre. The players, particularly those of us who played for Chief in high school, knew what it meant to him, but he was big enough to forget himself and, in the beginning, pay out of his own pocket the salary of the man who in his judgment could do a better job of coaching.

Followers of football remember that "Uncle Charley" Moran was the coach chosen, and believe me, he was a real coach. He knew the strategy and fundamentals of football from A to Z, and furthermore, he, too, was a man with a great heart.

Chief Myers became our athletic director. He was there with us—in body and in spirit—to see his dreams and ours come true. He was there every moment to see the pictures he had painted for us for so many years become a reality step by step. We won the Kentucky, the Southern and the national championship. Three of our members made Walter Camp's all-America team. Games were scheduled with Harvard. We lost in 1920 but we came back in 1921 to win an upset victory of 6–0. This was the first defeat suffered by Harvard since the Yale game of 1916. From this background emerged the "story-book" team of American college football.

Today these men of Centre College have made good. Matty Bell is a great coach at Southern Methodist University. Bill James is equally as successful as line coach at Texas A. & M. Howard Lynch and Ed Kubale are two other outstanding coaches. Bob Mathias and Tom Bartlett are calling signals as presidents of banks. Norris Armstrong, Terry Snowday and Minos Gordy are successful businessmen. Howard Van Antwerp, the valedictorian of his class, is an outstanding lawyer at Ashland, Kentucky. Red Roberts, Red Weaver, Ralph Montgomery, Allan Davis, Herbert Covington and Ben Cregor all are enjoying successful careers of various types of business.

To a man, the men of Centre College are not only successful financially but they are also leaders in the schools, churches and social life of their respective communities.

HOWELL STEVENS, *a member of the staff of* The Boston Post, *gave this complete account of the Centre College team and its victory over Harvard in* The Post *of January 1, 1949. It was one of a series of stories on the "Ten Top Sports Thrills of New England."*

One of the most dramatic sports events in New England's rich athletic history was the epic feat of Centre College's "Praying Colonels" from Danville, Kentucky, in conquering Harvard, 6 to 0 at the Stadium in 1921 as the result of magnetic "Bo" McMillin's memorable 32-yard reverse run after one minute of play in the third quarter. To the football firmament that amazing triumph was as significant as history's shot heard 'round the world at Lexington.

In the light of future events, it may be difficult for younger grid fans to appreciate the magnitude of Centre's accomplishment. If some obscure small college like the unheralded institution of learning in Kentucky should vanquish the Crimson today, the achievement would cause no particular surprise since the Cantabs were massacred by Virginia, 47 to 0 in 1947 and pulverized by Cornell, 40 to 6 and by Princeton, 47 to 7 last fall.

But the situation was entirely different in 1921 because Harvard was then the ranking football power of the East. When Centre invaded the Stadium, on the sunny afternoon of Oct. 29, 1921, the Crimson hadn't sustained a defeat on the gridiron since 1916 and had completed seven out of ten campaigns unbeaten. These were the seasons of 1908, 1910, 1912, 1913 and 1914 under Percy Haughton and those of 1919 and 1920 when Bob Fisher was generalissimo. And, operating under the latter's direction, the haughty Cantabs had engaged in twenty-eight tilts, three of which were ties, without a setback. Furthermore, Harvard had gained additional prestige by traveling to Pasadena and conquering Oregon, 7 to 6, on January 1, 1920. This was the first time that an Eastern team had gained the decision in the Rose Bowl classic.

Consequently, it was news of earth-shattering importance when the mystery team from the blue grass region of Kentucky, tutored by home-spun "Uncle" Charley Moran, a National League umpire who cobbled the players' shoes and mended their torn jerseys, humbled the grid Goliath of the North in its own citadel.

Founded in 1819, Centre suddenly burst into national prominence just a century later. With a squad composed of only sixteen players, the Colonels finished a nine-game slate in 1919 unbeaten and untied and numbered among their victims such highly respected outfits as Indiana and West Virginia. In the course of that historic campaign Centre amassed the staggering total of 485 points to its opponents' 23. The offensive-minded Kentuckians, whose attacking methods were reminiscent of those of the Carlisle Indians, scored more than 50 points in five of these frays and 49 in a sixth.

The supreme triumph, however, and that one vaulted Centre to dizzy heights, was the uphill 14 to 6 win over otherwise undefeated West Virginia, which had toppled a strong Princeton array, 24 to 0. It was in this stern test with the Mountaineers that Centre earned the nickname "Praying Colonels." Trailing at the half, 6 to 0, Moran's pupils knelt in prayer on the field during the intermission and then, inspired by their devotions, came roaring back to score two touchdowns in the second half and gain the verdict by a margin of eight precious points.

Walter Camp, "the father of football," was so impressed by that monumental victory that he picked two of Centre's participants, Quarterback "Bo" McMillin and Snapper-back Jim Weaver, who during his collegiate career converted 99 consecutive try points, on his first all-America team of that year and also heaped praise on James (Red) Roberts, who doubled in brass at fullback and end.

Next to Moran, the man most instrumental in fashioning this invincible outfit was Bob (Chief) Myers, director of athletics at the small Presbyterian institution at Danville. A graduate of Centre, Myers had coached high school football at Fort Worth, Tex., and he induced several of his most talented pupils there to enter his alma mater. They were McMillin, Weaver, Sully Montgomery, gargantuan lineman who later became a heavyweight boxer; Bill James, who performed capably both on the flank and at the tackle spot; end Madison (Matty) Bell, afterwards famed coach at Southern Methodist. These five stars, along with Red Roberts, formed the backbone of the unforgettable 1919 Centre combine.

Nothing succeeds like success, and after Centre's blazing 1919 campaign, the little college in the heart of Kentucky's blue grass region was deluged with schedule offers in 1920. *The Boston Post* and its then sports editor, Howard G. Reynolds, were the two chief factors in placing the Colonels on Harvard's slate and packing the Stadium in 1920 and 1921. Reynolds conceived the idea of a Centre-Harvard grid series while traveling to Princeton to cover the Crimson-Tiger game of 1919. On the train Reynolds met a former Princeton grid luminary, who extolled West Virginia as the nation's leading team. Directly after the Cantabs-Bengals tussle, the Saturday of that week, Howard noticed in the late scores that Centre had beaten this seemingly invincible Mountaineer unit. He immediately concluded that Centre would be a wonderful attraction for New England football fans.

Upon returning to Boston Reynolds put the proposition of popularizing and publicizing the little Kentucky college with an enrollment of less than 300 students up to his managing editor, the late C. B. Carberry. The latter approved the program and it was decided to send Reynolds to Danville along with Eddie Mahan, Harvard's immortal back of 1913, 1914 and 1915 and advisory mentor under Bob Fisher. Mahan and Reynolds were accorded a rousing welcome in Danville and they viewed Centre's final grid conflict of the year with Georgetown College of Kentucky on Thanksgiving Day. Georgetown was no match for the Colonels, the score being 77 to 0, but even so Mahan was intrigued by Centre's sparkling play and figured the plucky Southerners worthy foes of the Crimson. Eddie's technical report convinced Fred Moore, Harvard's director of athletics at that time, that Centre was entitled to a place on the Cantabs' schedule the following year.

The Colonels of 1920 were flashier offensively than the 1921 unit which made history by taking the Crimson's measure. But despite the brilliancy of this team, which was captained by McMillin, it lacked the balance and sturdy line play which the victorious team of the ensuing season possessed. In 1920, Centre unfurled all its magic and tricky stratagems in the first half, and the astute Harvard coaching staff had an opportunity to diagnose them and also check on the Colonels' defensive lapses. Captain McMillin's valiants scored a pair of sensational touchdowns before intermission to amass 14 points, which were matched by the Crimson, so the count was knotted when the third chapter began.

Harvard, much more rock-ribbed defensively and with a withering off-tackle assault, dominated the second half, tallying two touchdowns and Captain Arnie Horween punching over a field goal to make the final figures 31 to 14. But all the customers were satisfied because of Centre's breath-taking air and ground attack in the first half, which was the most dazzling witnessed at the Stadium since the days when Carlisle was in its heyday. Even in the last two quarters the Colonels were always dangerous when they had the ball.

The most electrifying play of this game came midway through the second quarter when, with the score deadlocked at 7 to 7, McMillin, sparkplug of the Colonels, volleyed a marvelous 40-yard pass which fleet halfback Eddie Whitnell cradled in his arms while on the dead run and converted into a touchdown. This gave the men from Dixie a temporary 14 to 7 advantage.

The public reaction to that high-scoring contest was so favorable that Centre was booked again for 1921, and the Colonels started preparations for that test immediately after their return to Danville. Moran, who had played on college teams in Tennessee and also with the noted Massillon, Ohio, pros and coached the Texas Aggies for eight years, realized that Centre would have to bolster its somewhat porous frontier to stand any chance of beating Harvard. Through his influence the Colonels secured the services of Claude (Tiny) Thornhill, former Pittsburgh star and afterwards a Stanford University Rose Bowl coach. And Thornhill moulded a tough-fibred forefront which was able to resist Crimson pressure.

Roberts was shifted from fullback, the position he had played in 1920, to left end, and James, who had performed at tackle the previous season, was installed at right flank to form as fine a pair of wingmen as any in the country. Minos Gordy and Ben Cregor were awarded the tackle berths while George Jones and Bill Shadoan were placed at guards and aggressive Ed Kubale took over the pivot post. The backfield consisted of McMillin at quarter, Captain Norris Armstrong and Terry Shoddy at the halves and Long Tom Bartlett at fullback. Five of these players, Roberts, Shadoan, Cregor, Shoddy and Bartlett, were natives of Kentucky; McMillin and James came from Dallas in the Lone Star State; both Kubale and Armstrong were residents of Fort Smith, Ark., while Gordy saw the light of day at Abbeville, La.

The trip from Danville to Boston in 1921 lacked the fanfare of the 1920 journey. Every member of the squad was in a grim and serious mood, determined if possible to avenge the setback of 12 months before. In each of these seasons Centre faced Harvard with an unblemished preliminary record.

The 1921 "Praying Colonels" didn't repeat their mistakes of the previous year in the Stadium. They used only routine offensive formations during the first two chapters and then hit the Cantabs with everything in the book in the opening minute of the melo-dramatic third period. Harvard enjoyed a slight advantage up to half time, advancing sufficiently close to the Colonels' goal line for Quarterback Charley Buell to essay two field goals, each of which missed.

No sooner had the second half started than Centre struck with the viciousness of King Cobra. Bartlett caught a high, booming Crimson punt on his own 48-yard mark, but was tackled by Clark Macomber after a 5-yard runback. Two other Crimson operatives were guilty of piling on and the home forces drew a disastrous 15-yard penalty to place the leather on Harvard's 32.

McMillin, blessed with rare intuition, sensed that the crucial, now-or-never moment had arrived. While Referee "Tiny" Maxwell was pacing off the distance, the smart Texan play director, who often designated his own blockers while a play was in progress, called the Centre players into a huddle.

"Now, men," shouted psychologist McMillin to his brother Colonels, but actually for Harvard consumption, "here's the break for which we've waited two years. Here's where we win the ball game!"

Every Centre warrior responded as Bo ordered a cutback. McMillin, expert at changing pace, started to lope around left end and then suddenly switched direction to shift through his scattered and baffled Crimson foes. Armstrong, Gordy and James performed crisp blocking jobs during the skillful operation, but his chief convoyer was Roberts. Bo himself took advantage of every scrap of interference offered, side-stepping the few Crimson defenders not taken out of play, and sprinted triumphantly across the goal line. Bartlett missed the try point, so Centre had to fight to the bitter end to preserve its hard won laurels.

Harvard almost came from behind in the final minutes as it had the week before to tie Penn State, 21 to 21. With the oval on Centre's 32, exactly the same distance from the Colonels' goal as McMillin had been from Harvard's when he staged his scoring run, Buell unloosed a long diagonal pass to Winnie Churchill which that speedster grabbed in full flight and carried to the 3 before he was gaffed simultaneously by Centre's two standbys, McMillin and Roberts. Had this play been allowed the Crimson would have had a first down perilously close to the Southerners' ultimate stripe, but a

Harvard player had been offside, so the oval was taken back to the 37 and Crimson hopes for victory went glimmering.

Herb Covington, a sub back, was a tremendous help to Centre during the last two periods as his long and brilliant runs from scrimmage permitted the Colonels to hold the ball more than half the time.

Just as the final whistle sounded, some delirious spectators swooped down on the field, gathered McMillin up in their arms and carried him in triumph to the locker room, while others who made the trip North, sang, with heads bared, "My Old Kentucky Home." Following an evening of rejoicing and hilarity at the Hotel Lenox, during which practically every kind of musical or noise device made its appearance, the Centre players started their unforgettable journey home.

The Colonels' Pullmans were cut off the main line at Cincinnati and hooked onto a Southern Railroad special. McMillin crawled up in the cab of the locomotive and took command of the throttle while Roberts acted as fireman and shoveled coal. The rest of the happy gang rendered "Casey Jones."

When Danville was finally reached the players were literally swept off the train into hundreds of arms and placed on a waiting fire truck. Up the main street they rode like Roman conquerors. World Series celebrations of the present day pale to insignificance by comparison.

Readers may be interested in what has become of some of those Centre idols who blazed such a luminous path across the gridiron horizon back in 1920 and 1921. McMillin took up a coaching career and tutored football teams at Geneva, Kansas Aggies and Indiana before joining the Detroit Lions in the National League professional circuit. Prior to his tragic death in a fire, Roberts, after a successful start in politics, ran for lieutenant governor on the Democratic ticket in his home state. According to the last reports, Whitnell, who scored in the 1920 game after receiving McMillin's pass, was in business in Florida. Armstrong was in the wholesale grocery trade and Bartlett was acting as a cashier in a bank at Owensboro, Ky. . . . Ed Kubale, who succeeded Weaver at center and played such a strong defensive game against Harvard in 1921, afterwards coached the Gold and White eleven but never had such promising material as did Moran or Thornhill.

After 1924 Centre's gridiron star declined, but memories of the Danville team's achievements in the "golden age" will be recalled as long as the great autumnal sport endures.

The following piece by RED SMITH *ran in* The New York Herald Tribune, *Dec. 19, 1945, after Bo McMillin had been named football's Coach of the Year for leading Indiana University to its first Big Ten championship with an undefeated record.*

There should have been at least one more guest in Bear Mountain Inn the other night when the lads were plaiting love-knots into the long, white hair of Bo McMillin, football's coach of the year. Wilmer Crowell, who ran one-two among the East's top referees and raconteurs until his death a year or so ago, would have loved to be there.

Nobody could spin a yarn better than Bill Crowell, and some of those he liked best to tell concerned button-nosed little McMillin and his colleagues on the Centre College team that trod on Harvard's classic profiles in 1921. Bill and his boon companion, the late Tiny Maxwell, were officials in that memorable game.

"Somehow," Bill used to relate, "Charley Moran got together a crew that not only could play a lot of football but also looked the part of the Kentucky hillbillies they were supposed to be. Great big, raw-boned guys that walked as though their feet had never been out of a plow furrow.

"They had a big gangling end with knobby wrists that stuck out of his sleeves this far. When Harvard snapped the ball he'd take one step forward and then wait. If the play went away from him he'd drop to one knee, prop his chin on a hand and watch with a dreamy, pleased smile while Centre flattened the runner.

" 'Didn't do so good with them rough boys, youngster,' he'd call to the Harvard quarterback. 'Better come around and see me next time.'

"They were just about the cockiest lot I ever saw on a field. It was traditional that Harvard quarterbacks calling signals would accent the second digit of each number in a sort of falsetto, like this: 'Twenty-*six*, thirty-*four*, forty-*nine*.'

"When Harvard was calling its first play, McMillin interrupted to yell, 'Time!' I asked him what was the trouble.

" 'Jes' wanted to tell that cute li'l old quarterback,' Bo said, 'that if he keeps that up I'm gonna kiss him sure.' "

Any more such levity, Bill warned, and Centre would be kissed with a penalty for delaying the game. But Crowell was grinning inwardly, remembering an encounter with McMillin just before the game.

A deplorably skeptical character, Bill had taken it for granted that Centre's team name, the Praying Colonels, was strictly a press agent's inspiration and didn't relate to any pious practice among the players. However, after getting into his own working clothes he happened to pass the door of Centre's dressing room.

"A clubhouse meeting was going on," he used to recall, "and through the transom I could hear somebody making with the oratory. I could catch only fragments of what was said, but from the rise and fall of the voice it was plain the eloquence was flying pretty thick. I stopped to eavesdrop.

"The voice went on and on, throbbing. Now and then I thought I could hear a sniffle. Now and then a sob. . . . Then there was silence, and then a number of voices in chorus, like group prayer.

"I hurried down the corridor to get the other officials and prove to 'em that the Praying Colonels actually did pray before a game. We stood and listened for a while, and then the chanting ended and we heard feet shuffling on the floor, so we ducked out of there.

"We stood just outside the field-house entrance, and the players filed past us. This one was drying his eyes with big, red knuckles. That one was choking back a sob. All the faces were downcast and some were tear-stained. To me—I was younger then, and impressionable—they looked devout.

"Bo was the last one out. He stopped and turned to me, and his lip was quivering.

" 'M-mmistah,' he said, 'out theah on that field today you're gonna see the blinkety blankest gang of fightin' such and suches you evah see in youah unexpurgated Yankee life.' "

FOOTBALL FORMATIONS AND TECHNIQUES

GLENN S. (POP) WARNER *wrote in a letter to the author in 1951:*

CONFLICTING CLAIMS have been made as to who invented or first used the many improvements and developments in football through the years. Some of these claims, I am sure, cannot be either proved or disproved but others can be verified and credit given where it rightfully belongs. I will therefore furnish what information I can to help arrive at the facts.

First, formations. Of course we all know that what is now called the T formation was the first formation generally used. It was called the regular formation because it was the original.

The positions on the team were descriptive of where the players were stationed. Ends were on the ends of the line. I do not know how the tackles came to get that name but guards were guarding the center, and the quarterback was one quarter as far back as the fullback.

I do not think anyone can say who invented the T or regular formation because it is probable that all teams that played the game when it first started used the same formation. . . . This formation was revived and became known as the modern T . . . and was so successfully used by the Chicago Bears and Stanford in 1940 that there was a stampede of coaches to that formation. In my opinion those two teams would have been just as successful if they had used most any other modern formation, because both teams that year had much better material than their opponents.

As a matter of fact the regular (T) formation was in use from the very beginning up to the present time. I remember very well that Cavanaugh and Doc Spears used it at Dartmouth when they coached there in the years 1911 to 1920. And of course the teams using the Notre Dame shift lined up in regular formation and ran some plays from it without shifting.

In the early days there were several different formations used up to the time in 1910 when the rules made it necessary to have seven men on the line and prevented helping the runner from behind. One of the most notable of these early-day formations was the close formation, first used by Princeton, in which the players lined up in an elliptical formation as close together as they could.

The ends were a little back and the backs very close to the line. The most effective plays from it were revolving plays to either side and power plays through the line. That was in the middle nineties.

Another formation which involved bringing linemen back of the line was the "guards back" formation first used (and very successfully) by George Woodruff at Pennsylvania (also the "ends back" formation of Alonzo Stagg in 1890). So successful was his formation that coaches all over the country made use of the idea in various ways, and guards back or tackles back formations became quite generally used. Doc Williams of Minnesota featured tackles back [as also did Stagg and Camp].

I do not think that George Woodruff has been given enough credit for the several ways he helped in the development of the game. In addition to his guards back formation, he was the first to use close-in crashing ends on the defense. Before this, the defensive ends generally played from three to five yards outside their tackles and their main duty against running plays was to make sure that the play did not go around them. They played a cautious game, tackling the runner if they could sift through the interference or turning the play inside so that the players backing up the line could nail the ball carrier. Woodruff's crashing ends played in very close to their tackles and their main duty was to rush in and break up the interference. That method of defensive end play in modified form has been in pretty general use ever since Woodruff proved its effectiveness.

I am quite sure that Woodruff was also the first to use starting signals to put the ball in play. Up to his time all teams started on the ball. That meant that they had to be able to see the ball (not always easy) and the defense had an equal opportunity to charge. The starting signals made it unnecessary for all the players to see the ball and gave the attacking team the big advantage of charging with the ball, helping the linemen particularly against their opponents. Starting signals of course have come to be used by all teams.

To get back to formations—in 1910 when the rules were radically changed, making it necessary to have seven men on the offensive line and preventing helping the runner from behind, guards and tackles back and practically all mass plays became unlawful. Up to that time the idea was to concentrate power in the backfield—some interferers to be ahead of the ball carrier and others in tandem or wedge formation pushing the ball carrier from behind. With that method of play ruled out, there was no longer any use of concentrating power in the backfield and the problem therefore now was to so place the backs that they would be in the position of greatest value.

Defensive tackles had always been difficult to keep out of the offensive backfield because they generally played outside the offensive ends and therefore could not often be blocked in on wide plays. I figured that one back could be used to very good advantage by placing him in a position where he would outflank the opposing tackle and still be in a position where he could run with the ball, as on reverse plays. I therefore started to use the formation which is known as the single wing formation.

That formation was referred to by Walter Camp as the Carlisle formation in the early days of its use. I originated it in 1906 and in later years I carried the idea a step further by placing both halfbacks in position close to the line and wide enough to outflank the defensive tackles. This became known as the double wing system. I therefore believe I should be credited with originating and first making use of the wingback system of play, both single wing and double wing.

As to who originated the Notre Dame shift, often alluded to as the Rockne or Notre Dame system, there seems to be some doubt. Jesse Harper used it, I understand, before Rockne. Harper was a former University of Chicago player under Stagg, and coach Stagg may have been the originator of it. [Rockne said the Notre Dame shift went back to Stagg.]

I do not know who was the first to use the spiral punt. I do known that Mt. Pleasant of Carlisle was kicking spirals in 1906 but I do not claim that he was the first to use it.

There have been several claims for the first to use the spiral pass. I do not believe that anyone has a provable claim to that method of passing. As soon as the forward pass was legalized by the rules committee in 1906, teams all over the country started using it in the same season, and it seems quite probable to me that players on several teams discovered that they could throw the ball spirally. I do know that Frank Mt. Pleasant of Carlisle was using the spiral pass very expertly in 1907. I was coaching at Cornell in 1906 and went back to Carlisle in 1907, and since the Indian backs were throwing the spiral so well in 1907, it seems reasonable to me that they must have started it the year before when the forward pass first came into use. As I stated above, it is possible that other backs used the spiral that same year.

Regarding the huddle system of giving signals, I notice that in the book *Football Through the Years* Herb McCracken claims to have been the first coach to use it exclusively. All through the early years the huddle had been used occasionally to call the play. [Stagg used the huddle indoors for a game in 1896. Zuppke claims to have been the first to make extensive use of it, in 1921.]

As to methods of getting the ball back from center to the ball carrier, I do not believe there is any record of proof as to who originated the different methods of passing the ball back to the quarterback or who was the first to use the direct pass from center to the ball carrier. [Stagg says he used the center snap in 1894 and Heisman claims to have used it in 1893. Heisman credits Camp with being the first to use the long snap from center to the punter. Parke Davis says that George Woodruff originated it. Zuppke claims that the spiral pass from center was used by his Muskegon High School team in 1906.]

I believe that Howard Jones at Southern California was the first coach to use the trap play (sometimes called sucker play or mousetrap). It was around 1928. [Walter Camp, Percy Haughton of Harvard and his predecessor there, W. Cameron Forbes; Ray Morrison of S.M.U., Tad Jones of Yale and Carl Snavely at Bucknell are other coaches credited with the trap.]

I believe I was the first coach to use the three- or four-point stance on offense in the backfield. I first had the backfield rest part of their weight on both hands, but later, on only one hand. I figured they could get a quicker start by taking a stance somewhat like a sprinter. Such a stance of the backs has been quite generally used. Up to the time I used this idea, all the backs stood up, resting their hands on their knees. A great many teams still use that standing stance, especially the T formation or shifting teams.

If you look at snapshots of football teams of the old days in action you will note that almost all of the players are on their feet. That was because in the early days blockers used only their shoulders, seldom leaving their feet. I figured that the use of the full length of the body provided a greater blocking surface than just the width of the shoulders and also made it less likely for the blocker to violate the rules by using arms or hands, and also making it harder for the defensive man to avoid the block. I therefore started using the body block or clipping block. The blocker leaving his feet and throwing his body across the defensive man's legs, following through with a body roll—the type of block the Indians used very successfully—was for several years alluded to by sports writers as the "Indian block." I believe I was the first to

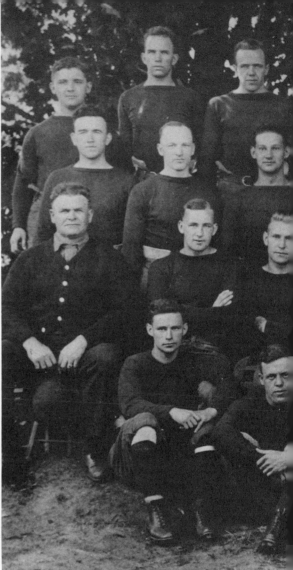

The 1916 Pittsburgh national champions, regarded by Pop Warner as the best team he ever coached.

use that block, which has since become the standard method of blocking in the open field.

I naturally had an inventive mind and I think I introduced some things in practice field equipment and protectors for the players which were a help in teaching fundamentals and giving the players better protection from injuries. Besides the tackling dummy, which most coaches used, I devised, among other things, a charging sled, used to practice quick starting by the linemen and as a developer of the leg and back muscles. I think I was the first to use such a machine, which now is in use on practically all prac-

tice fields all over the country. [Stagg said that he used a tackling dummy in 1889, suspending a rolled-up mattress in the gym, and that he had a charging sled in 1904.]

I remember that Bob Zuppke said in a talk that "Pop Warner has all kinds of gadgets for his boys to use in developing fundamentals without personal contact, and I don't think he will ever be satisfied until he invents a robot player which will yell 'Ouch' when tackled."

Regarding player uniforms and protectors in the old days, only soft padding was used on knees, hips, elbows and shoulders.

Such pads were clumsy. They became water-logged with perspiration and wet weather and they afforded little protection against severe contact with other players. Injuries to the large thigh muscles, called charley horse bruises, were common and very painful and slow to heal. Rattan or cane strips were commonly used to prevent thigh bruises but they afforded very little protection.

I figured that protectors which would fit closely to the parts to be shielded and distribute the impact of hard knocks over a large surface would afford much more protection and would be less clumsy and not act as sponges, becoming heavy with moisture. Sheet metal was against the rules. I couldn't think of any other material for such protectors until one day I bought a pair of shoes and was given a shoe horn. This shoe horn was made of a light fiber about 1/16th of an inch thick and I at once figured that was the material I had been looking for. I found where the fiber was manufactured and that it could be had in flat pieces of any shape and thickness. I sent patterns for making thigh and shoulder protectors, and when the fiber arrived I soaked the pieces in water to soften them and then bent them into the proper shape. When they were dry, I water-proofed them with a coat of varnish. They were lined on the inside with wool felt and they proved a big success.

Years after, the fiber company from which I secured the material wrote me and said that in looking through their files they learned that I was the first person to buy any of their product for use in athletic equipment and that since then the use of their product for athletic purposes had become a large business. They offered to supply me with any of their product whenever I could use it—free of charge.

Well, that about covers everything in the way of football inventions I can think of. I hope I have not blown my own horn too loudly. I was fortunate to be coaching in the early days when football was having growing pains and it was not then difficult to see how the game and the equipment could be improved.

I did not originate the use of linemen as interferers. Old Pudge Heffelfinger—that great old guard of Yale—was doing a great job as an interferer before 1890.

GLENN WARNER

By the author.

WITH THE EXCEPTION OF Rockne, Pop Warner was the most publicized coach in football in their heyday in the 1920's, when Zuppke, Stagg, Yost, Dobie, Neyland, Wade, Sutherland, Alexander, Heisman, McGugin, Spears, Andy Smith, Roper, Morrison, Tad and Howard Jones, Hawley, Cavanaugh, Biff Jones, Sanford, Bible, Wilce, Moore, McLaughry, Bezdek, O'Neill, Meehan, Kerr, Ingram, Stevens, McCracken, McEwan, Mehre, and Phelan, were holding forth. For years after, Warner, with Rockne, was written and talked about almost as much as the leaders who followed.

One of the pioneers and patriarchs of the game, who died at the age of eighty-three in 1954, after having coached from 1895 to 1939, Warner won national recognition as a coach of rare talents during his years at the Carlisle Indian training school at the start of the century, and even more so with his great Pittsburgh teams prior to our entry in the First World War. But it was not until Rockne usurped the national spotlight that Warner attained his greatest celebrity while at Leland Stanford University.

During the fabulous Twenties, when sports in general enjoyed their golden age of prosperity, and million-dollar stadiums went up all over the land, Warner and Rockne were the two magic names of the football coaching fraternity. Theirs were the two systems that led the parade and set the example for coaches throughout the country. The other coaches either jumped on the trickily designed Warner bandwagon, with double wingbacks flanking an unbalanced line, or piled into another famous Model T contraption bearing the Rockne stamp that got away to a fast start with its bitterly debated shift.

The rivalry beween the two coaches and their systems stood without precedent or parallel in football until approached by that between another Notre Dame coach, Frank Leahy, a pupil of Rockne's, and Earl (Red) Blaik of West Point in the Forties. The rivalry between Rockne and Warner, however, never developed the acrimony that tinged the philippics exchanged between Warner and Howard Jones of Southern California, another progenitor of the shift, which was anathema to Warner.

343

In his book, *Football for Coaches and Players*, Warner wrote scornfully of the shift as a "Rhythmic fancy movement such as is necessary for the success of a Russian toe dancer. . . . I firmly believe in dispensing with the Pavlova stuff and getting right down to the business in hand—that of gaining ground with the least possible fuss and feathers."

Glenn Warner was not the magnetic, vibrant personality that was Knute Rockne. He lacked the inspirational fervor and the mastery of psychology with which his South Bend rival lifted his teams for the supreme test. He was not a dominant, forceful leader of men, as was Rockne, though he could win their affection and loyalty as could few others. This was demonstrated at Carlisle, again at Pittsburgh and once again when, upon his signing a contract in December, 1932, at the age of sixty-one to go to Temple University, eighty-two members of his Stanford squad called on him and begged him, with tears in their eyes, to tear up the contract, declaring they would fight their hearts out for him if he stayed.

Warner had little of Rockne's biting sarcasm, penetrating wit, and genius for coining phrases, which were reflective of the spirit and tempo at which life was lived by the college youth in the tempestuous Twenties. His was the more contemplative and deliberative mind. And, though the roar of the crowd was music in his ears, it was not the atmosphere in which he excelled or found his metier, except as his individually fashioned machines carried out his precepts. It was behind the scenes, in the quiet of his study, that the genius of Warner, a tinkerer whose hobby was to take apart worn-out automobile engines and put them together again, found its expression. There he worked out the innovations, conceived the stratagems, and devised the departures from orthodox football that won him recognition as one of the two most fertile and original minds football has known, the other being Stagg's.

Rockne contributed little that was new in football. He himself readily acknowledged that the system bearing his name had its roots in the football taught at Chicago by Stagg and imbibed there by Jesse Harper, who brought it to Notre Dame in 1913 as Rockne's predecessor and mentor. Warner was pre-eminently a creator, and his fame is secure as one of the trail-blazers who led football out of the wilderness of massed, close-order, push-and-pull play into the open game of speed, deception, and brains that is so much more worthy a pastime for college youth.

As a player at Cornell, Warner was entirely familiar with the shortcomings of the game of beef and brawn and of the dangerous momentum mass plays. His was one of the more intelligent and visionary minds that helped to bring about the evolution of football from a mere physical test of unimaginative brute strength to a contest of skill in which the college youth was given the chance to show that there was something underneath his long hair besides a skull.

Warner was one of those who led in opening up the wider avenues of attack, ignored when the offense concentrated on pushing and pulling the ball carrier straight ahead five yards in three downs, and of putting finesse and mobility into the game. Initiative had been characteristic of him since his student days at Cornell, when he organized boarding clubs to help defray his expenses while studying law and winning his letter in football, baseball, boxing, and track. He also found time to express his artistic bent in water-color landscapes, which he sold to add to his income.

Warner was at Carlisle when the game began to take on this new and more attractive aspect. He had started his coaching career at Georgia in 1895, after getting his law degree at Cornell in the spring and hanging out his shingle for a few months. He was at Georgia in 1895 and 1896 and at the same time conducting pre-season practice at Iowa State. Then he went back to his alma mater to coach in 1897 and 1898. The following year he took charge at the government school for Indians at Carlisle, and he served there as athletic director and coach of football, baseball, track, and boxing through 1914, except for the years of 1904, 1905, and 1906, when he was back at Cornell.

Speed and deception characterized the football that Warner's Carlisle teams played. In the fast and comparatively light Indian athletes he had the type of material with which to build an open attack. These athletes loved to outsmart the white man and were adept in throwing the forward pass. Jim Thorpe was his star pupil along with many others.

It was while he was at Carlisle that Warner worked out the formation that was to win him his greatest renown as the founder of a system that became a standard national pattern. This was his single wing formation, with the ball carriers in Z alignment and one of the halfbacks flanking and in back of the end on the strong side of an unbalanced line, in which position he worked with his end in taking the defensive tackle out of the play. Then, taking the other halfback from his position five yards back of center and stationing him outside of and in back of the end on the short side of the unbalanced line, Warner had two halfbacks flanking the ends, with the quarterback a yard behind the right guard and the fullback four yards to the rear of center. This was the celebrated double wingback formation, projecting reverses, fakes, and spinners, and putting a big premium on a powerful, hard-running quarterback and fullback.

Just when Warner first used the single and double wing formations cannot be determined. Warner said himself on one occasion that it was against Army in 1912 that he first sprang the single wing, though at other times he put it as early as 1906, and shortly before he died he said that he could not recall the exact year. But, regardless of the year he first used the double wing, it provoked no comment while he was at Carlisle, if he used it there. Nor did it draw attention while he was turning out his great Pittsburgh team of 1916, so far as can be recalled.

It was not until he went to Stanford University on the Pacific Coast in 1924 that the double wingback formation, projecting smashes into the line and reverses off the tackles with equal facility, became Warner's system of attack to the exclusion of any other. To be specific, New Year's Day, 1925, is the date that should be encircled in red in football history. On that day, in the Rose Bowl game at Pasadena, California, between Stanford and Rockne's most famous of all Notre Dame teams, the Four Horsemen eleven, the double wingback formation was used exclusively for the first time by a Warner team. As time went by, Warner developed two varieties of this formation, the A and B, designed to add greater variety and deception to the attack and to fool the opponents into committing themselves in the wrong direction.

When Stanford defeated its traditional rival, California, in 1925, for the first time since the resumption of football relations between them in 1918, Warner silenced the skeptics who thought he was through when he left Pitt. But it remained for the visit of his team to New York in 1928 to sell his system to the whole country and to establish him as Rockne's greatest rival.

The exhibition that the Stanford Indians put on that year against Army at the Polo Grounds was an unforgettable one in football. Using a fake double reverse from the double wingback formation, the giant quarterback, Herb Fleishhacker, and Hoffman, Simpkins, and Smallings tore through the befuddled Army eleven at will. The multitude of coaches who looked on at this Eastern unveiling of the double wing were convinced that this was the football style of the future. Rockne and Notre Dame temporarily went into eclipse, particularly in view of the fact that Notre Dame in 1928 went through the worst season it had known under Rockne, losing four games, though in 1929 and 1930, Rock's last two years, he turned out masterpieces.

A month after the Army game, when Warner attended the American Football Coaches Association convention in New Orleans, his fellow coaches swarmed around him in the manner in which they had been accustomed to besiege Rockne. The Stanford sachem and quail shooter discoursed in detail on his famous A and B formations. Numerous coaches of major college teams in the East jumped on the Warner bandwagon in the next year or two, adopting either the double wing formation in toto or a variation of it, depending on the spacing between the ends and tackles and on the depth of the wingbacks behind the line.

As years went by there was a waning in the enthusiasm for the Warner system of attack. Many teams abandoned it for a simpler style of attack, finding that it required a type of quarterback not often available in the East, and that too much practice was required to achieve the delicate balance and timing of the delayed and complex maneuvers. Some of the critics of the system found it significant that on New Year's Day, 1935, three teams that were on the losing end of the score in the Rose Bowl, Sugar Bowl and East-West contests played Warner football.

Warner himself made departures from his system as he found that his attack was being stopped by a set defense on the Coast, where Southern California caused him much grief. The football world was greatly amused when, after Southern California had used an intricate shift to beat Stanford, 41–12, and California, 74–0, in 1930, Warner introduced a shift at Palo Alto. Here was Warner, the arch foe of the shift, who had fought Rockne and been largely instrumental in getting the rules-makers to impose a full second's stop on shifting teams, going over to the shift himself. A bit resentful of the teasing, the venerable, heavy-set patriarch of the gridiron grumpily announced, "It's nothing to get excited about. Just a little experiment I used once at Pitt."

Warner did not fare so well in his closing years at Stanford. And at the end of a rather disastrous 1932 season, although his agreement with the university still had four years to go, he startled the football world by signing a contract with Temple. Thus, at the age of sixty-one, he left the sunshine of California and returned to the East. In his second year at the Philadelphia university, his team was undefeated during the regular season. He remained at Temple through 1938. He resigned while wintering at his home in Palo Alto in 1939 and that fall accepted the position of advisory coach at San Jose State College. There he assisted one of his former pupils, Dudley De Groot, to develop a team that had a perfect record for the 1939 season.

In 1951, on top of many other honors that were accorded him, Warner was voted Coach of All the Years, a new award given to retired coaches for notable contributions to football.

There can be no question that Warner ranks among the greatest coaches football has known and second to none in the imagination, perception, and originality he brought to bear in moving eleven men upon a plane of turf. In addition to his wingback formations, he is credited with the crouching start, the clipping or body block, the reverse play, and other innovations. He was among the very first to appreciate the significance of the forward pass and to make full use of it.

At Cornell, Georgia, Carlisle, Pitt, and Stanford he had outstanding teams. His 1916 Pitt team ranks with the greatest. Three of his Stanford elevens—the 1924, 1926, and 1927 teams—played in the Rose Bowl, and he kept the Indians at the top until Howard Jones made Southern California a national power. Few coaches have developed so many notable players as did Warner. Among these were eight who were named on the all-America teams picked by Camp through 1924—Seneca of Carlisle in 1899, Johnson of Carlisle in 1903, Thompson of Cornell in 1906, Thorpe of Carlisle in 1911 and 1912, Peck of Pittsburgh in 1915 and 1916, Hilty and Davies of Pitt in 1918, and Stein of Pitt in 1920. After that he turned out such nationally known players as Nevers, Hyland, Post, Robesky, Shipkey, Corbus, Walker, Rothert, and Hillman of Stanford and Smukler and Stevens of Temple.

Warner's Pittsburgh team of 1916 was his particular pride. In a letter received from him a few years before his death, he wrote:

"The Pittsburgh team of 1916 was considered for many years as the best of all time. No doubt there have been better teams in later years because football standards of play have improved so much since then. But that team was the best I ever coached.

"Great players on that team were Jock Sutherland at guard, Tiny Thornhill, a tackle; Red Carlson and Pat Herron, ends, and Andy Hastings, Jimmie DeHart and George McLaren in the backfield. McLaren was a great fullback. At center was Bob Peck, one of the greatest of all time. In later years prominent players at

Pitt were Lloyd Jordan, an end, now coaching at Harvard; Harvey Harman, tackle, now coaching Rutgers; Herb Stein, center, and Tommie Davies, halfback. Pitt was unbeaten in 1915, 1916, 1917, 1918, and 1920."

In the letter Warner wrote also:

"I believe that Frank Hudson [of Carlisle] was the greatest drop kicker ever—I think he was better than Brickley of Harvard. The best place-kicking performance I ever saw was in 1901 when Mike Balenti [of Carlisle] kicked four goals from field against Navy, two of them from near the 40-yard line. What made the performance all the greater was the fact that Balenti was a substitute playing his first game."

THE FORWARD PASS REVOLUTION

GEORGE HALAS *wrote in* The Saturday Evening Post *of December 7, 1957:*

WHEN I BROKE INTO pro football, playing right end for the Hammond Tigers against Jim Thorpe and the Canton Bulldogs in the fall of 1919, I didn't have much trouble learning the offensive signals. By modern standards, our attack was stereotyped and unimaginative. We relied mostly on running plays. My basic job at right end was to help our right tackle block the defensive left tackle. I'd catch a pass only now and then.

In those days, smart quarterbacks never passed on first down, and seldom on second down. Usually they passed only on third down, and then only if they were in scoring territory and needed more than five yards for a first down.

Of course, there were reasons for this reluctance to throw the ball. For one thing, the football in the 1920's measured a plump twenty-two and a half to twenty-three inches around the middle. It wasn't until 1931 that the rules committee started slenderizing the "prolate spheroid," as a ball then was described in the manual. The legislators slimmed the ball by half an inch in '31, and another full inch in '34.

The importance of these changes cannot be overemphasized. The 1934 ball was designed for throwing. The passers in my playing days during the '20's had to palm our bigger cantaloupe-shaped ball. They threw it with a stiff-armed motion which sharply diminished their range and accuracy. In wet weather, that plumper ball was even harder to throw or catch.

We kept all ball handling to a minimum—forward passes, lateral passes, underhand tosses, pitchouts. When we wanted to move the ball we tucked it under an arm and ran with it.

Benny Friedman, the old Michigan all-America, was the first pro quarterback to recognize the potentialities of the pass. Benny starred for the New York Giants in 1929. He couldn't toss our "cantaloupe" with the accuracy which Sid Luckman and Otto Graham later achieved with a streamlined ball, but he was accurate enough to jolt our defenses with unexpected passes on first and second down. He demonstrated that the pass could be mixed with running plays consistently and effectively.

350

In my opinion, this was the first of three major steps in the evolution of pro football from a predominantly running game into the balanced running and passing game which prevails today. The second step took place in 1933, when the rules committee permitted the passer to throw from anywhere behind the line of scrimmage, instead of from at least five yards back, as previously required. The streamlining of the ball was the third step.

These developments opened the way not only for the passers but also for the pass receivers. The first of the great receivers was Don Hutson, who went from Alabama to the Green Bay Packers

Certainly, I'll never forget my introduction to the fleet and elusive Mr. Hutson in our 1935 opening game at Green Bay. On the first play of the game Hutson streaked downfield from his seventeen-yard line. Beattie Feathers was in the safety position for us, and well past midfield he allowed Hutson to get past him. Arnie Herber let fly with a tremendous pass. Hutson made an over-the-shoulder catch without breaking stride and raced to a touchdown. That was the only score of the ball game! For the next ten years Hutson was doing that sort of thing to every club in the National Football League.

All of the clubs began to look for receivers and strong-armed passers who could produce long touchdowns. The game was becoming more and more a crowd-pleasing spectacle. All too frequently, however, the competition was one-sided. A few teams dominated the league, and some of the weaker clubs were fortunate if they won two games a season.

At the league meeting in February, 1936, Bert Bell—now our commissioner—came up with the solution. Bell was then an owner, coach, ticket seller and head cheer leader with the Philadelphia Eagles, one of the "have-nots" of the league. He proposed a draft each year of college seniors, with the team that had finished with the worst record having first choice. So it would go, round after round, according to the standings, with the champions having last selection on each round.

Bell's plan was adopted. No longer was it possible for the wealthier teams to keep getting the cream of the talent by outbidding the others. Today any club in the league is capable of defeating any other on any given Sunday. Even the champions generally lose three or four games during a season. That's competition in the finest meaning of the word. . . .

Getting back to that initial draft meeting in 1936, the Bears surprised everyone by making Joe Stydahar, a little-known tackle from West Virginia, their first choice. However, Stydahar had been highly recommended to us. Our final pick, on the other hand, was strictly a shot in the dark—Danny Fortmann of Colgate.

Am I glad I took him! Danny was only nineteen and a medical student. He was small for a middle lineman at six feet and 200 pounds, but he had tremendous speed and tremendous desire. He was all-pro five times, and I'll rate him as one of the best guards who ever played football. He's now team physician for the Los Angeles Rams.

Stydahar, who later coached the Rams and the Cardinals, was a giant of a man, standing six-four and weighing a solid 245. He was a perennial all-star at tackle, and, playing alongside Fortmann, gave us a terrific pair. I recall one game when, blocked almost out of the play, Joe reached out and made a one-handed tackle with such a mighty swipe that he inflicted a knifelike cut. The officials actually stopped the game and searched Joe for concealed weapons!

The Bears picked up another mighty fine young football player that fall—Ray Nolting, a halfback from Cincinnati with an explosive start and high knee action which made him hard to tackle. We didn't choose him, though. He came to us. Everyone had passed him up in the draft.

With this nucleus of good youngsters, the Bears were ready to build another championship team, but it was a while coming. For one thing, we had to streamline our T offense. The thinking and planning which produced the Bears' modern T formation was a staff operation, with all our coaches making valuable contributions. Hunk Anderson, one of the great line coaches, had the knack of anticipating our opponents' probable defenses, and Paddy Driscoll and Luke Johnsos were adept at designing specific plays to crack those defenses.

Our biggest need was a quarterback—one who was exceptionally smart, could handle the fakes and feints and—most important—throw strikes with a football. We finally found our man. He was Sid Luckman, who starred for Columbia from 1936 through 1938. At Columbia, coach Lou Little was using the single-wing offense. Consequently, Sid had a lot to learn about playing quarterback in the T. We broke him into offense gradually, spotting him behind our veteran quarterback, Bernie Masterson. During the early part of the 1939 season, Sid played mostly at left half, where we could capitalize on his fine running ability and passing while he was still mastering the ball-handling tricks of a T quarterback.

When the 1940 season rolled around, Luckman was ready to

assume his role as "Mr. Quarterback"—the finest the game has known, in my estimation. By 1940 we had struck it rich at other positions too. The Bears' rookies that year included Clyde (Bulldog) Turner at center, George McAfee, Harry Clark and Scooter McLean at halfback, Ken Kavanaugh at end, and Lee Artoe and Ed Kolman at tackle. Each ranks among the best players ever to wear a Bear uniform.

At last we were ready to roll—and we rolled, although the club was still pretty green. We lost three games on the way to the championship playoff—one to the Cardinals, one to the Lions and one to the Redskins. The last defeat was especially significant in light of what was to follow.

We were losing by 7 to 3 with some forty seconds remaining when Bob Snyder passed to McAfee, who was finally brought down on Washington's one-yard line after a gain of forty-nine yards. McAfee feigned injury to get a time out. Unfortunately we had already used up our allotted four time-out periods, so we drew a five-yard penalty. That meant we had to pass. Snyder managed to throw two before the final gun, but both were incomplete.

On the last play Bill Osmanski complained that a Redskin was holding his arms, so that he had no chance to catch a pass which bounced off his chest. All our boys complained so bitterly about this bit of interference—which escaped the eyes of the officials—that the Redskins called them "crybabies."

This provided me with the exact psychology needle I wanted three weeks later when we played the Redskins in Washington for the championship. I kept throwing it in the faces of my players throughout the final week of preparation. We never drilled more thoroughly for a game. We knew what to expect from Sammy Baugh and that fine Washington team—trouble. Sammy always caused trouble when he was throwing a football around.

The best way to stop him, we decided, was to give him as little opportunity as possible to pass. Ball control—that was to be our strategy. To guarantee that ball control, we devised some new plays. We gambled that the Redskins would use the same defensive pattern which stopped us so thoroughly in the first game. Luckily, they did.

Luck was with us in everything that day. On the second play of the game the ball went to fullback Osmanski on what was intended to be a straight off-tackle slant, but McAfee's block hadn't taken out the right end, so Osmanski swerved and swung wide around end and ran sixty-eight yards to a touchdown.

I've seen plenty of hard blocks in my time, but never one

like the one which made this touchdown possible. George Wilson, who now coaches the Detroit Lions, threw it, and it flattened both Ed Justice and Jimmy Johnston.

Then we got another break. Baugh flipped a long pass to Charley Malone, his end, who was in the clear with no one between him and our goal line. Malone was one of the best pass receivers in the league, and wouldn't have dropped a pass like that once in a hundred times. This was the hundredth time. Had he caught that ball to tie the score, we would have been in for a rough afternoon.

At half time we had a nice 28–0 lead. Between halves, I reminded the boys, just in case they were getting complacent, what the Redskins had said about their being quitters and crybabies and a "first-half ball club." I said, "Show them that you are a second-half ball club too."

They did with a vengeance. In all, we intercepted eight passes that day, returning three for touchdowns. And ball control? We gained 372 yards rushing, to only 3 for the Redskins. The final score? 73–0!

Some observers said the Bears were a perfect football team that day. I can't quite agree. Looking over the movies, I can see where we should have scored another touchdown.

That was one of the most important games in football history, in my opinion. The lop-sidedness of the score focused nationwide attention on the T formation. A few weeks later Clark Shaughnessy's Stanford team, also using our T, scored a thumping victory in the Rose Bowl, and the stampede was on.

Shaughnessy had also played an important role in our victory over Washington. Clark joined us in Chicago in late November after Stanford's regular season ended and spent about two weeks with the Bears before rushing back to Palo Alto to begin his own preparations for the Rose Bowl. During those two weeks, Clark worked incessantly reviewing the movies of our 7–3 loss to the Redskins. He pinpointed every facet of the Redskins' defense, and his observations were incorporated in our explosive T-formation attack.

After those smashing successes by the Bears and Stanford, the T immediately became the dominant offense in football. The story of pro football since 1940 has revolved around the evolution of the T formation.

Probably the most graphic way to illustrate the evolution of Total Offense Football is simply to contrast the so-called "wide-open T" which triggered our 73–0 touchdown avalanche against Washington in 1940 with the "spread-slot" offense now widely used by the Bears and many other pro teams. The "spread-slot" offense splits both ends wide about fifteen yards from the tackles, and moves one halfback up into the "slot" on either the right or left side—that is, he's halfway between the tackle and end, and a yard behind the line of scrimmage.

The "spread slot" puts three potential pass receivers out wide where they can maneuver. What's more, the number of potential receivers can be increased to four simply by making use of a man-in-motion to produce the "double-slot" formation.

As a result of this, there have been some major changes in offensive tactics. For example, the spread ends—out on the flank anywhere from ten to fifteen yards from the tackle—have over-shadowed the running backs as long-yardage touchdown producers. It was a spread end named Elroy (Crazy Legs) Hirsch, of the Los Angeles Rams, who knocked the Bears out of the championship running in 1951 with the most spectacular catch of a touchdown pass I've ever had the misfortune to witness.

We had piled up a 14–0 lead in the first eight minutes and had the Rams in the hole—or so we thought—on their nine-yard line. But quarterback Bob Waterfield faked a hand-off to Tank Younger, held the ball behind his hip for a one-two-three count, then retreated to the goal line and arched a long pass. Hirsch made a leaping grab on the Rams' forty-four and raced another fifty-six yards for a touchdown —a ninety-one-yard scoring play. There was no holding the Rams after that. They stunned us, 42 to 17.

In twelve games during that 1951 season, Hirsch caught a total of seventeen touchdown passes and led the league in scoring, with 102 points. He also gained a total of 1,495 yards, shattering Don Hutson's pass-receiving mark of 1,211 yards set in 1942.

PRINCETON'S TEAM OF DESTINY VS. CHICAGO AND BILL ROPER

One of the unforgettable games of football was played in 1922 between Princeton and Chicago at Stagg Field in the Windy City. For thrills, excitement, suspense, and individual heroics in a surging comeback to victory, it stands with the Yale-Army game of 1929, starring Albie Booth, "Little Boy Blue"; the Notre Dame-Southern California game of 1931, in which Johnny Baker kicked the winning field goal for the Trojans in the closing minutes; the Ohio State-Notre Dame game of 1935, in which Andy Pilney won a place in the Fighting Irish pantheon of fame, and the Ohio State-Cornell game of 1939, the vehicle of little Pop Scholl's stardom in slaying the Buckeye goliath.

They called this Princeton eleven the "Team of Destiny." It was destiny's darling because it could not, would not lose, no matter what the odds or how desperate its plight. Largely inexperienced and not particularly big or powerful, it was considered to be no more than an average Tiger outfit at season's start. But week after week it won because it was one of the smartest, most daring, resourceful and fightingest outfits that ever wore the Orange and Black or any other colors. It was a team worthy of its coach, Bill Roper, superbly spirited and buoyed by the inspiration of his resolution and magnetism in firing up his men.

Three of its eight victories were gained by the margin of a field goal or conversion points after touchdowns. It was by the margin of three points after touchdown that it defeated ALONZO STAGG's *heavily favored Chicago team, which had run all over the Tiger in building up an 18–7 lead going into the final quarter and which went some seventy yards in the closing minutes, only to be stopped a yard short of victory by a granite defense that yielded only thirty-four points all season. Stagg said it was one of the greatest games of football he had ever seen.*

Mel Dickenson was the captain of this team of destiny and paired with Barr (Hoops), Snively at the guards. Herb Treat, an all-America, and Pink Baker were the tackles. The ends were manned by Howdy Gray and Saxby Tillson, and the center was Oliver Alford. At quarterback was little Johnny Gorman. CHARLIE CALDWELL, *who was to give Princeton two of its greatest teams as coach in 1950 and 1951, was at one halfback and Harry Crum was the other. The fullback was Jack Cleaves. Ken Smith kicked the extra points and the substitutes included Bob Beattie, Dinny Dinsmore, Don Griffin, Al Howard, Dick Newby, Harrison Thomson, Buzz Stout, and Willie Wingate.*

Caldwell said of the team as follows:

WE WERE A STRONG defensive team and we won on Ken Smith's kicking and the breaks. We were truly a team of destiny. Every Saturday they picked us to lose and we won, even though we weren't much on offense. Herb Treat at left tackle and Howdy Gray at left end were very fine players, and Captain Mel Dickenson at guard was too. We had no outstanding back except Jack Cleaves. He was by far the best. The rest of us were just so so. Cleaves was a fine football player: fast, a good runner, and a good competitor.

We had no blocking. We couldn't make a first down at times if we had to. We had no forward passing to speak of. When Cleaves passed to Johnny Gorman from behind our goal against Chicago, the play was made up in the huddle. Gorman went from our 1 to midfield before he was caught from behind.

We played a 7–2–2 defense all the time and I was the linebacker. I played wingback on offense, but we never ran reverses. I carried the ball once all season and had more actual playing time than anyone else on the team.

Roper felt that football was 90 percent fight. He was a great psychologist. He would use anything to advantage. He was wonderful in talking to the team. Football was just a fall proposition with him. It was not his profession. He was a lawyer, insurance man, and councilman—and a great man.

His offense consisted of the best plays other teams used. West Virginia and Ira Rodgers beat us in 1919. He kept Rodgers here for the weekend and tied Harvard and beat Yale that year with the West Virginia spread, which was new that year. The players were crazy about Roper as a person. He was a Princetonian and he would say that if you had a Princeton jersey on and the other man didn't, you had him licked. My senior year we had three different attacks. Roper would like something and put it in. We could have used a little more technique.

Stagg wrote of the game with Princeton in his book, Touchdown:

Chicago held a two-touchdown lead in the final quarter of the Princeton game and lost, 18 to 21, in a mad, wild last twelve minutes into which enough heart palpitation for forty games was packed. It ended with Chicago only a yard away from the winning touchdown and the crowd shrieking, "Hurry! Hurry!" and our quarter, confused in so desperate a crisis, hammering futilely at the Tiger's center. Never before or since has Chicago lost a game which it had tucked away so safely. . . .

John Thomas, with his brother Harry and Jim Pyott, had ripped the Tiger line to shreds and marched 60 yards in the first quarter for our first score, the bulk of the attack going inside the defensive tackles. We added a second touchdown early in the second quarter and a third near the end of the third quarter without once using a forward pass. . . .

Pyott opened the last quarter auspiciously with a smart 15-yard run. Princeton stiffened and Chicago kicked. Gorman caught the ball and attempted a daring backward pass to Cleaves, who was posted wide. But the pass was thrown forward, making it illegal, and Princeton was set back to her 2-yard line on the penalty—and we were leading, 18 to 7, with the end not far off.

A second time the Tiger outsmarted us. Instead of punting they passed [from the end zone] to their quarter, Gorman, who was out in end position, and he ran to the 40-yard mark. The tide turned swiftly here. . . . Chicago next got the ball on her 42-yard line. King, our center, was hurt. A substitute took his place. On the first play he passed inaccurately to Willie Zorn. The ball bounded off Zorn's shoulder and bounced into the hands of Gray, the Tiger left end, who . . . continued in full flight for 43 yards and a touchdown.

The score was 18 to 14. A 23-yard pass by Princeton to the quarterback (who had lined up far over near the sideline) carried the ball to our 33-yard line. Otto Strohmeier (who had been switched from end to quarterback) was playing left half on defense. He used his left hand on a Princeton end who was leaping for an out-of-range pass, giving the ball on a penalty to Princeton on our 15. They made 4 yards and on the next play gained 5 more on Chicago's offside play. From the 6-yard line Princeton carried it over by an eyelash in four downs (Crum catapulting across). Chicago was behind, 18 to 21, and time almost up.

Running the ball back to our 34 from the kick-off, we cut loose with the neglected forward pass, intermingled with five linebucks, and swept down to the Princeton 1-yard line. The attack was irresistible, but suddenly our tactics changed. With the frenzied crowd screaming a prayer for haste in the belief that only seconds remained . . . Princeton defended magnificently, and John Thomas butted his head into a stone wall. They were a smart and able team and played brilliantly the tricky, daring strategy of their coach, Bill Roper. No other athletic event in my memory so depressed the university as a whole for so many hours.

William W. Roper deserved the highest praise for the way he directed his team and the brand of football it played. At straight football the team was outclassed, for it had no powerful charging backs. But what the team lacked in rugged power it made up in versatility, keen football sense, its amazing resourcefulness, quickness to seize any advantage, and its daring—throwing a lateral after catching a punt, and passing from behind its goal line. The Princeton forward passing game was a thing of beauty. The amazing cleverness with which it was conceived and hidden made it extremely difficult to fathom.

When Bill Roper died on December 10, 1933, The New York Times *said:*

William W. Roper, insurance executive and political leader, who won national fame as a football coach, died at his home in Germantown, Pennsylvania today in his fifty-fourth year.

The names of Bill Roper and Princeton were associated in football, with a few interruptions, from 1899, when he played end on

Overleaf *Bill Roper's glamorous 1922 Princeton Team of Destiny.*

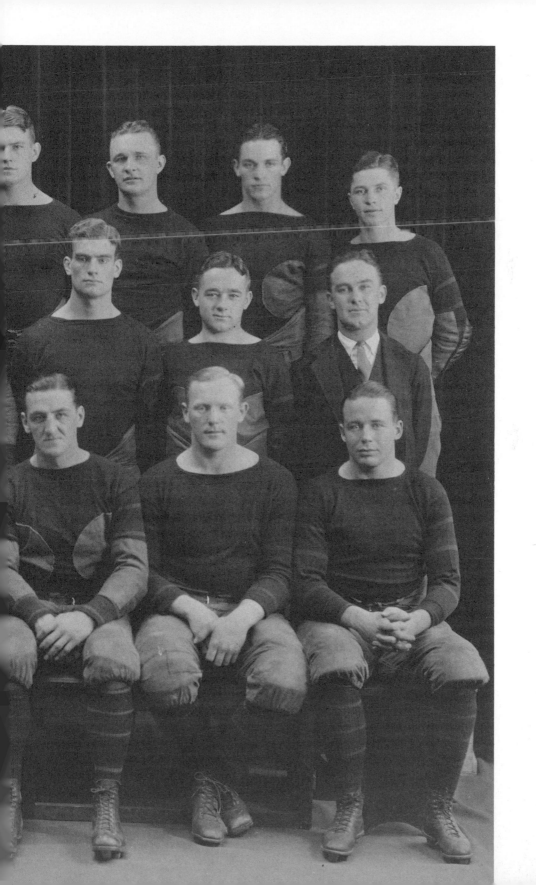

a championship team, until 1930, when he gave up his coaching career. . . . He became the outstanding independent member of the Philadelphia city council. The two great causes of his political career were prohibition repeal and modification of Pennsylvania's Sunday blue laws. . . .

Roper might have been called the last of the romantic coaches in football. . . . Where other coaches were remembered for systems of play, the name of Roper meant dramatic dressing room talk, last minute victories, and long runs with fumbled balls. There was no rule against picking up a loose ball and running with it when he was coaching.

Ill health in his youth turned Mr. Roper to his career of coaching. Born in Philadelphia in 1880, he attended Penn Charter School, where he played basketball, football, and baseball. He continued these sports at Princeton. He was an end on the football team, captain of the basketball team, and an outfielder in baseball. His health would not permit him to try medicine, as he planned. In order to remain out of doors he went to the University of Virginia as baseball coach and a law student. He also handled football there and in 1905 Princeton called him back.

He coached there through 1911, with the exception of 1909. That season he was head coach at Missouri. He returned to Princeton after the war and was head coach from 1919 through 1930. Teams coached by him during his career played 133 games, winning 89, losing 28 and tying 16. Under his teaching Princeton won three Big Three championships. The 1925 team had the famous Jack Slagle, and his 85-yard run from scrimmage against Yale is one of the highlights of the series history. Probably the most famous of the Roper teams was the 1922 eleven, which earned the nickname, "Team of Destiny." Mr. Roper used his . . . oratorical ability to great effect in his coaching, and was an intensely dramatic figure at football rallies.

President HAROLD WILLIS DODDS *of Princeton said:*

"Mr. Roper's death marks the passing of a vibrant personality. In football he was a distinguished coach, zealous for the honor of the game. In public life he valued independence and courage above private ambition."

Professor CHRISTIAN GAUSS, *Dean of the College, said:*

"No one ever had a more withering scorn for the dishonest, the hypocritical and the unsportsmanlike. No one ever had a higher faith in the human spirit and its possibilities or exemplified that faith more courageously in every act of his life."

ARTHUR SAMPSON *wrote in* The Boston Herald, *December 11, 1933:*

"It is almost impossible to believe that . . . one of the most vivid and forceful personalities who ever coached football . . . such an energetic and vital character could succumb, even to death. Of all the men closely affiliated with the game whom we have known intimately, Bill Roper was one of the most interesting. You never knew what to expect of him. Spontaneous in his decisions, he always kept you in the dark as to his next move. Roper teemed with energy. His day was full of action. . . . His mind was chock full of ideas. He changed his opinion as frequently as the weather, but he always was definite about his decisions.

"Roper never could be called an inventive genius of football tactics. He had neither the time nor the inclination to mull over new plays. His plan of attack was usually a series of plays some opposing team had executed well against his team. He was not a master of detail. His executive traits did not permit him the patience to drill over and over again what to him seemed insignificant things. His assistants were supposed to take care of those. But probably no coach had the faculty of preparing a team mentally for any one game better than Bill. He was the inspirational type. He could make his team play better than it knew how in the crucial game of the year. What it lacked in smoothness of execution it made up in sheer determination."

George Pfann, quarterback of Gil Dobie's Cornell Steamrollers of 1921, 1922, and 1923.

THE CORNELL STEAMROLLERS AND GIL DOBIE

Among the great teams in the decade of sports' Golden Age, the 1920's, were the invincible, overpowering Cornell elevens of 1921, 1922, and 1923. Piloted by GEORGE PFANN *at quarterback and operating from the single wing formation with a precision of timing, a faultlessness of execution and a destructiveness of blocking that moved the ball inexorably, the Big Red teams defeated twenty-four successive opponents. Never before nor since has Cornell put together three such successful seasons, and the names of Pfann, Eddie Kaw, Sunny Sundstrom, Swede Hanson, Floyd Ramsey and Charley Cassidy were nationally renowned.*

Pfann, one of the great quarterbacks of all time, a Rhodes Scholar at Oxford, a member of the staff of General George S. Patton Jr. during World War II, an assistant United States Attorney and a trustee of Cornell, made the following analysis of the three teams in a letter to the author in 1954.

IN 1915 CORNELL HAD its first undefeated, untied football team in its history, and the individual feats and names of its members are legendary. For the football seasons of 1921 through 1923, Cornell had undefeated, untied teams. We were invited to the Rose Bowl. We were picked in popular acclaim from Eastern to national champions. We had in that short span three so-called Walter Camp all-Americans. It was not necessarily the golden age, but certainly it was one of the highest peaks in Cornell athletics.

Of the three teams, I would rank them, for the reasons herein set out, as follows: The best all-around team was the 1922. A close second was the 1921. Easily the weakest was the 1923. . . .

Dobie needed for his offense two tandem guards who could swing out behind the line in lock step at full speed and block effectively down field as interference. On defense these same guards had to be able to charge and tackle. In Reno Jones and Turk Brayman, both about six feet, 195 pounds, Dobie had an almost perfect pair of guards.

The Dobie offense needed two blocking wingbacks who could also run and pass and buck. On the off-tackle play (a key in the offense), the wingback and end had to double team the tackle. Dobie picked his ends largely on their defense, although they had to handle the tackle alone on quick-opening plays and short and wide reverses. In 1921 Charley Cassidy at left end and Dave Munns at right end were ideally fitted for their jobs. . . .

The tackles played side by side in the middle of the unbalanced line on offense, and they were the key to the power plays. They opened the holes on the power plays in the line and made the key blocks on the off-tackle. They also ran interference on reverses. In Captain Wilson Dodge and Leonard (Swede) Hanson, Dobie had a top team. Dodge, six feet, five inches and 220 pounds, was a tough defensive man, and Hanson was one of the greatest football players ever to wear the Cornell uniform. He could do everything well and is the only man that Dobie let use his own judgment as to the amount of work he needed during practice.

The backfield consisted of Eddie Kaw, who kicked, passed, ran to the right and played left defensive halfback in a seven with a box, and safety in a 6–2–2–1; George Lechler, fullback, who blocked and hit the line, and two sophomores, Pfann at wingback on right formation and at tailback on left, and Floyd Ramsey at fullback on right formation and at blocking back on left. Lechler could get an end alone better than any other back I've seen, and Kaw was one of those rare individuals who delivered when the chips were down.

In addition, the 1921 team had tremendous reserve strength. At ends, Gouinlock and Baker were almost as good as Cassidy and Munns, and in some circumstances more experienced and smarter. Davidson and Sunny Sundstrom . . . were good substitutes for Dodge and Hanson, though with less experience and natural ability. Carl Olney, as a substitute for Lechler, was a much better ball carrier but could not block nearly as well. Charley Brayton was an awkward-appearing, hard-working, serious and steady center who contributed his full share. . . .

The reason I think the 1922 team was the best (and Dobie believed this, or at least said so in our conversations) is that there was more maturity and experience on this team than on the other two. The sophomores, Cassidy, Ramsey, Buckley, Sundstrom, Flynn and Pfann, were juniors now and the rest were seniors except Henderson. Gouinlock was an adequate replacement for Munns. Sundstrom in Captain Dodge's shoes was to become an all-American in 1923 and was smart and quick off the mark. There was as much savvy and teamwork by Gouinlock and Sundstrom, on both offense and defense, as I have seen. At center Bart

Richards made up in speed and skill what he lacked in brawn, and he was adequately protected by 220-pound Walter Rollo at left guard (6 feet, 5 inches) and Flynn (6 feet and 200 pounds) at right guard. Hanson, intercollegiate light heavyweight and heavyweight wrestling champion, was at left tackle and did the place kicking and some punting and passing. . . .

Dobie's whole theory of offensive football was power with timing, mixed with just enough passing and deception to keep the secondary from moving immediately toward the ball carrier, thereby keeping the defense sufficiently off balance to give his power plays a chance to develop. He had one or more plays for every possible hole in the defensive line, and his quarterback operated on the theory that if they shifted to stop one type of play, they weakened themselves in some other spot. Backs were instructed and trained to go three yards on a play, and anything more than that was just so much gravy. Consequently, Dobie-trained backs bucked more often than not when they hit the hole either off tackle, on a reverse or on a linebuck or a fake. The line and backs used both the shoulder block and hip block on offense.

Dobie believed that in order for a team to really become a team it must play together constantly, particularly on offense. Consequently, once Dobie had his first team picked in the fall (and the first three weeks were a survival fight to let him pick the eleven best men) no one except Dobie could touch the team. He kept it intact, so far as possible, and Dobie alone worked with its offense, adjusting backfield positions to fit the individual characteristics of the backs so that the entire team would charge *as a unit*. Dobie actually tried to make the ball carrier in each of his offensive plays hit at the time the maximum team pressure was being exerted to open the hole, on the often-proved premise that even a small opening at that stage could be exploited into three yards or more. He explained the 59–7 beating of Dartmouth in 1921 as an occurrence in which the teams were nearly equal but where the cohesion and unit striking force of the Cornell team in the second half reached a point of near perfection. He added that the Dartmouth team took a terrible physical beating because of that factor.

On defense, Dobie placed his men in positions which allowed for the least possible gamble. He never permitted two defensive linemen playing alongside each other to be spaced so that both could be double-teamed. He liked a seven-man line and a box defense and relied on rushing the passer to take care of the extra eligible receiver. His line was taught to play the cup defense, and he worked constantly to develop a fast, aggressive charge on the part of the line. His system of defense was so carefully worked out that there was no formation that we saw in football which his general system of defense did not fit. Consequently, his teams were rarely taken by surprise by new formations. He worried about crossblocks and trap plays by opponents more than anything else in looking at scouting reports. Perhaps this cup defense, with the least possible gamble, was not an outstanding reason for his success, but in one year (I think it was 1921) our opponents made only three first downs through the line.

Aside from insistence on careful execution of fundamentals and careful attention to detail, I think that the factors which made Dobie an outstanding coach were:

(1) His ability to select a team.

(2) His ability to keep a team in top condition mentally and physically.

(3) Obtaining an extremely high degree of coordinated team play.

(4) Getting the best performance of which they were capable out of the team.

About his equally famous teammate, Eddie Kaw, Pfann wrote:

Kaw was not exceptionally fast. In fact, when he, Ramsey, Cassidy and I played in the backfield we finished the 100-yard sprints about even, and this may have contributed to a very important timing factor in Dobie's offensive requirements.

Like Ramsey, Kaw took short, quick steps but, unlike Ramsey, he had a high knee action and was an exceptionally strong runner. Dobie always insisted that Kaw's greatest offensive ability lay in a semi-broken field where he could turn and twist, and he had an uncanny ability to use his blockers.

Actually, it was a Dobie type of offense with its powerful off-tackle and big reverse plays which gave Kaw the opportunity to exploit his offensive talents, and time and again, when they could get him through the line with two or three blockers out front, he would go all the way.

Kaw could also pass and, during the two years I played with him (1921 and 1922), did the passing for the team. We didn't take statistics in those days, but my recollection is that the number of his completions was above average. He also did the kicking.

*Eddie Kaw, running-mate of George Pfann on Cornell's
1921 and 1922 all-conquering teams.*

Most of the time he was an average kicker, but I never recall our opponents blocking one of his kicks.

He played safety man in the 6–2–2–1 defense and left halfback in the box defense. He was exceptionally good at intercepting passes and broke up many opponents' drives by such methods. Furthermore, I don't recall ever seeing him miss an open-field tackle.

Kaw was an exceptionally cocky individual and the greatest trouble that Dobie had was keeping him running in the spot where the play called. . . . My personal impression was that Eddie was inclined to loaf when the opportunity offered, although I never recall Dobie calling him for loafing.

Kaw had one quality above others which I think made him outstanding. When he had to produce, he delivered the goods. He kicked farther and better when he was behind his goal line than he did in the middle of the field. He made the necessary yardage when it was a must. He threw a block when he had to. I think of him more like Walter Hagen in his competitive attitude. I don't think he ever choked up when the pressure was on.

The following piece on Pfann was written by the author and published in the Cornell-Yale program of 1958, when Pfann was elected to the National Football Hall of Fame.

Willie Heston was the scourge of the Middle West with his explosive runs in leading the attack of Hurry-Up Yost's point-a-minute Michigan teams, and Walter Eckersall was about to make his appearance upon the football scene to win immortality as quarterback of one of Alonzo Stagg's greatest Chicago elevens when George Robert Pfann arrived on this terrestrial sphere in Marion, Ohio. Of course it had to be the month of October when he checked in, when the frost was on the pumpkin they called a pigskin and the shock was something fierce in those antediluvian days of massed, close-order football, before the advent of the forward pass.

The time was fitting and proper and just right. Michigan and Chicago were two of the great early rivals of Cornell, one of the first of the Eastern universities to build relations with the Middle West. And Eckersall and Heston had qualities on the football field in common with Pfann. With them he stands among the all-time elect of the gridiron, and today he joins them in the pantheon of the game's most illustrious heroes. Enshrined too in the hall of fame are their coaches—Stagg, one of Yale's greatest sons; Yost and Gilmour Dobie.

Let anyone start a discussion as to the all-time quarterbacks and inevitably the names of Eckersall and Pfann come up. Before them there were Vince Stevenson of Penn and Charley Daly of Harvard and Army. Between them there was Wally Steffen of Chicago. Contemporary with Pfann there were Benny Friedman of Michigan and Harry Stuhldreher of Notre Dame. Later came Frank Carideo of Notre Dame, Sid Luckman of Columbia and Sammy Baugh of Texas Christian, the last two standing as the greatest professional football has known as quarterbacks of the Chicago Bears and the Washington Redskins.

Pfann had the qualities of both a quarterback and a halfback, of Eckersall and Heston. Actually, his position in the single wing formation was halfback—tailback in formation left and wingback in formation right, except that in his senior year Dobie had him play tailback in both right and left formations. Wherever he was stationed, either to the rear of the center as tailback or working with his end on the defensive tackle as wingback, he ran the team as field general.

As a quarterback Pfann showed the qualities of Eckersall as a play caller, a passer and kicker, and on defense. He was not the field goal kicker that was Eckie, who booted five in each of two games, but he was a good punter. The forward pass was just coming into the game, in 1906, as Eckersall's career was closing, but Stagg was one of the first to appreciate the revolutionary nature of the change in the rules that permitted the ball to be thrown forward, and at Chicago he was far ahead of the coaches of the East in developing pass plays. And Eckie was his passer.

Pfann, playing in a period when the pass was beginning to be used far more extensively in the East, was feared for his looping passes, and he excelled also on the receiving end of aerials. He was most dangerous when he faked a pass and carried the ball off tackle.

As a ball carrier George invited comparison with Heston. He did not have Willie's speed, but he was fast off the mark, like the Michigan wonder, and he was murder when he got under way. Barrel chested and heavy of limb, he was a power runner who plowed ahead low with a terrific drive, seeming to run on his knees and throwing off tacklers even when they had a clear shot at him. It was no feat to catch him. Downing him was something else.

It was in 1923 when Pfann, now captain of the team, really had his chance as a ball carrier and passer. Eddie Kaw, who has preceded him into the Hall of Fame, was running wild from tail-back in 1921 and 1922, and quarterback Pfann was calling on Eddie most of the time. But with Kaw gone in 1923, George called his own signal more and he scored fifteen touchdowns and ninety-eight points that season. The two touchdowns he enjoyed the most were made against Penn. It was a strong Penn team and it set its defenses to stop Pfann, putting three men on him. George crossed them up, faking to carry and giving the ball most of the time to the late Bob Patterson, the newcomer in the backfield.

Powerful runner, cool, knowing field general, a good passer and kicker, rugged and smart on defense, and indestructible, George Pfann stands with Barrett, Kaw, Osgood, Wyckoff, Starbuck, Shiverick and Schoellkopf among the greatest of Cornell backs. Few football players have gone through their varsity career without once experiencing defeat. Pfann did that as a key man on Dobie's steamrollers of 1921, 1922 and 1923. . . .

Honors and distinctions have come George Pfann's way in profusion all through his adult life. He has excelled academically as well as on the athletic field, and also in the service of his country as soldier and attorney, and in the service of his university as a trustee. In the service of his family, too, and his friends, he has his own personal hall of fame on Triphammer Road [Ithaca], whence he goes forth with Nig and other cronies and his sons, George Jr. (Cornell '55) and Bruce (Cornell '59) for pheasant or a round of golf. . . .

After getting his degree in the College of Arts and Sciences, he spent two years in the Cornell Law School . . . then it was off to England in 1926 as a Rhodes Scholar, and he completed his study of law at Brasenose College at Oxford University. . . . From 1931 to 1937 he was United States Attorney for the Southern District of New York. Came the war and off he went to serve in the European theatre through the worst of the fighting. As a member of the staff of the brilliant General George Patton, he figured in the electrifying tank warfare that changed the attack from a slow, grinding, first-down affair to carry the ball all the way through the riddled defenses of the high-tailing Nazis. . . .

The author wrote of Gilmour Dobie in The New York Times *in 1931 as follows:*

Cornell University has had its full share of outstanding football coaches. Although most of its athletic traditions and more glorious

memories center around crew and track, around the revered Court-
ney and the beloved Moakley, the university founded on the isolated
hills above Ithaca by Ezra Cornell can lay claim to as brilliant a
lineage of gridiron preceptors as any school in the land.

Glenn (Pop) Warner, a guard in his undergraduate days at
Cornell and one of the country's most successful coaches at Cornell,
Carlisle, Pitt and Stanford; Percy Haughton, under whom Harvard
enjoyed its Golden Age, and Al Sharpe, who came from Yale as one
of the finest athletes to wear the Blue . . . have been among those
to direct Cornell's football destinies.

In the wake of this notable group came another figure of national repute . . . to revive the ebbing fortunes of Cornell, which had
gone into an eclipse after the days of Jim Munns, Gib Cool, Charley
Barrett, Fritz Shiverick, Fred Gillies, Murray Shelton and Jack
O'Hearn. . . . When Cornell defeated Penn in 1921, 1922 and 1923,
the years of Dobie's great juggernauts, Dobie was hailed as a
miracle man who had broken the spell of Franklin Field, on which
the Ithacans had gained only four previous victories in a series
going back to 1893. The names of Kaw and Pfann became football
bywords and the Dobie off-tackle smash the most dreaded and most
successful power play in football.

While the success of his unbeaten teams of those three years
brought the tall, spare-framed Scot into the forefront of American
coaches, Dobie years before had become a name to conjure with
on the Pacific Coast. There his Washington teams went through
nine seasons without sustaining defeat. . . . Hugo Bezdek will tell
you what manner of teams were those Huskies . . . and perchance
he will tell you of the time the skeptical Scot ordered his team to
take a couple of laps around the field for a workout after Washington had defeated California, 72–0. Just before he came to
Ithaca, through the initiative of Romeyn Berry, graduate manager
of athletics at Cornell, Dobie had added to his fame at Navy, not
only through the celebrated episode of one of his substitutes jumping up from the sideline to tackle a Great Lakes Naval Training
School back, but on the record of his teams. . . .

During the years when his teams were steamrollering all opposition . . . Dobie was acclaimed as the greatest drillmaster in
football. His elevens exemplified a mechanical perfection never
excelled on the gridiron. Such was the power and flawless execution of his off-tackle play that it was said by rival coaches the
Cornell quarterback could have called the play out loud and still
they could not have stopped it. It was as a stickler for detail, in
teaching every man his part until he was letter perfect, and in

tuning up and polishing his machine until the eleven component parts dovetailed into a perfectly synchronized unit, that Dobie's genius found its expression on the football field. . . .

Isolated . . . in the quiet retreat of Ithaca's hills and known to the public for his dire forecasts of disaster for his team, his philippics against Phi Beta Kappa players, and the Red hordes he turns loose upon the gridiron, Dobie has become something of a Merlin in the popular mind, a wizard, a prophet of doom who spends his evenings with Schopenhauer. . . . At heart he is the pessimist he has been made out. . . . The explanation is to be laid to the fact that he sets so high a standard to which a first-class player should measure up. His pessimism is born of skepticism. Kaw and Pfann were never "great" to him. They were no more than good players.

In The History of American Football *the author wrote:*

One of the legendary figures of football, ranking in the top flight of coaches with Warner, Stagg, Zuppke, Rockne, Yost, Haughton, and Dr. Williams, Dobie was no inventive genius. But neither was Rockne. Neither of them contributed much in the way of innovations in patterns of plays and formations. But they knew how to develop winning football teams as did few others. And they will be remembered for their personalities long after other winning coaches have faded into obscurity.

Dobie had none of Rockne's dynamic magnetism. He was no spell-binding, after-dinner speaker who could regale a gathering with an endless store of good stories, wit, withering scorn, biting sarcasm. Rockne was a born leader, at best in a crowd. Dobie did not attract crowds. He did not amuse people except when he sat down with a few friends in the evening, with a glass in his hand and with malice for the foe of the afternoon forgotten.

This tall, lean Scot, with the piercing eyes was no charmer. Flattery was not in his lexicon. He never buttered up anyone. He never used a superlative except in a derogatory sense. Someone might be the worst; never the best. He was the skeptic of skeptics. He had many unbeaten teams but he would never admit that he had an all-America player. On the football field he was hard as stone and wasted little sympathy on his men when hurt. Football to him was a form of war. Practice was not meant to be fun. It was hard work and lots of it. And yet, Gilmour Dobie was phenomenally successful until the late years of his coaching life, and most of those who played on his teams were loyal to him and came back when they could to spend an evening with him. How successful he was is shown by the bare record: In the thirty-three years he coached, fourteen of his teams were unbeaten. They won 180 games, lost 45 and tied 15.

When Dobie retired in 1938 he was independently wealthy. He lived simply, took good care of his money and added to his income by investments in the stock market. To whatever he set his legally trained mind he did well, whether it was football, investments, or golf. He was an inveterate reader, keenly interested in the affairs of the day. And those who enjoyed his company of an evening found him a conversationalist very much worth listening to, his remarks interspersed with the same dry humor that occasionally relieved the gloom of his dire prophecies to his squad in the lecture room.

Because of his occasional diatribes against Phi Beta Kappa football players, the idea got around that he was "agin" learning if it interfered with the success of his teams. On the subject he made the following statement to Louis Boochever, then director of public information at Cornell:

"Some people seem to have the idea that I object to a boy's coming to college to study. Let me say that I think this is the only reason a boy should come to college, and if football interferes with his studies he should drop football."

Dobie died at Hartford, Connecticut, in December, 1948, at the age of 69.

YALE'S INVINCIBLES AND TAD JONES

The 1923 Yale team is generally rated as the most potent ever to wear the Blue. Coached by Tad Jones, one of the most glamorous sportsmen in the history of football, and presenting an array of superlative running backs rarely matched on any campus, behind a big, fast, hard-hitting line, the Elis ran up 230 points in eight games and limited the opposition to 38, shutting out Harvard, Princeton, Georgia, North Carolina, and Brown.

Captain William (Memphis Bill) Mallory, Century Milstead, MAL STEVENS, Lyle Richeson, Ducky Pond, Win Lovejoy, Ted Blair, Flash Neidlinger, Dick Luman, Widdy Neale, and Charlie O'Hearn were among the top personnel of this team, the last Yale eleven to finish with a perfect record until 1960.

Stevens, perhaps the finest of the running backs, went to Yale from Washburn College in Kansas, where he was top man on the campus as an athlete, scholar, and leader of student activities. He won national acclaim at Yale, not only excelling on the gridiron but also graduating with honors and going on to medical school. In the years since, he has achieved added distinction in medicine in the field of gynecology and obstetrics, as well as having been football coach at Yale and New York University.

Dr. Stevens wrote the following analysis of the team in 1954 in a letter to the author.

I POLLED A NUMBER of players on our team and it seems to be the consensus that it was outstanding for these reasons:

Our team was well balanced with excellent reserve material.

Our material was composed of athletes who usually participated in more than one sport.

The team was coached mechanically by fine coaches.

Above and beyond that, we had in Tad Jones a wonderful coach who inspired us with the so-called Yale spirit.

Tad was above and beyond being merely a football coach. He was a Yale man, loved Yale, and felt that football was an integral part of Yale and that it was worth expending every effort to excel and worth making any sacrifice to attain perfection and to win.

Tad had excellent assistant coaches. Charlie Comerford coached the ends beautifully. Myron Fuller taught Yale line-play fundamentals, which, in my opinion, have never been improved upon. And in Milstead, Diller, Eckart, Miller, and Lovejoy he had superb operatives, flanked by Dick Luman, tall, rangy and rough, and by Hulman, fast (a track man and hurdler) and good offensively and defensively, as well as Bingham to back him up, or vice versa. All these gave Yale a line which made defense a pleasure for the backfield.

In using the single wingback and short punt, spread, and deep punt formations, Yale was equipped with running, passing, and kicking from all these alignments. A great deal of credit must be given Lovejoy, the center, whose passing was the best I have ever seen and aided the timing of the team immeasurably. He passed a wet ball or dry ball perfectly and can share in Mallory's two beautiful field goals against Harvard. Until Mallory started kicking field goals in the middle of the season (unfortunately for me, after talking Tad into it) I was the leading drop kicker in the country. Lovejoy's passes were also perfect for a drop kicker.

Defensively, the backfield was very solid. Mallory was a tremendous line backer and an inspiring leader. Tad and Mallory were pals and Mallory brought some of Tad's warmth to the squad. On the defense Pond was versatile at right half and Richeson was a good safety man. Stevens played left half and figured in many interceptions of passes as well as backed up against the strong side of the opponent's offense. On kicking downs, Stevens would drop back into safety position and, with the excellent blocking of Pond and Richeson and the holding up of the opposing ends, figured in many long punt returns.

We usually played a seven-man line overshifted a half or a full man to the strength. This allowed our tackles to be wide enough to operate on the outside shoulder of the offensive end or the wingback. Milstead and Blair were murder when released in this fashion. Our line became a six-man line against passes as we dropped our weak-side end back into the flat or back into a short zone, rushing the passer sharply with our overshifted guard, tackle and strong-side end.

We would crisscross our end and tackle to block punts and felt that with our good defense a blocked punt would win a game for us. We were drilled constantly on protection for our passer and particularly for our punter. I do not remember having a punt blocked while I was kicking at Yale, and stressed this feature in my coaching.

The only spring practice we had was Billy Bull taking me and one or two of the scrubs out in the spring for kicking practice. Although I punted in the West before transferring to Yale, Billy Bull taught me to kick and to kick away from the receiver, striving for out-of-bounds placements. Grantland Rice wrote of Stevens' kicking in the Harvard game that there had never been better kicking with a wet ball. So, I feel that spring practice does pay off.

Our team had a reputation for being alert. We recovered some twenty-three of our opponents' twenty-seven fumbles.

Our line was big and well balanced but not tremendous in size. Coaches in those days always put their big men down ten or fifteen pounds on the weight charts in the program. Milstead hit about 217 pounds, Blair 212, Luman 190–195, Eckart 195, Lovejoy 190, Diller 180–185, Bingham 200, Hulman 180. In the backfield Pond weighed 185 pounds, Mallory about 180, Richeson 176, Stevens 177. The other backs were the same—shifty and strong.

I wouldn't say that the team had any individuals who were terrifically fast. I think this was a blessing in disguise as our interference and backs all moved in unison, with speed and reckless abandon.

The team had a certain "anticipation," as shown by a fine doubles partner in tennis or exemplified by a sense when to pass for a shot in basketball or any other sport where teamwork rises above the mere mechanical and becomes a thing of beauty, exhilaration in accomplishment.

I don't want to sound like an old-timer, but I think our players were more versatile than they have been in recent years. For instance, Charlie O'Hearn was a terrific drop kicker, place kicker and passer, as well as runner. He has one 53-yard drop kick to his credit at Yale. In addition, he played hockey and baseball. Ducky Pond could pass and kick and was also an excellent baseball player and could have been on the basketball team. Eddie Bench, who was as good as any of us, was voted the best all-around athlete in our class. He had a fine burst of speed, was an all-around track man and was a champion swimmer as well as a good basketball player. Harry Scott was an excellent punter, drop kicker, place kicker, and played hockey and baseball. Stevens was a five-letter man in one year at Washburn College, in football, basketball, track, tennis and baseball. He also did the punting, passing, drop kicking, some of the place kicking and kick-offs. Widdy Neale was an all-around athlete, good kicker and passer, golfer and basketball and baseball player. Russ Murphy, substitute for Richeson, was a good all-around little athlete, and Neidlinger was a fine athlete.

Our team was never really forced into a consistent passing game. We had the receivers and passers and worked on our passing consistently in practice so that I really feel we could have set all kinds of records at that time in the passing game.

Another reason for our team play being so good was that we all, with the possible exception of a couple, loved to block and tackle. We loved scrimmages and I know that many on the team felt as I did, that scrimmages were almost as much fun as a game.

Our team members all liked and respected each other and have been, I think, uniformly successful and reputedly average good citizens. It was my first experience playing on a team which had two or three millionaires, and I was amazed to find that their feelings toward contact and love of football were the same as mine or Milstead's, which had been tempered in fire a little more primitive. I also think the success of this team and earlier Yale teams is partly due to the democratic spirit which was evident at Yale and I hope still persists.

George Connors, our trainer, had us superbly conditioned and we had very few key injuries. Our teams trained to the letter and spirit of the rules laid down by the coaching staff. It may sound a little silly but I know how shaken one of our players was when he confided that he had smoked a couple of cigarettes the week before a game and I advised him to talk it over with Tad Jones. He didn't smoke again and trained religiously.

From all of this it may be gathered that our team had material, a superb coaching staff, a great leader in Tad Jones, spirit (team and college), confidence, a good sense of humor, a genuine liking for each other, a feeling that football was a game but one to be played to win and a belief which persists today that we could lick any college team in the country. My teammates feel that we had imagination and the ability to improvise if necessary on top of a very solid and versatile offense.

GRANTLAND RICE *wrote of the 1923 Yale team in* The New York Sun *in 1945:*

The crash-death of Memphis Bill Mallory of Yale and the United States Army takes one back twenty-two years to what I consider the greatest Yale team of all time. . . . Mallory was captain of Yale's greatest all-around team, offensively and defensively, and Tad Jones was head coach. Tad had a great line that season— big, fast, and aggressive. But above all he had one of the greatest backfields I ever saw, and that includes the best of Notre Dame or Southern California backfields, or the Army and Navy backfields of 1944.

As a starter, Yale boasted of Lyle Richeson of Tulane at quarterback, a brilliant field general who could run a team perfectly and also block and tackle. He was a star quarterback. In this Yale backfield, to mention only a few, were Mal Stevens from Kansas, one of the greatest running backs I ever saw, and I'm not barring Jim Thorpe or Cliff Battles; Widdy Neale from West Virginia, Newell (Flash) Neidlinger, Mallory.

Tad told me once that Mallory was not only one of the best backs Yale ever had but one of Yale's greatest captains. "Mallory," Tad said, "was the most relaxed athlete under pressure I ever saw. . . . He had the full confidence of the team. They loved him and believed in him. Bill had all the backs any team needed to carry the ball. So he never tried to be a ball carrier. He was satisfied to block, to tackle and to kick field goals. He was our main inspiration."

That was the Yale team that beat a strong Army outfit, 31–10. My old pal, John J. McEwan, was coaching Army that year, and Army was leading until Jones sent in Stevens. Mal cut a fine Army squad into what is technically known as ribbons.

"I removed and bawled out four of my Army men," McEwan told me later, "for not stopping Stevens. Then I suddenly realized that nobody could stop Stevens with his speed and drive and high-flying knees that cut you down. What a back that fellow was! And so was Mallory. And so were most of the other Yale backs that year."

By the author.

Of all Yale's famous athletes and coaches, few rank with Thomas Albert Dwight Jones in glamour, if in accomplishment. He won renown both as a coach and player. Although he did not quite achieve the coaching success of his brother, Howard Jones, who had great teams at Yale, Iowa, and Southern California, he was a far more vivid personality, and the luster of his fame has been as lasting. Tad Jones stands for Yale, the Yale spirit, and the finest traditions of intercollegiate athletics.

"Gentlemen," he told his squad in the hushed silence of the dressing room, before sending Yale out to play Harvard in The Game, football's "holy of holies," "you are about to play football for Yale against Harvard. Never in your lives will you do anything so important."

When Jones retired as head coach at Yale following the 1927 season, declining the invitation to continue, the following statement was made on behalf of the Board of Control of the Yale Athletic Association by Professor George H. Nettleton, the chairman:

"The Board of Control . . . takes occasion upon the retirement of Mr. T.A.D. Jones from his long-accustomed position as head football coach to recognize cordially his service to Yale and to American college sport.

"On the field and in the councils of football he has stood firmly and constantly for the principles and practice of fair play and sportsmanship. He has won and held the loyal regard of many successive Yale teams. . . . His influence has counted clearly in maintaining scholastic and athletic standards in full integrity. . . ."

Tad Jones was a brilliant player of both baseball and football. He was a member of the varsity baseball team. But it was in football that he achieved his greatest distinction. He ranks among the finest Yale backs of all time. He was quarterback and was a superior field general and an exceptionally fine runner whose power and elusiveness and deadly straight-arm made him a dangerous man to bring down.

Jones' coaching experience began at Yale as assistant coach in 1908 after his graduation. He was head coach at Syracuse in 1909 and 1910, following his brother, and in 1911 and 1912 he was at Pawling School. In 1913 he went to Exeter Academy. There he turned out such strong teams for three seasons that he was called to Yale by Cupe Black in 1916, succeeding Frank Hinkey. The war intervened and Jones went into the shipbuilding business in Seattle. In 1920 he came back to Yale as head coach, remaining until he retired in 1927 to return to his coal business in New Haven, after which he was named chairman of the Graduate Advisory Committee.

As a coach Tad Jones compiled a record equaled by few other Yale coaches for over half a century. The first team Jones coached at Yale, in 1916, broke the Haughton spell and beat Harvard for the first time since 1909 (when his brother, Howard, was coaching the Elis) right after the two crushing humiliations the Blue suffered in 1914 and 1915. It lost only to Brown. His 1923 team may be Yale's best ever. His 1927 eleven, his final masterpiece, is given high rating. The 1921 team lost only to Harvard, and his 1924 varsity was unbeaten though tied by Army and Dartmouth.

Jones had his critics among the alumni who thought Yale should continue to rule the football roost as it had when there were few good teams other than the Big Three, and the finest material naturally gravitated to New Haven. They charged him with lacking smartness in his attack and with depending on sheer power rather than inculcating finesse. It was the same sort of criticism Gilmour Dobie was subjected to when his material fell off after the great years of 1921, 1922, and 1923.

Jones never made public answer to this criticism. He had a serenity that made him impervious to the barbs of his detractors. Even the latter could not question his high ideals of sportsmanship and his inspiring personal influence on youth. His 1923 team was its own answer to such criticism and his last varsity, in 1927, a beautifully synchronized machine that blended power, finesse, and deception admirably, put his detractors to rout.

RED GRANGE RUNS TO IMMORTALITY

October 18, 1924, is one of the historic dates in American football. On that day Harold (Red) Grange turned in the greatest perfor- mance of running with a football the game had known. It has not been surpassed to this time. In the space of twelve minutes, Grange, a halfback on the University of Illinois team, ran for four touchdowns against the University of Michigan in the open- ing quarter of the game at Champaign, Illinois, dedicating the Memorial Stadium.

The four times he scored were the only times he carried the ball, after which he was taken out of the game. Returning to the field in the third quarter, Grange ran for a fifth touchdown, and in the final period he passed for a sixth.

That same year the Four Horsemen of Notre Dame rode to immortality against Army, thanks in part to the lyrical prose of Grantland Rice in reporting the game. They became the most publicized team in all history, and their coach, Knute Rockne, the most famous of all mentors. But Grange's was the most sensational individual performance on record, and the "Galloping Ghost," the "Wheaton Iceman," the "Football Phantom" took his place with Thorpe, Mahan, Eckersall, Coy among the immortals of the game.

From then on to the end of his varsity career and during his professional career he was the most talked-of, written-about, and photographed single player in football. Millions of words were written about him, hundreds of thousands saw him play. Such was his fame, there were proposals to nominate him for Congress and to name a town after him. His blue jersey, adorned with the mystic orange numerals 77, became as famous as Joseph's coat from coast to coast and the number was retired by Illinois when he had played his last varsity game. In his three years on the team—1923, 1924, and 1925—he gained more ground than had any other player in history—totalling 3,647 yards from scrimmage and running back punts and kick-offs.

Grange's coach, BOB ZUPPKE, *ranks among the giants of the*

profession, rivaling Stagg and Warner for his originality and in-
genuity in devising plays and techniques and in challenging Rockne
with his wit and cleverness of repartee and in coining phrases.
"The Dutchman" they called him (he was born in Berlin) as well
as "Zup," and they loved this little man, the "painter-poet laureate
of Champaign," who was too small to make the varsity as an
undergraduate at the University of Wisconsin but became an
almost instant sensation when he went to Illinois as coach from
Hyde Park High School in Chicago in 1913.

In a letter to the author in 1951, Zuppke laconically tells what
happened on that 18th day of October, 1924.

*Illinois' Bob Zuppke, "the
Little Dutchman," one of football's wittiest, most successful, and most ingenious
coaches.*

G RANGE MADE FOUR TOUCHDOWNS against Michigan in twelve minutes, and no Michigan man laid a hand on him. I pulled him out, and he asked me why. I told him, "No Michigan man laid a hand on you and I want you to come out unsoiled."

Grange had taken the opening kickoff and returned it 95 yards for a touchdown. Michigan kicked off again and he went 67 yards for a touchdown. Grange got his hands on the ball again after an exchange of punts, and he went 56 yards for his third score. The fourth time he touched the ball he ran 44 yards for his fourth touchdown, in twelve minutes.

Later, I put him in again, and he made a 12-yard gain for a touchdown, and no Michigan man touched him. His first four touchdowns were very long runs. He had great blocking, and he made the utmost use of it—a very rare ability. He later passed 18 yards for one touchdown and he held the ball for Earl Britton's points after touchdown.

Grange could block, tackle, kick and pass.

I had Britton, who I think was one of the greatest punters and place kickers of all time and could do these better than Grange. In fact, Britton kicked a 55-yard place kick against Iowa in 1923.

In October, 1936, I wrote an article for *Esquire* and described Grange as follows:

"Grange was a genius of motion. I saw that and made a team picture with him at the focal point. He ran with no waste motion, like Eddie Tolan, Michigan's Olympic sprint champion of 1932. I once made a trip to the Kaibab Forest on the edge of the north rim of the Grand Canyon and as a deer ran out onto the grass plains, I said, 'There goes Red Grange!'

"The freedom of movement was so similar to Red's. Red had that indefinable something that the hunted wild animal has— uncanny timing and the big brown eyes of a royal buck. I sketched a team around him like the complementary background of a painting. These were not great teams . . . but they fitted around Grange, helped to set him off.

"The average person does not think of imagination as being necessary to an athlete. 'Brawn without brains' has become a by-word in athletics. But in real life brains and brawn teamed together excel. A brawny football player must be able to picture the entire scope of the play he is a part of. Otherwise, he cannot know how the other players are cooperating with him to make him an effective part of the picture.

"This requires the ability to orientate himself with teammates on the field. When Red Grange ran a play, his imagination pictured the part and duties of every one of his teammates.

"Due to his panoramic view and quick thinking, he had the

Red Grange, the "Galloping Ghost" of Illinois, carrying the ball against Chicago, 1924.

ability to spot instantly where the most effective blocking would carry him. He always carried a design of the play in his mind.

"We figured the percentages that Grange had to carry the ball thirty-one times to win a game for us. If he carried the ball only twenty times, we figured to lose. He thought in terms of long runs. He was not as effective from compact formations. You had to give him range and freedom of movement back of the scrimmage line."

Grange had courage and ability and cooperated well. He had an especially fast start and super speed. He was a climactic runner. Of the rangy type, he was very elusive with an imperceptibly fast start.

He had pick-up. Football is a series of pick-ups.

He had a great sense of balance, was very hard to knock off his feet. He had a panoramic eye and could survey the field quickly.

A long "figure S" was the design of the path of his long runs. He would start to his right around the end, cut back, and later

would reverse his field again. This is not a natural reaction, and Grange had to be drilled in it. But it was perfect for his style of running.

Grange was tough. He could "take it."

The following piece on an interview with Grange was written by w. w. EDGAR *in* The Detroit Free Press *in 1936.*

It has been a dozen years since Harold (Red) Grange earned his nickname of "The Galloping Ghost" by running roughshod over the University of Michigan eleven to score four touchdowns in something like eleven minutes.

The passing of the years has taken none of the glamour from that feat. Any mention of Grange immediately recalls that afternoon when he personally dedicated the Illinois Stadium with the most amazing open-field running the game has known before or since. But the real story of that triumph—the events that led up to the crushing of the Wolverines—was never told until the other evening when Grange, himself, disclosed during his visit here how wily Bob Zuppke "keyed" the players up for the battle.

"In all the years I have been connected with football," Grange remarked, "I never have seen a team aroused to such a fighting pitch as 'Zup' had us that afternoon. And I never expect to see it done again."

"You know, Zuppke is a wily little Dutchman," Grange went on. "He mapped our plans for that Michigan game weeks, yes, months in advance. When we reported for spring practice that year all he talked about was the game we were going to play with Michigan the afternoon the new stadium would be dedicated.

"Never for a minute would he let us forget it. He kept telling us the Michigan game would be the big game—the day the stadium would be dedicated—and that we just had to win."

Then Grange, pushing aside the years that have passed, smiled and continued, "Why, do you know what Zup did? The day spring practice ended he gave us a pep talk for the Michigan game. Told us to think about it all summer. He did even more than that. Before school closed for the year, we started to get letters from him. That is, each player got a letter from him daily. In these letters he spoke of the things he wanted done by the fellow to whom he was writing when the whistle blew in the Michigan game."

Grange shook his head. "Why those letters were like messages from the folks at home. They were little personal notes pointing out that if I, for instance, did what he had told me, I would be helping to dedicate the stadium properly.

"Those letters continued daily throughout the summer months. They implored each of us to keep in good condition so we'd be fit to face Michigan. When we reported for fall practice the first greeting we received from Zup was, 'Well, are you ready to face those Wolverines?' "

That all had its effect, Grange pointed out. Every player on the squad became sold on the idea that he had a part to play in the dedicatory exercises—and that little part was to help beat Michigan.

"When the day of the big game came," Grange reminisced, "we were ready if ever a team was. I'll never forget the talk Zup gave us in the dressing room. Outside, the old grads had gathered, the bands were playing, the beautiful new stadium was open to the public and we were to dedicate it.

"When he had finished talking to us, there wasn't a man on the squad who wasn't ready to do anything that he might be called on to do. We were fighting mad, raring to get at the Wolverines."

Grange hesitated a moment. Then he repeated, "I never saw a team raised to such a fighting pitch, and I never hope to see it again. Why, when that whistle blew, nobody could have beaten us. We weren't exactly playing a football game. We were meeting our most cherished rival—Michigan—but more than that, we were dedicating our stadium. No, sir, nobody would have beaten us that afternoon.

"Zup had taken care of all of that with his little personal notes every day throughout the summer. It wasn't a great stunt to score those four touchdowns in the first few minutes of play. The rest of the gang was fighting just as I was and all I had to do was to shift a bit now and then and keep on going toward the goal line. That's the story of how we beat Michigan and how I came to be known as 'The Galloping Ghost,' Grange concluded. "And that stadium down at Illinois was really dedicated—with wily old Zup playing the most important role."

GENERAL BOB NEYLAND'S TENNESSEE DYNASTY

During sports' Golden Age in the 1920's, while Knute Rockne and Notre Dame were skyrocketing to the top, Bob Neyland was leading the Tennessee Volunteers out of the wilderness and getting off to one of the most remarkably successful coaching records football has known.

A native of Texas and a graduate of West Point, where he played end on the unbeaten football teams of 1914 and 1915, was academy heavyweight boxing champion for three years, and established a record as a baseball pitcher, Neyland took over as head football coach at Tennessee in 1926, when the Volunteers were the doormat of the South. In his first season his team won eight games and lost one. In the next six years, from 1927 through 1932, the Volunteers lost just one game of 58, winning 52 and tying 5.

In 1938, 1939, and 1940, Neyland achieved even more spectacular success. Tennessee defeated all of its thirty opponents, scoring 807 points and yielding only 42. When General Neyland retired early in 1953, because of his health, he had a record of 172 victories, 25 defeats, and 12 ties in regular season games and his teams had scored 4,841 points to 1,116 for their opponents. His career had been interrupted twice when he was summoned back by the Army for tours of duty, first in 1935 and again from 1941 through 1945.

The late HERMAN HICKMAN, a member of the 1929, 1930, and 1931 teams, who is ranked among the greatest guards of all time, and who was on Colonel Red Blaik's staff at Army and head coach of Yale, wrote the author as follows in 1954:

THE BIRTH OF Tennessee's great teams took place in 1928 when Dodd, McEver, and Hackman were sophomores. I was a freshman that year. Gene McEver took the opening kick-off against Alabama that year and went 98 yards for a touchdown, and from that day on the Flaming Sophomores had the winning way. The records of the teams during these years were sensational both offensively and defensively.

In 1929 McEver was the high scorer of the nation, and until the era of Mr. B. and D. [Blanchard and Davis] at West Point, I never saw his equal. He suffered a knee injury playing baseball during the summer of 1930 and did not get to play football that year, but he came back in 1931 to finish when I did. Several operations and a clumsy brace that was the best they had in those prehistoric days hampered him, but he was still the "wild bull."

Bobby Dodd was the brains and the tailback on our 1929 and 1930 teams. He was a coach's player: calm, cool, a masterful punter, without the power of Beattie Feathers' leg, but more accurate. He was such a pin-point passer that the conservative Neyland allowed him to pass from behind his own goal line. Over a period of two seasons he did not have a pass intercepted. He was a slow but deceptive runner, and his running average was amazingly high.

Joseph (Buddy) Hackman was the most underrated member of this triumvirate. Buddy usually played wingback (but all the backs interchanged positions from play to play) and could "tickle" a tackle with the best. He was a brilliant runner, none was better as a pass receiver, and he was the best pass defense man I've ever seen. All these superlatives seem a little strong, but he filled the adjectives.

Beattie Feathers was a sensational sophomore on our great 1931 team, one of the great runners of all time. He was big, fast, and powerful. He could do it all and well. Later on with the Chicago Bears he established a record of 9.9 yards per try for an entire season, which, incidentally still stands [in 1954].

I was one of the youngest players that ever played for Tennessee, and for many years the largest. Neyland never went in for big linemen. I was his exception, weighing 225 pounds my senior year (203 in the program). I played my last year when still 19. To be egotistical for just a moment, Feathers and McEver were the only two men on the squad who could outrun me. All old guards get much better as the years go by. I guess that it comes from their vicarious hopes of being a backfield man.

Neyland (major, colonel, general) brought a new breadth to Southern football when he was assigned by the War Department to be Professor of Military Science and Tactics at Tennessee in 1925, and incidentally an assistant football coach at $600 a year. Tennessee football was in the doldrums. The wooden stands seated about 3,000 and there was only in name an athletic association. Neyland had been assistant to McEwan at West Point, along with Biff Jones and Ralph Sasse. He approached football scientifically and statistically—the approach of the engineer, which he was.

His heroes in those days—and now—were a young superintendent at West Point named MacArthur and his old coach, Charley Daly. He did a lot of scouting for West Point and when he came to Tennessee he first had a chance to put his composites of the best into his offense. He took over as head coach in 1926 with an offense of this model, a balanced single wing attack, with the quarterback halfway under the center, used as a threat for the quarterback sneak to force the middle lineman to play tight, but primarily as a blocker. He took his end run from Rockne, his off-tackle plays from Gil Dobie at Cornell and his general concept of football from the legendary Percy Haughton at Harvard.

However, with all this, Neyland's main forte was defense, coupled with an airtight, flawless kicking game. By kicking game he meant every phase of it: the return of punts (Tennessee led the nation for years), the kick-off returns (no team was as successful in this phase), and covering both. Up until a year or so ago, no team had ever returned a punt or kick-off against a Neyland coached team for a touchdown. He made a fetish of pass defense and the return of intercepted passes. Our linemen drilled incessantly on defense. I would estimate that we spent only 25 percent of our practice periods on pure offense.

This is a new note for most football fans. Neyland did not believe in too much scrimmage. Most of the time for rough work was divided into group work, in a day when a coach usually slammed eleven men against eleven every day to toughen them up. His practices were not long but his lecture periods were. He was a strict disciplinarian but not of the blood-and-thunder type. He was a far cry from the pre-game pep talk.

The order of the starting teams would be put on the blackboard (always the cadet), and a list of his game maxims, which he would always repeat before every game. The game maxims for the most part were always the same, but every Tennessee coach still uses them, and, by the way, Tennessee long supplanted Notre Dame as having the most coaches at colleges in the country. The maxims went like this:

The team that makes the fewer mistakes WINS.

Play for and make the breaks. When one comes your way, SCORE.

If a break goes against you, don't let down. Turn on MORE steam.

Press the kicking game. It is here that games are won or lost.

Against equal opposition a drive of over sixty yards is seldom successful.

Stop the long gains.

"OSKIE-WOW-WOW" (the signal to return an intercepted pass, a blood-curdling cry by the Tennessee team that brought doom to many an opponent).

GANG TACKLE (just what it meant) PROTECT AND COVER.

REMEMBER THE SPARROW (always a Tennessee story told on a winning streak about the sparrow who got so fat and happy when all the horses were on the street, and then came the automobiles, and no manure. The moral: Don't get it in your neck).

CHARLES A. (GUS) MANNING, *Athletic Publicity Director at Tennessee, wrote the following to the author in August, 1951:*

Neyland is a living legend in college football. That he holds a legitimate claim to such a title is shown by his outstanding records. . . . His defensive record is truly phenomenal. In 188 regular season games played during nineteen seasons, over a span of twenty-five years, his Tennessee teams have held the opposition to an average of only 5 points per game. As Herman Hickman, one of Neyland's star pupils, has pointed out on the basis of this record, "If Neyland could score a touchdown against you he had you beat. If he could score two, he had you in a rout."

Neyland had one of the longest consecutive winning streaks known in the history of football. His teams of 1937–1946 (Neyland was in the Army for five years during World War II) won thirty-six consecutive regular season games.

Neyland is known as the dean of Southeastern Conference coaches. He is the only coach to be named Coach of the Year in the conference as many as three times. In a recent Associated Press poll to select the coach of the mythical all-time all-America team, Neyland finished fourth, behind Rockne, Warner, Stagg.

The general's football philosophy may be summed up in a few words: "Hard tackling, hard blocking, make as few mistakes as possible, magnify your opponent's mistakes and turn them into scores."

The name of Neyland has become synonymous with the single wing system. He employs and always has employed the single wing with a balanced line. Coming from the huddle, the Tennessee backfield may line up in a single wing formation to either the right or to the left. The buck lateral series is used by Neyland for deception.

General Neyland lists as his great teams those of 1928, 1929, 1931, 1932, 1938, 1940, and 1950. Outstanding personnel on these teams were Gene McEver, Buddy Hackman, Bobby Dodd, Paul Hug, Fritz Brandt and Harry Thayer from the 1928–1929 teams, Herman Hickman, 1931 team; Beattie Feathers, 1932; Bowden Wyatt, Bob Suffridge, George Cafego, Ed Molinski, Abe Shires, and Bob Foxx of the 1938, 1939 and 1940 teams.

In 1928 and 1929 some of the great teams Tennessee played were Alabama, Florida, and Kentucky. Kentucky kept Tennessee from going to the Rose Bowl in both 1928 and 1929 by tying the Vols 0–0 in 1928 and 6–6 in 1929. However, Kentucky has never defeated a Neyland-coached team. In 1931 Tennessee defeated the great New York University team at the Polo Grounds in New York in a post-season game by a score of 13–0. It was there that Herman Hickman made his bid for fame. In 1938 Tennessee defeated Oklahoma in the Orange Bowl, 17–0. In 1939 Tennessee was beaten by Southern California in the Rose Bowl, 14–0 and in 1940 in the Sugar Bowl, 19–13 by a Boston College team coached by Frank Leahy which had such stars as Charley O'Rourke and Chet Gladchuck. In 1950 Tennessee defeated three of the finest teams of the country—Alabama, Kentucky, and Texas.

One game which stands out in General Neyland's memory is the 1932 game against Alabama, which turned into a great punting duel between Beattie Feathers of Tennessee and Johnny (Sugar) Cain of Alabama. The game was played in Birmingham in the rain. Both men kicked the ball twenty times. Feathers averaged 48 yards and Cain averaged 45 yards, even though both had a kick which carried only 10 yards. The general characterizes this game as the "best punting duel I have ever witnessed." Tennessee won, 7–3, Feathers scoring the winning touchdown.

General Neyland has the characteristics of a military strategist —tough and realistic, brilliant and meticulous. His success as a coach . . . is reflected in the men to whom he gave something of himself. Among these are some prominent head coaches throughout the country: Herman Hickman of Yale, Bowden Wyatt of Wyoming, Bobby Dodd of Georgia Tech, Bob Woodruff of Florida, Beattie Feathers of North Carolina State, DeWitt Weaver of Texas

Tech, Quinn Decker of The Citadel, Phil Dickens of Wofford, Ralph Hatley of Memphis State and Billy Meek of Kansas State. . . .

GRANTLAND RICE *in 1947 wrote of Hickman, "The Bard of the Smokies":*

Some years ago I happened to mention to Bob Neyland that Herman Hickman was the best guard the South ever produced.

"The South has ever produced?" Neyland combined a snarl and a glare. "Herman Hickman is the greatest guard football has ever known, South or North, East or West."

I still recall the time in New York University's years of glory when one of Chick Meehan's crack teams had the ball on Tennessee's 3-yard line. Some psychic quarterback decided to throw a series of plays at the Fat Man. After the fourth play the ball was on Tennessee's 14-yard line and the N.Y.U. attack was in a sadly disheveled condition. No one ever ran over Hickman, under Hickman, or around Hickman.

There was also the day that a smart Vanderbilt quarterback, in the huddle, gave out this information: "We'll go through the Fat Boy. He can't even move." So the play was called through the Fat Boy, who broke through, picked up the first blocker and threw him at the runner for an 8-yard loss.

Herman is Army's 310-pound line coach. Before the Hickman era, the two best line coaches I'd ever known were Hunk Anderson of Notre Dame and the Chicago Bears and Harry (Fats) Ellinger, also of Army. Both Anderson and Ellinger played against their pupils, selecting the survivors, who had to be tough. Hickman couldn't go quite that far. There would be no survivors. Tex Coulter was big and rough and fast. Coulter never saw the day he could move Hickman's 310 pounds two inches. Hickman is the only line coach or backfield coach I have ever known who is also a poet. He is widely known as the "Poet Laureate of the Smoky Mountains."

THE MODERN T FORMATION

The T is football's oldest and original formation. Glenn Warner said that it was in use from the very beginning and was called regular formation. Stagg said that the T dates from 1888, when the changes in the rule brought the linemen and also the backs in closer from the spread formation in vogue when the lateral passing of rugby was so prominent.

As early as 1894, Stagg said, he started having his quarterback take the ball from center in the modern standing position, instead of bending down almost on one knee. The man-in-motion is a distinguishing feature of the modern T, but Stagg says that in 1898 he was using a "flyer," a man outwardly in motion to receive a backward pass (the forward pass was not in the game then) and that in 1927 he used a "pedinger," a man outwardly in motion, mainly for forward pass purposes.

Warner said that Frank Cavanaugh and Doc Spears used the T at Dartmouth in the years prior to 1920 and that George Woodruff used backs in motion at Penn in the Nineties. Willie Heston said the T was "pretty standard, although we shifted from it," in his day at Michigan. Carl Snavely wrote that Penn State in 1906 lined up in T formation and the backfield shifted, the quarterback taking the ball and handing it off. Notre Dame under Harper and Rockne lined up in T formation but the backs shifted into a box except at times when inside the opponent's 20-yard line.

GEORGE HALAS was the man largely responsible for the revival of the T in its modern form and its universal adoption, displacing the Notre Dame shift and the Warner single and double wing formations. He and his staff on the Chicago Bears worked out the modern version, with the assistance of Clark Shaughnessy, then coaching at the University of Chicago, and their tremendous success with it in 1940 led to its adoption by Frank Leahy at Notre Dame and by Earl Blaik at Army, and the stampede was on. In a letter to the author in 1953 Halas wrote:

IN 1920, WHEN THE BEARS entered the newly founded National Football League, we used a variety of offensive formations, including the *loose* T. By splitting the ends and moving the halfbacks another two steps away from the fullback, we achieved greater mobility, particularly on end runs. . . .

What the Bears did was to put the T and the man-in-motion together and then gradually add refinements, such as the signal system (used by the majority of college and professional teams today) and the counter plays and *spreads*. This was a period of evolution spanning almost twenty years and was the product of the Bears' organization rather than of one individual.

Ralph Jones put additional T formation variations into the Bears' offense. It was during Jones' three-year term (1930–1932) as head coach of the Bears that he, Red Grange and quarterback Carl Brumbaugh first married the man in motion to the T, and Grange was the first T man in motion. [This seems to take direct issue with Stagg's statement that at Chicago he used a man in motion for forward pass purposes with his "pedinger" in 1927, except that Stagg in 1927 had his backs in trapezoid, and not T formation.]

It was in 1931 that the Bears tremendously increased the T's striking power by adding the man-in-motion to the basic T. Our quarterback started throwing laterals and forward passes to that man-in-motion, a development which forced our opponents to spread their defenses. Thus our man-in-motion served a double purpose. He was a fine pass target and, moreover, he forced the defense to spread out, and this gave our backs greater running opportunities.

Opposing teams developed ingenious defenses to blunt the power and mobility of the T. A revolving 5–4–2 concocted by Curly Lambeau of the Green Bay Packers and Gus Dorais of the Detroit Lions was an effective defense. The four-man defensive secondary would move with our man-in-motion, thus diminishing his effectiveness as a runner or potential as a pass receiver.

To counteract the sliding 5–4–2 defense, the Bears developed in 1939 a series of so-called counter plays, which enabled us to strike in the opposite direction from our man-in-motion. If our man-in-motion went to the right and the defense slid over to cover, we could send a ball carrier scurrying around the left end, thus catching the defense moving in the wrong direction. . . .

In 1933, after Ralph Jones went back to college coaching, I

again took up the reins as head coach of the Bears and added several innovations, such as stressing the importance of end runs, spreading the ends, off-tackle plays, etc. . . .

In 1937 Clark Shaughnessy joined our staff in an advisory capacity while head coach at Chicago. Shaughnessy, a man with a decided flair for the technical side of football, played a leading role in working out the numbering system which is still the basis of the Bears' signal system today. Shaughnessy also was a leader in staff planning on the development of "counter play." Luke Johnsos and Paddy Driscoll have dealt with individual plays to exploit the opposition's weak points. For example, the fullback delay play is one of Luke's original designs.

It was inevitable, since Shaughnessy right after having been associated with the Bears' organization, that his Stanford offense was patterned largely to Bear specifications. However, Clark is an extremely able coach, as his record attests, and he undoubtedly added individual touches to the T to capitalize on special abilities of his players. . . .

In 1940 the Bears employed a formation which spread the left end wide and sent a man in motion to the right. This was the start of the so-called wide-open phase of T-formation football.

From this wide-open formation the Bears touched off the touchdown avalanche which engulfed the Washington Redskins, 73 to 0 in the 1940 championship playoff. Thus the trend in total offense football has always been toward widening the area of attack. Today, with a new end split wide and a flanker, or man-in-motion (or both) on the right side, or vice versa, the Bears can deploy players virtually the width of the field.

Summing up, modern total offense football can be likened to a game of chess. . . . The maneuvers of the flankers, split ends and the man-in-motion are as sharply defined as the moves of the knights, bishops and the queen on the chessboard. Consequently, success in football, as in chess, goes to the team which can probe for a weak spot, disguise its point of attack, then strike swiftly and deceptively with the right combination of player maneuvers to produce a touchdown. . . .

During the all-important few seconds the quarterback calls signals, various Bear players perform all sorts of maneuvers. For instance: A halfback may race to a new position outside the end and close to the sideline. He becomes a flanker. The other halfback, or the fullback, may start running—left or right—toward either sideline and parallel to the line of scrimmage. He becomes the man-in-motion.

One or both ends may split out wide from the tackles into better pass-catching locations. The guards, tackles and ends may shift laterally, varying the spacing between their positions. The shifting sometimes enables them to get more advantageous blocking angles on linemen. On certain plays, nine of the eleven players in the Bears' T-formation line-up may shift positions during the three or four seconds the quarterback calls the signals; but this must be done prior to the halfback starting in motion. So when the center snaps the ball and the play actually starts, the Bears are rarely aligned in their celebrated T formation. Instead, our players are poised to attack from any one of literally hundreds of combinations, which can be worked out easily and quickly by moving out of the T.

There are times in every game when the Bears run from the T without shifting players. But this doesn't happen often. Primarily, we do not look upon the T as an attacking formation. Instead, we consider the T as a convenient way of lining up our players so that they can shift speedily into whichever attacking formation seems best calculated to overcome the opponents' type of defense.

Some of these attacking combinations, on closer scrutiny, resemble other well-known football formations. For example, when the Bears employ one halfback as a flanker, we actually shift into an attacking alignment similar to the Notre Dame box popularized by the late Knute Rockne. When the Bears employ one halfback as a flanker and use the other halfback, or the fullback, as a man-in-motion to the opposite side, we really shift into an attacking combination similar to the double wingback developed by Glenn (Pop) Warner. What's more, when we employ a flanker, a man-in-motion and split our ends out wide, we shift into an attacking combination which is not basically different from the tailback spread which Dutch Meyer has been using with spectacular success at Texas Christian for many years.

Consequently, when the Bears talk T-formation football, we aren't referring to any alphabetical pattern which the players fall into for an instant as they come out of the huddle. Instead, we're talking about the myriad attacking combinations our players can shift into before the play actually starts. Moreover, we are convinced that our players can shift into these attacking combinations more quickly, conveniently and deceptively from the T than from any other line-up.

So, in the Bears' football alphabet, T stands for Total. T-formation football is Total Offense Football because, from the T, the attacking team can shift into combinations which make up the sum total of virtually every known method of scoring touchdowns.

STANLEY WOODWARD *wrote in his column in* The New York Herald Tribune *following the Bears' 73–0 massacre of the Washington Redskins in the nation's capital on December 8, 1940—one of the red-letter days of football:*

Old Blues in turtle necks and slatted pants may now throw out their chests; for the Chicago Bears, using the original formation of football, the hallowed T, *sine qua non* of the early Walter Camp era, whaled the Washington Redskins, 73 to 0 before a capacity house in Griffith Stadium this afternoon.

The Bears did not score all their points with plays from the T. In fact, so wholeheartedly did the men of George Halas convert Washington passes into touchdowns that there was some question whether they were more dangerous when they had the ball or when Washington had it. But the T formation rolled up more points than are customary in big league football, and the conclusion that must be drawn is that hundreds, perhaps thousands, of football teams will be using it next fall. They will substitute quick openings, speed, head feints, and indirect handling for the ponderous and generally slow-moving line interference plays which have been popular in the last twenty years.

The great Halas has been fooling around with the T formation for years, but he has never given such a vivid demonstration of the virulence which may be forthcoming from it as he did today. . . . He is a second-growth pioneer into other realms which other football men have abandoned as fruitless, and he apparently is on the verge of starting a stampede back to first principles. . . .

There isn't much outside strength in this T alignment, but a back can run harder and faster if he gets the ball second-hand. . . . He can concentrate on his running if he doesn't have to worry about whether the center is going to hit him on the forehead or left knee. In Halas' system the quarterback takes the ball from center and hands it around, placing it lovingly in the very hands of the man who is going to lug it.

The lack of outside strength is made up in some measure by the variations Halas has introduced. He sends out flankers in varying profusion, and each time he sends one out a defensive man goes with him. It is much easier to decoy a man out of the play than it is to knock him down. In case men are not decoyed, Halas' flankers become receivers of forward or lateral passes. On most of the plays the quarterback hands the ball to a man who is hell-bent for one hole. In this system he gets there before the defensive men have been able to attain full momentum. It doesn't require much blocking to get the runner by the line of scrimmage, for he is shooting for an open space and planning to get there before the defense has time to close in.

It is old-time football, and Mr. Halas and aides proved today that it will work today as it used to work in the days when your agent was a nose-burying guard. The dive-tackle play . . . the cross-buck and sundry other maneuvers were proved this afternoon, in the middle of George Preston Marshall's heartbreak, to be plays of the hour.

The halfbacks and the fullback don't have to be anything except runners and blockers. You don't have to worry about placing a passer at left halfback and a spinner at fullback. The quarterback is the spinner and passer, and, in addition, he is the aloof man of the backfield. He has no blocking assignments and so does not dull his brain struggling with gigantic enemy ends and tackles. He hands the ball around. He fakes to a diving back and goes back to throw it. Except for the going-over the opposing linemen may be expected to give him when he passes, and the defensive work he has to perform, he is one detached, one able to concentrate on what must be done to advance the ball.

You wouldn't know what to do with an Evashevski or a Matusz-czak in this system. They are men whose duty it has been to put on the ponderous blocks of "modern" orthogenic football. Sid Luck-man, prize package of the current Bears, is the ideal quarterback for this game. He is a smart boy, also a passer without peer. He can fake the ball, drop back, and hit an ant in the eye with a 30-yard heave.

This game was like an assault of the Mongols on the citadels of modern civilization. Forgotten weapons were brought to bear, and plays of the past, abandoned because they were out of fashion, were proved to be more potent than ever.

The rush to get on the T bandwagon following the sensational success of the Bears and the Stanford Indians of Shaughnessy in 1940 marked one of the big turning points in offensive football. It was a turning back en masse to the original formation of the Camp-Stagg era, upon which had been grafted the man-in-motion and flankers to produce a fast-hitting, quick-opening attack that was totally different from the ponderous, close-order mass assault

projected from the original T in the 1880's, 1890's, and the first decade of this century.

By successive stages football had progressed from the dull, unimaginative push-and-pull game of those early years to the punting game of Yost's Michigan teams of the early 1900's, to the accelerated, more open style burgeoning with the forward pass, to the power and deception of the Warner wingback attack, with its overshifted line, and linemen pulling out as blockers; to the shifting offenses of Stagg, Heisman, Dr. Williams, Harper and Rockne, most spectacularly exploited by Notre Dame until the rule makers took the momentum out of it, and now, finally, back to the T with its modern, streamlined embellishments.

Numerous variations of the T have been devised since the stampede got into high gear with Frank Leahy's abandonment of the Notre Dame attack and development of the great team of 1943, directed at quarterback by the masterful Angelo Bertelli, with his fine Italian hand, and then by Johnny Lujack. The wing T, of which Lou Little at Columbia was a leading exponent; the split T, originated by Don Faurot at Missouri and exploited by Bud Wilkinson with spectacular success at Oklahoma and by Jim Tatum at Maryland; the slot T, the double wing T, the I (another type of T) and the pro spread have been among the varieties introduced in the never-ending challenge to keep ahead of the defense.

Red Grange, an immortal if there ever was one.

PHOTO CREDITS

INDEX

Ade, George, 83–92
Adee, George T., 66–68
Afraid of a Bear, 166, 169
Ahearn, M. F., 25
All–America teams, 11, 24, 50, 103, 112, 117, 118, 131, 142, 159, 165, 166–67, 168, 191, 200, 203, 205, 208, 209–10, 293, 294, 298, 312, 316, 327, 329, 348, 365
Allen, "Warhorse," 41
Allerdice (Michigan), 186
American Football Coaches Association, 51, 69, 347
American Intercollegiate Football Rules Committee, 11, 22, 25, 47, 50, 72, 149
American Professional Football Association, 307
Ames, Butler, 98
Ames, Knowlton L. "Snake," 85, 86, 87, 88, 95, 96
Ames, W. T., 239
Anderson, Heartley "Hunk," 212, 313, 352, 395
Anderson, Paul, 86
Andrus, Hamlin "Ham," 203, 205, 206, 208, 223
Appleton, William H., 23
Arcasa (Carlisle), 176
Armstrong, Norris, 331, 332, 333
Artoe, Lee, 353
Ayrault, Dr., 219

Babbit, James A., 23, 25
Bach, Joe, 281
Badenoch, Art, 144
Baker, Eugene V., 14, 15
Balenti, Mike, 159, 162, 166, 349
Ballard, Bland, 16
Bankart, Larry, 315, 316
Barnard, Charles, 228
Barrett (Cornell), 226
Bartlett, Tom, 331, 332, 333
Baston, Bert, 293, 305
Baugh, Sammy, 353, 354, 371
Bealle, Morris A., 149
Beecher, Harry, 23, 46
Bell, Bert, 351
Bell, Madison "Matty," 326, 327, 329

Benedict (Army), 290–91
Bentner, Max, 46
Berger (Notre Dame), 199
Bergie (Carlisle), 176
Bergman (Notre Dame), 199, 252
Bertelli, Angelo, 403
Bezdek, Hugo, 187
Bible, Dana X., 25
Bierman, Bernie, 232, 235, 237–39, 243
Big Four, 35
Big Ten Conference, 35, 84, 107, 110, 133, 214, 298, 322, 324, 334
Big Three, 63, 146
Black, Jeremiah, 95
Blacklock, Hugh, 307
Blagden, Crawford, 228
Blaik, Col. Earl "Red," 56, 343, 396
Blake, Bill, 229
Block game, 18
Body block, 164, 304, 339–40
Bowditch, "Pete," 228
Box formation, 56, 57, 217, 231, 236, 269, 396
Boyle (Pennsylvania), 115
Brayman, "Turk," 365
Brickley, Charley, 215, 216, 220, 223, 349
Britton, Earl, 385
Brooke, George, 65, 112, 114, 136
Brooks, William A., 23, 95
Brown, "Chigger," 148
Brown, "Three–Fingered," 246, 247
Brumbaugh, Carl, 397
Brush block, 281
Bryan, P. T., 18
Buell, Charley, 332
Bull, Billy, 79
Bullock (Dartmouth), 147
Burns (Penn State), 186
Burr, Francis, 218
Butterworth, Frank, 63, 136
Buttonhook pass, 232

Cabot (Harvard), 63
Cain, Johnny "Sugar," 394
Calac (Carlisle), 158–59, 169
Caldwell, Charlie, 356–57
Cameron, Forbes W., 339

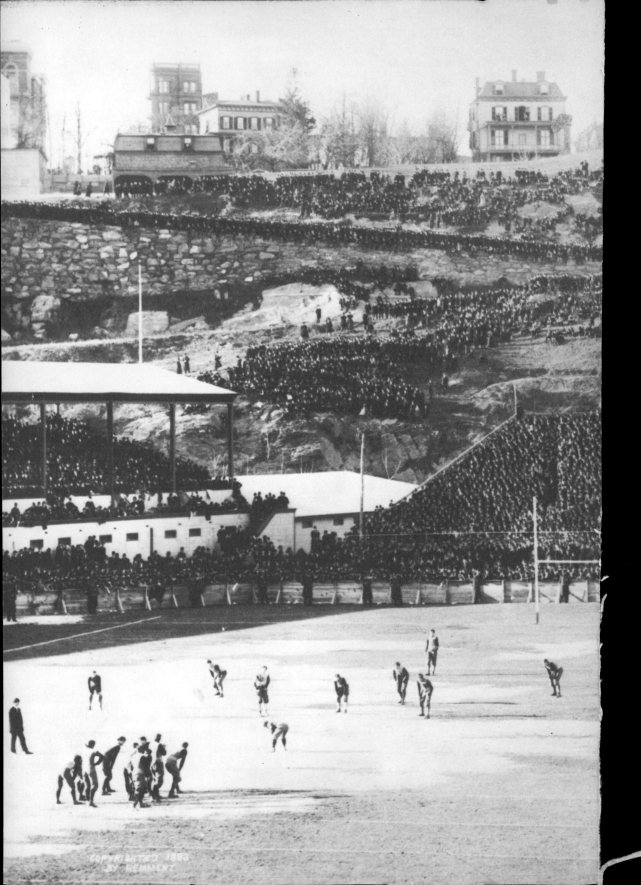

COPYRIGHTED 1893
BY HEMMENT.